SPACES OF CARE

The collection examines the ways in which the emerging interdisciplinary study of care provokes a reassessment of the connections and disjuncture between care and governance, ethics, and public, personal and professional identities.

Evolving from a project coordinated by the Cambridge Socio-Legal Group, *Spaces of Care* brings together leading international scholars to articulate what we may consider to be a useful analytic of care. Lawyers, anthropologists, sociologists and criminologists reflect on specific aspects of conceptualising caring relations in 'spaces'. These spaces include: communities of care and abandonment, self-care and kinship care, spaces as 'gaps' in care, the meanings of marketised care, and the ways in which care is constructed and constrained in different ways in venues such as homes, prisons, workplaces and virtual spaces.

Common themes include temporality (historical specificity) and the dynamics of care across time and place; subjectivity (including different experiences of care); the economies of care (including the commodification of care; public and private manifestations of care; privatised 'care'); disruptions of care (which generate vulnerabilities with regard to continuities of care); eligibility (those deemed to be deserving and undeserving of care); relationalities of care (collective and individual agency in caring relations, kinship care), and technologies and imaginaries of care (as in new notions of care forged by those in online virtual worlds such as Second Life).

Cambridge Socio-Legal Group titles published by Hart:

Marriage Rites and Rights (2015)
edited by Joanna Miles, Perveez Mody and Rebecca Probert

Birth Rites and Rights (2011)
edited by Fatemah Ebtehaj, Jonathan Herring, Martin H Johnson and Martin Richards

Sharing Lives, Dividing Assets: An Inter-Disciplinary Study (2009)
edited by Joanna Miles and Rebecca Probert

Regulating autonomy: sex, reproduction and families (2009)
edited by Fatemeh Ebtehaj, Emily Jackson, Martin Richards and Shelley Day Sclater

Death Rites and Rights (2007)
edited by Belinda Brooks-Gordon, Fatemeh Ebtehaj, Jonathan Herring, Martin Johnson and Martin Richards

Kinship Matters (2006)
edited by Fatemeh Ebtehaj, Bridget Lindley and Martin Richards

Sexuality Repositioned: Diversity and the Law (2004)
edited by Belinda Brooks-Gordon, Loraine Gelsthorpe, Martin Johnson and Andrew Bainham

Children and their Families: Contact, Rights and Welfare (2003)
edited by Andrew Bainham, Bridget Lindley, Martin Richards and Liz Trinder

Body Lore and Laws (2002)
edited by Andrew Bainham, Shelly Day Sclater and Martin Richards

What is a Parent? A Socio-Legal Analysis (1999)
edited by Andrew Bainham, Shelley Day Sclater and Martin Richards

Spaces of Care

Edited by
Loraine Gelsthorpe
Perveez Mody
and
Brian Sloan

•HART•
OXFORD • LONDON • NEW YORK • NEW DELHI • SYDNEY

HART PUBLISHING

Bloomsbury Publishing Plc

Kemp House, Chawley Park, Cumnor Hill, Oxford, OX2 9PH, UK

1385 Broadway, New York, NY 10018, USA

29 Earlsfort Terrace, Dublin 2, Ireland

HART PUBLISHING, the Hart/Stag logo, BLOOMSBURY and the Diana logo are trademarks of Bloomsbury Publishing Plc

First published in Great Britain 2020

First published in hardback, 2020

Paperback edition, 2023

A catalogue record for this book is available from the British Library.

Library of Congress Cataloging-in-Publication data

Names: Spaces of Care: Socio-Legal Workshop (2018 : University of Cambridge) | Gelsthorpe, Loraine, editor. | Mody, Perveez, editor. | Sloan, Brian, 1984- editor. | Cambridge Socio-Legal Group, sponsoring body.

Title: Spaces of care / edited by Loraine Gelsthorpe, Perveez Mody and Brian Sloan.

Description: Oxford ; New York : Hart, 2020. | Includes bibliographical references and index.

Identifiers: LCCN 2019053915 (print) | LCCN 2019053916 (ebook) | ISBN 9781509929634 (hardcover) | ISBN 9781509929641 (Epub)

Subjects: LCSH: Social legislation—Congresses.

Classification: LCC K1700.A6 S67 2018 (print) | LCC K1700.A6 (ebook) | DDC 344.01—dc23

LC record available at https://lccn.loc.gov/2019053915

LC ebook record available at https://lccn.loc.gov/2019053916

ISBN: PB: 978-1-50997-426-9
ePDF: 978-1-50992-965-8
ePub: 978-1-50992-964-1

Typeset by Compuscript Ltd, Shannon

To find out more about our authors and books visit www.hartpublishing.co.uk. Here you will find extracts, author information, details of forthcoming events and the option to sign up for our newsletters.

ACKNOWLEDGEMENTS

We would like to acknowledge the generous financial support for the project and symposium which has led to this book from Pembroke College, King's College and Robinson College, Cambridge, where Loraine Gelsthorpe, Perveez Mody and Brian Sloan are respective Fellows. We would also like to thank the Cambridge Socio-Legal Group, University of Cambridge (www.law.cam.ac.uk/researchfaculty-centres-networks-and-groups/cambridge-socio-legal-group) for their sponsorship and support. We are also grateful to the anonymous reviewers of the book proposal who grasped our intentions and offered constructive comments. We would also like to express our sincere gratitude to Siôn Hudson for his skilful initial copy editing, and to our contributors and our colleagues in Hart Publishing for their patience in regard to the production of this book.

TABLE OF CONTENTS

LIST OF CONTRIBUTORS

Tom Boellstorff is Professor of Anthropology at the University of California, Irvine.

John Borneman is Professor of Anthropology at Princeton University.

Susanne Burri is an Associate Professor at Utrecht University School of Law.

Rob Canton is Professor in Community and Criminal Justice at De Montfort University, Leicester.

Helen Carr is Professor in Law at the University of Kent.

Jane Dominey is a Senior Research Associate at the Institute of Criminology at the University of Cambridge.

Loraine Gelsthorpe is Professor of Criminology and Criminal Justice at the University of Cambridge, and a Fellow of Pembroke College.

Jonathan Herring is Professor of Law at the University of Oxford, and a Fellow of Exeter College.

Elena Khlinovskaya Rockhill is an Institute Associate at the Scott Polar Research Institute at the University of Cambridge.

Ed Kirton-Darling is a Lecturer at Kent Law School, University of Kent.

Perveez Mody is a University Lecturer at the Department of Social Anthropology, University of Cambridge, and a Fellow of King's College.

Koreen Reece is an ERC Postdoctoral Research Fellow in Social Anthropology at the University of Edinburgh.

Maria Fernanda Salcedo Repolês is an Adjunct Professor of Law at the Federal University of Minas Gerais, Brazil.

Brian Sloan is a College Lecturer and Fellow in Law at Robinson College in the University of Cambridge.

1

Introduction

Spaces of Care: Concepts, Configurations, and Challenges

LORAINE GELSTHORPE, PERVEEZ MODY AND BRIAN SLOAN

I. Origins and Aims of the Project

This edited collection of essays emerges from a project on space and care, drawing on different legal, criminological and social anthropological perspectives and particularly on a symposium held in Cambridge in April 2018. The aim of the collection is not to provide a general overview of the now extensive and fertile literature on care, but rather to interrogate the ways in which the emerging interdisciplinary study of care challenges and provokes a reassessment of the points of connection and disjuncture between contexts, meanings and acts of care and the wide variety of spaces and locales in which they emerge. It also emerges from a concern with understanding the ethics of care, and the multiple (and diverse) public, personal and professional enactments of care that emerge through a critical engagement with the spaces in which we study care. The symposium brought leading international scholars together to discern and articulate what we may consider to be a useful analytic of care. Lawyers, anthropologists, sociologists and criminologists reflected on varying socio-legal aspects of conceptualising caring relations in 'spaces', including regimes of care and abandonment (Khlinovskaya Rockhill; Borneman), self-care and kinship care (Carr, Kirton-Darling and Salcedo Repolês; Mody), spaces as 'gaps' in care (Burri), the meanings of marketised care (Sloan; Dominey and Gelsthorpe), and the ways in which care is imagined, made, constrained and engendered in different ways in places such as homes, prisons, workplaces and virtual worlds (Gelsthorpe and Canton; Boellstorff). The symposium allowed the exploration of the complex and varied cultural registers and spaces in which care is being transformed (such as practices of kinship and mobility, migration, law, new regimes of bureaucracy and governance) with important theoretical consequences for how we understand and evaluate what counts as 'care' and what constitutes its abdication.

The original idea for this project, however, emerged in 2008 as an outcome of an interdisciplinary undergraduate course in Social Anthropology & Sociology at the University of Cambridge, which was designed to address new developments within the social sciences on the subject of care. Four members of the Cambridge Socio-Legal Group with different disciplinary backgrounds (Anthropology, Criminology, Law and Sociology) came together to teach on the course (Mody on kinship practices of care, Gelsthorpe on women in prisons, Joanna Miles on family law and care, Darin Weinberg on learning disability and care); the paper was conceived and run by a member (Mody) and it encouraged the start of some important conversations about the conceptual and disciplinary points of departure and connection for our teaching of 'care'. Over the intervening years, what has become increasingly obvious is how productive the interdisciplinary methods and insights have been to the study of care and how this has continued to inform its study in a wide range of academic contexts in subjects as diverse as Law, Medicine, Social Anthropology, Sociology, Politics and Philosophy, amongst other fields. We offer this volume as a further contribution to that engagement.

The two-day symposium associated with the *Spaces of Care* project took place at Pembroke College, Cambridge. All papers were presented, and the authors pre-circulated drafts. A number of discussants from various disciplines were invited to respond to the papers (Patrick McKearney, Jo Cook, Barbara Bodenhorn, Megha Amrith, Sam Cole, and Alice Ievins), and the discussion was lively and fruitful. In the final session of the workshop, participants reflected on themes that emerged from the event, including temporality, subjectivity, economy, 'imaginaries', relationality and the 'dark side' of care (Fine 2007). These themes guide the connections that we make through this book, and are further considered in section III of this introduction below.

II. Setting this Book in the Context of Existing Literature

It would of course be impossible even to summarise the vast body of existing scholarship on care. Here, we therefore highlight literature that has particularly helped to frame and/or distinguish the approach that we take in this book.

Notable amongst previous research in relation to this book is *ReValuing Care in Theory, Law and Policy: Cycles and Connections* edited by Harding, Fletcher and Beasley (2017). Collectively, the authors seek to explore the different dimensions of care that shape social, legal and political contexts. They address these dimensions in four key ways. First, the contributors expand contemporary theoretical understandings of the value of care, by reflecting upon established conceptual approaches (such as the 'ethics of care') and developing new ways of using and understanding this concept. Second, the contributors draw on a wide range of methods, from doctrinal scholarship through ethnographic, empirical and biographical research methodologies. Third, the book enlarges the usual subjects of care research, by expanding its analysis beyond the more typical focus on familial interconnection to include professional care contexts, care by strangers and care for and about animals. Finally, the collection draws on contributions from academics working in Europe and Australia, across law, anthropology, gender studies, politics, psychology and sociology. Harding, Fletcher and Beasley's book has informed some of the thinking underpinning this edited collection. Like ours, *ReValuing Care* is an international as well as interdisciplinary collection and provides helpful support as an intellectual interlocutor for our joint endeavours.

A special issue of *Social Studies of Science* (2015) acknowledges the slippery nature of the concept of care. As the introduction to the issue indicates (Martin, Myers and Viseau 2015: 625–26):

> Any attempt to define it will be exceeded by its multivocality in everyday and scholarly use. In its enactment, care is both necessary to the fabric of biological and social existence and notorious for the problems that it raises when it is defined, legislated, measured, and evaluated. What care looks and feels like is both context-specific and perspective-dependent. Yet, this elusiveness does not mean that it lacks importance. In our engagements with the worlds that we study, construct, and inhabit, we cannot but care: care is an essential part of being a researcher and a citizen.

Again, this relates strongly to our project, and has informed our thinking about the fluidity and unsettled quality of the concept of care (Cook and Trundle, forthcoming).

Other interdisciplinary texts and articles have focused on single elements of care, particularly in primary and secondary health care settings. For example, Deborah Swingleton edited a collection of papers in the *British Medical Education Journal* on 'The Many Meanings of "Quality" in Healthcare: Interdisciplinary Perspectives' (2015). Ayse Gurgess and Yan Xiao (2006) carried out a systematic review of the literature on design information technology in care settings, particularly relating to multi-disciplinary rounds in hospital wards. Sociologies of care have similarly tended to focus on health care. One example is *Dead on Arrival: The Politics of Health-Care in Twentieth Century America* by Colin Gordon (2003).

Political conceptions of care include: *Intimate Labours: cultures, technologies and the politics of care* edited by Eileen Boris (2010) – a book which focuses on those around the world who make their living from offering 'personal care' in one form or another. A new wave of books and articles about care focus on ecological care for the environment: *Beyond Mothering Earth: Ecological Citizenship and the Politics of Care* by Sherlyn Macgregor (2006) and 'Local and green, global and fair: the ethical foodscape and the politics of care' by Kevin Morgan (2010). Our collection may touch on such matters, but its focus is considerably broader.

Very recent texts on dimensions of 'care' include *Stories of Care: A Labour of Law* by LJB Hayes (2017). This is an interdisciplinary study of the interactions of law and labour that shape paid care work. Based on the experiences of homecare workers, this highly topical text unpicks doctrinal assumptions about class and gender to interrogate contemporary labour law. It demonstrates how the UK's crisis in social care is connected to the gendered inadequacy of labour law and argues for transformative change to law at work. The book is fascinating and compelling, but the focus on individual experiences is at some distance from our collection of essays. A related book is *Obligation and Commitment in Family Law* by Gillian Douglas (2018). She takes a contextual approach (drawing on history, sociology and social policy) to examine the concept of obligation as developed in family law and the difficulties the law has had in translating it from a theoretical and ideological concept into the basis of enforceable actions and duties. Thus the book has been of interest to us, but it focuses on a much narrower concept of care than was unfurled during our symposium. The same can be said for Bottomley and Wong's (2009) edited collection of essays: *Changing Contours of Domestic Life, Family And Law: Caring And Sharing*, which broadly offers a reflection on the changing contours of what is generally thought of as 'domestic relations' and on the impact which legal recognition carries in making visible some relationships rather than others. The book also explores the potential for normative values encapsulated within patterns of legal recognition and regulation and the intersections between private law and public policy; the role of private law in the allocation of responsibility and privilege; and the differential impact of seemingly progressive policies on economically vulnerable or socially marginal groupings. Further, the editors examine tensions between family law models and models carried within other fields of private law; and, unusually, architectures in law and the built environment designed to facilitate broader accounts of domestic relationships.

In our deliberations, we have found particularly interesting ideas of 'carescapes' in regard to the environment and planning (Milligan and Wiles 2010; Bowlby 2012; Ivanova et al 2016). Equally, applying feminist ethics to topics such as well-being, social justice, and the ways we relate to one another and the places in which we live, this volume has been enriched by Barnes' (2012) examination of the public debate on care in social policy. The role of the voluntary sector in regard to care (Milligan 2001; Ticktin 2011) and the ethics of care in everyday practice (Barnes 2012) have provided helpful reminders of the need to restore care as a fundamental value in private lives and public policy, and encourages us not to assume the virtue of any regimes of care without interrogating its politics and sources of moral legitimacy. Our intention in this book is to focus particularly on the ambiguities and fluidities of care as conceived and practised. We have sought to offer here a distinctive contribution to multi-locational conceptions of care; considering 'care' beyond those areas and debates most often associated with caring (such as health care, family care, caring for elderly people, for disabled people and other vulnerable populations, as well as care of the body and carescapes). In so doing, we argue that care and caring are deeply ambiguous, fluid and inter-subjective, and that wherever we study care we are inevitably confronted with this changeability and its potential to be transformed through acts of resistance, reinterpretation and reimagination.

III. Organising Principles and Emerging Themes

'Care' is one of the foremost issues of our age and 'spaces of care' is our organising theme. Our approach is to consider 'care' as fundamentally contingent, and as a way of building capacities, imaginaries and relationships. The contingency of care makes us alert to the open-endedness of caring relationships such that we cannot easily detect the agencies of those involved, bringing to mind the disruptive potential of care. In addition to contingency, we argue that care is often reciprocal (even multi-directional) and that it serves as a technology with the potential to assist, maintain, transform, harm and disrupt (for instance, maintaining good documentation can be a technology of care). In this sense, care is a form of social reproduction with the potential to also reproduce inequality and oppression. Canton and Dominey (Chapter two this volume) draw our attention to the way in which punishment invites people who have offended to change, and the authors reflect on the process of bringing about change, causing them to question whether punishment shares the reciprocal characteristics of care, and whether the anticipated desire to bring about change (in those who are incarcerated) transforms the nature of the punishment/caring relationship.

However, this recognition of the potential relationality of care (see, in particular, Herring's contribution – Chapter nine) does not allow us to predict its outcomes. On the contrary, numerous contributors to this volume argue for the need to mobilise care as a strategy and a form of imagination, allowing us to better apprehend the creative and potentially disruptive aspects of care. In this vein, care is a constitutive element in the meaning-making of place (such as the *gae* in Reece's work in Botswana (Chapter eleven), cities as spaces of care in Carr, Kirton-Darling and Salcedo Repolês' chapter (Chapter six), and Ethnographia Island in Boellstorff's account of Second Life (Chapter thirteen)). While a more simplistic understanding of 'space' and 'care' might focus only on the physical and geographical aspects of 'care', we have deliberately adopted a broad understanding of 'space' to encompass its conceptual nature whilst also capturing the making and un-making of care in actual places.

The themes which cut across the chapters and characterise this volume (many of which emerged during our symposium discussions) include: contingency and temporality (historical specificity) and the dynamics of care across time, place and generations; subjectivity and inter-subjectivity – are intentions of care experienced in that way and how is care reciprocally experienced, and what does care feel like?; the economies of care (including the commodification of care; public and private manifestations of care; privatised 'care'); disruptions of care (which generate vulnerabilities with regard to continuities of care); eligibility (those deemed to be deserving and undeserving of care); relationalities of care (collective and individual agency in caring relations, kinship care); and technologies and imaginaries of care – as in new notions of care forged by those in online virtual worlds such as Second Life.

The book also attends to flows of care, asking whether care is better thought of as sitting on a spectrum of relationality rather than being defined as absent or present, 'good' or 'bad'? Are there communities of care and who defines and recognises these (recipients or givers of care; individuals or states)? Are there tensions between policy designed to define 'care' and everyday practices of care? Does care necessitate reciprocity? Is reciprocity difficult? What are the materialities of care? What is the relation between formal and informal dimensions of care and public and private economies of provision?

Another set of themes relate to the 'dark side' of care (lived realities), with paradoxes of care coming to the fore, as well as harm done in the name of 'care'; this also relates to the rhetoric and reality of care and to the apparent ineptitude of organisations in delivering care in some instances; euphemisms of care; care as a human condition; what does 'good enough' care look like?; and the 'scales of care' and whether organisations as well as individuals can 'care', are also relevant to organisational culture and continuities of care.

The unifying argument here is that care transforms the relational sphere and confounds distinctions between the apparently 'public' and 'private', 'personal' and 'professional'. The authors in this volume are all engaged in the task of interpreting how people understand the professional or personal obligations of caring and in so doing, drawing lines between these categories almost to reconfigure them, whilst allowing us to engage with and discern their notions of care. These practices of demarcation and re-signification are often sneakily transgressive of dominant cultural models of care, and reveal the importance of imagination and contingency that shapes and transforms the care we study.

IV. Structure and Contents of the Book

We end this introductory chapter with an overview of the contents of the book's chapters. Chapters two, three and four form a trilogy which revolves around concepts and experiences of care in the criminal justice system, traditionally conceived of as a space in which 'hard' or 'unpleasant' things happen in the form of punishment. In Chapter two, 'Punishment and care reappraised', Rob Canton and Jane Dominey examine the variable and uncertain place that 'care' has had in the discourse, policies and practices of punishment. Punishment by the state has been called 'the inflicting of pain, intended as pain' (Christie 1981: i) and almost all definitions of punishment insist that it must involve the imposition of some form of 'hard treatment'. All of this seems starkly opposed to care. Yet probation, responsible for giving effect to many non-custodial punishments, has sometimes been listed among 'the caring professions' and closely aligned with the values of social work; at other times it has had to contend with political proposals that it should be punishment and to distance itself from any traditions of caring. In particular, probation has long been preoccupied with the question of whether it is (or should) 'care or control' or whether it could do both – debates that, oddly, have largely taken place without reference to the reported experiences of service users. Again, prison is not usually regarded as a place of care, but sometimes prisoners say that they do feel that some staff care about (and even for) them, while many prison staff take caring to be part of their work. The relatively few attempts that have been made to apply an 'ethics of care' approach to questions of punishment have tended to make a case for restorative justice. This paper argues that care is compatible with – and indeed entailed by – almost all legitimate penal objectives. Being cared about is a precondition of caring for others and this is already sufficient to place it at the centre of any attempt to bring it about such that fewer crimes come to be committed. It concludes (following Coverdale 2017) that caring responses to crimes have indeed many beneficial consequences, but that care is of intrinsic value and a moral entitlement of all people.

Chapter three focuses on 'Who cares? Probation practice and the private sector'. Here, Jane Dominey and Loraine Gelsthorpe outline some of the tensions between public and private provision in relation to support for offenders post-release from prison and supervised in the community, or supervised under Community Orders in the community. Supporters of privatisation have argued that a mixed market of supply in relation to services for offenders brings efficiencies and innovations beyond the usual scope and capacity of the public sector. The authors suggest that care for offenders was an important value of the probation service originally, and question how far this is challenged or compromised by the privatisation of the service; thus exposing the potential tension between public and private notions of care.

In 'Parodoxes of Care: women in the criminal justice system' (Chapter four), Loraine Gelsthorpe and Rob Canton further explore ideas of how care is expressed and experienced in the context of the penal system. They discuss aspects of the 'dark side' of care, pointing to ambiguities in regard to recent developments relating to recognition of 'personality disorder' amongst women in conflict with the law, and more generally to some of the questions which need to be asked in relation to seemingly progressive developments in provision for women both in the community and in prisons in England and Wales.

The next several chapters focus on care in spaces outside the criminal justice system: children's homes, cities, workplaces, private homes and adult care homes. At times, the authors highlight common themes concerning 'caring institutions' and care as an exercise of power present in the earlier criminological contributions. In her chapter '"All children are our children": care and kinship in residential children's homes in the Russian Federation' (Chapter five), Elena Khlinovskaya Rockhill explores some of the ambiguities and coercions of the state by looking at the impact of residential care on children in Russia – on their lives, sense of belonging, and relationship with their biological family and the state. In the Russian Federation, social orphans, or children without parental care, are placed either with members of their extended family or family substitutes in a chain of state residential care institutions. The latter placement is the beginning of a construction of specific social relations in the context of institutional space where children, kinship, care and the state are all entwined. At the heart of this social organisation lies the process of re-kinning. Shortly after children are removed from their 'unfit' biological parents, the kin ties between them are (often) severed. While being raised in residential care they are supposedly stripped of the 'spoilt' identity of their parents and re-kinned to the state. Now their parent, the state aspires to provide children with comprehensive care during their childhood and include them into its polity as unpolluted children of the state. The chapter analyses the construction of these kinship-like relationships, based on the expectation of mutual care obligations between social orphans and the state in all its multiplicity, both embodied and abstract. It explores the ideology and practice of this 'kinship based on care' arrangement within and outside the institutional space, showing that neither removal of 'spoilt' identity, nor kinning to the state, are unproblematic. Finally, it considers some implications that this type of relatedness has for children's lives, sense of belonging, and the relationships with their biological family and the state.

Chapter six, by Helen Carr, Ed Kirton-Darling and Maria Fernanda Salcedo Repolês, 'Re-imagining cities as spaces of care – a perspective from street homelessness' invokes the city as the space under scrutiny. Their chapter tells a tale of three cities in particular, London and Canterbury in England and Belo Horizonte in Brazil. They concede that in contemporary politics, cities are often conceived as spaces either of economic development or of insecurity, with potentially very negative consequences for their homeless populations. Such populations, whose numbers have been increased by such political concepts of the modern city in the first place, are often expected either to participate in entrepreneurship or to be subject to legal discipline, exclusion and/or schemes aiming to remove them from the streets but also protect private property. Carr et al nevertheless argue that cities can be re-imagined as spaces of care via the universality of vulnerability and insecurity and what they term the 'disruptive potential' of care. They provide examples of two projects through which homeless people provide a form of care for cities and their inhabitants by running library projects, in one case in the face of opposition from civic authorities and business owners, but with the support of other relevant groups. In the 'city of care' that Carr et al describe, 'potential for liberation and self-realisation is made possible by encounter and self, collective management', with benefits for both the homeless and housed populations. The library projects illustrate 'that citizenship is based on the acknowledgement of interdependency', and that 'protection extends beyond physical protection, to encompass protection of a common space, of a community founded in care'. The authors contrast the city of care with the neoliberal city, which 'see[s] as positive the dependency of women and children in the private sphere, whilst any dependency in the public and labour spheres [is] considered highly objectionable'. They claim that analysing the city in terms of care 'can be a starting point for progressive re-framings of the relationship between liberty, security and control'.

Brian Sloan's Chapter seven on formal and informal care in England and Australia begins with the provocation that any attempt to distinguish between public and private spheres as spaces of care gives rise to immediate difficulties. For example, while formal adult social care tends to be associated with the public responsibility and the state, in England few local authorities are involved in the direct delivery of care services, with most services operated by private, for-profit providers. He argues that much formal care takes place in private homes, and such homes and other private property can be appropriated to fund the social care system. Moreover, privacy is an important value in the context of a care home that might in other respects be characterised as public. Conversely, the recognition of, and reliance on, *informal* care (which might legitimately be characterised as a matter of private arrangement) by the state arguably gives it a public character. Sloan's chapter compares the relationship between formal (associated with the public sphere) and informal (associated with the private sphere) care in England and Australia in terms of their legal recognition and funding. Both jurisdictions have recently passed legislation reforming their social care funding systems, but several Australian States and Territories recognise informal caring *relationships* in a much more coherent manner than is true in England, drawing attention to the importance of conceptions of care that recognise it as based on a system of generalised reciprocity. Sloan asks inter alia whether it is justifiable to seek to limit liability to pay for formal public care while at the same time mandating wealth transfers through the recognition of private informal care relationships.

There is something of an irony in Susanne Burri's chapter on care and the workplace (Chapter eight). She considers strategies that allow workers to spend *less* time in the particular space with which she is concerned so that they can provide care in another space (often, as she points out, the worker's own home). The workplace itself thus arguably becomes a space of care by implementing policies that facilitate care elsewhere, even if this is not always considered possible in practice. Burri analyses what she describes as the unique Dutch model with its focus on providing strong rights to adjust working time (including leave) and/or place, and compares it to an EU proposal on work-life balance. It is noteworthy that, despite the often gendered nature of care work, both men and women work part-time more often in the Netherlands than elsewhere. That said, Burri highlights that there are still significant gender differences in both the take-up of flexible working opportunities and the amount of care provided. She also argues that, while the strategies of the Dutch employment legislation do enable care, they still result in financial disadvantages for the carer, particularly in light of the unpaid nature of several types of leave. She emphasises the importance of tax incentives and viable facilities for the care of children and disabled people as part of the wider context of the relationship of employment and care.

The 'space' addressed in Jonathan Herring's Chapter nine might be characterised as the gap in understanding between advocates of disability rights and of the ethics of care respectively. That space is therefore more conceptual than some of the previous chapters, notwithstanding its concern with highly physical activities. Herring argues that the debate between the two schools of thought can be resolved if care is understood in a relational way. He rejects the idea that care should be regarded as a flow of benefits from one person to another, but argues that the realities of care mean that the line between the 'disabled' and the 'able-bodied' person become blurred. One part of the 'ethics of care' approach that he outlines is that care should be understood subjectively in the sense that it needs to be tailored to individual circumstances. More broadly, it regards care as an inevitable and positive part of life (albeit one that can produce disadvantages for the carer). Herring nevertheless highlights the disability rights critique that care has a 'dark side', can be oppressive, and should be replaced with a notion of recipient-directed assistance. Herring's reconciliation of these two schools of thought involves a focus on caring relationships so that the contributions of both parties are recognised, but without a focus purely on the value of the services provided or the autonomous direction of a person requiring assistance. He relies on the temporal nature of care to show that such a relationship will develop over time. Herring's preference for a relational approach also casts doubt on an understanding of 'economies' of care that seek to value care services in monetary terms, and highlights the universality and positive nature of vulnerability of interdependence (while accepting that people's needs vary). As he puts it, '[d]owngrading care works to the disadvantage of disabled people', while '[d]owngrading disabled people impacts on those in relationships with them'.

The remainder of the book concerns anthropological perspectives on care and space, drawing attention to the earlier themes on contingency and imagination. Chapter ten focuses on 'forced marriage' and kinship care amongst British South Asians (Mody), Chapter eleven, on kinship and the 'crisis of care' in Reece's study of movement in Botswana, and Borneman (Chapter twelve), on the collapse of the state and security, refugees and flight to safety from war-torn Syria. Finally, Boellstorff's Chapter thirteen presents us with an account of the imaginaries of care that generated a real place (Ethnographia Island) in which his disabled informants were able to explore and experiment with their own creativity as forms of care.

The potentially coercive context of care comes to the fore in Perveez Mody's paper, alongside the fact that understandings of what constitutes 'care' can be extremely subjective and variable. In a contribution entitled 'Kinship Care', she considers the phenomenon of 'forced marriage', including the differences in how it is understood and viewed by the state and within British South Asian communities. One of Mody's subjects illustrates how a coercive form of perceived 'care' by parents in forcing a daughter to enter and remain in an abusive marriage could be used to exact care from those parents for the daughter and her children, without recourse to legal protections for those forced into marriage. Another retains a very complex relationship with her parents, having endured a similar experience. Mody highlights the 'importance of recognising the complex ways in which narratives of care (and demands for it) are marshalled to the cause of kinship values but also change them', emphasising that '[w]e can't say where precisely care resides because it is manifestly inter-subjective', particularly over a long period of time. For her informants, spaces of care emerge 'through their ownership and more thoroughgoing and critical appraisal of what was given to them as kinship care'. Mody is left with questions about the morally positive nature of both kinship and care.

Koreen Reece explores mobility from a different dimension, examining the ways in which the movement of families in Botswana produce spaces of care. Her strong argument is that the AIDS epidemic in Botswana is frequently cast as a 'crisis of care' wherein family breakdown and HIV transmission are explicitly linked to mobility. Paradoxically though, she found in her own work that Tswana kinship relied on movement precisely as a means of providing and provisioning care. The Tswana *gae* (home) is characterised in her work as a multiple and scattered space – including the *lelwapa* (courtyard), farmlands and cattle-posts – integrated by constant movement and crucially, care-work. The characteristic multiplicity of the *gae* also generates risks and crisis ('*dikgang*' in Setswana) that she argues are ameliorated by families through compromises of closeness and distance; staying together and moving apart. The figure of elderly Ntate ('father') arriving unexpectedly back at the *gae* from the cattle-post with his swollen feet and allegations of a sexual dalliance is juxtaposed against the rest of the family attending to care obligations that included the attentive stirring of a pot in which a cow-head was being cooked, being present at a neighbouring village to plan a wedding, visiting a relative who had taken sick and going to the cattle-post to free animals that had been bogged down in mud around their watering holes. Reece draws our attention to the specific expectations and contributions of care that differentiate kin along generational and gender lines (see also Yaris 2017). As she puts it, 'Movement … is not only a key practice of care used to mark out specific spaces of care, but also a means of identifying, ordering, and delimiting relatedness'. Reece's work demonstrates the ways in which 'care is emplaced ("housed"), but also produces space ("houses")' in Tswana kinship.

John Borneman's chapter builds upon his ground-breaking anthropological work on caring, which challenged the normativities and ethnocentricity of earlier accounts of gender and kinship with a provocation to engage with 'a concern for the actual situations in which people experience the need to care and be cared for' (Borneman 1997: 583). His chapter here is an attempt to make sense of his own experience of watching his Syrian informants and interlocutors enduring horror in the shape of war and displacement. As an anthropologist who had spent a considerable period of time in Syria, he found himself struggling professionally and personally to 'digest' the experiences that his informants were documenting through social media before and after they took flight from the war. He argues for the need to go far beyond 'witnessing' and 'representation' (the two standard modes of anthropological engagement with extreme suffering) and instead to extend relationships of 'holding' and 'loving care' towards informants whose lives have been deeply damaged by their experiences, so that the anthropologist asks more profound questions: in Sontag's (2003: 114) terms, what can we do to 'moderate hell's flames' for those being engulfed by them? For the refugee who has experienced a profound rupture in their own holding environment, the self is further experienced as 'fragmented, discontinuous and disintegrated'. For Borneman, adequate 'holding' (in addition to 'witnessing') allows a 'sense of security' in which the self can be re-integrated. His paper explores the meanings of spaces and relationships of care as 'containers' and 'holders' across national, material and communicative registers and between Germans and Syrians as they seek to create relationships of reciprocity, welfare, refuge and care for each other. Borneman begins with Todorov's (1996) claim that of the three 'ordinary virtues' (dignity, care and life), caring is morally superior because it involves establishing reciprocity and the possibility of a reversal of roles. Reflecting on the nature of care as evidenced in the receiving German welfare state (where he subsequently followed many of his informants' lives), Borneman explores the nature and meanings of flight and care for his refugee informants.

Finally, more than any other contribution in this volume, Tom Boellstorff's work speaks critically of the anthropology of place in the context of the virtual. His work on Second Life, the online social world, caused him to embark on a methodological innovation, setting up 'Ethnographia Island' in Second Life, and inviting disabled persons on a first-come, first-served basis to build upon individual and collaborative parcels of virtual land to respond to and reflect upon their disability experience. This allowed the anthropologist to engage, participate and observe in a collaboratively created field-site. Boellstorff explores the nature of ableist physical environments and logics through this study of the uses of an emerging digital technology that challenges geographies of ability beyond the usual registers of access and mobility so prevalent in disability studies of care. With John Law (2004: 45), he argues that methods do not 'discover and depict realities' but participate in the 'enactment of those realities'. Digital embodiment and creativity, agency, place-making and digital topography become the central objects of study rather than the mere connectivity afforded by linking two places. As Boellstorff is at pains to stress: 'Second Life is not just a place: it is a place that is built' and on Ethnographia Island, disabled persons reconfigure and interrogate ableist lifeworlds through their building activities. One of his informants, Phoebe, says movingly of the digital place she inhabits in Second Life: 'What we have here are experiences, "There is a 'here' here"'. A further aspect of the digital place is that it allows co-presence, with proximity of adjacent parcels of virtual land raising problems as well as serving as a resource. This chapter provides a unique and powerful insight into the ways in which digital place can provide 'capability-diverse' creativities and experiences of pleasure and discomfort; often speaking back to exclusions of ableist discourse and the possibilities of virtual human care.

Thus it will be clear that this book is not simply about geographical 'spaces of care', although prisons, spaces of probation, residential care, the workplace, trading markets, agricultural land, kinship groups and family, for instance, give the book material grounding. But together the authors explore notions of 'care' as it adapts, and is adapted, to fit social space. It speaks to concern for 'care' as a spatially fluid, spatially dependent and spatially revealed dimension of humanity.

References

Barnes, C (2012) 'Re-thinking Disability, Work and Welfare' *Sociology Compass* 6: 472.

Boris, E (ed) (2010) *Intimate Labours: Cultures, Technologies and the Politics of Care* (Stanford CA, Stanford University Press).

Borneman, J (1997) 'Caring and Being Cared for: Displacing Marriage, Kinship, Gender and Sexuality' *International Social Science Journal* 49(4): 573.

Bottomley, A and Wong, S (eds) (2009) *Changing Contours of Domestic Life, Family And Law: Caring And Sharing* (Oxford, Hart Publishing).

Bowlby, S (2012) 'Recognising the time-space dimensions of care: Caringscapes and carescapes' *Environment and Planning A: Economy and Space* 44(9): 2101.

Christie, N (1981) *Limits to Pain* (Oxford, Martin Robertson), available online at: www.prisonpolicy.org/scans/limits_to_pain/ (accessed 6 August 2019).

Cook, J and Trundle, C (forthcoming) 'Introduction: Unsettled Care' *Anthropology and Humanism: Special Issue on Unsettled Care*.

Coverdale, HB (2017) 'Punishment and welfare: defending offender's inclusion as subjects of state care' *Ethics and Social Welfare* 11: 1.

Douglas, G (2018) *Obligation and Commitment in Family Law* (Oxford, Hart Publishing).

Fine, MD (2007) *A Caring Society? Care and the Dilemmas of Human Services in the 21st Century* (New York, Palgrave Macmillan).

Gordon, C (2003) *Dead on Arrival: The Politics of Health-Care in Twentieth Century America* (Princeton NJ, Princeton University Press).

Gurgess, AP and Xiao, Y (2006) 'A Systematic Review of the Literature on Multidisciplinary Rounds to Design Information Technology' *Journal of the American Medical Informatics Association* 13(3): 267.

Harding, R, Fletcher, F and Beasley, C (eds) (2017) *ReValuing Care in Theory, Law and Policy: Cycles and Connections* (London, Routledge).

Hayes, LJB (2017) *Stories of Care: A Labour of Law* (London, Palgrave Macmillan).

Ivanova, D, Wallenburg, I and Bal, R (2016) 'Care in place: A case study of assembling a carescape' *Sociology of Health & Illness* 38(8): 1336.

Law, J (2004) *After Method: Mess in Social Science Research* (London, Routledge).

Macgregor, S (2006) *Beyond Mothering Earth: Ecological Citizenship and the Politics of Care* (Vancouver BC, University of British Columbia Press).

Martin, A, Myers, N and Viseu, A (2015) 'The politics of care in technoscience' *Social Studies of Science* 45(5): 625.

Milligan, C (2001) *Geographies of Care: Space, Place, and the Voluntary Sector* (Abingdon, Ashgate).

Milligan, C and Wiles, J (2010) 'Landscapes of care' *Progress in Human Geography* 34(6): 736.

Morgan, K (2010) 'Local and green, global and fair: the ethical foodscape and the politics of care' *Environment and Planning A: Economy and Space* 42(8): 1852.

Sontag, S (2003) *Regarding the Pain of Others* (New York, Farrar, Straus, and Giroux).

Ticktin, M (2011) *Casualties of Care: Immigration and the Politics of Humanitarianism in France* (Berkeley CA, University of California Press).

Todorov, T (1996) *Facing the Extreme: Moral Life in the Concentration Camps* (New York, Metropolitan Books).

Yaris, K (2017) *Care Across Generations: Solidarity and Sacrifice in Transnational Families* (Redwood City CA, Stanford University Press).

2

Punishment and Care Reappraised

ROB CANTON AND JANE DOMINEY[1]

I. Introduction

This chapter considers what space there may be for care in the practices of punishment. Punishment is thought to make us safer by contributing (in one way or another) to a reduction in offending; it is also expected, by imposing hardships or deprivations on offenders, to vindicate the experience of victims and to affirm the values that bind a community. Does pursuit of these objectives leave any space for care?

Discussion begins with some reflections on the idea of care and its contribution to ethical thinking, before turning to a short historical account of its changing significance in penal policy in England and Wales. The discourse and practices of the principal institutions of punishment – the probation and prison services – are then explored, with a particular scrutiny of the relationship between care and control. The ethics of care – a relatively unfamiliar paradigm within the philosophy of punishment – is then adduced to appraise the moral dimensions of penal practice. It is concluded that activities and attitudes characterised by caring better support the objectives that are set for principled punishment as well as having an intrinsic ethical worth.

This discussion of punishment and care will touch upon a number of the themes that are common to the chapters in this book. There will be illustrations of a *dark side* of care, when harm and oppression can be concealed behind pretensions to care. Again, debates about punishment often centre on *eligibility* for care, on who is deserving of care and who, by contrast, has no such entitlement. Even when claims to care are sincere, there can be a dissonance between the *rhetoric and the reality*; between the avowals of caring and the lived experiences of the supposed beneficiaries. And, as we have already seen, there will be a consideration

[1] The authors would like to thank Professor Loraine Gelsthorpe and the other editors, as well as the contributors to this volume, for their advice and encouragement. Sam Cole read the paper carefully in draft and we are indebted to him for his suggestions for improvement. Alice Ievins chaired a constructive discussion at a seminar when this and other contributions to this volume were considered.

of *care and control*, objectives and activities that are often assumed to be in stark opposition, although it will be argued that the relationship between them is far from straightforward.

II. What is Care?

Care is said to be one of humanity's most fundamental moral foundations – 'innate and universally available psychological systems' that form the foundations of our moral judgements (Moral Foundations 2013). While societies construct their distinctive moral codes, their 'virtues, narratives, and institutions' (ibid), the foundations on which these are built have been argued to be constant. Jonathan Haidt and colleagues argue that societies and individuals with a sensitivity to these foundations will thrive and that in their absence individual and social flourishing could not be achieved (Haidt 2012). Emotions of compassion and empathy and an aversion to harming, leading to (and enhanced by) practices of caring, bring clear evolutionary benefits. Most obviously, care for and protection of children ensure the continuation and thriving of families and communities. This extends to other kin, to communities, perhaps to other people and maybe to all sentient beings in an 'expanding circle' of concern, as an innate drive transforms into a deliberately chosen ethic (Singer 1981).

Care, as an emotion, prompts courses of action. Haidt regards caring as a *moral* emotion, of which one defining criterion is that 'the emotion puts the person into a motivational and cognitive state in which there is an increased tendency to engage in certain goal-related actions which … either benefit others, or else uphold or benefit the social order' (Haidt 2003: 854). Thus care will prompt actions like aiding, supporting or comforting. The willingness to act may be a litmus test of the sincerity of a claim to care: someone who professes to care is expected to take some action or at least to call upon others to do so and a failure to do so raises doubts about their words.[2] If care remains a mere private sentiment, it is also of uncertain worth. Further, the actions to which the emotion gives rise must be experienced *as care*. The caregiver cannot determine on their own whether they have succeeded in evincing or accomplishing care: this will also depend on the perceptions of the supposed beneficiary. It will be argued later that the failure of criminological scholarship to inquire sufficiently into the experiences of defendants and offenders makes accounts of care at best incomplete and at worst significantly misleading.

In (probably all) human societies, manifestations of caring are extolled as virtues (kindness, compassion, gentleness); their opposites (cruelty, callousness)

[2] This is not to overlook the possibility that there may be circumstances when genuine intentions to care are thwarted by a lack of power or resources. Staff may be over-burdened, for example, or the organisation may frustrate their ability to express their care. See also Dominey and Gelsthorpe, Chapter 3 this volume.

are condemned as vices. Indeed reflections on the 'opposites' of care can be instructive. Amartya Sen (2009) has perceptively noted that while not many of us could elaborate a theory of justice, we all think we can spot an injustice when we see one. Similarly, if care is not easy to define, there are certain attitudes and behaviours with which it seems starkly incompatible and thinking about these opposites can be a useful heuristic device to explore the concept. Thus, malevolence or the imposition of deliberate harm seem incompatible with care; so too do neglect or indifference to a person's interests or a failure to accord respect or to honour their intrinsic human dignity. It seems plausible to infer that care, whatever else it entails, involves a concern for the interests and well-being of another.

Care and compassion for *victims* are prominent in reactions to crime: some crimes are outrageous, provoking an anger that commonly leads to a punitive response (Nussbaum 2016). These sentiments are not difficult to understand. Retributive emotions often reflect a decent compassion for a victim's distress and a virtuous expression of solidarity with members of our community, especially since 'we are offered limited opportunity to express our civic involvement, empathy with others' suffering, or indignation in the face of iniquity in any other way' (Sparks 2011: 319). At the same time, if care and aversion to harm are the only moral emotions at work, we may wonder why they are not extended to the *offender* too.[3] Punishment by the state typically involves the deliberate imposition of pain, hardship or at least deprivations – behaviour which the moral foundation of care could not usually countenance. But so far from being troubled by this, there often seems to be a widespread satisfaction in contemplating the suffering of the wrongdoer. Other moral emotions are at work as well, interacting in ways that make the practices of punishment inherently unpredictable and even contradictory (Canton 2015). Whatever the explanation of this selective compassion, it is a vivid example of the question of *eligibility* for care. Histories of welfare commonly reflect on distinctions between deserving and undeserving recipients of care, and offenders, considered reductively only in terms of their criminal conduct, are often thought to be undeserving and therefore ineligible. As we shall see, characterised in other ways, people with criminal convictions have a strong claim to be entitled to care.

Care can hold a central place in some forms of ethical thinking. The *ethics of care*, associated with and inspired by Carol Gilligan, is an approach to morality that is commonly contrasted with the traditional focus on duties, rules and rights (see also Herring, Chapter nine this volume).[4] Rather than emphasising the duties

[3] There is a risk of over-generalisation here, no doubt. Norbert Elias wrote of changes in sensibilities over time that reflect an increased (albeit selective) aversion to infliction of pain and have had an influence of forms of punishment. See in general Garland (1990: especially ch 10) and Smith (2008).

[4] Virtue ethics, which has its own and different focus, has many similarities with care ethics, but there are ways in which they should be distinguished (Slote 2007). Slote also argues against those who hold that care ethics can be reconciled with formal abstract principles, holding that it is better seen not as an 'add-on' or complement to those approaches, but as a distinct and comprehensive morality. Held (2010) takes a different view, arguing there is no necessary incompatibility between justice and care: 'When justice should … prevail in certain contexts, it need not oppose or cancel the care on which legal systems should be built' (Held 2010: 117).

or rights of an abstract autonomous individual, care ethics attends to responsibilities and, especially, to relationships. As Virginia Held puts it:

> The ethics of care understands the value and necessity of caring labor and it emphasizes the values of empathy, sensitivity, trust, and responding to need. It cultivates practices such as the building of trust, and practices of responding to actual needs. At its most basic level it understands persons as interrelated, in contrast with the model of the independent, self-sufficient individual of liberal theory. (Held 2010: 117)

This entails what Gilligan referred to as 'its insistent contextual relativism' (2016: 22). Care ethics thus restores the context that gives a moral problem its meaning and significance, seeking responses that express care for all affected and centring on the restoration and nurturing of personal relationships.[5] The implications of this for punishment – the extent to which care is, could or should be part of the way in which punishment is put into effect – is the subject of this chapter, and the place of care in penal policy is next to be considered.

III. Care in Policy

For much of the twentieth century, a model of penal welfare is said to have dominated crime policy in England and Wales (Garland 2001). Offenders were considered to be deprived and neglected, their offending commonly attributed to these disadvantages. In that case, punishment was unfair (offending was behaviour they could not help – or at least they had fewer choices than most people) and irrelevant (for unless the problems bound up with their offending were addressed, further offending was likely). Care was due to them as vulnerable people with troubled biographies, and care was the way to bring about change – for example, through the therapeutic processes of social casework. Whether the aspirations of policy were matched by the realities of practice is, of course, another matter (Cohen 1985). Any historical account is inevitably dominated by formal statements of theory and policy, and little can be said with any confidence about what these policy aspirations entailed for individual offenders, who may well often have been dealt with in ways that were not experienced as care at all. Within and beyond criminal justice, even sincere claims to care, as we have seen, are not always matched by the experience of the supposed beneficiary. A prominent example is the use of indeterminate sentences. If the purpose of a sentence is to determine the right treatment, how can it be possible to anticipate how long

[5] Gilligan argued persuasively that these different approaches are *gendered*: women and girls look for solutions to moral problems that express principles of caring; men and boys typically favour ostensibly dispassionate and abstract reasoning. These ideas are developed in other chapters in this volume (for example, Gelsthorpe and Canton, Chapter 4).

a period of detention may be required for the treatment to have its effects? In the USA especially, it became common to impose a term of (say) 5–20 years, with the length of time served depending on an expert's perception of how well the individual had 'responded to treatment' (Bean 1976; Mitford 1977). This naturally led to enormous resentment and was felt as anything but the caring that this approach purported to represent.

In any event, the treatment model of rehabilitation associated with this understanding of crime notoriously fell into theoretical and political disrepute (Canton 2017: chapter six and references there cited). Policy-makers and practitioners were discomfited by the difficulties of finding evidence to show that treatment was effective in reducing reoffending. The model was argued to be condescending and disrespectful to offenders, intrusive and even manipulative in its methods to effect change, and masked the origins of much offending by regarding crime not as a function and symptom of social injustice but as the product of individual sickness or weakness (Bean 1976). It was no less coercive or (at least potentially) oppressive than other punishment ideologies, and was all the more insidious for purporting to do this in the name of care. This could be described as a 'dark side of care' where the declaration of caring masks a very different form of intervention which can be paternalistic or otherwise oppressive.

The rehabilitative ideal was accordingly challenged robustly by a *justice model* that insisted that the least and the most the state was entitled to do was to punish people in proportion to what they deserved (American Friends Service Committee 1971; von Hirsch 1976). Punishment became its own self-evident justification. The discrimination and disdain for proportionality in sentencing that had marked the treatment model were to be eradicated by minimising or at least structuring sentencer discretion. At the extreme, sentencers (especially in the USA in some States and at the federal level) were to be guided by sentencing tables or grids. The index offence and the record of previous convictions were all that were relevant and should, accordingly, determine the sentence. All other factors were deemed to be irrelevant, their introduction risking unfair discrimination: context did not matter.

Nils Christie was among those who protested against these developments. Once recourse to individual mitigating (or indeed aggravating) factors has been prohibited, 'Lady Justice does not need to be blindfolded. She has nothing to look at, except a table' (Christie 2000: 169). Years earlier, Christie had objected to responses to crime that amounted to 'inflicting pain, intended as pain' (Christie 1981: i) and argued that, for all its shortcomings, the '[treatment] ideology and the acts – also contained realities of pain-reduction' (ibid 17). As Bottoms had put it, 'The rehabilitative ethic, and perhaps still more the liberal-reformism which preceded it, was an ethic of coercive caring, but at least there was caring' (1980: 20). In an era of 'just deserts', or where imprisonment aspired to no more than 'humane containment', care might be jettisoned altogether. As we have seen, it is not only the deliberate infliction of pain that is incompatible with care, but the disregard for the individual which follows from the abstraction of the crime from the context that gives it its meaning and significance, dealing mechanistically with people now reduced to their offending behaviour or carriers of risk factors (see further Dominey and Gelsthorpe, Chapter three this volume).

These changes in policy from penal welfare to (one conception of) justice and control were accompanied by shifts in the 'emotional tone' of crime policy in the final quarter of the twentieth century. When welfare was dominant, 'The affect invoked to justify penal reforms was most often a progressive sense of justice … a compassion for the needs and rights of the less fortunate' (Garland 2001: 10). In the transition, compassionate sentiments did not disappear, but there was now a 'new discourse of crime policy [that] consistently invokes an angry public, tired of living in fear, demanding strong measures of punishment and protection' (ibid).

Care, then, came to be seen as something due not to offenders, but to others – to victims of crime, to the vulnerable, to people with backgrounds of abuse, neglect and disadvantage, to people in poor health, those with mental illnesses, learning disabilities or addictions, to care-leavers and to those with no homes or jobs. But the truth, however politically inconvenient, is that all of these groups are and always have been strongly represented and often heavily over-represented in penal populations (Reiman and Leighton 2013; Muller and Wildeman 2013; for England and Wales, Prison Reform Trust 2017). The stark rhetorical polarities between the deserving and undeserving, offenders and victims, goodies and baddies, do scant justice to the realities. For example, offenders and victims are often the same people. Today's abused and neglected child is tomorrow's hooligan or worse (Boswell 1996). A recent report by Her Majesty's Inspectorate of Probation found that, where information was available, 81 per cent of the young people in their sample (of users of the services of youth offending teams) had 'experienced trauma or other adverse events' (Her Majesty's Inspectorate of Probation 2017: 5). Baroness Corston (2007) argued this was especially true of girls and women, many of whose offending histories cannot be understood outside the context of the abuse they have experienced (see Gelsthorpe and Canton, Chapter four this volume).

If Haidt and colleagues are right to regard care and an aversion to harm as a moral foundation, how is it that care is withheld from so many people with such marked disadvantages, and so clearly apparent needs? Part of the explanation, no doubt, is that the master status of 'offender' suppresses all other ways of understanding people with convictions (Becker 1963). Defined by their worst behaviour, 'offenders' are denied their full humanity and are thus rendered ineligible for compassion and care. The anger that is provoked by crimes is a strong emotional stimulus to punishment (Nussbaum 2016), and anger towards someone typically suppresses any sentiments of care – at least in the short term. The language in which debates are often conducted is another contributory factor. The rights and needs of 'offenders' and 'victims' are rhetorically opposed to one another as if there were a 'zero-sum', such that the more care due to victims, the less there must be for offenders (for example, Zimring 2001). Again, if care is taken to be incompatible with control (further to be discussed below) the anxiety to reduce offending may lead to a repudiation of care.

IV. Care and Probation

The criminal justice institution most associated with care, in the public mind and in the professional self-awareness of its practitioners, is probation. For most of the twentieth century, the probation service aligned itself closely with social work, its traditions and professions of caring (Bochel 1976; Vanstone 2004).[6] Probation officers and social workers were felt to need the same skills, knowledge and values and they followed the same training. The professional qualification for probation officers was the Certificate of Qualification in Social Work and, later, the Diploma in Social Work. For a time, the correct title of the service was the 'Probation and After-Care Service', while *throughcare* was how probation referred to its work with serving prisoners, including its work with their families.[7]

In the late 1980s, however, even as it became increasingly apparent that prison was an expensive failure, any attempt to reduce prison numbers risked estranging those who believed that punishment was the answer to crime. The government tried to resolve this dilemma by presenting probation and other community sanctions as *punishment in the community*: punishment would indeed be the response to crime, but there was no reason why this could not as well take place outside of prison, enforced by a vigilant and strict probation service (Brownlee 1998). Connotations of caring seemed quite at odds with this conception of probation. This was perhaps the most salient of the reasons why the government repudiated social work as a characterisation of probation and abandoned social work training as the appropriate preparation for the profession (Canton and Dominey 2017).

Since much of the knowledge and probably many of the skills needed by social workers are also required by probation staff, it was the government's understanding of a social work ethos or its values that was being rejected (Aldridge and Eadie 1997). 'Care' was not at all what was to be expected from an agency charged with

[6] It must not be forgotten that social work, like the other caring professions, may sometimes be practised in ways that are incompatible with claims to care. Social work practice may sometimes be negligent, judgemental, mechanistic or even unkind. Yet it purports to be a caring profession and this characterisation is broadly accepted, such that shortcomings in care are received as failure. The public expects social work to care; this is not always or everywhere its expectation of probation.

[7] The term *after-care* has largely fallen out of use now in England and Wales, although it is interesting to note that it survives in the lexicons of the Council of Europe (for example, 2010). Distinguished from *resettlement* – the formal supervision following release from prison – after-care is voluntary on the part of the client, but recognised as a duty of the state and the community.

administering punishment in the community. There also were more sophisticated critiques of probation's reliance on 'social work values' from others, including some sympathetic to its work. Nellis commented on a lack of political resonance (do 'social work values' mean anything much to most people?) and their incompleteness as an ethical characterisation of probation's work. Many of the guiding principles of working with offenders could be retained, but probation's commitment to its 'clients' had to be complemented with a recognition of the rights and interests of victims and of the wider community (Nellis 1995). Nor, once a 'zero-sum' assumption has been rejected, is there any need to compromise caring for offenders in respecting these other interests.

The rejection of social work coincided with (or perhaps just slightly anticipated) an emphasis on evidence-led practice – on 'what works'. Not only in penal policy but across all areas of government, the claim was that there was to be rigorous research to determine if a policy is working, and policy and practice should adapt in response to the findings (Davies, Nutley and Smith 2000). But, perhaps to the discomfort of those who felt there was no place for social work in the new era of rigour and effectiveness, Peter Raynor was to argue that the social work literature included many useful ideas about how probation supervision should be managed and these insights should therefore continue to inform probation's thinking. As he put it, 'the search for effective practice cannot afford to ignore relevant research just because it goes under a currently disparaged label' (Raynor 2003: 84). The continuing relevance of social work was similarly asserted by David Smith:

> [F]or all the rhetoric of punishment and public protection, risk management and enforcement, when practitioners decide what they are actually going to do to engage and motivate clients, help them access resources and convey a sense of hope in the possibility of constructive change, they will find themselves using ideas and skills that have emerged from social work theory and research. (Smith 2005: 634)

The place of care in the thinking and the professional culture of probation is discussed further in Dominey and Gelsthorpe (Chapter three this volume). For all the political positioning, many characteristics of probation practice are shared with social work, even if they have come to be articulated in a rather different language. They are tenacious because respect for people, kindness and a commitment to care are indispensable elements in what it takes to do the job well. They cannot be eradicated for political expediency, even when they are regarded as subversive of the attempt to present probation as punishment.

V. Care and Control

Even when professionally aligned with the caring traditions of social work, probation was exercised about (at least) two aspects of caring. First was the worry about the very idea of compulsory care. There seems a risk that purported caring, without the consent of the cared-for, will be experienced as intrusion or condescension and not at all as care. And as we have seen, care cannot be ensured just by the benevolent sentiments or even the actions of the caregiver, but fundamentally depends, too, upon the perceptions of the (supposed) cared-for. It was true, for most of the twentieth century, that probationers were asked to express formal consent in court, but the formal obligations of the Probation Order were one thing, further intrusion quite another. To resolve this, Bryant and colleagues (1978) proposed that a probation order should be seen as being made up of a 'primary contract' between the offender and the court, which would constitute the formal, compulsory imposition, and an optional 'subsidiary contract', between the client and the probation officer, which could include social work help. Opportunities for help, support and caring would be made available, but it would be for the client to decide whether or not these offers were accepted.

The second concern was a perception that care was incompatible with control. It may be that some offenders are disadvantaged and deserving of care, but no more so than many other people who do not commit crimes. The justification for an agency providing services for offenders, then, must lie in its attempts to change their behaviour – which looks like a practice of control. What space would and should be left for care?

Before considering its relationship with care, however, it is worth asking why it is that, in most circumstances, control is morally problematic and its exercise stands in need of justification. Control may be an imposition in its own right – the 'hard treatment' that is an element of many definitions of punishment – being and being meant to be an unwanted burden. At least as commonly, however, control has an instrumental function: to constrain people's conduct or movements in an attempt to influence their behaviour. In both respects, control appears to violate one of our most fundamental moral entitlements – the right of autonomy. One conception of human rights is grounded in 'the values of personhood' and to be a person entails rights of: autonomy (to decide on one's pathways and projects for oneself); choice (and genuine choice requires adequate information); ability to act (which requires a minimum provision of resources and capabilities); and liberty (against anyone blocking this) (Griffin 2008: 34). All of this is violated or at least threatened by control.

To this extent, since care includes a respect for rights and interests, control does seem to fit uncomfortably with claims to care. It is to be noted that this problem is shared by social work and perhaps by other 'caring professions'. Social work involves many authoritative interventions, however defensible they may be, that amount to control and even coercion. For example, in most countries, child protection is a prominent duty of social work and can involve a separation of children from their parents, which the family may vehemently oppose and which can cause considerable distress. There are further duties with regard to people who are believed to be mentally ill, with social workers often being involved in processes of compulsory detention. These activities are plainly coercive (Handler 1973), but it would be a mistake to think that they somehow disqualify social work from being a caring profession. These activities are to be justified on the grounds of their enhancement of the rights and interests of others. In safeguarding procedures, the children's right to be safe and properly looked after is paramount. In the case of mental health detentions, there may be concerns about risks of harm to others and/or to patients themselves.[8] Even in these cases, however, the *manner* in which these statutory duties are fulfilled can evince care. The attempt to engage with, attend to and take account of those whose preferences are being over-ridden can make the encounter qualitatively different from behaviour which, callously or bureaucratically, ignores them and shows that it *doesn't care* about them.

Considered as punitive hard treatment, control is neither more nor less problematic than other punishments and should be regulated by the same principles, especially desert and proportionality. Considered instrumentally, the exercise of control to safeguard the interests of others is no more or less problematic for probation than for social work or other authoritative interventions of the state.

In spite of (though perhaps because of) an awareness of the controlling aspects of its work, social work has often affirmed as a central value the principle of *self-determination* (Biestek 1961; McDermott 1975). While this is arguably nowadays less prominent in the profession's expression of its own values, it still finds its place in the Code of Ethics of the British Association of Social Workers (2014). In this Code (page 8) it is defined as the principle that

> [s]ocial workers should respect, promote and support people's dignity and right to make their own choices and decisions, irrespective of their values and life choices, provided this does not threaten the rights, safety and legitimate interests of others.

Perhaps this is best understood as an insistence that people must never be treated in ways that simply ignore their preferences and interests, whether through a mechanistic disregard of their position or in a blinkered pursuit of some general conception of the public interest. Practice must always express the principle that social work *cares about* its clients. This is a principle to which probation can and should also subscribe. While there will certainly be times when actions must be taken against the expressed preferences of service users, both principle and pragmatism insist their wishes and interests should never be disregarded.

The probation counterpart to self-determination is the idea of *self-efficacy*. That people are and ought to be in charge of their own lives, albeit that their courses of action are circumscribed by the law and by respect for the interests of others, seems a compelling moral principle. *Self-efficacy* is also associated with

[8] Justification may also involve the claim that the patient, at least for the time being, lacks the competence to exercise their autonomy – their liberty, as it were, already compromised by their mental condition.

desistance – the process whereby people come to stop offending. There is reason to think that, typically, persistent offenders often see themselves as subject to forces outwith their control, while 'desisting offenders maintain a distinctly optimistic sense of control over their future and strong internal beliefs about their own self-worth and personal destinies' (LeBel, Burnett, Maruna and Bushway 2008: 136). All this implies that control, considered as more than punitive imposition and as a way of changing behaviour, is best achieved in ways that nurture self-control.

To summarise: the 'opposites of care' were said earlier in this chapter to be cruelty, malevolence, neglect, and indifference to (*not caring about*) the rights and interests of the individual. No doubt control can be exercised in these ways, but to do so is neither necessary nor effective. Legitimacy and therewith compliance are enhanced by a respectful attention to the interests and indeed the preferences of clients, even when these are not the only considerations to be taken into account and cannot always be decisive.

VI. Care and Imprisonment

While probation practitioners have wanted to retain a professional commitment to caring (Dominey and Gelsthorpe, Chapter three this volume), even when this has been politically unfashionable, the occupational culture of prison staff has typically – perhaps stereotypically – had other kinds of association. Some have gone so far as to refer to a 'culture of machismo' in prison, where practices and personal qualities of caring are thought to be precisely antithetical to its mission (Crawley and Crawley 2008). The position, no doubt, is more complex and variegated than this, and as ever it is important to reflect on the possibility of discrepancies between policy statements, staff accounts of their attitudes, their behaviour and how this is experienced by prisoners.

There is some irony even so that just as probation was about to be instructed to renounce caring, the Head of the Prison Service (1991–93), Joe Pilling, was insisting on 'care' as one of the 'pillars' of prison work (see discussion and references in Liebling, Price and Shefer 2011: 91–92). The Prison Service was thinking hard about its purposes and practices at that time in the aftermath of the riots that had taken place in several prisons in 1990. In his inquiry into the disturbances, Lord Woolf reported that 'the Prison Service had failed to *persuade* [several of the rioting] prisoners that it was treating them fairly' (quoted by Cavadino, Dignan and Mair 2013: 24; see also Prison Reform Trust 1991; Dunbar and Langdon 1998). Woolf insisted on the importance of *justice* and emphasised its relationship with good order and security. A prison in which people are – and can have confidence that they are – fairly dealt with will be safer and better-ordered, which will also make it more secure. Others have developed these ideas through the concept of *legitimacy* (Cavadino, Dignan and Mair 2013) and it is broadly agreed that this is indispensable to the character of any justifiable form of detention. Prisoners need to be able to give their experience meaning and to feel trusted and recognised as human beings to experience the prison as legitimate (Liebling, Price and Shefer 2011).

'[R]espect, care, fairness, meaning and personal development in prison matter, in a deep way, shaping, and if absent, damaging our identities as human beings' (Liebling 2011: 545). These characteristics and the quality of the personal relationships through which they are realised are accordingly prominent in the criteria by which prisons evaluate their 'moral performance' (Liebling assisted by Arnold 2004; Liebling, Hulley and Crewe 2011). The National Offender Management Service (now superseded by Her Majesty's Prison and Probation Service) adopted the *Measuring the Quality of Prison Life* survey (and a counterpart survey for staff), developed by Alison Liebling and colleagues, in appraising performance in all prison establishments in England and Wales, enabling the implementation of a 'decency agenda' (Prisons Research Centre 2016).

The extent to which respect and fairness mark prisoners' experience is a matter for empirical inquiry and is no doubt variable. But where prison staff fail in these respects, it would be difficult to speak of care: they are, in other words, necessary conditions of care. But are they also sufficient or is there more to care than this? In a valuable study of caring in prison, Sarah Tait (2010) found that care was interpreted and practised in different ways. She came across staff who offered help actively, whose empathy, compassion and own emotional investment amounted to caring, in their own understanding, in speaking to others about their work and in the way in which it was received by prisoners. Others spoke very differently about care. Personal and professional experience, as well as the type of institution and its 'culture', were influences on the ways in which care was understood and accomplished in practice: 'caring is a malleable concept shaped by personality, experience and the working environment' (Tait 2010: 449).

Tait proposed a typology of caring, assigning staff to one of five categories. An instructive example is the category she calls 'old school' – staff with extensive experience whose helping and caring was often conditional (in exchange for prisoner compliance):

> But they were also paternal and protective, with a keen eye for detecting exploitation. 'Care' was a complex and loaded term for most of these officers; however, prisoners identified them as caring and enjoyed their sociability and humour. They provided a reliable and trustworthy presence on the wing, and prisoners could count on their responsiveness and straightforward approach. (Tait 2010: 446)

Caring, then, was not prominent in their own accounts of what they did, but their dealings with prisoners were, at least sometimes, experienced as caring nevertheless. Just as (intended) care may be experienced as something less or different, so too there are occasions when behaviour towards prisoners, however it was meant, could come across as caring. This is a more positive example of the dissonance between how punishment is talked about and the lived experience, between the rhetoric and the reality. Tait concludes that caring means different things to different staff members, and no doubt to prisoners too.[9]

To summarise: while care may not always be an explicit objective of the Prison Service (Tait 2010), the prominence of indices of humanity, respect and caring in the methods that prisons use to evaluate their moral performance is evidence of their appreciation of the importance of relating to prisoners in these ways. It is plain that caring conduces to good order, as Woolf insisted, and that both make for a safer and more secure prison. Perhaps caring can also be a contribution to reduced levels of reoffending. The findings from probation research (see Dominey and Gelsthorpe, Chapter three this volume) suggest that possibility, and arguably both probation and prison are examples of the general truth that to get the best out of people you must treat them well. However that may be, the value of care does not rest upon such contingent achievements, but is a moral entitlement that is grounded in what it is to be a person (Coverdale 2017).

VII. Punishment and the Ethics of Care

At first sight, crime and punishment seem very much the province of justice – a setting where rules should be applied, rights affirmed and protected. Can this leave any space for care? The beginning of an answer is to recall Gilligan's reference to the 'insistent contextual relativism' of care ethics (2016: 22). Instructively, this attention to context chimes with the conception of fairness held by some of the prisoners whose experiences are cited in the study by Liebling, Price and Shefer. They found that

> [p]risoners were asking for flexibility within a framework of consistency. They were asking that their individuality, their own needs, be attended to when rules were enforced or decisions taken. *There was thus an understanding that straight consistency and rule enforcement could lead to unfair treatment.* The prisoners were asking for discretion to be exercised in their cases (Liebling, Price and Shefer 2011: 108, emphasis added).

Here a care ethics approach calls for a regard to the circumstances in which the question of the rule's application arises. The right decision is one that takes account of the implications for everyone affected and with a suitable respect for their needs. Allegations of (at least potential) inconsistency can be met by the reply that justice requires not only that like cases should be treated alike, but also that relevant differences are respected: cases may differ one from another in any number of ways and the interests of the parties affected constitute proper grounds for differentiation.

[9] Anecdotally, there are many accounts of prisoners' experiences of care, and the ways in which it can be accomplished, alongside experiences of a very different kind (for example, Padel and Stevenson 1988). See further the discussion of experiences of probation in Section VII.

Duties, rules and rights cannot in any case always determine what is the best thing to do: rights may conflict, for example, and courses of action may involve more than one obligation, such that all relevant rights and duties cannot be honoured. A pertinent example in the present context is the purposes of sentencing. The Criminal Justice Act 2003 (section 142) requires courts to

> have regard to the following purposes of sentencing –
>
> a) the punishment of offenders,
> b) the reduction of crime (including its reduction by deterrence),
> c) the reform and rehabilitation of offenders,
> d) the protection of the public, and
> e) the making of reparation by offenders to persons affected by their offences.

Yet, plainly these several objectives do not always point to the same sentence: the most appropriate punitive imposition may be very different from that sanction which will best support rehabilitation, while deterrent, protective/incapacitative or restorative objectives could call for something else again. The proliferation of sentencing purposes to which courts must have regard, not ranked in any order of priority, can lead to worrying inconsistencies and has been derided as a 'cafeteria' approach to sentencing (Ashworth 1995: 331). But the attempt to constrain sentencing to a single criterion, as attempted by the Criminal Justice Act 1991,[10] proved unsustainable. The several purposes are all legitimate penal objectives – which is not to say that they are always achievable (Canton 2017).

As well as its insistence on the relevance of context, care ethics also foregrounds the importance of *relationships*. Crime can be understood as a disruption of relationships: 'Whether or not they ever meet, offenders and their victims are locked into a relationship. Without knowing each other in reality, they know one another intimately in their imagination' (Marshall and Merry 1990: 1, quoted by Masters and Smith 1998: 10). In more than a metaphorical sense, moreover, the offence represents a disturbance of the relationship between the offender and the community of which she is a member. Care ethics would commend a response that tries to respect the needs and interests of all affected, but also, and prominently, to make good these relational disruptions. Further, care ethics attends to the *processes* of repair: responses to crimes should be managed in a way that expresses care for all concerned.

Masters and Smith (1998) were among the first to apply care ethics to thinking about criminal justice and to commend responses to wrongdoing that attend to repairing relationships disturbed by an offence. Drawing on the work of John Braithwaite (1989), they argue that reintegrative and restorative responses to offending are 'contextual immediate and relational, rather than universalist, remote

[10] CJA 1991 specified that seriousness and therefore desert should determine sentence (with some exceptions in cases of risk of serious harm). Objectives of rehabilitation and deterrence could be pursued, but within the parameters of desert (Wasik and Taylor 1991).

and abstract' (Masters and Smith 1998: 14).[11] They therefore propose restorative justice responses to wrongdoing. Centring on victims, offenders and a need for a repair of the relationships damaged by the offence, restorative justice rejects coercion, exclusion or denunciation. Transcending any assumption that the interests of victims and offenders are inherently opposed, this approach seeks resolutions that satisfy the legitimate interests of both, with due regard to others affected as well. As we have seen, an accusation that is levelled at this approach, and to which care ethics would be vulnerable for the same reasons, is that this leads to 'inconsistency'. But it can be argued that the satisfaction of the principal parties with the outcome is more important than compliance with abstract principles (Brooks 2012: chapter 4).

In sympathy with the approach of care ethics, Braithwaite (1989) proposed that punishment by the state should be done against a background of confidence and trust – shared by those who implement the punishment, the community and the offender – that the status of 'offender' is temporary and opportunities for reintegration and restoration will be keenly sought. Restorative justice most plainly represents these principles, but it may turn out that care ethics should inform practices that support most of the conventional objectives of punishment.

While retributive punishment can be imposed for its own sake as deserved hard treatment, several theorists have advanced a persuasive case for a justification based on censure.[12] Punishment does and should convey a clear message (to the offender and others) that the conduct was wrong – not as mere scolding, but as a demand on the wrongdoer to acknowledge their offence as a member of a community bound together by its shared values and as a precondition of their full reintegration.[13] Censure and restorative justice theorists have accordingly recognised a synergy between their respective projects, uniting around this notion of membership of a moral community (von Hirsch et al 2003; Shapland, Robinson and Sorsby 2011). Duff (2003) has gone so far as to say that, far from being incompatible, restorative justice and retribution are better understood as two sides of a coin.

Again, while it can be argued that rehabilitation is in opposition to restorative justice (eg Carlen 2012), a broader conception of rehabilitation can find this same common cause (McNeill 2012). Rehabilitation

[11] This, incidentally, encourages them to reject, as we have done, the rhetorical opposition between care and control: 'An effective method of control is to care about others, since care expresses their value in the community and hence maximizes the shame felt at the prospect of breaching community norms' (Masters and Smith 1998: 14).

[12] See among others von Hirsch 1993; Duff 2001; Bennett 2008. For all the differences in their positions, these scholars set censure at the centre of their respective accounts of punishment.

[13] Some forms of restorative justice, notably victim-offender mediation, have been suspected of turning the offence and the response into a private transaction between individuals. One way of ensuring that the interests of society are fully respected and given an influence, however, is through enabling a wider participation, including a community representation, in restorative encounters (see Canton 2017, ch 8).

> is not just about sorting out the individual's readiness for or fitness for reintegration; it is as much about *rebuilding the social relationships without which reintegration is impossible.* Any would-be supporter of rehabilitation has to do more than try to sort out 'offenders'; s/he needs to mediate relationships between people trying to change and the communities in which change is impeded or impelled; s/he also has to mediate the role and limits of the state itself in the process. (McNeill 2012: 17, emphasis added)

As with censure theory and restorative justice, this understanding of rehabilitation lays emphasis on the value of relationships to be restored and nurtured.

For all their different origins, approaches and emphases, then, these three conceptions of an ethical response to wrongdoing – censure theory, restorative justice and rehabilitation – all align with care ethics in recognising the value of affirming the responsibility of wrongdoers, attempting to elicit their commitment to make amends and keenly anticipating their subsequent acceptance in the moral community from which their offending estranged them. They also can (though only variably do) insist on the reciprocal duties of the community. As Duff writes, 'Reconciliation is what the repentant wrongdoer seeks with those she has wronged – *and what they must seek with her if they are still to see her as a fellow citizen*' (Duff 2001: 109, emphasis added). Processes that evince care are most likely to achieve this aspiration and to avoid further damage that other ways of implementing punishment may risk.

Two other statutory purposes of sentencing remain. First, incapacitation involves a period of forcible detention. At least to begin with, there is usually little or no attempt to mend the relationships that have been damaged by the (usually very grave) crimes that lead to incapacitative sentences. On the other hand, in almost all cases,[14] there will come a point when attention must be given to release and reintegration. During the period of detention, too, the custodial experience can and should be managed with care and concern in a manner entirely consistent, as we have seen, with secure confinement. Second, deterrence addresses offenders (and prospective offenders) in the language of threat alone. Since it gives no moral reasons to refrain from offending, it can be taken as providing nothing more than an incentive not to get caught. This is incompatible with care. Deterrence has no interest in (*doesn't care about*) the needs or interests of the individual and is solely preoccupied with threat. It is true that, like any response to crime that is concerned to reduce offending, there is a sense in which deterrence expresses care for potential victims, but it represents mere coercion of offenders and cannot lead to any mending in relationships. If care ethics cannot accommodate deterrence, this is not a sign of its own shortcomings, but rather calls into question the morality of grounding penal policy or sentencing decisions on that foundation (Canton 2017: chapter 5).

[14] Capital punishment is the most obvious exception. 'Whole life' sentences and 'Life without the possibility of parole' also set aside attempts at repair. That said, restorative justice meetings have taken place between people awaiting execution and bereaved families with plain benefits to all involved (Beck, Britto and Andrews 2007).

To summarise: punishments can be imposed and administered in ways that are incompatible with care. Punishment can be imposed as hard treatment for its own sake (because deserved); ostensibly rehabilitative measures can be oppressively intrusive, mechanistic, careless or heedless of the individual's interests and preferences; even reparation could be debased into some token and possibly humiliating imposition that loses what this ought to mean for offender and victim. Yet, retribution can take the form of a censure that affirms the wrongdoer's membership of a community; rehabilitation can be inclusive, encouraging and offer support to people striving for desistance; restorative justice can evince care for offender, victim and community. Care, it is concluded, is not only compatible with punishment, but required by the principled pursuit of most penal objectives.

VIII. Caring for 'Offenders'

As we have seen, even as probation has long debated whether its mission should be to care or to control or perhaps both, there had been little attention given to the way in which its interventions were understood by its clients. Was probation experienced as care? And was it felt to be any less or more caring when it regarded its main duty as to control? Indifference to these experiences in itself looks like a failure to care. Desistance studies, notably, have paid more attention to these questions (Maruna 2001; Farrall and Calverley 2006; McNeill and Weaver 2010; King 2013). This work has been complemented by related inquiries into the impact of punishments and what they mean for those subject to sanctions, whether in the community (Weaver and Armstrong 2011; Weaver and Barry 2014; Hayes 2015; van Ginneken and Hayes 2017) or in prison (Liebling, assisted by Arnold 2004; Hulley, Liebling and Crewe 2012; Armstrong and Weaver 2013; Schinkel 2014). These studies are instructive generally and are of particular importance for those theories that focus on censure (see above) or other penal communications. Any accounts of punishment that ground its justification on communication cannot disregard what is in fact communicated. For example, does prison succeed in conveying the intended censure (Schinkel 2014)?

These studies have not usually focused on 'care'. One general difficulty here is that many offenders may feel uncomfortable using the language of care in this context (or indeed at all). Still, there are many accounts that refer to experiences that could be described in this way. For example, some people recall not only the practical help that a probation officer provided, but also and especially *the sense of personal interest and concern that they experienced and appreciated* (Farrall 2002).[15]

[15] Incidentally, the benefits of this are not always understood at the time, but may be recalled and interpreted in this way some time afterwards, with a positive influence on the process of desistance (Farrall 2002; Farrall and Calverley 2006).

A recent research study (into the effects of a training programme for prison staff) found that prisoners reported that some officers, even during brief exchanges, gave them the opportunity to express and alleviate negative feelings and were supportive and encouraging in affirming their achievements and acknowledging their difficulties. Personal qualities of staff that prisoners appreciated included their being non-judgemental, willing to help, willing to listen and treating them as a human and with respect (Tate, Blagden and Mann 2017). This is caring, whether or not the word itself is used to reflect on the experience.

Inquiry into service user experiences tends to show, unsurprisingly, that these are variegated, and it seems likely that the same would be found for experiences of care. Some supervisors would no doubt be found more or less caring by some offenders. There are many factors at play here, including not only the personal characteristics of those involved, but also organisational processes (for example, pressures of workload, processes of implementation and enforcement, office location or physical conditions of a prison, efficiency of the organisation) that bear on this experience (see also Dominey and Gelsthorpe, Chapter three this volume). In prison, caring by individual members of staff can be undercut by

> participants' sense that imprisonment failed to achieve any penal purpose beyond incapacitation, while creating a number of unintended negative consequences, [which] undermined the punishment's ability to connect to a person's sense of wrongdoing. User experiences of punishment offer an important opportunity to explore how penal legitimacy works, and under what conditions it is achieved or damaged (Armstrong and Weaver 2013: 302).

Once again, we find this tight conceptual connection between legitimacy and care. Where one is absent, the other is immediately in jeopardy. And legitimacy, as has been argued here (and also by Dominey and Gelsthorpe, Chapter three this volume), is indispensable to the implementation of punishment.

IX. Conclusions

'What works?' has been the besetting problem for policy-makers in recent years, as we have seen. This question makes assumptions about the purposes of punishment and the chances that they can be achieved, but it also suppresses matters of process, of *how* punishment is put into effect. How things are done is always a salient ethical consideration. And care relates to *how* we act: *care* is a verb and a noun, but it should have been an adverb.

Restorative justice proponents have looked in detail at the processes and relational transactions that take place in meetings (Rossner 2011, 2013; Shapland, Robinson and Sorsby 2011; Sherman and Strang 2011). Rehabilitation has similarly insisted upon the central value of relationships in supporting change and desistance (see Dominey and Gelsthorpe, Chapter three this volume; Canton and Dominey 2017, especially chapter seven and references there cited). The quality of relationships has been emphasised too, as discussed above, as an aspect of prison's 'moral performance'. Principled punishment must be grounded in an ethic of respect, decency and compassion, and the manner of its implementation ought to reflect those values.

Caring for offenders should not be seen as a passive process for the offender or one in which people are infantilised (Coverdale 2017). On the contrary, caring can nurture self-efficacy and indeed people's capacity to give care to others. Care elicits care and, by these means, 'we can normalise care-giving and care-receiving; and provide an opportunity to learn practical and social skills for self-care and care for others' (Coverdale 2017: 10). The concept of *generativity* originally referred to a concern for and commitment to the well-being of one's children or, more generally, the next generation, but can be extended naturally to include caring for others. This has been argued to be associated with desistance, as people come to create and then to assert new identities for themselves (Maruna 2001; McNeill and Maruna 2008). The offender's identity as 'taker' is transformed into that of 'giver', with a powerful impact on individuals' perception of themselves and on how they come to be regarded by others. In the best prisons, there are opportunities for people to offer support to others in many ways, through mentoring, counselling and educational support, and such peer work is also undertaken in the community (Nixon 2017). Establishments and agencies have to make these activities possible and bestow trust and respect. To be trusted like this is a way to become trustworthy; to be cared about makes caring more likely.

As Coverdale argues, withholding care compounds the disadvantages that have marked the lives of some many people subject to punishment. By contrast, care can amplify caring resources. The instrumental advantages of caring in the implementation of punishment are thus clear and considerable. Yet at the last its value depends less on this than its intrinsic moral worth in respecting the fundamental human entitlement to be cared for and about. Many crimes 'say' to victims: *I don't care about you, you don't matter*. The interests of the victim are suppressed in the relentless pursuit of whatever gain the offence is supposed to bring. To administer punishments with a lack of care is to echo some of the worst aspects of such crimes.

References

Aldridge, M and Eadie, T (1997) 'Manufacturing an issue: The case of probation officer training' *Critical Social Policy* 17(50): 111–24.

American Friends Service Committee (1971) *Struggle for Justice: A Report on Crime and Punishment in America* (New York, Hill & Wang).

Andrews, D and Bonta, J (2010) 'Rehabilitating Criminal Justice Policy and Practice' *Psychology, Public Policy, and Law* 16(1): 39–55.

Ansbro, M (2008) 'Using attachment theory with offenders' *Probation Journal* 55(3): 231–44.

Armstrong, S and Weaver, B (2013) 'Persistent punishment: User views of short prison sentences' *The Howard Journal of Crime and Justice* 52(3): 285–305.

Ashworth, A (1995) *Sentencing and Criminal Justice*, 2nd edn (London, Butterworths).
Bean, P (1976) Rehabilitation and Deviance (London, Routledge).
Beck, E, Britto, S and Andrews, A (2007) *In the shadow of death: Restorative justice and death row families* (New York, Oxford University Press).
Becker, H (1963) *Outsiders* (New York, Free Press).
Bennett, C (2008) *The Apology Ritual: A Philosophical Theory of Punishment* (Cambridge, Cambridge University Press).
—— (2010) 'Punishment and Rehabilitation' in J Ryberg and J Angelo Corlett (eds), *Punishment and Ethics: New Perspectives* (Basingstoke, Palgrave Macmillan).
Biestek, F (1961) *The Casework Relationship* (London, Unwin University Books).
Bochel, D (1976) *Probation and After-Care: Its Development in England and Wales* (Edinburgh, Scottish Academic Press).
Boswell, G (1996) *Young and dangerous: The backgrounds and careers of Section 53 offenders* (Aldershot, Avebury).
Bottoms, A (1980) 'An Introduction to "The Coming Crisis"' in A Bottoms and R Preston (eds), *The Coming Penal Crisis: a criminological and theological exploration* (Edinburgh, Scottish Academic Press).
Braithwaite, J (1989) *Crime, Shame and Reintegration* (Cambridge, Cambridge University Press).
British Association of Social Workers (2014) BASW Code of Ethics, available online at: cdn.basw.co.uk/upload/basw_95243-9.pdf (accessed January 2018).
Brooks, T (2012) *Punishment* (Abingdon, Routledge).
Brownlee, I (1998) *Community Punishment: A Critical Introduction* (Harlow, Longman).
Bryant, M, Coker, J, Estlea, B, Himmel, S and Knapp, T (1978) 'Sentenced to social work?' *Probation Journal* 25(4): 110–14.
Canton, R (2015) 'Crime, punishment and the moral emotions: Righteous minds and their attitudes towards punishment' *Punishment & Society* 17(1): 54–72.
—— (2017) *Why Punish? An Introduction to the Philosophy of Punishment* (London, Palgrave Macmillan).
Carlen, P (2012) *Against Rehabilitation: For Reparative Justice* (22nd Eve Saville Memorial Lecture, 2012), available online at: tinyurl.com/p8bcrtm (accessed January 2018).
Cavadino, M, Dignan, J and Mair, G (2013) *The Penal System: An Introduction*, 5th revised edn (London, Sage).
Christie, N (1981) *Limits to Pain* (Oxford, Martin Robertson), available online at: www.prisonpolicy.org/scans/limits_to_pain/ (accessed December 2017).
—— (2000) *Crime Control as Industry: Towards Gulags, Western Style*, 3rd edn (London, Routledge).
Cohen, S (1985) *Visions of Social Control* (Cambridge, Polity Press).
Corston, J (2007) *The Corston Report: A Review of Women with Particular Vulnerabilities in the Criminal Justice System* (London, Home Office), available online at: www.justice.gov.uk/publications/docs/corston-report-march-2007.pdf (accessed December 2017).
Council of Europe (2010) *Recommendation CM/Rec (2010)1 of the Committee of Ministers to Member States on the Council of Europe Probation Rules* (adopted by the Committee of Ministers 20 January 2010), available online at: tinyurl.com/7gr523w (accessed December 2017).
Coverdale, HB (2017) 'Punishment and welfare: defending offender's inclusion as subjects of state care' *Ethics and Social Welfare* 11: 1–16.
Crawley, E and Crawley, P (2008) 'Understanding prison officers: culture, cohesion and conflict' in J Bennett, B Crewe and A Wahidin (eds), *Understanding Prison Staff* (Cullompton, Willan).
Davies, H, Nutley, S and Smith, P (eds), (2000) *What Works? Evidence-based policy and practice in public services* (Bristol, Policy Press).
Duff, RA (2001) *Punishment, Communication and Community* (Oxford, Oxford University Press).
Duff, A (2003) 'Restoration and Retribution' in A von Hirsch, J Roberts, A Bottoms, K Roach and M Scheff (eds), *Restorative Justice and Criminal Justice: Competing or Reconcilable Paradigms* (Oxford, Hart Publishing).

Dunbar, I and Langdon, A (1998) *Tough Justice: Sentencing and Penal Policies in the 1990s* (Oxford, Blackstone).
Farrall, S (2002) *Rethinking what Works with Offenders: Probation, Social Context and Desistance from Crime* (Cullompton, Willan).
Farrall, S and Calverley, A (2006) *Understanding desistance from crime: Theoretical directions in resettlement and rehabilitation* (Maidenhead, Open University Press).
Garland, D (1990) *Punishment and Modern Society: A Study in Social Theory* (Oxford, Oxford University Press).
—— (2001) *The Culture of Control: Crime and Social Order in Contemporary Society* (Oxford, Oxford University Press).
Gilligan, C (2016) *In a Different Voice: Psychological Theory and Women's Development* (Harvard MA, Harvard University Press). (Original edn 1982).
Griffin, J (2008) *On Human Rights* (Oxford, Oxford University Press).
Handler, J (1973) *The coercive social worker* (Chicago IL, Rand McNally College Publishing Company).
Haidt, J (2003) 'The Moral Emotions' in R Davidson, K Scherer and H Goldsmith (eds), *Handbook of Affective Sciences* (Oxford, Oxford University Press).
—— (2012) *The Righteous Mind: Why Good People are Divided by Politics and Religion* (London, Allen Lane).
Hayes, D (2015) 'The impact of supervision on the pains of community penalties in England and Wales: An exploratory study' *European Journal of Probation* 7(2): 85–102.
Held, V (2010) 'Can the ethics of care handle violence?' *Ethics and Social Welfare* 4(2): 115–29.
Her Majesty's Inspectorate of Probation (2017) *The Work of Youth Offending Teams to Protect the Public*, available online at: tinyurl.com/yc37otaz (accessed December 2017).
Hulley, S, Liebling, A and Crewe, B (2012) 'Respect in prisons: Prisoners' experiences of respect in public and private sector prisons' *Criminology & Criminal Justice* 12(1): 3–23.
King, S (2013) *Desistance transitions and the impact of probation* (London, Routledge).
LeBel, T, Burnett, R, Maruna, S and Bushway, S (2008) '"The chicken and egg" of subjective and social factors in desistance from crime' *European Journal of Criminology* 5(2): 131–59.
Liebling, A assisted by Arnold, H (2004) *Prisons and their Moral Performance: A Study of Values, Quality and Prison Life* (Oxford, Oxford University Press).
Liebling, A (2011) 'Moral performance, inhuman and degrading treatment and prison pain' *Punishment & Society* 13(5): 530–50.
Liebling, A, Price, D and Shefer, G (2011) *The Prison Officer*, 2nd edn (Cullompton, Willan).
Liebling, A, Hulley, S and Crewe, B (2011) 'Conceptualising and measuring the quality of prison life' in D Gadd, S Karstedt and S Messner (eds), *The SAGE Handbook of Criminological Research Methods* (London, Sage).
Marshall, TF and Merry, S (1990) *Crime and accountability: Victim/offender mediation in practice* (London, HM Stationery Office).
Maruna, S (2001) *Making Good: How Ex-convicts Reform and Rebuild their Lives* (Washington DC, American Psychological Association).
Masters, G and Smith, D (1998) 'Portia and Persephone revisited: Thinking about feeling in criminal justice' *Theoretical Criminology* 2(1): 5–27.
McDermott, F (ed) (1975) *Self-determination in Social Work* (London, Routledge and Kegan Paul).
McNeill, F (2012) 'Four forms of "offender" rehabilitation: Towards an interdisciplinary perspective' *Legal and Criminological Psychology* 17(1): 18–36.
McNeill, F and Maruna, S (2008) 'Giving Up and Giving Back: Desistance, Generativity and Social Work with Offenders' in G McIvor and P Raynor (eds), *Developments in Social Work with Offenders* (London, Jessica Kingsley).
McNeill, F and Weaver, B (2010) *Changing Lives? Desistance Research and Offender Management*, Scottish Centre for Crime and Justice Research Report No. 3/2010, available online at: www.sccjr.ac.uk/publications/changing-lives-desistance-research-and-offender-management/ (accessed January 2018).

Mitford, J (1977) *The American Prison Business* (Harmondsworth, Penguin).
Moral Foundations (2013) www.moralfoundations.org/ (accessed January 2018).
Muller, C and Wildeman, C (2013) 'Punishment and Inequality' in J Simon and R Sparks (eds), *The Sage Handbook of Punishment and Society* (London, Sage).
Nellis, M (1995) 'Probation values for the 1990s' *Howard Journal* 34(1): 19–44.
Nixon, S (2017) *'I just want to give something back': Peer work and desistance* (PhD thesis, De Montfort University, Leicester, unpublished).
Nussbaum, M (2016) *Anger and Forgiveness: Resentment, Generosity, and Justice* (New York, Oxford University Press).
Padel, U and Stevenson, J (1988) *Insiders: Women's Experience of Prison* (London, Virago).
Prison Reform Trust (1991) *The Woolf Report: A Summary of the Main Findings and Recommendations of the Inquiry into Prison Disturbances* (London: Prison Reform Trust), available online at: www.prisonreformtrust.org.uk/Portals/0/Documents/Woolf%20report.pdf (accessed January 2018).
Prison Reform Trust (2017) *Prison: The Facts* (Bromley Briefing) (London: Prison Reform Trust), available online at: www.prisonreformtrust.org.uk/Publications/Factfile (accessed January 2018).
Prisons Research Centre (2016) *Measuring the Quality of Prison Life – MQPL+*, available online at: www.prc.crim.cam.ac.uk/directory/research-themes/mqpl (accessed January 2018).
Raynor, P (2003) 'Research in Probation: From "Nothing works" to "What works"' in WH Chui and M Nellis (eds), *Moving Probation Forward: Evidence, Arguments and Practice* (Harlow, Pearson Longman).
Reiman, J and Leighton, P (2013) *The Rich Get Richer And The Poor Get Prison: Ideology, Class and Criminal Justice*, 10th edn (New York, Pearson).
Rossner, M (2011) 'Emotions and Interaction Ritual: A Micro Analysis of Restorative Justice' *British Journal of Criminology* 51(1): 95–119.
—— (2013) 'Reintegrative Ritual: Restorative Justice and Micro-Sociology' in S Karstedt, I Loader and H Strang (eds), *Emotions, Crime and Justice* (Oxford, Hart Publishing).
Schinkel, M (2014) 'Punishment as moral communication: The experiences of long-term prisoners' *Punishment & Society* 16(5): 578–97.
Sen, A (2009) *The Idea of Justice* (London, Allen Lane).
Shapland, J, Robinson, G and Sorsby, A (2011) *Restorative Justice in Practice: Evaluating What Works for Victims and Offenders* (Cullompton, Willan).
Sherman, L and Strang, H (2011) 'Empathy for the Devil: The Nature and Nurture of Revenge' in S Karstedt, I Loader and H Strang (eds), *Emotions, Crime and Justice* (Oxford, Hart Publishing).
Singer, P (1981) *The Expanding Circle: Ethics and Sociobiology* (Oxford, Oxford University Press).
Slote, M (2007) *The Ethics of Care and Empathy* (Abingdon, Routledge).
Smith, D (2005) 'Probation and social work' *British Journal of Social Work* 35: 621–37.
Smith, P (2008) *Punishment and Culture* (Chicago IL, University of Chicago Press).
Sparks, R (2011) 'Divided Sympathies: David Hume and Contemporary Criminology' in S Karstedt, I Loader and H Strang (eds), *Emotions, Crime and Justice* (Oxford, Hart).
Straw, J (2009) 'On community punishment', speech at the University of Portsmouth, available online at: www.crimlinks.com/News2009/Feb42009.html (accessed July 2018).
Tait, S (2011) 'A typology of prison officer approaches to care' *European Journal of Criminology* 8(6): 440–54.
Tate, H, Blagden, N and Mann, R (2017) *Prisoners' perceptions of care and rehabilitation from prison officers trained as Five Minute Interventionists* (HMPPS Analytical Summary), available online at: www.gov.uk/government/publications/prisoners-perceptions-of-care-and-rehabilitation-from-prison-officers-trained-as-5-minute-interventionists (accessed January 2018).
Van Ginneken, E and Hayes, D (2017) '"Just" punishment? Offenders' views on the meaning and severity of punishment' *Criminology and Criminal Justice* 17(1): 62–78.
Vanstone, M (2004) *Supervising Offenders in the Community: A History of Probation Theory and Practice* (Aldershot, Ashgate).
Von Hirsch, A (1976) *Doing justice: The choice of punishments* (New York, Hill and Wang).

Von Hirsch, A, Roberts, J, Bottoms, A, Roach, K and Scheff, M (eds) (2003) *Restorative Justice and Criminal Justice: Competing or Reconcilable Paradigms* (Oxford, Hart).
Weaver, B and Armstrong, S (2011) *User Views of Punishment – The dynamics of community based punishment: insider views from the outside* (The Scottish Centre for Crime and Justice Research), available online at: www.sccjr.ac.uk/publications/user-views-of-punishment-the-dynamics-of-community-based-punishment-insider-views-from-the-outside/ (accessed January 2018).
Weaver, B and Barry, M (2014) 'Managing high risk offenders in the community: Compliance, cooperation and consent in a climate of concern' *European Journal of Probation* 6(3): 278–95.
Wasik, M and Taylor, R (1991) *Blackstone's Guide to the Criminal Justice Act 1991* (London, Blackstone).
Zimring, F (2001) 'Imprisonment rates and the new politics of criminal punishment' in D Garland (ed), *Mass Imprisonment: Social Causes and Consequences* (London, Sage).

3

Who Cares? Probation Practice and Privatisation

JANE DOMINEY AND LORAINE GELSTHORPE

I. Introduction

Public services in England and Wales are increasingly provided by private companies. Since the 1980s, governments of all political colours have used mechanisms of out-sourcing and contracting to bring private providers into areas of welfare provision from housing to health, railways to criminal justice (Ascher 1987; Garland 2001). Supporters of privatisation argue that a mixed market brings efficiencies and innovations beyond the reach of the public sector. However, one criticism of private sector provision is that it puts profit before people and, inevitably and inescapably, leads to a poor quality of practice in which traditional values such as care are put at risk.

This chapter takes as its focus the recently privatised probation service in England and Wales. The probation service had not been immune from the neo-liberal turn in political thinking (Burke and Collett 2015; Dominey and Gelsthorpe 2018), but significant organisational change did not take place until the Coalition Government of 2010–15 which oversaw the privatisation of much of the service's work.

Defining care as a quality expressed in (or absent from) the relationships between staff and service users, this chapter explores the ways in which care is changed when probation services are delivered by the private sector. It illuminates ways in which care is shaped by economics and the processes of commodification and marketisation. It exposes the link between care and time, and contrasts the official rhetoric of care with the lived experience of practitioners and service users.

As yet, there has been little research exploring the impact of privatisation on the quality of probation practice. This chapter draws on evidence from other areas of public policy, including prisons and adult social care, considering the extent to which experience from these sectors has relevance for probation work. It asks whether the new private providers of probation services have space to care.

II. What does Care have to do with Probation Practice?

Debates about whether probation is (or should be) a caring profession are evident throughout probation's history. A central theme is that caring is often set as the opposite of controlling, raising questions about the compatibility of these two purposes. The contribution by Canton and Dominey (Chapter two this collection) explores this discussion in detail, setting it in the context of punishment and of the ethics of care.

There is also debate in the probation world (and not just in the UK, see Herzog-Evans 2011) about which words should be used to describe the people who receive the probation service. Policy documents prefer 'offender', a term unpopular with many probation staff for its derogatory labelling quality. 'Supervisee' and 'probationer' are accurate, if ungainly, words for someone subject to supervision or on probation. 'Client' and 'service user', terms employed elsewhere in the helping professions, are both used in probation work, although both downplay the involuntary nature of the interaction. This chapter, reflecting these tensions, uses a variety of terms.

Care in probation matters for two reasons. First, care matters because we can be increasingly confident that good relational practice (which reflects care) supports positive outcomes across probation. Secondly, and significantly, care matters because the moral quality of probation matters (Canton and Dominey 2017). The aims and objectives set for probation (both by itself and by others) are important but, in the absence of an ethical foundation for practice, they lead to priorities which shift with political imperatives and permit practice which fails to recognise the worth of the individuals involved.

Many studies highlight the significance of the relationship between supervisee and supervisor for the quality of probation supervision (Shapland et al 2012 provide a review). Probation's embrace of evidence-led practice (Canton and Dominey, Chapter two this volume) led to the creation of a practice model based on methods derived from cognitive behavioural psychology that made much use of programmes with precisely specified content. Critics of this approach (known as 'what works' (Home Office 1995)) argued that its focus on correcting thinking skills neglected the social causes of crime (Kendall 2004) and that the prescribed nature of interventions did not respect the diversity of service users (Shaw and Hannah-Moffat 2004). 'What works' was characterised as a way of working in which offenders were assessed (using structured assessment instruments) and then allocated to inflexible programmes. Probation, it was argued, had lost sight of the importance of human interaction.

In response, advocates of 'what works' argued that their work did, and always had, recognised the importance of the relational aspects of practice (Lösel 2012; Bonta and Andrews 2010). However, in England and Wales 'what works' approaches were implemented at pace and in a climate of managerialism

(Raynor 2003). As a consequence, it appeared that little space was left for the building of relationships and the practice of care.

In 2004 Dowden and Andrews, both prominent contributors to the development of 'what works' initiatives, published an influential research review which tried to identify the core elements of effective practice. They pointed to five such components and concluded:

> The fifth and final component of CCP [core correctional practice], relationship factors, is also arguably the most important. Essentially, this approach argues that the interpersonal influence exerted by the correctional staff member is maximized under conditions characterized by open, warm, and enthusiastic communication. An equally important consideration is the development of mutual respect and liking between the offender and correctional staff member (Dowden and Andrews 2004: 205).

Other research findings pointed to a similar conclusion. 'What works' had placed emphasis on method, but there were emerging findings that some characteristics common to all well-delivered therapeutic interventions – warmth, empathy, engagement, congruence, therapeutic alliance, fairness, encouragement – were both more valued by clients and more efficacious than any particular method (McNeill and Burnett 2005; McNeill, Batchelor, Burnett and Knox 2005). The National Offender Management Service subsequently created its Offender Engagement Programme as a response to these findings and as a means of renewing an organisational commitment to good-quality, one-to-one work between supervisor and supervisee (Rex 2012; Canton and Dominey 2017: chapter 11). The relational dimension of practice is, therefore, important for engaging involuntary clients (Trotter 2006) and for supporting the effectiveness of interventions. The rehabilitative potential of probation work is enhanced when it is delivered by staff who demonstrate care for service users.

The importance of relationship – and associated expression of care – is significant across the probation caseload. It is relevant to work with high-risk offenders in the community as well as to practice with individuals who cause less concern. Risk management strategies that rely entirely on externally imposed controls lack the benefits that come from engaging the cooperation and participation of the offender. Discussing the findings from their study of interviews with practitioners and (high-risk) service users, Weaver and Barry argue that

> authentic supervisory relationships underpinned by clear communication, negotiation and mutual trust have more potential to encourage service users' active engagement and, in turn, are more likely to create the conditions within which cooperation and change might be enabled (Weaver and Barry 2014: 292).

Reducing re-offending is one key objective for probation work; ensuring that offenders comply with the requirements of court orders and post-release licences is another. Here, too, there is evidence that care – or something very like it – supports positive outcomes. Bottoms (2001) explained that among the influences on compliance were normative factors, which included the idea of attachment.

Attachment to someone who demonstrates concern for and personal interest in the supervisee is associated with compliance. This insight, that a good working relationship with a supervisor can bring a reason to cooperate, has also emerged from empirical studies of compliance and engagement (Rex 1999; Ugwudike 2010). Lewis (2014) worked with supervisees in a collaborative research project to identify characteristics associated with a positive supervisory relationship. One characteristic was mutual caring, associated with loyalty to the practitioner and an investment in the personal relationship. 'For example, it was stated that "I didn't want to let her down", "I almost wanted to protect her" and "I cared about what she thought"' (Lewis 2014: 170).

The work of Hayes (2015), which also explores supervision from the perspective of the supervisee, points to the complexity of the supervisory relationship and its potential to both intensify and ameliorate the pains of community penalties. There are tensions and subjectivities in probation relationships. Care offered, even authentically, by workers may be perceived as something quite different by their involuntary clients.

In addition to attachment, Bottoms (2001) identifies the importance of legitimacy in enhancing compliance. McNeill and Robinson (2013: 117) develop this concept, conceptualising the legitimacy of community sanctions as liquid, ebbing and flowing as 'a community sanction is negotiated, constructed, contested and reconstructed by the various actors and audiences involved'. The legitimacy of probation, from the perspective of service users, is threatened where decisions appear unfair and arbitrary, and where supervisory relationships are fragmented and lack warmth. Legitimate supervision also requires respect for individuality, the right 'to be treated not as a composite offender but as fully human, socially and culturally differentiated offender' (Gelsthorpe 2007: 301). Paying attention to building relationships, ensuring procedural justice and responding to diversity all serve to improve compliance with community supervision, and contribute to a practice culture of care.

Attending to relationships and demonstrating care do not in themselves guarantee effective and good-quality probation practice. Enabling rehabilitation, supporting desistance and managing court orders also require practical resources and well-running organisational processes. Conversely, many aspects of probation work can (and frequently do) take place effectively as brief transactional encounters between staff and service users who barely know each other. For example, someone subject to a community order may attend a reporting centre, speak for a few minutes with the staff member on duty, and receive useful practical advice or information. Such an interaction may be carried out in a respectful way and the staff member may communicate concern for the circumstances of the service user, but this is an example of supervision that is practical and impersonal rather than based on the development of relationships.

The probation service has been pushed to reposition itself as a law enforcement rather than social work agency (Canton and Dominey Chapter two this volume). Despite this, a culture of care still appears to be important for its staff.

While practice has been influenced by changes in political rhetoric and public policy, practitioners have continued to perceive at least aspects of their job as providing help and facilitating change (Annison et al 2008; Deering 2010). Worrall and Mawby (2014: 347), drawing on their study of probation cultures (which developed a typology of workers), identified that a commitment to the importance of the supervisor/supervisee relationship was widely shared:

> Despite differences in social and employment backgrounds, training received and perspectives on the politics of probation work, we conclude that belief in the importance of the relationship between probation worker and offender is one of the ties that bind these types into what one of our interviewees described as an 'honourable profession'.

The idea that probation practice is best delivered in the context of caring about the service user is, therefore, central to probation's idea of itself. It has proved resilient through political and organisational changes to the probation service. Official rhetoric about the importance of positive relationships and continuity in supervision may often be matched in reality by an experience of brief encounters and fragmented interventions, but the empirical evidence points to the benefits of practice that expresses care. Does the privatisation of probation pose a significant and new challenge to the future of care?

III. Does the Privatisation of Probation Raise Concerns about the Future of Care?

In 2014 the probation service in England and Wales was subject to a major reorganisation which, among other changes, saw private companies contracted to deliver statutory services (including the community supervision of individuals deemed to pose a low or medium risk of causing harm). This reform programme was named *Transforming Rehabilitation* (Ministry of Justice 2013). The *Transforming Rehabilitation* reforms were implemented in the face of near universal objection from within the probation service (Burke and Collett 2015) and with precious little support from commentators beyond the service, for example from the voluntary sector or from academia (Howard League 2013; Senior 2016). The Government's reasoning in support of the reforms (that the private and voluntary sectors would bring creativity and innovation to probation practice, enable an expansion of rehabilitative services and provide value for money) was dismissed in favour of the view that held the reforms to be ideological, a rejection of public sector provision, and a means by which the Ministry of Justice could manage its required budget cut.

While *Transforming Rehabilitation* marked a dramatic shift in private sector involvement in the probation service, the processes that permitted marketisation had begun some years earlier (Dominey 2012). Historically the voluntary sector had worked alongside the probation service, providing services which complemented or supplemented the work of the public sector. These working arrangements took various forms, varying from informal local joint work through to services governed by commercial commissioning and contracting arrangements. Prior to *Transforming Rehabilitation* the private sector had had little involvement with probation, its input limited to contracts for discrete pieces of work like electronic monitoring and accommodation for people on bail.

The Government's *Transforming Rehabilitation* reforms were not introduced gradually. Rather, the Ministry of Justice divided England and Wales into 21 'contract package areas' and ran a competitive process to appoint 'prime providers' to lead the new Community Rehabilitation Companies (CRCs) tasked with running probation services for low- and medium-risk offenders (court work and work with individuals identified as high risk fell to a newly created public sector National Probation Service (NPS)). Consultation and policy papers ahead of the reforms stressed the Government's desire to see a significant role for the voluntary sector in new probation services (Ministry of Justice 2010; Ministry of Justice 2013). However, the logic of the funding model (which included a payment-by-results mechanism) resulted in all but one successful prime provider coming from the private sector.

At the same time as making a significant change to the organisation and governance of the probation service, the Government added to its workload. It did this by extending statutory post-custody supervision to prisoners serving short (less than 12-month) sentences. Previously, unlike those serving longer sentences, short sentence prisoners were released with no requirement to comply with probation supervision. The absence of a formal resettlement service for this group (known to have a high likelihood of reoffending) had long been identified as a gap, but previous efforts to address it had been deemed too expensive (Justice Select Committee 2008).

Transforming Rehabilitation was launched in the continuing period of Government spending cuts that began in 2010. The real-terms budget change for the Ministry of Justice in the period 2010/11 to 2019/20 is anticipated to be a 40 per cent cut (Institute for Fiscal Studies 2017). The private companies running the new CRCs have entered into contracts that require them to do more work for less money than the public sector probation trusts that they replaced. The financial context has a significant impact on the quality of practice; economics, alongside relationships, shape the expression and experience of care.

Many critics of privatisation in the probation service (and in the criminal justice system more widely) argue that there is no place for profit in punishment (McNeill 2013; Teague 2016). Sandel (2012) carefully sets out the shifts that the introduction of market practices bring to services and to the network of relationships between the people involved as providers and recipients. McNeill (2013: 85) argues that, transformed 'from being a moral good into a market good' the nature of rehabilitation is inevitably corrupted. Privatisation has an impact on how policy-makers and practitioners think about their work (*Transforming Rehabilitation* expanded the probation vocabulary to include words like 'supply chain' and 'rate card') and also on the quality of the interactions between service users and staff. Probation has been commodified, both in the formal sense that interventions are bought and sold but also in a substantive sense with products and processes reconfigured for consumption by an anxious public (McCulloch and McNeill 2007).

Proponents of privatisation in criminal justice argue that the stimulus of competition and the innovation of private providers has been responsible for a culture change which has improved the quality of prison regimes (in both public and private sectors) and, as a consequence, the care afforded to prisoners (for example, this argument is made in the report that led to the creation of the National Offender Management Service (Carter 2003)). Research findings contrasting regimes in private and public prisons in England and Wales suggest complex patterns. As with public sector prisons, not all private sector prisons are the same; they differ from each other (and from public sector prisons) in a number of ways (Crewe et al 2011; Liebling and Ludlow 2016).

An explicit aim of prison privatisation (Ludlow 2017) was to shift an organisational culture seen as an obstacle to improvement. One of the findings from the subsequent research was that newly appointed private prison staff adopt a more friendly, less rigid and cynical style of interaction with prisoners. However, they are often less confident users of their authority and power, and lack the knowledge needed to deal with prisoners' requests and needs. Crewe et al (2011: 112) conclude:

> [E]ven in high-performing private sector prisons, the under-use of power seems to reflect an uneasy balance of power between prisoners and staff. That said, critics of privatization should not disregard the fact that some private prisons have succeeded in recruiting, training and managing staff in a manner that produces relatively humane and respectful prison environments.

Learning from prison privatisation has some lessons for privatisation in the probation service, but there is a limit to the parallels that can be drawn. More than a decade ago, Liebling (2006) identified that the Home Office had successfully shifted the probation service in the direction of punishment in the community (see Canton and Dominey Chapter two this volume) without recourse to the threat of privatisation. At the point of *Transforming Rehabilitation*, the probation service was not identified as a failing service unwilling to accept new ways of working and stuck with a negative and punitive organisational culture. Ludlow (2014) pointed to the particular challenges that the National Offender Management Service (NOMS) faced in applying contract mechanisms to probation: first, the difficulty of measuring the performance of the service since many of its outcomes depend on work done by other agencies; and second, achieving the aim of improving a service already judged to perform well and provide good value for money.

One outcome of prison privatisation (an outcome found across the out-sourcing of public services) is that staffing costs are lower in private prisons than in public prisons. This results from differences in basic salaries, but also in funding for pensions and other employment benefits. In addition, changes to working practices led to a requirement for fewer staff. That said, one consequence of Ministry of Justice spending cuts has been a reduction in staffing levels across the public prison estate too (Prison Reform Trust 2017; Crewe and Liebling 2018).

Away from the criminal justice system, adult social care provides another example of the out-sourcing of a public service argued on the basis that marketisation offers both efficiency and the potential for innovation. However, Rubery et al (2013) argue that the evidence suggests that government commissioning policies result in arrangements that prioritise cost above quality. Further, they suggest (2013: 433) that 'overriding costs constraints' and the 'rising influence of national providers' have blunted the extent to which local authorities can influence the shape and quality of provision. The influence of national providers is significant in *Transforming Rehabilitation* too. The two private companies, Sodexo and Interserve, together own 11 (of 21) CRCs.

As with prisons and probation, in adult social care minimising cost means reducing the amount of money spent on staff. Working with fewer staff results in shorter home visits, lack of payment for travelling time between visits, longer delays in setting up care packages and increased staff turnover. Hayes and Moore (2017: 330) explicitly make the link between care and time, explaining that 'under conditions of austerity, home-care services are reconfigured and care itself is reductively constructed as a consumption of time, service users are constructed as needy (or greedy) time-consumers and home-care workers as resource-wasting time-takers'. Rubery et al (2013) argue that any increase in the quality of home care and in user satisfaction with the service depends on an improvement in the human resource practice of care providers from the independent sector.

These experiences, from adult social care and from the prison, suggest that one consequence of probation privatisation will be downward pressure on staff costs and increased focus on lean working practices. Maintaining the quality of relationships, through which care in probation practice is expressed, will consequently be a challenge.

IV. What is Happening in Practice?

The new probation arrangements are still less than five years old and, as a consequence, there is little evidence about their impact on the quality of care. The majority of the evidence that does exist (and is publicly available) comes from two main sources: independent inspection reports undertaken by Her Majesty's Inspectorate of Probation (HMIP) and a modest number of small pieces of academic research.

For the most part, the findings from inspection reports are not positive about the overall quality of the service provided by the CRCs. HMIP has produced Quality and Impact Inspection reports investigating the work of all private providers and highlighting practice across England and Wales. In her 2017 Annual

Report, HM Chief Inspector of Probation made clear her concerns, questioning whether *Transforming Rehabilitation* had created a model for probation that was capable of delivering an acceptable service (HMIP 2017a). By 2019 (HMIP 2019: 3) she had concluded that 'the probation model delivered by *Transforming Rehabilitation* is irredeemably flawed'. The inspection criticisms are levelled at the implementation of the new operating models but, crucially, also at the structure of these models.

The inspection reports provide evidence that anticipated downward pressure on staff costs has indeed led to high workloads, staff shortage and lack of continuity for supervisees. HMIP (2017a: 6) notes that some CRCs have undertaken more than one round of staff redundancies and 'in some, we find staff with exceptional workloads working long hours and still unable to deliver to the professional standards that they know are right'. By way of example, the inspection of CRC work in Suffolk (HMIP 2017b) found caseloads for full-time officers to be much higher than the target of between 55 and 70, with one staff member dealing with 106 cases. In the report on work in Gloucestershire (HMIP 2017c: 4), caseloads were described as 'plainly unreasonable'. Even in areas which HMIP judged to be more successful, workload pressure was a real concern. For example, inspectors calculated that staff in Cumbria were working with an average caseload of 65, an experience leading workers to explain that they were 'always chasing their tail' (HMIP 2017d: 22).

In the north of London, HMIP (2016) found the CRC to be struggling with poor staff morale, high vacancy rates and an increasing level of sickness absence. MTC Novo, the company that owns the London CRC, introduced the strapline BIONIC (Believe It Or Not I Care) from its work in the USA to English probation practice. This approach to branding was, perhaps, always going to sit awkwardly with probation culture, but the mention of 'care'. at a time when staff felt neither cared for by their employers nor able to care about service users as they wished, led to expressions of both ridicule and anger (Brown 2016). Returning to the London CRC in 2018, HMIP (2018) did find improved performance, but nevertheless concluded that neither public protection nor rehabilitative work was good enough.

For service users high caseloads mean little chance of establishing a link with a supervising officer that provides more than a brief and short-lived relationship. Staff may behave with respect and politeness to service users, but will struggle to get to know them well. Supervisors who do not know their supervisees well are poorly placed to understand their needs, encourage their compliance and engagement, or demonstrate mutual caring (Lewis 2014).

However, the work of HMIP goes beyond suggesting that the quality of probation practice is hindered by staff shortages and high workloads. HMIP (2017a; 2019) raises questions about the new probation operating models themselves, particularly where these operating models appear to hamper the development of a productive working relationship between supervisor and supervisee. Two practices come in for particular criticism: supervision by telephone and the use of public rather than private spaces for meetings. For example, telephone supervision for individuals identified as posing the lowest risk forms part of the way of working implemented in the CRCs owned by the company Working Links. In its inspection of Gloucestershire (HMIP 2017c) the inspectors noted with concern that junior staff were responsible for the telephone supervision of between 190 and 200 cases each.

CRCs are also developing 'Community Hubs' – places where probation supervision takes place away from the probation office but where other community services are available to the supervisee. The merit of this approach is its potential to introduce supervisees to agencies and charities providing help, advice and opportunities in their neighbourhood. One drawback, a problem where Community Hubs are established in premises poorly equipped for privacy, is the lack of opportunity for sensitive and difficult conversation (Brewer 2017). The operational model developed by the company Sodexo for its CRCs provides open-plan booths, rather than interview rooms, for much of the day-to-day interaction between staff and service users. The booths are unpopular with those who use them. Speaking to inspectors, a service user said: 'It's embarrassing. You get asked things like "how did the meeting with social services go?"' (HMIP 2017b: 22) and a member of staff commented 'The office booths are appalling! They create issues of confidentiality, trust, openness, and relationship building' (HMIP 2017d: 23).

These operating models, with details including the use of telephone contact and the move away from the use of traditional interview rooms in probation offices, formed part of the bids made by the new probation providers to the Ministry of Justice. For HMIP (2017a: 6) the Ministry of Justice's decision to award contracts that allowed these practices was 'inexplicable'. However, the learning from outsourcing elsewhere in the public sector suggests that the Government's behaviour can be well explained as an inevitable consequence of asking private providers to do more work with fewer resources. It is too often the case that CRC staff are given neither the time nor the space to care.

There is, as yet, little academic research addressing the process, experience or outcome of *Transforming Rehabilitation* and exploring the practices of the CRCs. The work that has been done has a focus on occupational culture and on the experience of staff rather than on service users. It reflects the period of upheaval and transition that followed the swiftly implemented creation of the NPS and CRCs. Robinson et al (2016) undertook fieldwork in the early days of a CRC. They gathered data from interviews and focus groups with practitioners and managers, as well as from observation of meetings. Their findings revealed a workforce caught between the old and new, feeling the loss of relationships with former colleagues and service users, and fearing that they had been moved to an insecure position, lacking professional status and threatened by private sector values.

The focus of Birkett's (2017) work is on the supervision of female offenders. She interviewed 36 practitioners (18 probation staff and 18 workers from agencies providing a specialist service for women offenders). Her findings support the argument (made ahead of *Transforming Rehabilitation* by authors including

Gelsthorpe and Hedderman (2012)) that the privatisation of probation would lead to particularly unsatisfactory outcomes for women service users. Women form a minority of the probation caseload and, as a group, are lower risk but often with complex needs (Gelsthorpe and Canton, Chapter four this volume). Community women's centres, established prior to *Transforming Rehabilitation* to provide a holistic service for women offenders and women at risk of offending, have faced significant funding cuts as CRCs have not found the money to continue this provision. Some centres have closed (Gelsthorpe and Russell 2018).

Kay's (2016) research did include interviews with probationers who were subject to supervision at the time of the creation of the NPS and CRCs. His finding that probationers began to think differently about the two organisations (identifying the NPS with punishment and the CRC with help) merits further investigation. There remain other important research gaps too. There is, as yet, no evidence about the impact of probation privatisation on the relational aspects of CRC practice. While it seems likely that the factors highlighted in inspection reports (high caseloads, increased use of routine reporting and poor staff morale) will curtail the extent to which supervisors and supervisees develop professional relationships that express care and support change, research exploring this issue would be welcome.

V. What Might the Future Hold for Care and Probation?

One reading of the available evidence is that probation staff come to work caring about service users and wanting to help them make positive changes in their lives. Delivering practice in this spirit of care is not incompatible with the responsibilities of probation (for enforcing orders and managing risks) that inevitably require the exercise of control. Indeed, the argument that probation is best undertaken with an ethos of care is supported by research indicating the importance of relational factors for outcomes such compliance, engagement and effectiveness. Service users identify some (certainly not all) experiences of probation as caring; they talk of the value of working with staff who listen carefully, take an individualised approach and go the extra mile to help.

Perhaps there is no reason why privatisation should inevitably harm the quality of probation practice. As we have seen, the evidence from prisons in England and Wales does not demonstrate that privatisation inevitably results in loss of quality; it shows that private providers in criminal justice are capable of running regimes that perform well, including on dimensions that are related to care (like respect, fairness and trust).

However, the marketisation of public services changes the relationship between existing stakeholders. In the probation context, civil servants switch from policy development to contract monitoring, CRCs employ staff whose function is to ensure that the company achieves the metrics specified in the contract, and service users risk being increasingly understood as metric-meeting units. Marketisation also creates new stakeholders (the senior managers and shareholders of private companies) with a direct interest in the profitability of the contract and no incentive to share ideas about best practice with competitors. While there may be little evidence of corruption in the English experience, there have been high-profile failures of out-sourcing companies (Carillion in the facilities management sector and Southern Cross in the social care sector), investigations into overcharging (Serco and G4S in the electronic monitoring sector) and fraudulent behaviour (for example A4e in the employment sector). The first commercial failure in the probation world came at the end of 2018 when the private company Working Links went into administration. Its CRC contracts were transferred to another private provider.

Yet more organisational change is coming to the probation service. Responding to the evident shortcomings of *Transforming Rehabilitation* – many highlighted in a strongly critical Select Committee report (Justice Select Committee 2018) – the Government plans further reform. It has announced that the current CRC contracts will end early (in 2020 rather than 2022), conceded that more money is needed now to improve the quality of supervision, and required CRCs to provide more face-to-face contact time for supervisees (Ministry of Justice 2018). The Government appears committed to marketisation and the role of the private sector. At the time of writing (May 2019) the proposed new shape for probation was subject to consultation with the Government (Ministry of Justice 2018: 13) undertaking to

> explore with the market how in future we could establish a more effective commercial framework which better takes account of changes in demand for probation and ensures that providers are adequately paid to deliver the core services which are essential to a successful probation system.

As with private prisons, private probation services conceivably have the potential to provide a service which operates with a culture of care and respect, for staff as well as service users. However, this potential will not be realised for as long as the Ministry of Justice and private providers make contractual arrangements that are financially unsustainable. The position in the probation service resembles that in out-sourced adult social care, where increasing levels of demand and restricted funding have restricted the availability of services, suppressed the wages of staff and impacted negatively on the quality of care.

The quality of care in probation practice depends partly on the motivation and values of probation staff. However, it also requires that those staff have time to build relationships with service users and training to develop the knowledge and skills required by the role. When caseloads are too large supervisors lose the capacity to see service users as unique individuals and practice becomes mechanistic. Probation staff typically do want to care about the people that they supervise and, as a society, there are empirical and moral reasons why we should all want to see probation practised in a culture of care. However, in order to achieve this, practitioners need a structure that gives them the time, knowledge and confidence to construct positive working relationships with service users. This is not the structure that has been provided by *Transforming Rehabilitation*.

Perhaps there are approaches to privatisation that would have resulted in service innovation and an increase in the quality of probation practice. However, the privatisation model chosen for the probation service is not able to achieve this. The *Transforming Rehabilitation* reforms pose a threat to care in probation practice because private providers have contracted to do too much work with too little money.

References

Annison, J, Eadie, T and Knight, C (2008) 'People First: Probation Officer Perspectives on Probation Work' *Probation Journal* 55(3): 259–71.

Ascher, K (1987) *The Politics of Privatisation* (London, Macmillan).

Birkett, G (2017) 'Transforming women's rehabilitation? An early assessment of gender-specific provision in three Community Rehabilitation Companies' *Criminology and Criminal Justice* 19(1): 98–114: https://doi.org/10.1177%2F1748895817743286.

Bonta, J and Andrews, D (2010) 'Viewing offender assessment and rehabilitation through the lens of the risk-needs-responsivity model' in F McNeill, P Raynor and C Trotter (eds), *Offender Supervision: New directions in theory, research and practice* (Cullompton, Willan).

Bottoms, A (2001) 'Compliance and community penalties' in A Bottoms, L Gelsthorpe and S Rex (eds), *Community Penalties: Change and Challenges* (Cullompton, Willan).

Brewer, K (2017) 'Why are privatised probation services using public libraries to see clients?' *The Guardian* 1 November, available online at www.theguardian.com/society/2017/nov/01/privatised-probation-services-libraries-ex-offenders (accessed 18 December 2017).

Brown, J (2016) 'Pick of the Week 15' *On Probation Blog* Weblog 25 September, available online at: probationmatters.blogspot.co.uk/2016/09/pick-of-week-15.html (accessed 21 January 2018).

Burke, L and Collett, S (2015) *Delivering Rehabilitation: The Politics, Governance and Control of Probation* (London, Routledge).

Canton, R and Dominey, J (2017) *Probation*, 2nd edn (London, Routledge).

Carter, P (2003) *Managing Offenders, Reducing Crime: A New Approach* (Correctional Services Review) (London, Home Office).

Crewe, B and Liebling, A (2018) 'Quality, professionalism and the distribution of power in public and private sector prisons' in A Hucklesby and S Lister (eds), *The Private Sector and Criminal Justice* (London, Palgrave Macmillan).

Crewe, B, Liebling, A and Hulley, S (2011) 'Staff culture, use of authority and prisoner quality of life in public and private sector prisons' *Australian & New Zealand Journal of Criminology* 44(1): 94–115.

Deering, J (2010) 'The purposes of supervision: practitioner and policy perspectives in England and Wales' in F McNeill, P Raynor and C Trotter (eds), *Offender Supervision: New directions in theory, research and practice* (Cullompton, Willan).

Dominey, J (2012) 'A mixed market for probation services: Can lessons from the recent past help shape the near future?' *Probation Journal* 59(4): 339–54.

Dominey, J and Gelsthorpe, L (2018) 'Competing to control in the community: What chance for a culture of care?' in A Hucklesby and S Lister (eds), *The Private Sector and Criminal Justice* (London, Palgrave Macmillan).

Dowden, C and Andrews, D (2004) 'The Importance of Staff Practice in Delivering Effective Correctional Treatment: A Meta-Analytic Review of Core Correctional Practice' *International Journal of Offender Therapy and Comparative Criminology* 48(2): 203–14.

Garland, D (2001) *The Culture of Control: Crime and Social Order in Contemporary Society* (Oxford, Oxford University Press).

Gelsthorpe, L (2007) 'Dealing with Diversity' in G McIvor and P Raynor (eds), *Developments in Social Work with Offenders, Research Highlights in Social Work 48* (London, Jessica Kingsley).

Gelsthorpe, L and Hedderman, C (2012) 'Providing for women offenders: The risks of adopting a Payment by Results approach' *Probation Journal* 59(4): 374–90.

Gelsthorpe, L and Russell, J (2018) 'Women and penal reform: Two steps forwards, three steps backwards?' *Political Quarterly* 89(2): 227–36.

Hayes, D (2015) 'The impact of supervision on the pains of community penalties in England and Wales: An exploratory study' *European Journal of Probation* 7(2): 85–102.

Hayes, LJB and Moore, S (2017) 'Care in a Time of Austerity: the Electronic Monitoring of Homecare Workers' Time' *Gender, Work and Organization* 24(4): 329–44.

Herzog-Evans, M (2011) 'What's in a name: Penological and institutional connotations of probation officers' labelling in Europe' *EuroVista* 2(3): 121–33.

HMIP (2016) *Quality & Impact inspection The effectiveness of probation work in the north of London*, available online at: www.justiceinspectorates.gov.uk/hmiprobation/wp-content/uploads/sites/5/2016/12/North-of-London-QI-Report.pdf (accessed 18 December 2017).

HMIP (2017a) *2017 Annual Report*, available online at: www.justiceinspectorates.gov.uk/hmiprobation/corporate-documents/annualreport2017/ (accessed 18 December 2017).

HMIP (2017b) *Quality & Impact inspection The effectiveness of probation work in Suffolk*, available online at: www.justiceinspectorates.gov.uk/hmiprobation/inspections/suffolkqi/ (accessed 18 December 2017).

HMIP (2017c) *Quality & Impact inspection The effectiveness of probation work in Gloucestershire*, available online at: www.justiceinspectorates.gov.uk/hmiprobation/inspections/gloucestershireqi/ (accessed 18 December 2017).

HMIP (2017d) *Quality & Impact inspection The effectiveness of probation work in Cumbria*, available online at: www.justiceinspectorates.gov.uk/hmiprobation/wp-content/uploads/sites/5/2017/10/Cumbria-QI-report.pdf (accessed 18 December 2017).

HMIP (2018) *Quality & Impact inspection The effectiveness of probation work by the London Community Rehabilitation Company*, available online at: www.justiceinspectorates.gov.uk/hmiprobation/inspections/qilondoncrc/ (accessed 2 August 2018).

HMIP (2019) *Annual Report 2019*, available online at: www.justiceinspectorates.gov.uk/hmiprobation/wp-content/uploads/sites/5/2019/03/HMI-Probation-Chief-Inspectors-Report.pdf (accessed 7 May 2019).

Home Office (1995) *Managing What Works: Conference Report and Guidance on Critical Success Factors for Probation Supervision Programmes* Probation Circular 77/1995 (London: Home Office).

Howard League (2013) *Response to Transforming Rehabilitation* (London: Howard League).

Institute for Fiscal Studies (2017) *Autumn 2017 Budget: options for easing the squeeze*, available online at: www.ifs.org.uk/uploads/publications/comms/BN135.pdf (accessed 2 February 2018).

Justice Select Committee (2008) *Fifth Report – Towards Effective Sentencing*, available online at: www.publications.parliament.uk/pa/cm200708/cmselect/cmjust/184/18402.htm (accessed 18 December 2017).

Justice Select Committee (2018) *Ninth Report – Transforming Rehabilitation*, available online at: publications.parliament.uk/pa/cm201719/cmselect/cmjust/482/48202.htm (accessed 29 September 2018).

Kay, C (2016) 'Good cop, Bad cop, Both? Examining the implications of risk based allocation on the desistance narratives of intensive probationers' *Probation Journal* 63(2): 162–68.

Kendall, K (2004) 'Dangerous thinking: a critical history of correctional cognitive behaviouralism' in G Mair (ed), *What Matters in Probation* (Cullompton, Willan).

Lewis, S (2014) 'Learning from success and failure: Deconstructing the working relationship within probation practice and exploring its impact on probationers, using a collaborative approach' *Probation Journal* 61(2): 161–75.

Liebling, A (2006) 'Lessons from Prison Privatisation for Probation' in M Hough, R Allen and U Padel (eds), *Reshaping Probation and Prisons: The New Offender Management Framework* (Bristol, Policy Press).

Liebling, A and Ludlow, A (2016) 'Privatising public prisons: Penality, law and practice' *Australian & New Zealand Journal of Criminology* 50(4): 473–92.

Lösel, F (2012) 'Offender treatment and rehabilitation: What Works?' in M Maguire, R Morgan and R Reiner (eds), *The Oxford Handbook of Criminology*, 5th edn (Oxford, Oxford University Press).

Ludlow, A (2014) 'Transforming Rehabilitation: What lessons might be learned from prison privatisation?' *European Journal of Probation* 6(1): 67–81.

—— (2017) 'Marketizing Criminal Justice' in A Liebling, S Maruna and L McAra (eds), *Oxford Handbook of Criminology*, 6th edn (Oxford, Oxford University Press).

McCulloch, T and McNeill, F (2007) 'Consumer Society, Commodification and Offender Management' *Criminology and Criminal Justice* 7(3): 223–42.

McNeill, F (2013) 'Transforming Rehabilitation: Evidence, Values and Ideology' *British Journal of Community Justice* 11(2/3): 83–85.

McNeill, F and Burnett, R (2005) 'The place of the officer–offender relationship in assisting offenders to desist from crime' *Probation Journal* 52(3): 221–42.

McNeill, F and Robinson, G (2013) 'Liquid Legitimacy and Community Sanctions' in A Crawford and A Hucklesby (eds), *Legitimacy and Compliance in Criminal Justice* (Abingdon, Routledge).

McNeill, F, Batchelor, S, Burnett, R and Knox, J (2005) *21st Century Social Work: Reducing Re-offending: Key Practice Skills*, available online at: www.gov.scot/Publications/2005/04/21132007/20089 (accessed 19 January 2018).

Ministry of Justice (2010) *Breaking the Cycle: Effective Punishment, Rehabilitation and Sentencing of Offenders* (Cm 7972) (London, Ministry of Justice).

Ministry of Justice (2013) *Transforming Rehabilitation: A Strategy for Reform*, available online at: consult.justice.gov.uk/digital-communications/transforming-rehabilitation/results/transforming-rehabilitation-response.pdf (accessed 29 November 2017).

Ministry of Justice (2018) *Strengthening Probation, Building Confidence*, available online at: consult.justice.gov.uk/hm-prisons-and-probation/strengthening-probation-building-confidence/supporting_documents/strengtheningprobationbuildingconfidence.pdf (accessed 2 August 2018).

Prison Reform Trust (2017) *Bromley Briefings Prison Factfile*, available online at: www.prisonreformtrust.org.uk/Portals/0/Documents/Bromley%20Briefings/Autumn%202017%20factfile.pdf (accessed 2 February 2018).

Raynor, P (2003) 'Evidence-based probation and its critics' *Probation Journal* 50(4): 334–45.

Rex, S (1999) 'Desistance from Offending: Experiences of Probation' *Howard Journal of Criminal Justice* 38(4): 366–83.

—— (2012) 'The Offender Engagement Programme – rationale and objectives' *EuroVista* 2(1): 6–9.

Robinson, G, Burke, L and Millings, M (2016) 'Criminal Justice Identities in Transition: The Case of Devolved Probation Services in England and Wales' *British Journal of Criminology* 56(1): 161–78.

Rubery, J, Grimshaw, D and Hebson, G (2013) 'Exploring the limits to local authority social care commissioning: Competing pressures, variable practices, and unresponsive providers' *Public Administration* 91(2): 419–37.

Sandel, M (2012) *What Money Can't Buy: The Moral Limits of Markets* (London, Allen Lane).

Senior, P (2016) 'Privatising Probation: The Death Knell of a Much-Cherished Public Service?' *Howard Journal of Crime and Justice* 55(4): 414–31.

Shapland, J, Bottoms, A, Farrall, S, McNeill, F, Priede, C and Robinson, G (2012) *The Quality of Probation Supervision: A Literature Review* (The University of Sheffield Centre for Criminological Research Occasional Paper 3).

Shaw M and Hannah-Moffat, K (2004) 'How cognitive skills forgot about gender and diversity' in G Mair (ed), *What Matters in Probation* (Cullompton, Willan).
Teague, M (2016) 'Probation, people and profits: The impact of neoliberalism' *British Journal of Community Justice* 14(1): 133–38.
Trotter, C (2006) *Working with Involuntary Clients: A Guide to Practice*, 2nd edn (London, Sage).
Ugwudike P (2010) 'Compliance with Community Penalties: The Importance of Interactional Dynamics' in F McNeill, P Raynor and C Trotter (eds), *Offender Supervision* (Cullompton, Willan).
Weaver, B and Barry, M (2014) 'Managing high risk offenders in the community: Compliance, cooperation and consent in a climate of concern' *European Journal of Probation* 6(3): 278–95.
Worrall, A and Mawby, RC (2014) 'Probation worker cultures and relationships with offenders' *Probation Journal* 61(4): 346–57.

4

Paradoxes of Care: Women in the Criminal Justice System in England and Wales

LORAINE GELSTHORPE AND ROB CANTON

I. Introduction

Over the past 30 years or so the use of imprisonment for women has increased enormously as a worldwide phenomenon (Walmsley 2018). Whilst there is no evidence to support changes in crime rates or the seriousness of crimes committed by women, the increase in the number of women in prison can be conceived as a logical outcome of critical scrutiny and campaigns in the UK since the 1980s and 1990s to improve prison regimes (see, for example, Carlen 1990; Social Work Services and Prisons Inspectorate 1998; Prison Reform Trust 2000; Scottish Government 2002). There was further scrutiny in 2007 when a major review of vulnerable women in prisons took place (Corston 2007). The Corston review was partly triggered by the deaths by suicide of six women in Styal Prison in Cheshire, England. Within a 12-month period in 2002 to 2003, Julie Walsh, Nissa Ann Smith, Anna Baker, Sarah Campbell, Jolene Willis and Haley Williams committed suicide soon after entering the prison. Each woman's story reflected her personal struggles and profound sadness. Typical of so many incarcerated women, they had faced a combination of addictions, mental health difficulties, homelessness, bereavement and trauma, together with numerous other debilitating challenges. Typical of imprisonment, there was evidently all too little 'care'. Following a fundamental re-thinking about services to support women in conflict with the law and how they are delivered in custody and in the community, there have been many changes since 2007, but these developments too, must fall under critical scrutiny, for gendered discourses of provision repeat earlier misconceptions, myths and muddles. Care and control are interwoven in paradoxical ways.

This chapter contributes to the critical scrutiny required to really understand the seeming 'care' offered to women in the criminal justice system. It is in three parts. We begin by outlining some policy developments (and reverses). We then move to consider developments in regard to the creation of special provision for women in the community and the shadows underlining seemingly positive developments. The final substantive part of the chapter addresses whether prisons in particular might be conceived as refuges and places of rehabilitation (which can be broadly interpreted as 'care') as well as being places of control, constraint and coercion. Do new psychological interventions relating to personality disorder help, for instance, if these emphasise individual pathology rather than broader social and structural issues relating to women's pathways into crime?

Thus there are questions as to whether criminal justice interventions can be viewed positively, or whether there are always shadows which signal neglect, an absence of care, or control (see Canton and Dominey, and Dominey and Gelsthorpe Chapters two and three in this volume for instance). How do we treat women who are both offenders *and* victims, for instance? We do not give attention to this particular issue in this chapter, but mention it to emphasise that what this chapter covers is merely illustrative of more general issues concerning the 'shadow' of care for women in the criminal justice system. As this chapter will show, there are differences between the rhetoric and reality of care, difference between policy and practice, and lived realities which expose the 'dark side' of care.

II. Control and Care: A Patchwork Quilt

In 2001 David Garland published *The Culture of Control*, an insightful historical-cultural account of how the crime control developments witnessed in the late twentieth century in particular have 'adapted' and 'responded' to the late modern world (broadly conceived as being the period from the 1950s onwards), and to its political and cultural values. In essence, his thesis was that the socially conservative politics, including the adoption of free market solutions to social problems, that came to dominate the USA and the UK in the 1980s shaped new strategies of control and punishment which were emerging. Garland (2001) thus offered a genealogical account of the contemporary 'crime complex' which is animated and sustained by cultural assumptions and social and economic factors; it is a 'history of the present'. The book has been widely acclaimed, with even the most critical responses hailing it as a significant contribution to our understanding of events. One of the authors of this chapter, Gelsthorpe, nevertheless drew attention to the fact that the treatment of women as both offenders and victims received very little attention in the book (Gelsthorpe 2005). This was surprising, since the conventional treatment of women might be said to epitomise the penal-welfare strategies that Garland was suggesting were been replaced by crime control strategies.

Penal welfarism as defined by Garland (2001) is a structural response to crime that is composed of two ideological strands. Firstly, due process and proportionate punishment, with their inherent liberal ideologies, ensure that all the rights of the offender are respected. The punishment is fitting to the crime and the circumstances of the offender. Rehabilitation and offender welfare are approached from a correctionalist viewpoint. These elements ensure that the punishment given to the offender maintains a focus upon rehabilitation, as does the approach of professionals who work with the offender during the punishment period. In short, penal-welfarism suggests that rehabilitation will be most effective if the offender is provided with positive motivation while in the care of the penal system. The logic behind the practice is that if the offender is provided with the opportunity to progress during 'punishment' – whether in custody or in the community – they will wish to continue to do so when their sentence has been completed. By the 1960s, in both the USA and the UK, penal-welfarism commanded the attention of all the key groups involved in criminal justice – and the enthusiastic support of government department administrators, social work and probation professionals, and liberal elites. The idea of 'progress in penal reform' was a conventional idea, and a persuasive one, because it captured the sense of the gradual implementation of a progressive programme that was widely shared and respected. The programmes and working ideologies were integral elements of the post-war welfare state and its social democratic politics.

Garland reminds us that the basic axiom of penal-welfarism is that:

> [P]enal measures ought, where possible, to be rehabilitative interventions rather than negative, retributive punishments … giving rise to … sentencing laws that allowed indeterminate sentences linked to early release and parole supervision; the juvenile court with its child welfare philosophy; the use of social inquiry and psychiatric reports; the individualization of treatment based upon expert assessment and classification; criminological research focusing on etiological issues and treatment effectiveness; social work with offenders and their families; and custodial regimes that stressed the re-educative purposes of imprisonment and the importance of re-integrative support upon release (2001: 34).

Turning to the treatment of women in the criminal justice system, critiques of criminology have demonstrated that beliefs about female offenders which locate their offending behaviour in the discourse of the pathological have long persisted, despite the introduction of more sociological and social constructionist ideas in relation to males' offending behaviour (Gelsthorpe and Morris 1990; Heidensohn and Hahn-Rafter 1996). The discourse of the pathological lends itself to penal-welfarism and it also fuels the quest for the special treatment of women.

Calls for differentiation in the treatment of male and female offenders led to a significant number of changes in the nineteenth century (Zedner 1991). In the twentieth century, of particular note was the attempt to provide a distinctive therapeutic regime for women offenders within the (then) new Holloway prison in 1968 (Rock 1996),[1] a development, which at the time, was very much seen as a demonstration of particular 'care' for women. The notion of Holloway as a therapeutically-orientated prison quickly became outmoded in that period, however, alongside opposition from the staff in the prison. There is now limited Therapeutic Community (TC) provision for women in HMP Send and some psychologically-informed planned environments (PIPEs) in other women's prisons, as well as in men's prisons.[2] The main point here is that the treatment of women offenders and girls in conflict with the law has long reflected elements of the 'penal-welfarism' to which David Garland refers – except that it has not been replaced by a culture of control in quite the way suggested. Penal-welfarism for women lives on, and with it, a confusion of care and control.

There are perhaps three main themes that infuse the treatment of women in the criminal justice system: pathology, domesticity and respectability. A woman who appears in the court room can be seen as 'incongruous' or 'out of place' and so explanations for her presence are sought within the discourse of the pathological and the irrational (Worrall 1990): menstruation, mental illness, poor socialisation and the menopause have all featured in explanations, and all have been subject to strong critique (one of the first major critiques can be found in Carol Smart's *Women, Crime and Criminology* (1976) for instance). In contrast, men's offending is seen as both 'rational' and 'normal'. Women's social problems and welfare needs, which might be interpreted as 'care' for them, are seen to be important influences in sentencing (Carlen 1983; Farrington and Morris 1983). Other research – based on analysis of sentencing patterns and interviews with magistrates – has revealed that women are seen as 'troubled' more than 'troublesome' (Gelsthorpe and Loucks 1997). This sort of thinking reflects the notion that women's offending behaviour can be seen as a reflection of their own 'caring' roles in the family (stealing to feed or clothe their children, for instance, as a matter of survival), or as the result of provocation from or coercion by abusive men, or attributable to mental disturbance.

Similar familial themes can be identified within prison regimes. Pat Carlen and Chris Tchaikovsky captured the nature of the penal-welfare direction of the treatment of women offenders in their memorable claim that women's prisons 'Discipline, Infantalize, Feminize, Medicalize and Domesticize' (1985: 182). Writing about women's imprisonment at the turn of the twenty-first century and the dual nature of women's treatment – 'caring' on the one hand, but dishing out

[1] HMP Holloway was closed in July 2016, with prisoners being moved to HMP Downview and HMP Bronzefield, both in Surrey.

[2] There is now one such prison – HMP Send, and (for men) HMP Grendon. The story of how these prisons survive in a context of ever-increasing security and control would take us beyond the main arguments in this chapter, however (see Genders and Player 2010).

harsh punishment on the other and removing women from their caring roles in the family – Carlen explained:

> [W]omen's family responsibilities and previous family histories interact (variously) with dominant ideologies about women's place in the family and (contradictorily) with the rigours of state punishment – to increase several-fold the pains of penal incarceration (1998: 82).

Thus the treatment of women has been closely linked to their characterisation as being essentially 'bad, sad or mad', or uncaring or neglectful mothers.

Women did not escape the punitive turn which Garland (2001) outlines so vividly. Receptions of women into prison more than doubled between 1990 and 2000 (Home Office 2001). How could this be explained? Gelsthorpe and Morris (2002) explored possible changes in demographics, in crime, and in the levels and lengths of sentencing, whilst Deakin and Spencer (2003) looked at possible changes in women committing burglary offences (given the emphasis on giving custodial sentences for burglary at the time). Changes in offending were acknowledged, but drug and violent offences occurred at the lower end of seriousness and these factors could not account for the huge increase in the number of women in prison.

One other explanation for the huge increase in the use of imprisonment for women relates to campaigns for reform. Academics, liberal penal reformers, feminist reformers and criminal justice professionals alike have argued for the prison conditions for women to be ameliorated since the early 1980s in particular. The issue is whether the practical reforms which have emerged as a result of the campaigns, in an effort to 'care' for women in prison and to ensure that their needs are addressed, have led to the unintended consequence of making prisons more attractive to sentencers as suitable places to send women. The evidence in England and Wales does not go far enough to support this idea, but in the context of this chapter it is an idea we should keep in mind. There may be a three-fold effect of the interweaving of punitive and penal-welfare discourses: an increase in the use of imprisonment as part of the general wave of punitiveness (Garland's (1991) 'culture of control' idea); an up-tariffing of women in sentencing because of a reluctance to fine them (recognition of poverty and child-care responsibilities) which in effect means that the 'ladder' of sentencing options is shorter for women than men; and a perception that a prison sentence creates a sense of women's needs being able to be met in 'improved' prisons (especially in the relative absence of community-based social services). Pat Carlen (2002) refers to this as 'carceral clawback'; interestingly, Kelly Hannah-Moffat (2001) has also written about this in the context of improvement to prisons for federally sentenced women in Canada.

Alongside other aspects of the reinvigoration of 'law and order' from the 1980s onwards, increasing reliance on the use of imprisonment is often described as the most notable penal development of the mid-1990s, reflecting increased fears of crime and a climate in which protection, incapacitation, and 'risk management' became government priorities. Punitive and penal-welfare approaches are thus combined, in a way that makes 'care' in prisons for women in conflict with the law seem both reasonable and realistic. This creates a patchwork quilt of control and care.

III. Contemporary Criminal Justice 'Care' for Women in Conflict with the Law: Towards Special Provision for Women in the Community

When the Labour Party came to power in the UK in 1997 there was clear expectation that progressive ideas about appropriate ways of addressing the needs of women in conflict with the law, mooted by various academics and campaigning groups, would become practice. There was general interest in 'what works', a recognition of individual pathways into crime (acknowledging social dimensions such as poverty), and consideration of the need to examine research evidence in relation to women offenders. Whilst there was no avowed interest in decarceration, there was unmistakable interest in making imprisonment more effective. Importantly, it was acknowledged that women's needs often were greater than men's and were often overlooked, or not prioritised, in a system designed for men. There was also renewed recognition that the women's prison population was growing at a greater rate than that of men, yet with no evidence that women were committing more crime or more serious crime. Indeed, the Cabinet Office's Social Exclusion Unit produced a report which outlined the prospect of a Women's Offending Reduction Programme (WORP):

> The Programme's plan of action, to be formally launched later in 2002, will provide a framework for building on existing good practice to reduce women's offending. It will also enhance the growing recognition across the criminal justice system that there needs to be a distinct response to the particular needs of women (SEU 2002: 142).

An Action Plan followed in 2004 – designed to give full attention to women's needs and to 'care' for women in this way. There was no new funding at this point; rather the aim was to embed a consideration of women's needs into existing systems and approaches. The Sentencing Guidelines Council was invited to produce guidance and instructions on how the new sentencing powers established by the Criminal Justice Act 2003 might impact differently on women.[3] The Women's Policy Team within the Ministry of Justice set up a cross-departmental liaison group in 2006, encouraged the development of guidance concerning services for women on probation, and lent support to existing initiatives to improve community-based

[3] The Sentencing Guidelines Council became the Sentencing Council in 2010.

responses to women's mental health needs. Supported by an exceptional number of female ministers in government, the Policy Team negotiated £9.15m in funding to build on best practice developed by small-scale initiatives such as the 218 Centre in Scotland and the Asha Centre in England and Wales. It supported a demonstration programme *Together Women* (TW); five community-based projects across two regions of the country, which sought to provide holistic 'wrap around' support (help with dealing with debts, housing, substance misuse and so on, as well as addressing temptations to commit further offences) for women who were former or current offenders or whose social exclusion needs were thought to put them at risk of offending (Hedderman et al 2008). Finally, there was articulation of and a clear response to the need to care for women in conflict with the law in a particular way.

The Ministry of Justice's own analysis of the implementation of special community provision for women offenders and those at risk of offending which was introduced between late 2006 and early 2007 suggested that TW was seen by local stakeholders as filling an important gap in provision (though at the time there were still concerns about the supply of suitable accommodation, access to counselling, and mental health outreach services). Individual care plans were important, and most service users interviewed early on were optimistic about their chances of avoiding further offending through their involvement in the centres delivering the special community provision for women. There was acknowledgement that those who were struggling most could still turn to TW long after other agencies, family and friends had given up on them. In terms of holistic support, a number of stakeholders and staff noted that finding the right representatives from local health services had been slow and difficult, but that this reflected the complexity of local health arrangements rather than a lack of interest (Hedderman et al 2008: 16). More generally, and notwithstanding difficulties in measuring diversion from crime and from custody via the new community services for women, the overall impression of the services was positive. The service users who had sustained contact with TW in its first year of operation very much valued the assistance provided and the facilitated access to other agencies (Hedderman et al 2011).

As mentioned in the Introduction to this chapter, the suicides of six women in HMP Styal prompted the Labour Government to commission Baroness Jean Corston to review women 'with particular vulnerabilities' in the criminal justice system. She interpreted her brief broadly, seeing most women in prison as 'vulnerable':

> There are many women in prison, either on remand or serving sentences for minor, non-violent offences, for whom prison is both disproportionate and inappropriate. Many of them suffer poor physical and mental health or substance abuse or had chaotic childhoods. Many have been in care (Corston 2007: i).

And as a consequence she very much promoted the idea of community-based holistic support for women offenders. Despite all preceding developments and initiatives as described above, Baroness Corston expressed dismay when she introduced her report in 2007:

> I have been dismayed at the high prevalence of institutional misunderstanding within the criminal justice system of the things that matter to women and at the shocking level of unmet need. Yet the compelling body of research which has accumulated over many years consistently points to remedies. … There can be few topics that have been so exhaustively researched to such little practical effect as the plight of women in the criminal justice system (Corston 2007: 16).

We can translate this into an evident lack of care. Corston produced 43 recommendations which revolved around the need for holistic care of women in the community. Readiness for action was reinforced by the Fawcett Society's commissioned survey of existing community centres and services which might be adapted for women offenders (Gelsthorpe, Sharpe and Roberts 2007) published within weeks of the publication of the Corston Report. The report attempted to fuel debate by identifying nine lessons to be taken into account in providing for women in the community, ranging from women-only workshops to practical help with child care (Gelsthorpe et al 2007: 54).

Drawing on the initial favourable impact of the TW project, existing expertise from practitioners (via voluntary sector organisations such as *Women at the Well* and *Women in Prison*, for example), and with support from the Equalities Office and the Corston Independent Funders Coalition (a collaboration of grant-making trusts and foundations who wanted to see action following the report), the Ministry of Justice produced further funding to promote the extension of women's centres around the country to make special provision for women in contact with the criminal justice system. As part of this funded work, a forum was developed for women's centres to share good practice and learning, and out of their meetings came an understanding that if community-based services stood any chance of survival past the two-year window of committed funding then a strategic approach by the voluntary sector was needed. The forum eventually became Women's Breakout, a national network of some 47 women's community services. However, these positive developments were not all straightforward or sustained, and there were some missed opportunities. 'Care' was not consistent (see Gelsthorpe and Russell 2018).

Firstly, although the Government distributed funding across a number of organisations, the failure to insist on a rigorous monitoring and evaluation system led to the effectiveness of the sector's contribution being challenged when the initial funding came to an end and continuation funding was being sought. It also allowed those with the power to allocate further resources to delay and minimise those resources with circular arguments relating to how successful outcomes could be 'assigned' to specific interventions (or not). Secondly, the National Offender Management Service's report entitled *A Distinct Approach: A Guide for Working with Women Offenders* (2012) outlined two key issues which affect women: violence and self-harm. These issues did not feature large in discussions beyond the criminal justice system in terms of creating a 'holistic approach'.

There is broad agreement that there was evidence of real progress during the Labour years of 1997 to 2010 (Gelsthorpe and Russell 2018). Indeed, with renewed momentum inspired by Baroness Corston's Report, the Ministry of Justice committed millions in funding to voluntary organisations to take the lead in working with statutory agencies to provide additional and enhanced community support for women at risk of offending or reoffending. And the creation of a national network of community-based programmes and centres is undoubtedly one of the major achievements in demonstrating care for women in conflict with the law. There are numerous positive evaluations of individual community-based services.[4] But, as already indicated, there were missed opportunities to ensure monitoring and evaluation across the services, and failure to implement aspirational policies. In particular, there was a general 'silence' on women offenders' needs when the Coalition Government came to power in 2010 with resultant closure of some community centres for women offenders.

Since 2010 we can see that energies to reform provision for women have dissipated and it is arguable that the much vaunted Corston Report has lost its power. The funding (£15.6m) that the Ministry of Justice allocated to implement the recommendations of the Corston Report in 2009 was time-limited – two years. At the end of that time there was no firm plan to continue to fund gender-specific, holistic, community services for women impacted by the criminal justice system, but late in the final year, a one-year rescue package was pulled together by the Corston Independent Funders Coalition (CIFC) (with some financial support from the Ministry of Justice, drawing on what was called the Women's Diversionary Fund One),[5] on the understanding that mainstream funding would be identified. It was very late on in 2011 that limited further funding was identified through the National Offender Management Service (Women's Diversionary Fund Two) and CIFC. The National Offender Management Service produced funding for 2012–13 (£3.78m).[6] There was then a trickle of support from Probation Trusts, but from 2014 services were wholly commissioned through Community Rehabilitation Companies (CRCs). CRCs were created as part of the *Transforming Rehabilitation* agenda which came from the Coalition Government in 2010, with commitment to reduce reoffending and reduce the size of the prison population. In the context of austerity and ideological commitment to competition, a Competition Strategy for Offender Services followed in 2011 and, in 2013, indication that Probation Trusts were to be replaced by a new National Probation Service (NPS), responsible for the public sector duties, and by private or voluntary sector organisations (the CRCs). The CRCs were commissioned by

[4] See Easton (2011); McCoy et al (2013); Radcliffe and Hunter (2016); and Brighton Women's Centre's 'Inspire' at: http://www.womenscentre.org.uk.

[5] The Women's Diversionary Fund was a new fund that was set up in February 2010 with the specific aim of working with both offenders and vulnerable women considered to be at risk of offending, to divert them from crime.

[6] On 1 April 2017 NOMS was replaced by Her Majesty's Prisons and Probation Service (HMPPS).

the National Offender Management Service to work in 21 'contract package areas' (Canton and Dominey 2018; see also Chapter three by Dominey and Gelsthorpe in this volume, which looks at care and the privatisation of probation). This made a number of campaigning groups and commentators concerned that the positive developments regarding the creation of appropriate 'care' for women offenders would be reversed (Gelsthorpe and Russell 2018). *Together Women* had surely served as a 'beacon of hope' that there could be proper provision for women in conflict with the law.

So what has happened since? A very high proportion of women continue to be sentenced to short custodial sentences. Over 80 per cent of women entering prison under sentence in 2017 had committed a non-violent offence and 70 per cent of women entering prison in the year to December 2016 were serving six months or less (Ministry of Justice 2018a). This figure has grown enormously since 1993, when only a third of imprisoned women were given these very short sentences (Ministry of Justice 2018a). There has also been a failure by sentencers to understand *Together Women* and other similar community-based provision for women. For instance, it became clear that magistrates did not fully understand the use of Women's Centres and special provision for women as a resource in sentencing. This is a point which has been re-emphasised by Gemma Birkett (2016: 504) following focus group discussions with magistrates in 2014; as one focus group participant put it 'we have no awareness of what might be out there, where the probation send them, what they actually do'. Moreover, and as indicated above, the lack of consistency in monitoring and evaluation has not helped the case for community-based services for women. An analysis of re-offending following TW (Jolliffe, Hedderman, Palmer and Hollin 2011) highlighted the lack of standardised measures and systems for recording data, and a lack of consistency in how service users were defined, along with the differing nature of support provided.[7]

Other examples of the shadows of care include evidence to suggest that whereas the police previously referred women to Women's Centres on an informal basis, they began to refer them formally (via a Women's Specific Conditional Caution) (Easton et al 2010) with related concerns about net-widening (that is, drawing people into the criminal justice system, rather than diverting them as is often more appropriate for those who have committed less serious offences). Notwithstanding positive feedback from users of Women's Centres referred in this way, there has been confusion about the requirements, services and support available at the centres (Easton and Matthews 2011). Alongside insufficient bail accommodation for women, mental health liaison schemes have been under great strain, which has meant that women have not always been referred to the specialist services which they need. There is particular evidence of an absence of dual diagnosis

[7] It is of course questionable whether such services can be evaluated using only official measures of proven re-offending, but that is another matter.

resources (drug misuse and mental ill-health, for instance), and the whole policy of commissioning (putting services out to tender so that organisations are forced to compete for scarce contracts) means that services are competing against each other rather than co-operating or trying to provide a collaborative and holistic service for affected women (Page 2013; Grace et al 2016).

The introduction of the Offender Rehabilitation Act 2014 (ORA 2014) and what has emerged from the restricting of probation and the privatisation of elements of provision (see Dominey and Gelsthorpe, Chapter three this volume) merits further attention too. The legislation extended statutory post-prison release supervision to short sentence prisoners (those serving less than 12 months in custody). ORA 2014 (implemented 1 February 2015) states (in section 10) that 'in providing supervision or rehabilitation the Secretary of State must comply with the public sector equality duty under the Equality Act 2010 as it relates to female offenders and must also identify anything in the arrangements that is intended to meet the particular needs of this group'. Notwithstanding every suggestion of increased 'care' for women through the increased attention to their needs, from the outset there were concerns that these changes would not bring unalloyed benefits to women. Indeed, Clinks (2014) published study of the experiences of initiatives and centres providing community support to women offenders (*Who Cares? Where next for women offender services?*) within which 89 per cent of initiatives and centres felt that their service was less secure or as insecure as 12 months earlier. Probation Trust funding stopped at the end of January 2015 when the CRCs took over responsibility. *Changing Lives*, the women's centre in Cardiff, for example, was told that its contract would not be renewed, despite having been named as a subcontractor in the original bid submitted by Working Links (a CRC company). Consequently, *Changing Lives* has now closed. Thames Valley CRC withdrew funding for work delivered by Alana House, an award-winning centre in Reading, having worked with probation services to deliver a quality service to women offenders for a number of years. There are similar stories which have affected provision for women offenders in other areas; some contracts have been extended; some have become part of complicated supply chains and funding is uncertain; some centres for women have had to close as a result of the new probation landscape. Women's Break Out, the national network of women's centres and initiatives has now been absorbed by Clinks, following recognition that there was insufficient sponsorship to continue, with government support for the initiative having been cut.

It is difficult to gain a full picture of how different CRCs are addressing the need to give attention to women given protected commercial interests. We certainly know that community service providers have been struggling to engage with some CRCs; we also know that some CRCs have decided to create their own programmes for women rather than investing in existing community provision (London CRC, for example, has created a Structured Supervision Programme for women).

The Justice Committee's follow-up on women offenders (House of Commons Justice Committee 2015: paras 3 and 4) noted:

> We are concerned that funding appears to be a recurring problem for women's centres and that future funding arrangements have not been put on a sound basis as we recommended … we reiterate our recommendation that sustainable funding of specialist women's services should be a priority.

The current climate of austerity and competition for funding has also militated against a coherent national agenda in regard to provision for women offenders, with the Government being slow to produce a long-promised Strategy for Women (Ministry of Justice 2018b). The long-awaited published strategy rather homogenises women; there is little attention to older or younger women's needs, mere mention of Black, Asian and Minority Ethnic women, and no attention to intersectionality. This means that whatever good intentions there are within the strategy will be 'blunt instrument[s]' rather than tailored to suit different groups of women. The limited funding which has accompanied the strategy has also attracted criticism (Hine 2019).

Having outlined something of the complexities, insufficiencies and inconsistencies in developments in regard to community provision for women, we now turn to some of the complexities of 'care' in terms of prison regimes, focusing on one particular element of the regimes: provision for those with 'personality disorder', which serves to show that there is a shadow to special provision for women there too.

IV. Care for Women via Mental Health Provision: The Paradox of 'Personality Disorder'

Women form about 16 per cent of the probation caseload and five per cent of the prison population (Ministry of Justice 2018a). Focusing specifically on women in prison in England and Wales, overall, it is widely argued that the prison population in England and Wales contains a high prevalence of mental health problems, with one particular study suggesting that over 90 per cent of prisoners have one or more psychiatric disorders (Singleton, Meltzer and Gatward 1998). It could be argued, of course, that if they did not have such problems before being imprisoned, they might have problems as a result of the incarceration. This study drew on Office for National Statistics data which has been criticised for using a very broad definition of mental disorder. However, another large-scale prison survey of psychiatric morbidity in the UK found that 14 per cent of women had a psychotic disorder, and 50 per cent had a personality disorder. 63 per cent of sentenced women and 76 per cent of those on remand were found to have a neurotic disorder, a rate three times higher than in the general population, with women prisoners significantly more likely to suffer from mixed anxiety and depressive disorder (O'Brien, Mortimer, Singleton and Meltzer 2009). Bebbington et al (2017), using data from two London prisons, are among recent researchers who claim that prisoners have very high rates of mental disorder. And Jakobowitz (2017) assessed 80 per cent of women and 70 per cent of men to have at least one mental health treatment need. Women prisoners, whilst making up only five per cent of the prison population, are considered to be more likely to experience mental health problems and to have more complex levels of mental health need. How far ordinary problems and anxieties are magnified and intensified by experience of imprisonment it is difficult to say of course, and it may be that women's problems are medicalised (via drugs) in order to contain them, rather than rates of medication being an accurate descriptor of rates of mental ill-health. Certainly, the idea of the pathologisation and medicalisation of women offenders is not new. It ranges from early theoretical accounts of women which suggested that responses to women reflected their psychological deficiencies (Leonard 1982) to more recent accounts which focus on HMP Holloway as exemplification of the continued tendency to medicalise female criminality (Rock 1996; Lacey 2018). Carlen et al's claim, as noted above, that women's prisons 'Discipline, Infantalize, Feminize, Medicalize and Domesticize' (1985: 182) is part of the received wisdom passed on through generations of researchers in criminology.

At the same time, the higher rates of mental health problems amongst women in prison have been explained by a multiplicity of disadvantage and damage, and the Corston Report (2007) mentioned above gives ample illustration of this. 'Women in Prison' (2017), as one of the main service providers in the voluntary sector, similarly outlines clear evidence of early childhood trauma, domestic violence, substance addiction, and chaotic lifestyles experienced amongst women in prison. Add to this the high rates of suicide and attempted suicide and it becomes clear that it is entirely appropriate to think of ways of addressing the underlying problems (including personality disorder) via different kinds of interventions (Trebilcock and Weston 2020). Recent research conducted by the Disabilities Trust and Royal Holloway, University of London (2019) which found that '64% [of] female offenders … reported a history indicative of a brain injury' will undoubtedly support claims that it is right to be concerned about offenders' mental health.

It is worth looking at personality disorder classifications more closely. The term encompasses complex psycho-social disorders, and indeed, there have been and continue to be numerous debates about definitions. Durcan and Saunders, for example, have indicated that it is not uncommon for there to be multiple personality disorders and co-occurrence with specific mental illnesses and substance misuse:

> For some personality disorders, there can be over 100 different possible presentations and therefore some people with the same diagnosis will have very different presentations. Many people will also have more than one diagnosis of personality disorder, and people given the same diagnoses may have very different problems (2015: 2).

Beyond debates about definitions and the ways in which substance abuse can mask diagnoses of both mental disorder and personality disorder, there are other observations to make. Firstly, in the UK, section 1(2) of the Mental Health Act 1983 provides a restrictive legal definition of 'psychopathy' which requires personality disorder to be 'persistent and result in abnormally aggressive or irresponsible conduct'. A clear policy objective that mentally disordered offenders should be diverted from imprisonment to health, social and psychiatric services ensued. However, as Player (2016) has set out, diversion from prison rested not only on offenders' diagnosis, but on the testimony of two psychiatrists that their condition was 'treatable'. A combination of a shortage of hospital places, reluctance on the part of the courts to relinquish control over serious offenders, and some resistance from offenders to being labelled as 'psychopaths' resulted in most offenders being sentenced by the criminal courts, and not diverted to other services.

Secondly, sections 1(2) and 4 of the Mental Health Act 2007, represent a further attempt to ensure appropriate responses to offenders with 'any mental disorder or disability of mind' by replacing the 'treatability test' with 'an appropriate medical treatment test', regardless of their clinical diagnosis. This more inclusive approach thus acknowledged unmet need for mental health services amongst offenders, but a lack of substantial investment in forensic services across the health sector means that the policy of diversion has remained rhetoric rather than reality.

Thirdly, Lord Bradley's 2009 review of services offered to people with mental health issues in the criminal justice system thus accepted the inevitability of personality disordered offenders remaining in custody rather than in the 'care' of health services. Lord Bradley suggested the development of a national strategy, coordinated by the Department of Health, the National Offender Management Service and the NHS, for the management of all levels of personality disorder in custody, through to resettlement in the community. It is out of this context that the Offender Personality Disorder Pathway (OPDP) was born. Building on some pilot work initiated a decade earlier, on Dangerous and Severe Personality Disorder (DSPD), the Pathway project aimed to channel resources normally destined for special hospitals to prisons in order to increase treatment capacity (O'Loughlin 2014). This arguably reflected broader aspirations relating to rehabilitation espoused by the Coalition Government in their Green Paper, *Breaking the Cycle* (Ministry of Justice 2010).

The OPDP for men depends on them representing a high risk of serious harm to the public, specifically through repeat sexual or violent offending that is clinically related to severe personality disorder, but for women, the route is rather different. The offender personality disorder strategy for women was put out for consultation in October 2011 and published in 2012. Respondents to the consultation stressed the need for a strong community element, a holistic approach to women's needs and better transitions between the criminal justice system and health services. The implementation team was thus charged with the task of ensuring appropriate integrated care pathways across the country. The Offender Personality Disorder Pathway for women indicated that women would be included if they met the following criteria: (i) a current offence of violence against the person, criminal damage including arson, sexual (not economically motivated) offences and/or where the victim is a child; (ii) assessed as presenting a high risk of committing another serious offence; (iii) likely to have a severe form of personality disorder; and (iv) a clinically justifiable link between the above.

Given that the prevalence of personality disorder for women in prison was thought to between 50 and 60 per cent at the time, the Department of Health and Ministry of Justice (2012) estimated that this definition would include approximately 1,500–2,000 women – of whom 40 per cent would be in prison and 60 per cent would be under community supervision at any one time. A different definition was justified for women compared to men on the grounds that the same entry criteria for men and women would mean that only a very small number of women would be identified, thus presenting challenges in terms of having sufficient numbers of participants in the right place, at the right time, to participate in interventions. This 'making up the numbers' approach thus led to there being a wide target group, with a focus on risk of re-offending, not just risk of harm to others.

But whether or not this should lead to a focus on 'offender personality' disorders is highly questionable. It may be argued that such a focus individualises and pathologises women for their responses to oppressive circumstances of their lives (see Warner and Wilkins 2003).

The OPDP for women has been designed in the context of other developments regarding the recognised need for gender-responsive provision for women (as described above; see also Annison et al 2015; Gelsthorpe 2018; Moore et al 2018). Although the post-Corston argument has been that women offenders require a multi-agency, women-centred, holistic approach based in the community wherever possible, the gender-responsive mantra has impacted on prison regimes in a number of ways. Few would dispute the need for such an approach, whether this be 'trauma-informed' training for staff, or general offending behaviour programmes. Female offenders who meet these criteria are eligible, of course, but *so too* are those diagnosed with a severe personality disorder who *do not* constitute a risk of serious harm (Player 2017).

What are the consequences of this? Firstly, on the positive side, there is seeming response to the cumulative evidence that women in conflict with the law reveal a high risk of suicide and self-harm, as well as experiences of trauma relating to histories of sexual and violent victimisation, with high levels of social disadvantage (Corston 2007; Hollin and Palmer 2006). We can add to this Jakobowitz et al's (2017) outline of unmet needs amongst prisoners. Thus by adopting an inclusive approach to prisoners classified as having a personality disorder it is thought that women suffering from mental health problems will have access to programmes in prisons (and in the community) and to an independent monitoring and advocacy service. D'Cruz (2015) suggested a slightly lower figure than the Department of Health, but nevertheless claimed that the opening up of the OPDP for women who do not necessarily present a risk to others but who nevertheless have personality disorder difficulties relating to their offending means that up to 1,500 women will be eligible for support, instead of just the 200 or fewer who meet the same criteria for the pathway as do men (the reality, in terms of capacity to provide this level of support to so many women, may be rather different of course). Secondly, the response perhaps marks a move away from the traditional reliance on medication (Noyce 2012), although a Howard League for Penal Reform and Centre for Mental Health (2016) research report indicated that many prisoners continued to regard mental health services in prison as those which revolve around medication, with concomitant concerns about treatment as control rather than treatment as care. Indeed, an earlier study by Mills et al (2011) had indicated that some prisoners feel coerced into taking medication in order to avoid the threat of sanctions and they believed that any parole applications would only be viewed positively if they continued to take prescribed medication.

There are a number of cautions to exercise regarding expansionist 'treatment' on grounds of personality disorder.[8] Firstly, there could be a 'self-fulfilling prophecy' phenomenon whereby negative interactions with providers may promote further distress and dysfunction. Secondly, there are issues of self-identity and confidence to deal with as a result of the classification. Thirdly, the idea of treatment in prison (whether for personality disorder or indeed other perceived needs) runs the risk of there being an expansionist approach to custody, with sentencers sentencing women to imprisonment 'to help them' or 'for their own good'. But imprisonment must be recognised for what it is in terms of control, and there needs to be caution in thinking that rehabilitative ambition or 'care' can be delivered via prisons in unalloyed and unambiguous fashion. One particular danger is that a focus on the mental health of women, via the broad Offender Personality Disorder Pathway, will lead to a de-contextualisation of offending behaviour so that the specific behaviour of women in prison becomes the focus rather than the complex situations which have led to the problematic behaviour. More generally, the prison environment can be traumatic for women with borderline personality disorder due to the hostile, punitive environment (Fossey and Black 2010).

Feminist perspectives add to this negative analysis, given the role of power in the diagnostic and clinical processes (Shaw and Proctor 2005). It is argued that the diagnosis of personality disorder individualises and pathologises women for their responses to oppression because of its fundamental failure to locate and understand distress within its social context. Moreover, personality disorder diagnoses

[8] Whilst women are over-represented in a number of psychiatric diagnoses, they are significantly less likely than men to be classified with an Antisocial Personality Disorder (they are more likely to receive a diagnosis of Borderline Personality Disorder (Fazel and Danesh 2002). Whilst there are some similarities in these conditions, the significance of this relates to ASPD involving few emotions and a lack of empathy or sense of intimacy, and BPD involving extreme emotions and difficulties in regulating emotions, low self-esteem and so on. In the former case, there is impulsive and antagonistic behaviour, in the latter behaviour which is self-punishing and sometimes self-harming (Trebilcock and Weston 2020). Perhaps this distinction does not matter, however, as long as there are interventions.

are situated within dominant Western discourses on identity, a conception of selfhood that values autonomy and goal-directed behaviour, assuming that there is consensus on these values. These characteristics are linked to cultural norms of self-provision through work. Deviation from these norms thus render people vulnerable to personality disorder diagnoses. Thus women who are affected by the sequelae of childhood abuse and disempowerment, women who fail to live up to the culturally determined gender roles because they express anger and aggression, and women who conform too strongly by internalising anger and expressing this through self-harm are all rendered vulnerable to classification of personality disorder. Covington (2012), one of the prime instigators of 'trauma-informed' training for prison service staff in the UK, has long argued that a medical approach to trauma can be alienating and disempowering.

Thus the Offender Personality Disorder Pathway has been tailored to deliver services to a relatively wide population of women prisoners, going well beyond the 'dangerousness' criteria which determine access for men (Player 2017). We should remind ourselves here that very few women are in prison for violent or otherwise 'dangerous' offences; most are in prison for persistent acquisitive crime (Ministry of Justice 2018a). Thus there is a possibility that women are being drawn into programmes for personality disordered women, without fully recognising the power dynamics of diagnosis, and the consequences that derive from the coercive environment of prisons. The label of 'personality disordered' may be unwarranted, unjustified in terms of offence seriousness, and damaging to women's self-esteem and sense of empowerment. Seeming 'care' for women in prison via the Offender Personality Disorder Pathway may be double-edged. (We might add that this is a point which could be made about other circumstances that lead to women being sent to prison for 'care'; for example, for drug treatment or alcohol detoxification).

V. Conclusion

We have reviewed a number of developments in regard to women offenders in the criminal justice system in England and Wales, pointing to some complexities and challenges when it comes to assessing the quality of 'care' provided. We have also looked at some of the actual and inadvertent consequences of policies (for example, the possibility that following improvement in prisons for women, sentencers might have come to see them as ameliorative environments within a failing wider social care network). The consistent theme across the narrative in this chapter is that 'care' may be hidden, inconsistent, insufficient, contradictory, or dual-edged in the treatment of women in the criminal justice system. It is perhaps axiomatic that the state should 'care' for those who are made subject to its interventions, notwithstanding aims to punish and control at the same time. Thus the chapter has focused on both general and specific illustrations of the need to pose searching questions whenever we witness criminal justice policy commitments which seemingly express 'care'. The 'discovery' of the concept of personality disorder and its application to women with a background of trauma and oppression is arguably just the latest example of seeing women as in need of treatment and 'care'. Interestingly, while new approaches to desistance have focused on ways in which offenders can be effectively rehabilitated via positive changes in personal identity or sense of self (Maruna 2001), the intention to 'care' for women offenders via a route of classifying them as 'personality disordered' may have the opposite effect, in making it more difficult to refuse or resist an 'offender identity'. The pathologisation may become part of a woman's identity, with all the deleterious consequences that we might imagine.

References

Annison, J Brayford, J and Deering, J (eds) (2015) *Women and Criminal Justice. From the Corston Report to Transforming Rehabilitation* (Bristol, Policy Press).

Bebbington, P, Jakobowitz, S, McKenzie, N, Killaspy, H, Iveson, R, Duffield, G and Kerr, M (2017) 'Assessing needs for psychiatric treatment in prisoners: 1. Prevalence of disorder' *Social Psychiatry and Psychiatric Epidemiology* 52(2): 221–29.

Birkett, G (2016) '"We have no awareness of what they actually do": Magistrates' knowledge of and confidence in community sentences for women offenders in England and Wales' *Criminology & Criminal Justice* 16(4): 497–512.

Bradley, Lord (2009) *The Bradley Report* (London, Department of Health).

Canton, R and Dominey, J (2018) *Probation*, 2nd edn (London, Routledge).

Carlen, P (1983) *Women's Imprisonment* (London, Routledge and Kegan Paul).

—— (1990) *Alternatives to Women's Imprisonment* (Milton Keynes, Open University Press).

—— (1998) *Sledgehammer: Women's Imprisonment at the Millennium* (London, Macmillan).

—— (2002) *Women and Imprisonment. The Struggle for Justice* (London, Routledge).

Carlen, P, Hicks, J, O'Dwyer, J, Christina, D and Tchaikovsky, C (1985) *Criminal Women* (Oxford, Polity Press).

Clinks (2014) *Who Cares? Where Next for Women Offender Services?* (London, Clinks).

Corston, Baroness (2007) *The Corston Report: A Review of Women with Particular Vulnerabilities in the Criminal Justice System* (London, Home Office).

D'Cruz, L (2015) 'Implementing an offender personality disorder strategy for women' *Prison Service Journal* 218: 47–53.

Deakin, J and Spencer, J (2003) 'Women Behind Bars: Explanations and Implications' *Howard Journal of Criminal Justice* 42: 123–36.

Department of Health and Ministry of Justice (2012) *Offender personality disorder (PD) strategy for women. Summary of strategy and implementation plan* (London, Department of Health and Ministry of Justice).

Disabilities Trust and Royal Holloway, University of London (2019) *Making the Link: Female Offending and Brain Injury*, available online at: www.thedtgroup.org/media/163444/making-the-link-female-offending-and-brain-injury.pdf (accessed 12 August, 2019).

Durcan, G and Saunders, A (2015) *Personality Disorder and Complex Needs: Bradley Commission Briefing 3* (London, Centre for Mental Health), available online at: www.centreformentalhealth.org.uk/sites/default/files/2018-09/bradpersonality.pdf (accessed 27 June 2019).

Easton, H and Matthews, R (2011) *Evaluation of the Inspire Women's Project* (London, London South Bank University).

Easton, S, Silvestri, M, Evans, K, Matthews, R and Walklate, S (2010) *Conditional Cautions: Evaluation of the Women Specific Conditional Pilot* Ministry of Justice Research Series 14/10 (London, Ministry of Justice).

Farrington, D and Morris, A (1983) 'Sex, sentencing and reconviction' *British Journal of Criminology* 23(3): 229–48.

Fazel, S and Danesh, J (2002) 'Serious mental disorder in 23,000 prisoners: A systematic review of 62 surveys' *The Lancet* 359(9306): 545–50.

Fossey, M and Black, G (2010) *Under the Radar. Women with Borderline Personality Disorder in Prison*, available online at: www.ohrn.nhs.uk/resource/policy/UndertheRadar.pdf (accessed 7 July 2019).

Garland, D (2001) *The Culture of Control. Crime and Social Order in Contemporary Society* (Oxford, Oxford University Press).

Gelsthorpe, L (2005) 'Back to Basics in Crime Control: Weaving in Women' in M Matravers (ed), *Managing Modernity. Politics and the Culture of Control* (London, Routledge).

—— (2018) 'Women, Crime and Criminal Justice: Tales of Two Cities' in E Milne, K Brennan, N South and J Turton (eds), *Women and the Criminal Justice System. Failing Victims and offenders?* (London, Palgrave Macmillan).

Gelsthorpe, L and Loucks, N (1997) 'Magistrates explanations of sentencing decisions' in C Hedderman and L Gelthorpe (eds), *Understanding the Sentencing of Women*, Home Office Research Study 170 (London, Home Office).

Gelsthorpe, L and Morris, A (eds) (1990) *Feminist Perspectives in Criminology* (Milton Keynes, Open University Press).

—— (2002) 'Women's Imprisonment in England and Wales: A Penal Paradox' *Criminal Justice* 2(3): 277–301.

Gelsthorpe, L and Russell, J (2018) 'Women and Penal Reform: Two Steps Forwards, Three Steps Backwards? *Political Qaurterly* 89(2): 227–36.

Gelsthorpe, L, Sharpe, G and Roberts, J (2007) *Provision for Women Offenders in the Community* (London, Fawcett Commission).

Grace, S, Page, G, Lloyd, C, Templeton, L, Kougali, Z, McKeganey, N, Liebling, A, Roberts, P and Russell, C (2016) 'Establishing a 'Corstonian' continuous care package for drug using female prisoners: linking Drug Recovery Wings and Women's Community Services' *Criminology & Criminal Justice* 16(5) 602–21.

Hahn-Rafter, N and Heidensohn, F (eds) (1996) *International Feminist Perspectives. Engendering a Discipline* (Buckingham, Open University Press).

Hannah-Moffat, K (2001) *Punishment in disguise: Penal governance and federal imprisonment of women in Canada* (Toronto, University of Toronto Press).

Hedderman, C, Gunby, C and Shelton, N (2011) 'What women want: the importance of qualitative approaches in evaluating work with women offenders' *Criminology & Criminal Justice* 11(1): 3–19.

Hedderman, C, Palmer, E and Hollin, C, with the assistance of Gunby, C (2008) *Implementing Services for Women Offenders and Those 'At Risk' of Offending: Action Research with Together Women*, Ministry of Justice Research Series 12/08 (London, Ministry of Justice).

Hine, J (2019) 'Women and Criminal Justice: Where are we Now?' *The British Journal of Community Justice* 15(1): 5–18.

Hollin, C and Palmer, E (2006) 'Criminogenic need and women offenders: A critique of the literature' *Legal and Criminological Psychology* 11: 179–95.

House of Commons Justice Committee (2015) *Thirteenth Report. Women Offenders. Follow-Up. Government's Response to the Committee's Thirteenth Report of Session 2014–15* (London, House of Commons).

Howard League for Penal Reform and Centre for Mental Health (2016) *Preventing Prison Suicide: Perspectives from the Inside* (London, Howard League for Penal Reform and Centre for Mental Health).

Jakobowitz, S, Bebbington, P, McKenzie, N, Iveson, R, Duffied, G, Kerr, M and Killaspy, H (2017) 'Assessing needs for psychiatric treatment in prisoners: 2. Met and unmet need' *Social psychiatry and Psychiatric Epidemiology* 52(2): 231–40.

Jolliffe, D, Hedderman, C, Palmer, C and Hollin, C (2011) *Reoffending Analysis of women offenders referred to Together Women (TW) and the scope to divert them from custody*, Ministry of Justice Research Series 11/11 (London, Ministry of Justice).

Lacey, N (2018) 'Women, crime and character in the 20th century' *Journal of the British Academy* 6: 131–67.

Maruna, S (2001) *Making Good. How Ex-Convicts Reform and Rebuild Their Lives* (Washington DC, American Psychological Association).

McCoy, E, Jones, L and McVeigh, J (2013) *Evaluation of the Liverpool Women's Turnaround Project* (Centre for Public Health, John Moore's University, Liverpool).

Mills, A, Lathlean, K, Bressington, D, Forrester, A, Va Veenhuyzen, W and Gray, R (2011) 'Prisoners' experiences of anti-psychotic medication: Influences on adherence' *Journal of Forensic Psychiatry and Psychology* 22(1): 110–25.

Ministry of Justice (2010) *Breaking the Cycle: Effective Punishment, Rehabilitation and Sentencing of Offenders* (London: The Stationery Office).

Ministry of Justice (2018a) *Statistics on Women and the Criminal Justice System 2017. A Ministry of Justice Publication under Section 95 of the Criminal Justice Act 1991.* (London, Ministry of Justice), available online at: assets.publishing.service.gov.uk/government/uploads/system/uploads/attachment_data/file/759770/women-criminal-justice-system-2017.pdf (accessed: 1 June 2019).

Ministry of Justice (2018b) *Female Offender Strategy for women in the criminal justice system* (London, Ministry of Justice).

Moore, L, Scraton, P and Wahidin, A (eds) (2018) *Women's Imprisonment and the case for abolition. Critical reflections on Corston ten years on* (London, Routledge).

National Offender Management Service (2012) *A Distinct Approach: A Guide for Working with Women Offenders* (London, NOMS).

Noyce, G (2012) 'The Mental Health Act: Dual diagnosis, public protection and legal dilemmas in practice' in A Pycroft and S Clift (eds), *Risk and Rehabilitation: Management and treatment of substance misuse and mental health problems in the criminal justice system* (Bristol, Policy Press).

O'Brien, M, Mortimer, L, Singleton, N and Meltzer, H (2009) 'Psychiatric morbidity among women prisoners in England and Wales' *International Review of Psychiatry* 15(1/2): 153–57.

O'Loughlin, A (2014) 'The offender personality disorder pathway: Expansion in the face of failure' *Howard journal of Criminal Justice* 53(2) 173–92.

Page, G (2013) *Risks, Needs and Emotional Rewards: Complexity and Crisis in the Drugs Intervention Programme* (Unpublished PhD, University of Cambridge).

Prison Reform Trust (2000) *Justice for Women: The Need for Reform*, a report on the findings and recommendations of the independent Committee on Women's Imprisonment, chaired by Professor Dorothy Wedderburn.

Player, E (2014) 'Women in the criminal justice system: the triumph of inertia' *Criminology & Criminal Justice* 14(3): 276–97.

—— (2017) 'The offender personality disorder pathway and its implications for women prisoners in England and Wales' *Punishment & Society* 19(5) 568–89.

Radcliffe, P and Hunter, G (2016) '"It was a safe place for me to be": Accounts of attending Women's community Service and moving beyond the offender identity' *British Journal of Criminology* 5: 836–56.

Rock, P (1996) *Reconstructing a Women's Prison. The Holloway Development Project, 1968–88* (Oxford, Clarendon Press).

Scottish Government (2002) A Better Way: The Report of the Ministerial Group on Women's Offending (Scottish Executive), available online at: www.webarchive.org.uk/wayback/archive/20170107102049/http://www.gov.scot/Publications/2002/02/10714/File-1 (accessed 7 July 2019).

Shaw, C and Proctor, G (2005) 'Women at the Margins: A Critique of the Diagnosis of Borderline Personality Disorder' *Feminism and Psychology* 15(4): 483–90.

Singleton, N, Meltzer, H and Gatward, R (1998) *Psychiatric Morbidity Among Prisoners in England and Wales* (London, Office for National Statistics).

Smart (1976) *Women, Crime and Criminology: A feminist critique* (London, Routledge and Kegan Paul).

Social Exclusion Unit (2002) *Reducing Reoffending by Ex-Prisoners* (London, Office of the Deputy Prime Minister).

Social Work Services and Prisons Inspectorate (1998) *Women Offenders: A Safer Way: a review of community disposals and the use of custody for women offenders in Scotland* (Scottish Executive).
Trebilcock, J and Weston, S (2020) *Mental Health and Offending. Care, Coercion and Control* (Abingdon, Routledge).
Walmsley (2017) *World Female Imprisonment List*, 4th edn (London, Institute for Criminal Policy Research).
Warner, S and Wilkins, T (2003) 'Diagnosing Distress and Reproducing Disorder: Women, Child Sexual Abuse and 'Borderline Personality Disorder' in P Reavey and S Warner (eds), *New Feminist Stories of Childhood Sexual Abuse* (London, Routledge).
Women in Prison (2017) *Corston+10. The Corston Report Ten Years On* (London, WIP).
Worrall, A (1990) *Offending Women* (London, Routledge).
Zedner, L (1991) *Women, Crime and Custody in Victorian England* (Oxford, Oxford University Press).

5

'All Children are Our Children': Care and Kinship in Residential Children's Homes in the Russian Federation

ELENA KHLINOVSKAYA ROCKHILL

I. Introduction

When I started my research into children's homes and social orphans, or children who have living relatives but grow up in residential care institutions in the Russian Federation, 'care' was implicitly weaved into the fabric of the child welfare and child care institutional network. Residential care facilities such as baby homes, children's homes, boarding schools/homes, children's shelters and rehabilitation centres, performed child care duties in the most basic sense: feeding, clothing, keeping children warm, clean, healthy under the constant gaze of carers, nannies, and pedagogues, as well as an army of cooks, cleaners, drivers, doctors, social pedagogues, psychologists, administrators, with all expenses paid by the state. There are very few biological orphans there; most children are social orphans. Part of that network were also children's departments of local police, guardianship departments, centres for temporary isolation for under-age delinquents, committees for minors, maternity homes and children's hospitals. These facilities deal with children from 'problem' families and vagrant children; again, they are seen as social orphans. Four ministries oversee the work of this network: Ministry of Health (baby homes and children's hospitals), Ministry of Education (children's homes and boarding schools), Ministry of Labour and Social Protection (children's homes for disabled children), and Ministry of Internal Affairs (vagrant and delinquent children). All these institutions are connected to form a heterogenous whole, charged with looking after children's best interests.

Hence the first thing that draws one's attention is how vast and encompassing the child welfare network is. A few numbers will demonstrate the scale of the system. Since statistics are not synchronised either between various state departments in the official statistics, or in estimates by independent organisations, we shall treat them as rough estimates only. In general, the residential care network is constituted by approximately 1,500 facilities (depending on the source, anywhere from 1,400[1] to 1,655[2] to 1,850[3]), with their numbers constantly fluctuating. Thus, according to Gosstat, the Federal Statistics Bureau, in 2009 this number was 1,957 institutions, with 136,599 children (and 577,400 children in 'family substitutes');[4] and the overall number of children aged 0-18 in the Russian Federation was 26,055,000. In 2015, these numbers were 1,399 and 84,600 children (695,023 in family substitutes),[5] respectively; and the overall number of children stood at 27,374,000. Included here are residential homes for children with developmental delays and for disabled children. These Homes are grouped into eight types, depending on the nature of the disability (ie deafness, speech, cerebral palsy, blindness, etc), each with their own facilities. The above numbers do not include other institutions, such as rehabilitation centres, shelters (some 615 of them, apparently), centres for temporary isolation of juvenile delinquents, and disabled children with families but who live and study in residential care.

Looking at the financial side of the family/institutional distribution of children, residential care is expensive. Currently the annual cost of keeping a child in a baby home is 802,000[6] Roubles (R), while child benefits paid to mothers are considerably less: for a working woman calculated at 40 per cent of her average monthly salary for the past two years.[7] In the attempt to stimulate the falling birthrate, in 2007 the government introduced a one-time payment of 'maternal capital' paid for the birth of a second child (453,026 R in 2017), with strict stipulations as to how it could be spent.[8] In the 2010s, financial support of substitute families and a consistent push towards choosing family and not institutions for such children resulted in a reduction of the number of children in institutions and in the number of institutions themselves. These are very positive changes towards a change of paradigm.

[1] tsput.ru/res/other/Bschool/Forms/forms2.htm.

[2] neodin.takiedela.ru/wiki/text_popup1.html.

[3] statref.ru/ref_polujgmeryfs.html.

[4] www.gks.ru/doc_2009/deti09_rus.pdf, p 108.

[5] www.gks.ru/free_doc/doc_2015/year/efegod-15.pdf, p 191.

[6] ac.gov.ru/files/publication/a/9403.pdf. In Sterling, around £10,000.

[7] Currently, monthly child benefits constitute 40% of a woman's salary for the last two years. So if we take a 50,000 R average monthly salary, she will be paid 240,000 R a year (additionally there may be regional payment scheme, which would depend on the local budget). But many women get a fraction of this salary: on average in the Russian Federation some 11% of the working-age population gets less than 10,000 R a month (www.newsru.com/finance/07dec2017/ruwagesrated.html). For unemployed women monthly payments are still less, and calculated on the basis of the minimum wage at that time.

[8] These stipulations were as follows: the 'maternal capital' was payable when a second child reached the age of 3, and could be spent only on education of children, improvement of home conditions, and payment towards a mother's pension, and (more recently) rehabilitation of children with disabilities. For the duration of the programme (2007-) some 8.5 million families have received this form of state (public) support and 5 million of them spent it improving their home conditions: https://www.gazeta.ru/business/2017/11/28/11014820.shtml?updated.

But these efforts are an uphill battle. While in the 2010s families with children enjoy much greater financial support than in the 2000s – when I conducted the bulk of my study – monthly parental benefits are still less than the cost of keeping a child in a baby home. Considering that the main reason for a mother to request an institutional placement is a 'difficult material situation' due to unemployment, single motherhood, or an absence of accommodation, paying a mother less than the cost of keeping her child in a baby home is rather telling. But as was the case 18 years ago when I started my study, the subject of social orphans and their relationships to the state is not about money. It is about the consequences of a certain configuration of public and private, made visible in the workings of the child welfare network – Actor-Network-Theory-style (Latour 2007; Law and Hassard 1999; Mol 2010). This becomes clear if we consider the simultaneous and symbiotic working of current and historical family- and child-related policies, conceptual apparatus, legal framework and binding documentation, moral values, infrastructures, and the adults, administrators, pedagogues, nurses, etc, engaged in the decision-making and working in this system. The child welfare network was engendered by the Soviet political economy and is still constituting an 'ordering' mode (Law 1992, 1994) for the making of the contemporary post-Soviet social world, where Soviet, post-Soviet and hybrid social forms intertwine. The system proved to be extremely persistent in the face of social, economic and political changes, and resistant to restructuring. It is an expression of care as a virtuous act that the state extends to all children in need.

Social orphans growing up in institutions, a group of children that is at the same time privileged, disadvantaged and marginalised, is the result of care relationships. What sort of relationship is that? Among multiple definitions of care there some that are directly applicable to the case of social orphans. Certainly, care for children without parents points at human need and the responsibility for meeting it (Thelen 2015). Care can be seen as social relations that sustain life in both mundane and dire moments (Robbins 2013), which would include 'the work of looking after the physical, psychological, emotional and developmental needs of other persons, and it has the dual sense of work activities ("to care for somebody") and feeling states ("to care about somebody")' (Martin 2013). A wider interpretation of care is situated in the context of the anthropology of kinship, understood as a mode of social belonging, 'since kinship, like other forms of social belonging, must be actively chosen, made or maintained, care practices are needed to contribute to the making and maintaining kinship' (Drotbohm and Alber 2015: 2).

In this view, care is understood as a social practice that connects not only kinsmen, friends, neighbours and communities, but also collectivities such as states and nations (ibid). This is building on previous work on kinship that uncoupled kinship and biological relatedness, such as Anderson (1983) who saw the welfare state as an abstract entity that offered to all citizens horizontal membership based on imagined connections of kinship; Schneider (1980, 1984) who maintained that domains other than blood and marriage, such as nationality and religion, can produce the same relationship of diffused enduring solidarity; Carsten (2004) who explained kinship as a particular set of affinities, obligations and emotional connections which are created by care; and Borneman (1997) who viewed kinship as 'relations of affinity based on care alone' (ibid 40).

I would like to take John Borneman's conceptualisation of care forward to show how in post-socialist Russia social orphans are a product of an asymmetrical power relationship between the state, family, and child; relationships that could be described as 'virtual kinship' and 'kinship based on care', two sides of the same coin, one more symbolic and another more practical. We shall see how the intersection of kinship and care in virtual space and in the physical space of an institution produce a certain kind of family where the state, both in its embodied and abstract forms, and social orphans are tied up by an implicit contract of mutual obligation and responsibility for each other, and where a child's biological family is demonised and cut off. I wish to show that although caring seems to be seen in an unquestionably positive light as the 'morally superior act' (being among the three 'ordinary virtues' of dignity, care and life of the mind) (Todorov 1995 cited in Borneman, Chapter twelve this volume), and one of humanity's most fundamental moral foundations, caring – as a moral emotion prompting actions like aiding, supporting or comforting (Haidt 2003, Singer 1981, cited in Canton and Dominey, Chapter two this volume) – can in fact have a dark side, as lived realities do not always live up to lofty aspirations on which the system has been built.

So first let's look at the perceived source of the problem: that biological family of social orphans, called the *neblagopoluchnaya* ('unfit', 'problem', 'crisis' family), for there are no social orphans without the *neblagopoluchnaya* family.

II. The *Neblagopoluchnaya* Family: Inadequate Child Care and What it Says about the Family

In August of 2015 in a small community in Krasnodar region, a young child died. He was a three-month-old boy, Rodion, who was still breastfed, and who was taken away from his parents by employees of the local administration and police and placed in a local children's hospital. The boy died six days later. The cause of death was head injuries, although upon admittance he was found to be in good health. Here we go again, I thought. Another typical case, where the state, the family and the child become locked in a deadly embrace; this encounter results either in the symbolic death of a parent, or in the death or injury of a child.

Rodion's parents were known to the authorities because they were registered as a low-income family (*maloimuschiye*) and because both were former residential care wards. Rodion's father lost his job and was in search of another. That day his mother went to collect their older child, a three-year-old girl, from a kindergarten, leaving Rodion in the care of an unrelated adult – either a neighbour or the girl's godmother. At this time, the Guardianship Department came for a home visit, found that their flat was dirty, messy and there was no food in the fridge; they owed 30,000 R in monthly fees for the apartment. So both children were forcefully removed from home and placed in the children's hospital some miles away. The mother was not allowed to visit and breastfeed Rodion. There was no custody order or any other documents left with the parents. Soon after, some undetermined state employees were walking around the community asking whether these children were neglected or abused. Neighbours said that the family was a good family; they did not drink or use drugs. Some considered their flat messy, yes, but the parents were not dangerous to their children. They were former residential care wards; they were unemployed, and socially unprotected (*sotsial'no-nezaschischenniye*). Dispensing with euphemisms, they were poor and vulnerable.

In the eyes of the authorities, Rodion's parents belonged to a particular type of the family called the *Neblagopoluchnaya Family* (NF, literally: family without any goodness), the culprit of all cases of social orphanhood. The use of this term constitutes a puzzle, as this category is ubiquitous and elusive at the same time. The NF has no legal definition in the Russian legal system, yet state agents use it and act on it in official settings, such as in a court of justice. In popular imagination the NF is very real and it assumes a place next to homeless people, criminals or ex-convicts. They all live on the margins.

So what is the NF, exactly? In Russia normal childhood is seen as familial, ie, embedded in the family (as it is elsewhere in Europe) (Qvortrup 1990), as children are viewed as dependent, vulnerable, and in need of protection from harm. They belong in a family but it has to be a 'good' family that provides 'good' care to their children. As Mol has maintained, 'care is involved in complex negotiations over competing notions of the "good", always seeking to craft "more bearable ways of living in – or with – reality"' (cited in Buch 2015: 280).

The NF epitomises the opposite of 'good'; it is a category of social differentiation, an umbrella term for a range of family situations where numerous risk factors are believed to impact negatively on the development and well-being of the child. This is of course very vague. Looking for a definition, I found that the NF is a sociological concept, a descriptive one at that (Yakovleva and Velichko 2009: 3). One can find a truly dizzying disarray of descriptions, typologies, and (excessive) labelling. Elsewhere I gave a list of such typologies given by various authors, where the NF is a family with low social status that cannot cope with family responsibilities successfully; where a child experiences discomfort, stress, neglect or violence; where families are defined by the lack of love, care, do not satisfy the child's needs and do not protect their child's interests and rights; a family that is distrusting, careless, and sly(!); conflict in the family and pedagogical incompetence; an unhealthy moral atmosphere and unhealthy emotional atmosphere; an amoral single parent and lacking material goods (ie poor); and even a family that is structurally defective (Sidorova and Khlinovskaya Rockhill 2016: 39–40). Based on these classifications, Yakovleva and Velichko summarise the main characteristics of unfavourable conditions in a family that in their opinion are attributive of an NF: poverty, pedagogical incompetence, single-parent household, and incorrect moral and legal orientation. Together the classifications add up to what in contemporary parenting studies might be called deficient parental behaviour, which must be subject to correction (Lee et al 2014). I shall come back to this. In practice, parents can have their children taken away because there is not enough food in a fridge, or having a messy flat; or not having an indoor toilet or having a wood stove for heating; or losing a job and not having income; or for a child not to have been vaccinated; not enough toys; or because children may have been under supervision of an adult but not a parent, as was the case with Rodion. One case was about a female 'care leaver' who was given a run-down flat by the state, who went on to have a child, and that child was taken away because she had a run-down flat.[9] Most of such cases of removing children were unlawful, according to then the Children's Ombudsmen Pavel Astakhov, and yet they are ubiquitous.

So the category exists as a social fact, even without a legal definition, and most people know what it is. As soon as the NF is uttered, imagination paints a picture of decay, eliciting strongest condemnation ('these people should be shot for treating children this way'). In the realms of good and evil they are definitely evil. The NFs without children are inconsequential – just incorrigible human refuse. But if there are children, the concept of NF becomes a powerful tool that justifies state intervention, which often leads to separation of children from their parents to avoid harm and for providing good child care elsewhere. This is because at this stage, children are seen as a product of their environment: if they grow up in a *neblagopoluchnaya* family, they will become the same – for like reproduces like, it is believed.

III. How the State Decides the Family is 'Unfit': The Importance of Home Conditions

Let me start with a case study of Maria, a story showing how a child ends up in residential care institutions. Maria was a 25-year-old woman with three children: a son (six) who lived with her mother and step-father, a daughter (two) who lived with her and her informal partner Peter, and a son (one) who was in state care since birth. We met at the court hearing for termination of her parental right for the oldest and the youngest of her children. At the time of the birth of her third child neither Maria nor her cohabitant Peter, the father of Maria's two youngest children, had permanent jobs with a steady income. So she was advised by the maternity home doctors to leave the baby in state care for a year, and Maria, who did not have enough money to buy things necessary for the newborn, agreed. To have their child returned to her she had to adhere to two sets of requirements. The first was spelled out in the beginning: she was expected to come to the baby

[9] www.mk.ru/social/2015/08/30/pochemu-organy-opeki-zachastuyu-zabirayut-detey-izblagopoluchnykh-nonebogatykh-semey.html and juvenaljustice.ru/statji-yuvenalnaya-yusticiya/50-organy-opeki-zabrat-rebenka-iz-semji.html.

home, visit her child, bring gifts and take him for walks. That was clear, although casually stated in the beginning. But the second set of requirements was revealed to her only after the placement and they had to do with providing appropriate home conditions (*nadlezhaschiye sotsial'no-bytoviye usloviya*) that would, from the vantage point of the state, ensure the proper development of her child. 'Proper' is a key concept because it presupposes a set of norms upon which value judgement will rest. This is where many women get trapped.

Here we can deduce what is considered a good family. To be considered suitable, parents must ensure they have a well-furnished, warm and well-lit, clean and orderly dwelling with a separate room or at least a designated area for the child and with enough food and clothing. Parents must demonstrate evidence of being good parents through the creation of artefacts and atmosphere, producing simultaneously, on different levels, the required signifiers: material sufficiency signals income; cleanliness and orderliness mean that the parents understand the importance of these virtues for the whole family; and a separate space allocated to the child means that the child was expected and desired. The 'performance of love' as I call it, is scrutinised as evidence of their determination to raise the child, and these signifiers, ticked and recorded during brief home inspections, may be sufficient to release the child back to the family. Any departure from this line is interpreted as a punishable moral insufficiency and the proof that the family is indeed an NF. Here, then, moral qualities are expressed through the outward form of material sufficiency, which is assumed to ensure the psychological and emotional well-being of a child. The 'performance of love' serves as a resource to the state: to prove the lack of the appropriate parental behaviour and/or appropriate home conditions would automatically point to a parent's inadequacy.

Suspecting parents to be an NF is to move them into the liminal zone where a family is under close scrutiny and where the fate of the child and his family will be decided upon. Proven evil, the multiple connections between the parent and the child will be severed and the state becomes the sole parent. Redeeming themselves as good, parent(s) would be moved back into the moral community of good parents, albeit with a black mark, while the children will be left with them.

But here comes a twist. It may seem that once parents have complied with all the guardianship authorities' and institutional administration regulations, they should get their children back. Yet in the 2000s, only six per cent of children were returned to their biological parents. I have seen some cases when none of the compliance efforts would have helped! Children were not returned to their mothers even if the mothers had more or less decent accommodation – (Guardianship Department's verdict: accommodation not good enough, not clean enough); even if they had a job (Guardianship Department's verdict: not enough monthly income); or even if they applied time and again to get their children out. Why is that? Morality enters the stage.

At first, women who voluntarily place their children in residential care appear not to be condemned, but this is misleading, for it turns out only immoral mothers would let their children out of their hands. By agreeing to the separation in the first place, they fail the main test for mothers: the presence of 'maternal instinct', seen as an inherent trait and not a learned skill. The essentialised gender differences see a woman as having an immutable nature that necessarily incorporates an innate maternal instinct, the basis of mother love and care. If it were present, maternal instinct should guide a mother through any difficulties to ensure the child will stay with her. But if it is absent, then the child is in danger. A seemingly innocent offer of an institutional placement, then, is not *just* state assistance but also a precaution with a covert test written into it. Once the initial act of a child transfer happened, regardless whether it is the doctors that suggested it, or whether she did it out of love, it is very difficult to get out of it; she now had to demonstrate through her action of compliance (with the authorities and their demands) that her maternal instinct was there. The other trials to which she was subjected were a further 'testing', which mothers consistently fail through their inability (apathy or passivity) to overcome their problems, such as getting employed or fixing up theirs house. This was seen as further proof of the absence of her maternal instinct. Hence in this interplay between the ideas of failure of essence and failure of action, it would take a conspicuous action to correct suspicion about a mother's essence, while failure of action may readily indicate failure of essence. A child would be better off without such mother because, as state agents say, she is not going to give him anything.

Personal disintegration and inadequacy are expressed in the absence of work and income, alcoholism, multiple sexual partners, messiness, and dirtiness, and all this is evidence of the bad seed that was first suspected and has now revealed itself in all its ugly glory, or so the thinking goes.

To win, she must fight and have enough resources. I have seen children being returned to their parents or grandmothers but in most cases these were mature women with some forms of capital, and in the position to 'perform love' correctly. But this is not the catchment population of the child welfare network. Implicitly, being young, inexperienced, unmarried, unemployed, and a poorly educated mother, or a single father, with no accommodation and problems with a housing registration, contributes to the state agents' suspicion that a parent lacks the vital resources to ensure the well-being of the child. A suspicion of alcohol or other substance abuse only speeds up the process, as this allows the state to pull together readily available and observable elements without further proof of parental inadequacy, helping to move them into the liminal, grey area of NF, invariably seen in a morally negative light and as a threat to their children.

This is worrying as we are now moving into the realm of socio-economic circumstances that are outside these people's control, with poverty being one of them. Marginality (being an NF), poverty, and immorality are becoming fused together and children should not be raised in such families. Undoubtedly, this is why the government has introduced in 2018 a monthly payment of just over 10,000 R to low-income families having their firstborn; this measure is thought to alleviate poverty.

Although poverty and 'morality' are mutually constitutive to produce an NF, 'morality' may assume a leading role. The two latest examples are the case of a single mother, Irina, who brought up her own three children and adopted two boys. The local authorities took away her adopted boys because she has undergone a breast reduction surgery; she also had a blog related to transgender issues. She was suspected to be planning to undergo transgender surgery herself and that was the reason for removal of the children: being anything but heterosexual is morally wrong even if the parents are not poor. Children should not grow up in such a family; therefore an LGBTQ family is *a priori* an NF. Irina filed a law suit in the regional court against a district court's decision and won.[10] The second case involved a professional mother of seven children. All children were removed because her four-year-old son had hair reaching below his shoulder blades. The local Guardianship department decided this would affect the children's gender stereotypes negatively (Tarasov 2017).[11]

Hence we established that the *neblagopoluchnaya* family is considered to be the main supplier of social orphans. Whether a family deemed *neblagopoluchnaya* is a real threat to their children or they are cast as such for other reasons, ie settling scores using 'morality' or 'poverty' cards as culturally-accepted ways of solving real or imagined problems with the family, is a moot point. There is no tangible practical support for the family and, consequently, no real understanding of what is taking place there. Spaces of care are still dichotomic. Children are either left in their families (private setting) and viewed as being at a disadvantage, or placed in institutional care (public setting). These two settings rarely cross each other in Russia as elsewhere in Eastern Europe. For example Read (2007) analysed ideologies of (nursing) care in the Czech Republic, showing the distinction made between forms of care associated with the state (which were rational, modern and applied equally to all regardless of context) and those associated with more personal relationships and networks, such as kin, friends, or neighbours. Care for elders was strongly divided between residential care within state institutions and care in the home performed by kin. Health care provided by the state, she maintains, was spatially and morally distinct from care offered by family and friends, creating a problem for the chronically ill and elderly, for whom the state provided few services that enabled them to remain at home or within their communities. The options were either to face permanent residence within state health institutions or to rely almost exclusively on the care and support of their families (ibid: 206). The two care settings, private and public, rarely cross each other in this context.

What does it mean for the decision-making regarding children from NFs? I already referred to contemporary parenting studies that view deficient parental

[10] www.newsru.com/russia/06dec2017/courtsunebrg.html.
[11] www.novayagazeta.ru/articles/2017/12/20/74982-bogsud-i-sleza-rebenka.

behaviour as necessitating correction (Lee et al 2014). What practices of correction do we find in the Russian child welfare field? They are disciplinary: since targeted individualised assistance to the NF family is not uniformly set up country-wide, guardianship departments identify areas of parental deficiency and order parents to fix their problems or their children will be taken away. How the family is supposed to deal with their problems is up to them and there is ample evidence that many problems cannot be fixed in a timely manner. Since nobody knows what is really going on in these families, local guardianship departments' agents apply their own intuitive criteria as to whether a child's life and health are in danger. In most cases these agents play on the safe side: remove the children and make them the state's responsibility.

So once moved into this category, parents are at an increased risk of losing their children. It is not only about the *quality* of care that is a derivative of the *moral standing* of the parents. It is about a belief that child care by immoral parents is in itself woefully inadequate, and if the parents are unable to mend their ways very quickly, children must be moved to a better environment with correct upbringing to ensure a proper development for the child. This is where the chain of residential care institutions comes in. Some children enter into this chain at birth or as toddlers and leave only when they finish their secondary or vocational schooling. They never experience family life. They enter into a kin relationship with the state which from then on will be their (uneasy) parent, while their biological families are cut off, left to fend for themselves. I call this the symbolic death of a parent.

IV. A Society of Virtual Kin

The Soviet state created and maintained extensive and comprehensive frameworks for healthcare, education, housing and employment for all its citizens – all state-owned and state-run. With regard to children, a chain of crêches, day-care centres, schools, after school activities and pioneer camps created an institutional network where caring for a child was done by both the family and the state. The engagement between the state and the family was variously described as a partnership (Alt and Alt 1959; Madison 1968) whereby the state took the role of a super-parent, with the parental rights delegated to the parents (Alt and Alt 1959); an alliance between the state and mother (Issoupova 2000) at the expense of the father (Kukhterin 2000); and a cooperation between the family and the state (Heitlinger 1979). Verdery saw the state as an extended family 'composed of individual nuclear families, but these were bound into a larger familial organisation of patriarchal authority with the "father" Party at its head' (Verdery 1996: 64). The construction of the state as an extended family facilitated the development of what I call 'virtual kinship' where, by assuming financial, social and educational responsibility for the well-being of each family member, and especially children, the state had actually become a part of the family, beyond the symbolic figure of the Father, into a practical fusion with the family, constructing a relationship of co-parenthood in relation to children. This familialisation of the state and etatisation of the family gave rise to the issues of childhood belonging, responsibility and accountability: Did children belong to the family or to the state; Whose responsibility was it to bring them up?; Who is accountable for mistakes in upbringing?

I wish to write about a practical extension of this 'virtual kinship' we can call 'kinship based on care' that would explain how children get into residential care institutions in the first place. Why is it so easy and quick for the family to place their children in residential care, and for the state to remove children and raise them as its 'own'? Why does the separation between parents and their children seem so unproblematic? As one of my informants from a guardianship department told me, 'The place for children is in the family. But only a good family. If I am to prioritise, then first comes a good family, then an institution, and then the *neblagopoluchnaya* family'. How did this happen, that an institution is seen as a good family substitute? And what does it really mean for the child and his parents? I argue that 'kinship based on care' is an ideological construct written into a well-developed over-structure and complete with its own history, conceptual apparatus, legal frame and infrastructure, where the state, family, child, particular typology of parents, co-parenting, kinship and care are all intimately entwined. This Actor-Network-Theory-style over-structure, both symbolic and practical, ensures that the production and reproduction of social orphanhood is a continuous process. It plays an enabling role in allowing children to grow up in a kind of 'family' vastly different from what home-raised children know. To put it simply, the state and social orphans are intimately connected because the state raises these children, invests in them, provides for them, and children are expected to reciprocate later in life. How different is it from a normal parent-child relationship?

In the post-Soviet period much of the social welfare system has been dismantled – secure employment, guaranteed income, accommodation, affordable day-care facilities, free medical care – these and other elements that allowed parents to share parental responsibility with the state were lost. So was lost an explicit ideological connection between the state and its citizens that made up the relationship of 'virtual kinship' of the previous era. But the 'kinship based on care' relationship survived, written into the chain and network of child welfare and residential care institutions, which not only continued but whose role seems to have been strengthened. Which is only logical: once family became more incapacitated by the social and economic ordeals, the flow of children to institutions only increased. As many carers in the baby home I studied complained in 2000, 'In the Soviet times we did not have so many perfectly good healthy children. But now mothers reject their children and they end up here. Mothers have lost their maternal instinct'. My study has shown that it is not only mothers that leave their children in state care, whether temporarily or permanently, but it is very often the state that tries to take control of the children if their mothers did not measure up to the vague standards of child care. Said my informant (in 2000) from a guardianship department: 'In our difficult times it is a normal thing to do to place a child in a baby home temporarily and go on fixing their problems and take children back home'. What is omitted in this comment is how extremely difficult it is to get the child back. They become children of the state (*gosudarstvenniye deti, detdomovtsy*).

V. The State as a Parent

We shall now scale down into the physical space of the residential care institutions. Discourses on care are often built on dichotomies such as public and private, good and bad, and often a juxtaposition of the expectations of 'warm' care in a private sphere and 'cold' impersonal care in institutions (Thelen 2015), if we talk about ideologies of care (Read 2007). But residential care institutions (as are other institutions in socialist and post-socialist contexts) are the hybrid between public and private as these institutions not only serve as homes for children, they are in themselves an expression of the care the state takes of its children. An extension of kinship to embrace the state institutions makes it logical that as a better parent, institutions will provide good care. An ideal to strive for was that paid care work would not obviate parental care for the children.

Child care and child welfare organisations are spaces where the notions of 'caring about' and 'caring for' have the same dual meaning as in English, where 'care' connotes both affective concern and practical action. In the Russian language *zabota o detyakh, ukhod za det'mi* mean exactly that, although the latter is implied in the former. In most cases however, it leans towards the practical side: *zashchita interesov* (protection of interests), *sotsial'noye obespecheniye* (social benefits and economic provisions), and *podderzhka detei-sirot* (support for orphaned children) are all tropes of caring for children.

Child care in a baby home is in its most basic form. Children from birth to the age of three or four are fed, clothed, nursed, cleaned, and kept warm and healthy. Pre-school children's homes (for those 3–7 years old) are essentially residential kindergartens, where in addition to receiving basic care children are subjects of pedagogical work of correct character formation (*vospitaniye*) by teachers and carers. In boarding homes/schools they receive formal schooling but are still wards of large residential homes with their own army of carers, cleaners, cooks, drivers and administration. Each of these stages is patterned after typical health and educational institutions for 'home children', such as crêches, day-care centres, and schools, except at the end of the day home children go home to their relatives, while social orphans remain in an institution with multiple and ever-transient unrelated adults.

Moving from their failed family to a 'good' institution is supposed to solve numerous problems for the child: to give him or her a fresh start away from the 'corrupting' influence of their parents, to provide a suitable environment for the child's proper development, and 'to surround children with true love and care' – so the institutional staff are called upon to love these children as if they were their own. It is an extension of the oft-repeated sentiment regarding all children of the Soviet Union and now the Russian Federation: 'All children are our children'. This is taken as a sign indicative of a caring society which is not indifferent to children's needs. Consider the case of sisters Anna and Nastya. They lived in a small regional community. Their mother became disabled and her disability benefit was not sufficient to support the family. In bold, a single disabled mother had not enough money to support her children. The girls, then aged nine and seven, were placed in an *internat* (boarding school). Their mother died a few years later. Particularly Anna was bitter about the authorities' decision to remove them from their mother instead of supporting the family, financially or in any other way. The girls have fond memories of their *internat* years with good teachers and *vospitateli* (upbringers), and many interesting activities. Nastya especially believes that the state gave her more opportunities than her mother would have been able to provide. Anna agreed reluctantly with Nastya but thought that it was wrong to abandon her mother. She feels guilty and responsible for her mother's death. At the time of my study she was a single mother to a two-year-old, working and living in a modest room in a dormitory. She was trying to get another of her sisters, Ira, out of a children's home but the authorities had a better idea: they found a well-to-do middle-aged adoptive family and planned to give the third sister away for adoption. Anna concluded with some pain that yes, perhaps she would not be able to provide for her sister as well as that adoptive family but it was still wrong, having destroyed her natal family, now to take her sister away. Many of her attempts to secure the return of her sister were blocked by the authorities. Anna was not even informed that the authorities had prepared documents for the adoption. When I discussed Anna's case with one of them, she replied:

> Yes, according to the law it is necessary to notify her and ask her permission, but we shall do without her consent. All we need to do is to collect enough convincing documents that will make a strong case proving she is not suitable to raise this girl.

And that is exactly what happened. Thus, although Anna made many attempts to reunite with Ira, she lost the battle and Ira was adopted by a local couple. Quite clearly, children's needs were seen as separate from those of their family: providing for the girls at a state institution and leaving their mother to deal with her problems alone seemed to be a suitable solution to the problem.

VI. How the 'Bad Seed' Belief Kills the Environmental View on Child Development (Or Genetic vs Environmental Determinism)

'Problem' mothers and their children come from all walks of life. Maria placed her child in a baby home temporarily because she experienced what was seen as a 'difficult material situation'. Anna and Nastya's mother experienced difficulties of a different kind: she became disabled and could not provide adequately for her girls on her own. Rodion was simply taken away because his family was seen as *neblagopoluchnaya*. Irina's adopted boys were taken away because she did not conform to the dominant framework of the neo-traditionalist Russian Orthodox moral code for sexuality. If Rodion had lived and Irina had given up on her two boys, they could have ended up in state care like hundreds before them.

But these nuances of family situations are lost on the institutional staff. For them, the family that left their children in state care (for this is a common view) cannot possibly be a good family; otherwise children would not end up there. And children from the *neblagopoluchnaya* family carry their family's 'bad seed'; it is in their genes. Consider this case: I worked in a baby home for a few weeks and was going through children's files when I noticed that a one-year-old boy, who was removed from his parental custody by guardianship authorities when he was two months old, had a medical diagnosis of 'delayed mental and speech development'. I asked one carer who was especially adamant that the state is taking really good care of the children by 'giving them everything' as to why the child was delayed in his development. She was taken aback for a moment, and then she said, 'But look what families they are coming from. Their parents are prostitutes and thieves!' I heard these words many times. Although some children residing in that baby home came from families that experienced 'difficult life situations' and some mothers were trying their best to get them out, invariably they were seen as women who had lost their maternal instinct, and who were 'prostitutes', and fathers who were 'thieves' and 'from prison'. This stands in stark contrast to the initial intention of the state agents to remove the polluting influence of the unfit parents from an 'innocent' child. So the process of 're-kinning' (Howell 2006) had partially failed – biological ties were severed and yet simultaneously reconstructed within the institution as a stigma, a polluted identity.

VII. The State as an Uneasy Parent: A Mixed Bag

A new relationship forged with the state as a parent is also problematic. If we look at the content of this relationship, it is indeed based on 'care'. When a child is taken into state custody, all the expenses related to residential living are now coming from the state purse, which includes not only feeding, clothing and educating children but also paying for maintaining the extensive residential care network and other auxiliary institutions (ie children's department of the police or children's shelters) and the salary of its staff. 'The state has given you everything', so goes the sentiment regarding what the state has done for the children: full parental responsibility for caring and providing for the children until they become of age (18), or until they graduate from an educational institution approximately in their late teens or early twenties, and the state gives these children preferential treatment as far as access to vocational and higher education institutions is concerned. After that, the state terminates its parental responsibility, and here we see the disruption of care written into the system from the beginning: unlike the parent-child relationship, the state supports children, not adults. Local authorities are also obliged to provide care-leavers with accommodation, although there are numerous accounts of local administration cheating: teenagers are either not given any, as there is always a shortage of flats, or they are offered inferior rooms in dormitories but if taken, the chances of getting their own flat is close to zero. But what is now expected is reciprocity – the flow of care is expected to be both ways. Young people are considered to be self-sufficient and must start contributing back to society, however unprepared for the life outside institutions they may be. That includes following the 'normal' life course for a person, having a job and income, getting a family, living an independent life. Anna and others I met (Andrei and Mila, see below) managed to do so, although still under attack from the authorities, but if young people fail, resorting to thievery and getting imprisoned, that is seen as them being ungrateful and unappreciative, pointing to their polluted origins.

This is about 'caring for'. What about 'caring about'? In the official discourse carers were supposed to treat and love children as their own. In real life, chance and personalities play a very significant role in the life of many children in care and former residents. Within institutions, the grouping of children and teachers is accidental. Whether or not a child will encounter a particularly cruel or caring caregiver is unforeseeable. Institutional cultures – that is, the set of rules and practices, the composition of the staff, the personality of an administrator and the location – are peculiar to a given institution and determine the quality of a child's experiences. Receiving help when they need it upon leaving an institution, as well as finding a job, are also a matter of chance: some receive timely and crucial assistance, while others do not. For those young people who did not get much out of their institutional life, there are very few organisations of post-*internat* adaptation, or post-prison rehabilitation, which is also pertinent to many of the former inmates. None were in the town where I did my study.

When the (abstract) state terminates its legal obligation towards these children, and the child-parent relationship may come to an end, it will depend on individual former carers whether or not to continue helping a former resident. Indeed, I have some examples of teachers forming warm supporting relationships with their selected wards and who continued supporting them beyond institutions. Andrei and Mila are a young couple who grew up in the same *internat*. Once they left their boarding home/school, one of their former teachers helped them in finding jobs, fighting off the guardianship authorities when they wanted to take away the couple's child (care leavers are always under closer scrutiny), and to fight for accommodation that the city authorities were supposed to give to the couple but were in no hurry to do. So, some people like this teacher felt responsible for a child's home and children. The feeling of ownership and a caring attitude is acquired through love of their work and children, many years of experience working in an institution, and identification with it both personally and professionally.

Such a person was Kim Moskovskiy, the director of a children's home, who invested himself completely into his 'home', developing a sense of belonging and professional identity, and caring for these children as his own. Being an orphan himself, and never having had his own family, this children's home was his home and family. He hosted a former resident, a young indigenous man, in his one-room flat because he did not have anywhere else to go except to Kim, his 'father'. According to Kim's memoirs and letters from former students, many treated their children's home as their home, their childhood friends as brothers, and Kim as father. Kim himself participated vigorously in keeping in close contact with his former students. Indeed, his Children's Home was his home and his students were his children.

Three of my informants, Misha, his sister Lyuba and their friend Igor whom they call their 'brother', remember good and bad carers, calling a kind one 'mother', while the bad were called the derogative 'gorilla'. But even having a beloved carer and calling her 'mother' does not ensure that feelings are mutual. Kim Moskovskiy gives an example of such a disjunction. There was a student of a particular teacher, whom she liked and called her favourite. In the 1970s, this teacher got into a conflict with the boy because he was disobedient, and repeatedly hit him on the head. Later they made up and she gave him a motherly kiss, which the boy was only too happy to receive: 'my mother kissed me!' Many years later he came back to the community where he grew up in the children's home. By that time he was married to a girl from the same home and they were expecting their second child. He wanted to meet his 'mother' to show her that his life had turned out well, that he made decent money and had a good family. They invited the teacher to visit them. They prepared a meal and were constantly looking outside the window in anticipation of her visit. When they saw her walking down the street they told their child: 'Look! Your granny is coming!' They listened to her footsteps, waiting for the doorbell to ring. But the steps went further up the stairs. After an hour of waiting, his wife started to take everything back to the kitchen. A few minutes later she told him, 'Come and look, there she is going back, your "mother"'. He saw his former teacher and 'mother', going back after visiting a new *vospitatel* ('upbringer') who had moved into a flat upstairs. While conveying this story to Kim 10 years later, the young man was bitter and perplexed: 'I was her favourite … I wanted so much to talk, to see her, to make her be proud of me'.

There were also numerous examples of carers/teachers for whom this work was only a job and a source of income, and this most often comes through as the staff's indifference. A director of one baby home told me:

> We depend on these children and we need children in institutions. We receive our salaries here, and if caring for children with some deviations in their health, we get paid more. All children are diagnosed with 'delayed mental development'. Nobody removes this diagnosis because for carers it is a source of higher salary.

I asked one doctor why the teachers do not use more developmental activities. She replied: 'Who cares? Everyone's basic concern is their salary, and it does not depend on the quality of their work. Why should they bother if it means more work for them?' The director of another baby home told me that financing the work of an institution depends on the number of children. If that number drops, so does financial support and it is very difficult to increase it in the next financial year.

Not everything is cynicism though. An expectation of treating children as their own has unexpectedly revealed itself in reprimands. Thus, in an official letter, the Vice-Head of a Department for Education admonished particular *vospitateli* for 'not treating children with genuine motherly love and care; when children from the remedial *internat* were placed in a hospital, no-one visited them for a year, nobody sent them letters or gifts'. This was found to be unacceptable. But I wonder how different it is from a mother who is reprimanded for not bringing gifts and not visiting her child in residential care. For her this will be a black mark against her name and a reason why the authorities may retain her child. What happens when a state child is not visited in a hospital for a year? The same offence but different consequences?

Despite all the care lavished on them by the state, Misha, Luyba and Igor walked away with a firm belief that 'nobody cares'. They saw it all. By the time the young men were 25, they had gone through the chain of institutions, army, and prison (for theft). The theft happened in the difficult 1990s, when Misha who worked for a private employer was not paid for a few months, and with no family or relatives to fall back onto, robbed a flat and was caught. They had families and their own children but were unemployed with no income. I saw them coming to the Guardianship Department looking for their personal files that had either been lost or misplaced. A strong healthy young man, Misha, was asking for money. One of the employees nervously dipped her hand in her purse and, handing over five roubles, said:

> For how long are you going to ask for favours? You have to be self-sufficient by now, the state has provided everything for you, it is time that you give back to the state, not the other way around. You are so ungrateful. All you know how to do is ask for more.

The shamed young man was standing in the middle of the room, slightly bent forward, and speaking with a childish weak voice, just like a guilty child in front of his scolding mother, the only difference being that she was not his mother. He was caught in a vicious circle but no-one there was interested. He tried to explain that the reason why he did not have any money was that he could not find a job because he did not have housing registration (*propiska*). He did not have registration because he did not have a flat. To get a flat he had to show the evidence that he had the status of an orphan, and he could not do this because his file had been lost. She waved her hand and said: 'Ah, you people always come up with some excuses'. The appointment ended and he left, but the problem was not solved. Two years later I found Misha and Lyuba living in somebody's flat:

> We gave up trying to find our documents. We were going between the Guardianship Department, our *internat* and the vocational school, and nobody knows where they

> are. They told us, 'go and find these documents yourself'. At 25 they are no longer responsible for you. Nobody cares [*nikomu eto ne nuzhno*].

At the same time I heard the same employees discussing what help they give to their own grown up children, whether it was buying an expensive fur coat, contributing towards buying a flat for their children or providing child care as a grandmother. Care leavers do not have family to turn to. They turn to the only embodied state-parent they know, those state employees, many of whom were responsible for placing them in residential care in the first place. And they were expressly taught to do so. In the words of Misha:

> If in the *internat* we were taught some skills, to take care of ourselves, to work, make money, to shop. I wish they explained more about what life is like outside of an *internat*. They did not give us any idea of what to expect, what one is going to experience and confront in life, what are the relationships, and how to solve problems. Over there we had a communist upbringing, all people are brothers, put rose-tinted glasses on our eyes, but when you leave the *internat*, these pink glasses are difficult to take off, they are more likely to be broken off, and life is seen very differently. In a family, a father tells his son, you better take this job, because you'd be better off financially, and you will step over this or that person and will make enough money for yourself. What have we been taught? Go and *ask* this or that person for help, do not step on anyone's head, you must be polite, as if we were not people but Jesus Christ. Not only were they doing everything for us in the *internat* but the Guardianship Department helped us to get prepared for the army. We didn't have to worry about a thing, just go to a store and choose what we needed. The state tamed, domesticated us, the state made us its own, and we cannot live without it anymore. It should be responsible for us.

But as we see, many of these 'parents' turn their former wards away. Care leavers are often not welcome to visit their former 'homes' either.

Who else is left? Their 'mates'. So it is here, at the boarding homes/schools, that they acquire their future 'family' as some of their mates not only will be their friends in the *internats* but also beyond. These friends, whom some of my informants called 'my brother' or 'my sister', will form a support group where children are connected by their common past and experiences. They understand each other much better than the outside world understands them. But their mates are in the same disadvantaged position as themselves. Hence many young men turned to theft and other criminal activities while the girls sometimes sell their bodies in exchange for favours (room and board), and their children are at an increased risk of being taken away. The circle has closed.

VIII. Conclusion

In post-Soviet society children without parental care are an outcome of the engagement between the state-constructed category of *neblagopoluchnaya* family and the state-run child welfare network. They are called social orphans and they grow up in the chain of residential care institutions under parental care of the state. The number of these institutions and the number of children in them fluctuates depending on changes to federal family policy, changes to moral codes (ie from Soviet to neo-traditional Russian Orthodox), availability of financial support to individual families, or local initiatives.

There are no social orphans without the *neblagopoluchnaya* family, which in turn is the interface between the two domains: economic and social. They are poor (in a new post-Soviet way) and they are unsuitable (normative value); this category is a moral judgement as well as an economic description. In the new post-Soviet environment, normative values do not take into account economic realities: expectations of motherhood are similar to Soviet times, but the economics do not allow women to fulfil these expectations. Children from such families are placed in the chain of residential care institutions and very quickly become the children of the state. In this re-arrangement of kinship, children are de-kinned (parental rights of their parents are terminated) to make them susceptible to re-kinning, and this is the point at which the state comes in. Institutions are set up in a way that requires a constant supply of artificial orphans, and children are re-kinned to the abstract state. The residential care institutions are not simply last-resort possibilities for child placements. On the contrary, they are intertwined with the social fabric of the community, being an integral part of the child welfare network, a logical continuation of the state's parental responsibility beyond the family, an extended arm of the state. An institutional placement, then, is comparable to moving a child from one family member (family) to another (an institution), where a child would receive better care. Whether accepted (Liarskaya 2004) or resisted (Bloch 2003), used enthusiastically, reluctantly, or out of resignation, residential care institutions became a part of the infrastructure through which the state's parental care was operationalised. Although the explicit socialist ideology is gone, the infrastructure, practices and even judgements within the child welfare network remain.

When the state takes over the role of a supposedly good parent, a new type of kinship is set up – 'kinship based on care' – constructing relations of obligation in which a child must 'repay' the state for this provision. This care by the state is matched by the child's sense of obligation, reciprocity and loyalty. Children are expected to be grateful, and the feeling of obligation towards the state runs deep in the consciences of many former residents. Pavel, a 22-year-old resident of the *internat* for the disabled, was very aware of his responsibility towards the state:

> I am striving towards a good life. I have a plot of land I can farm. I want to live, to have a family, and to be useful for the state, because I can no longer hang around the state's neck.

But this quite idealistic arrangement has certain consequences. One is an intergenerational break between parents and children. The relationship between social orphans, and the state as a parent, is profoundly ambiguous; more so for the children who have never known their parents and family. De-kinning of the child removes the sense of loyalty and responsibility to their families in the same way as an 'unfit' family is relieved of the responsibility to care for their children. As such, in the individual-family-state (society) chain, the middle unit, the family, is eliminated, connecting a child directly to the state. The concept of the 'state as a parent' renders most issues concerning kin and family relations ambiguous: family, parents, relatives, home and belonging. However, the biggest problem seems to be not with the issue of 'home' (some children consider their last *internat* their home, or can make one for themselves), and not even with 'family' (they manage to substitute it with their 'brotherhood', partners or their own children), but with a 'parent' and a relationship with a parent, constituting an intergenerational break. Thus re-kinning to the state ensures social reproduction over time but not across generations.

Another issue is understanding what the state as a parent looks like. There are actually two 'states' that carry out parental responsibility: an abstract state that uses the public purse to pay for children's needs while they are brought up in institutions, and an embodied state, that is, those adults who work in the system of child welfare. From the social orphans' point of view, both are problematic and the feelings of reciprocity, responsibility and obligations towards an imagined state are very abstract. As far as the embodied state is concerned, depending on the age of the child, different adults have different responsibilities towards him or her, being temporary, transient and job-related in character. They do not focus on an individual child or two but many children at once. Similarly, the responsibility for the child-parent relationship on the part of a social orphan also cannot focus on one or even a few people. An image of the state as a parent is now a de-personified and disembodied collage of all the faces of adults who have ever participated in the child's upbringing over the years. As children grow, they have passing relationships with nannies, teachers, staff and administrators from at least three institutions, the summer camp and the staff members of the Guardianship Department. The nature of contact in the relationships varies from close personal to distant, eliciting a range of feelings, from attachment and love to ambiguity, confusion and hate. There is no certainty in who is considered to be a 'parent'. Children love some carers and can't stand others. Relationships between children are formed and dissolved over the long years. People come and go: carers, nannies, cleaners, teachers, and a different combination of children in each age group. Institutions themselves change as children are moved from one building to another, each of which is supposed to be their 'home'. The transience and multiplicity of relationships entails multiple losses and gains, leaving children unsure of what type of relationship they can expect and have with each new carer and where to find support when they need it. Complex human relations and attachments do form, but these are subject to chance and may or may not be long term. These people stand for the more abstract entity of the state as a family, to which the child is ultimately indebted.

No less problematic is the expected feeling of obligation towards the abstract state for everything it has provided for the child. Since these provisions were paid for using taxpayers' money, does a child 'owe' all citizens? If, as Igor indicated, parents provide for small children, and children take care of their old parents, how would this work in the case of the abstract state? Should they begin working and thus contributing to the state and society, despite jobs not being guaranteed in post-Soviet times? Or should they do what society wants them to do without failing, whether serving in the army, going to war, taking a job in which they are not interested or being thankful for a room in a dormitory that the embodied state decided to give them instead of the separate flat they are entitled to, because otherwise they will be called ungrateful? Do they 'owe' concrete carers, including abusive staff? What do they owe to those who provided them with room and board but took away their disabled mother, as in case with Anna?

Finally, the aspiration of the state agents to give future social orphans a fresh start by placing them in institutions does not remove their spoilt identity. When the state intervenes and breaks the ties between the 'unfit' parent and a child, this connection is transformed from being a kinship tie into a stigma. Here we see the reworking of the 'bad' origin: with one stroke it is broken, but with another it is being simultaneously reconstructed. The deployment of the 'bad seed' biological model is a fall-back defensive position: when things go wrong, it enables staff to claim that it is not their failure, but the individual's.

Hence in this child welfare and residential care domain the concept of care serves as a basis of kinship relations between the state and the child. But it is also a way of separating 'good' from 'bad' (parenting and persons), a cleansing tool to create and maintain moral boundaries. Care is applied only to those in the moral universe. The 'bad' are cut off and abandoned. So does care always have a positive and moral connotation? Could care be indifferent and still count as care? Could care be a threat to one's well-being?

References

Alt, H and Alt, E (1959) *Russia's Children: A First Report on Child Welfare in the Soviet Union* (New York, Bookman Associates).

Borneman, J (1997) 'Caring and Being Cared for: Displacing Marriage, Kinship, Gender and Sexuality' *International Social Science Journal* 49: 154.

Buch, E (2015) 'Anthropology of Aging and Care' *The Annual Review of Anthropology* 44: 277–93.

Carsten, J (2004) *After Kinship* (Cambridge, Cambridge University Press).

Drotbohm, H and Alber, E (2015) *Anthropological Perspectives on Care: Work, Kinship and the Life-course* (New York, Palgrave Macmillan).

Heitlinger, A (1979) *Women and State Socialism: Sex Inequality in the Soviet Union and Chechoslovakia* (London, Macmillan).

Howell, S (2006) *The Kinning of Foreigners: Transnational Adoption in a Global Perspective* (New York, Berghahn Books).

Issoupova, O (2000) 'From Duty to Pleasure? Motherhood in Soviet and Post-Soviet Russia' in S Ashwin (ed), *Gender, State and Society in Soviet and Post-Soviet Russia* (London, Routledge).

Kukhterin, S (2000) 'Fathers and Patriarchs in Communist and Post-Communist Russia' in S Ashwin (ed), *Gender, State and Society in Soviet and Post-Soviet Russia* (London, Routledge).
Latour, B (2007) *Reassembling the Social: an Introduction to Actor-Network Theory* (Oxford, Oxford University Press).
Law, J (1992) 'Notes on the Theory of the Actor-Network: Ordering, Strategy and Heterogeneity' *Systems Practice* 5: 379–93.
—— (1994) *Organising Modernity* (Oxford, Blackwell).
Law, J and Hassard J (eds) (1999) *Actor Network Theory and After* (Oxford, Blackwell).
Lee, E, Bristow, J, Faircloth, C and Macvarish, J (eds) (2014) *Parenting Culture Studies* (Basingstoke, Palgrave Macmillan).
Madison, B (1968) *Social Welfare in the Soviet Union* (Stanford CA, Stanford University Press).
Martin, J (2013) Review of: 'Rethinking Care: Anthropological Perspectives on Life Courses, Kin Work and Their Trans-Local Entanglements' International Research Centre 'Work and the life cycle in global history', Humboldt-Universitat zu Berlin, 6-8 December 2012. H-*Soz*-u-*Kult*, April.
Mol, A (2010) 'Actor-Network Theory: Sensitive Terms and Enduring Tensions' *Kolner Zeitschrift fur Soziologie und Sozialpsychologie. Sonderfeld* 50(1): 253–69.
Mol, A, Moser, I and Pols, J (eds) (2010) *Care in Practice: On Tinkering in Clinics, Homes and Farms* (Bielfield, Netherlands, Transcript).
Qvortrup, J (1990) 'Childhood as a Social Phenomenon: an Introduction to a Series of National Reports', *Eurosocial Report 36/1990* (Vienna, European Centre).
Read, R (2007) 'Labour and Love: Competing Constructions of 'Care' in a Czech Nursing Home' *Critique of Anthropology*, 27(2): 203–22.
Robbins, J (2013) 'Beyond the Suffering Subject: Towards an Anthropology of the Good' *Journal of the Royal Anthropological Institute* 19: 447–62.
Schneider, D (1980) *American Kinship: a Cultural Account*, 2nd edn (Chicago IL, University of Chicago Press).
—— (1984) *A Critique of the Study of Kinship* (Ann Arbor MI, University of Michigan Press).
Sidorova, L and Khlinovskaya Rockhill, E (2016) 'Family on the Edge. *Neblagopoluchnaia* Family and the State in Yakutsk and Magadan, Russian Federation' *Sibirica* 15(3): 31–63.
Thelen, T (2015) 'Care as Social Organization: Creating, Maintaining and Dissolving Significant Relations' *Anthropological Theory*, 15(4): 497–515.
Verdery, K (1996) *What Was Socialism, and What Comes Next*? (Princeton NJ, Princeton University Press).
Yakovleva, N and Velichko, O (2009) 'Pravoviye Problemy Zaschity Prav Detei, Nakhodyaschikhsya v Usloviyakh Semeinogo Neblagopoluchiya' ['Legal Problems in Defending the Right of Children Found in Unfavourable Home Conditions'] in O Pristanskaya, N Yakovleva, O Velichko and P Razumovskaya (eds), *Pravoviye i Kriminologicheskiye Problemy Zaschity Prav Nesovershennoletnikh* [*'Legal and Criminological Problems in Defending the Rights of Minors'*] (Moscow, Academy of Prosecutor-General of the Russian Federation) 3-14.

6

Re-imagining Cities as Spaces of Care – A Perspective from Street Homelessness

HELEN CARR, ED KIRTON-DARLING AND MARIA FERNANDA SALCEDO REPOLÊS

I. Introduction

Since the 1980s, and on a global scale, cities have played a critical role in the political/economic imaginary, and, most critically, by those in power, have been simultaneously constructed as spaces for economic development and as spaces of insecurity. Our starting point is to examine the consequences of this for homeless people by comparing and contrasting the experiences of the homeless in London and Canterbury in the United Kingdom, and Belo Horizonte in Brazil. These street sleepers have been required to position themselves as entrepreneurs, selling for instance the Big Issue, or organising car parking for restaurants, and at the same time are made subject to sanitary and security regimes which seek to remove them from the streets. What we note here is a shift from welfare politics, which sought to deliver a particular, paternalistic and non-inclusive programme of care for the vulnerable, to a neoliberal and urban politics, which requires the reformation of the subject via entrepreneurialism. However, recent political events have arguably destabilised urban entrepreneurialism, and it is this destabilisation which provides the main argument of our chapter. Whilst many commentators fear the consequences of a politics of retrenchment and despair, this chapter takes the suggestion of Rose (2017) that it is important to explore the progressive possibilities provided by the language of liberty, security and control that have fuelled populist rejections of neoliberalism, seriously. For Rose the language and the events reveal something particular:

> We are not so much 'insecure' as 'vulnerable'– our daily lives are vulnerable, our values are vulnerable, our people are vulnerable, our nation is vulnerable – we live in a state of pervasive vulnerability (Rose 2017: 317).

In the face of such politically potent engagements with vulnerability and drawing on Harvey's observation that 'cities are important power bases from which to work' (Harvey 1989: 16), the chapter makes the suggestion that cities can and should be re-imagined as spaces of care and argues that there is disruptive and progressive political potential in doing so.

The chapter begins by considering the urban space of our project and the emergence of urban entrepreneurialism and urban insecurity. We examine the consequences for homeless people and the charities and the NGOs which support them, noting in particular the work of law in constituting and regulating marginal populations. It then turns to reflections on the future, on politics and imaginaries, and a juxtaposition of the place of vulnerability in the work of Rose, Butler and Lorey. What we draw from this juxtaposition is that there is a need, not addressed by these theorists, for an engagement with care in a radical reframing of social protection. This necessary reframing, which we suggest can be seen as protection without exclusion, seeks to ensure its distinctiveness from the patriarchal and excluding practices inherent in much of twentieth-century welfare politics, and would provide more than the arguably chimerical solidarities emerging from an acknowledgment of shared precariousness.

Drawing these theoretical threads together, we move to re-imagine the city as a space of care. Taking inspiration from other re-imaginings of the city, we suggest that in the margins of the neoliberal city, simultaneously, forms of resistance have built real possibilities for cities to be spaces of transformation. We then consider what a city conceived of as a space of care might look like, working from the perspective of the street homeless and drawing on a case study of the Tree House in Belo Horizonte. Such a re-imagination also requires a re-imagination of law. The chapter concludes by considering resistance to such a project, and the extent to which the re-imagination the chapter proposes can be more than a provocation and instead become a practical and progressive project of political disruption.

II. The City in Contemporary Politics

Politics, as many scholars have noted (see Harvey 2005), has for several decades been dominated by a disruptive combination of free-market ideology and coercive state practices designed to extend the market and manage consequent social insecurities. We use the term 'neoliberalism' to describe this politics, although the term is contested (see Venugopal 2015) and carries with it notions of universal coherence that are not necessarily convincing. As Brenner and Theodore point out, this form of politics is better understood as a set of messy practices which should be seen as an

> historically specific, ongoing, and internally contradictory process of market-driven sociospatial transformation, rather than as a fully actualized policy regime, ideological form, or regulatory framework (Brenner and Theodore 2002: 353).

Nonetheless, certain generalisations can be made about the characteristics of neoliberal politics. As Gough points out, 'Neoliberal strategy is centrally concerned with depoliticising economy and society by weakening or removing historically accumulated forms of socialisation' (Gough 2002: 410). In the UK, for instance, welfare entitlements have been eroded and replaced with increasingly conditional benefits set at minimal levels. Council (local state) housing, which used to house a significant percentage of the population, has been residualised via the Right to Buy and other privatisation measures. Private renting has been deregulated and housing benefit, a state subsidy particularly for those in low-paid work faced with increasingly unaffordable housing costs, has been capped. The trajectory in post-dictatorship Brazil, despite the different context of a peripheral capitalism where notions of the welfare state were only loosely applied, is not dissimilar. It was not until the Worker's Party administration that a housing policy appeared, but its purpose, as described by then leader Lula, was not welfare housing per se, but to unite the acquisition of housing for low-income families with the economic interests of banks and economic elites and projects of job creation. This was done through the guarantee of interest rates, the financing of infrastructure with subsidised mortgage credits, the provision of public lots, the regularisation of land, and subsidies for private construction consortiums which operated publicly-funded contracts to build residential units. This apparently dream formula revealed itself as way of sustaining the neoliberal policies of privatisation of social rights and gentrification of the largest Brazilian cities, in the wake of the global financial crisis.

It is clear that the city plays a particular role in this form of politics. Brenner and Theodore note that cities

> have become increasingly important geographical targets and institutional laboratories for a variety of neoliberal policy experiments, from place-marketing, enterprise and empowerment zones, local tax abatements, urban development corporations, public–private partnerships, and new forms of local boosterism to workfare policies, property-redevelopment schemes, business-incubator projects, new strategies of social control, policing, and surveillance, and a host of other institutional modifications within the local and regional state apparatus (Brenner and Theodore 2002: 368).

It is possible to debate whether these cities are real in any meaningful sense, or whether they are utopian creations of neoliberal imagination. Whatever our conclusion, this way of thinking about cities has material effects. As far back as 1989, Harvey noted the characteristics of urban entrepreneurialism, which

> [t]ypically rests, then, on a public-private partnership focussing on investment and economic development with the speculative construction of place rather than amelioration of conditions within a particular territory as its immediate (though by no means exclusive) political and economic goal (Harvey 1989: 8).

Harvey here refers to a distinct spatial shift, from the nation state, to the city as locus of political and economic life. This shift, we would argue, is critical to the de-socialisation and re-commodification of the social, broadly conceived

(Macleod 2002). For Sassen the new and distinct significance of cities emerges from a complex duality, 'a spatially dispersed, yet globally integrated organization of economic activity' (Sassen 2001: 3). So, as global forces diminish the power of the nation state, they simultaneously strengthen cities because, as Sassen makes clear, key structures of the world economy are necessarily situated in cities (Sassen 2001: 3). Globalisation is spatial and urban.

There are two particular consequences which Sassen identifies which are of significance to this paper, the proliferation of high and low wage jobs, and the elimination of middle earning jobs. She notes for instance, that

> a vast supply of low-wage jobs [is] required by high-income gentrification in both residential and commercial settings. The increase in the numbers of expensive restaurants, luxury housing, luxury hotels, gourmet shops, boutiques, French hand laundries and special cleaners that ornament the new urban landscape illustrates the trend (Sassen 2001: 9).

So cities become significant generators of wealth and simultaneously generators of socio-economic inequalities.[1] The inequalities are made manifest not only in low wages but in insecurity. In order to inhabit these neoliberal cities, citizens become imagined as entrepreneurial and mobile. For some highly skilled citizens, cultured and cosmopolitan success is assured. Others scrape together fragile portfolios of work, forced to rely on short-term, insecure contracts, and increasingly bearing the costs of their employment. And more than this happens: in order for the city to thrive it increasingly excludes and disciplines – through architectural design, institutional practices and laws – certain marginalised groups. As Macleod puts it, 'the new urban glamour zones conceal a brutalizing demarcation of winners and losers, included and excluded' (Macleod 2002: 605). This is an important dimension of the imagined city, it is not to be 'compromised by the visible presence of those very marginalized groups' (Macleod 2002: 602), otherwise it might lose the sophisticated, cosmopolitan elite on which its success depends. So there are two consequences of urban entrepreneurialism that are relevant to this chapter: homelessness increases because of increasing socio-economic inequalities, and homeless populations are increasingly disciplined and excluded.

The implication is that another city exists alongside, and entwined with the entrepreneurial city, the product of a more dystopian, but equally potent urban imagination; the insecure city. As Monroe, an urban anthropologist, points out, albeit in the context of the extreme example of Beirut,

> [t]heories of security and insecurity have helped us understand the ways in which contemporary human life is besieged by a whole host of challenges and fears from imminent ecological or financial disaster to the avoidance of toxins and crime that make the management of risk and insecurity a central feature of our lives (Monroe 2016: 3).

[1] www.urbancentre.utoronto.ca/pdfs/curp/tnrn/Three-Cities-Within-Toronto-2010-Final.pdf.

From London to São Paulo and Belo Horizonte, from cities in the epicentre of capitalism or in the periphery, shared fears of terrorism and the violence that emanates from gang warfare compete with health risks from polluted air, an overburdened health service and a never-ending crisis of unaffordability. Anxieties appear irresolvable. House prices and the cost of renting are extortionate, but a collapse in house prices would impoverish everyone.[2]

The homeless are caught up in this atmosphere of insecurity. A longstanding source of official concern, they embody these heightened anxieties; their figures are visual and tactile representations of many of these fears – fears which are then further bolstered by the arguments used by authorities to justify disciplinary measures. The move by these authorities was prefigured by the social danger associated with pauperism (Procacci 1991); that their state risks contaminating us all. They (or their belongings or their animals) may cause disease, may hamper commercial activity, may provoke crime or bring down house prices.

III. Practices of Discipline and Exclusion in the Neoliberal City

Actual existing practices of discipline and exclusion of homeless people, like those of neoliberalism from which they emanate, vary, dependent in part upon particular social welfare histories and the priorities of certain national governments (Brenner and Theodore 2002). So in England and Wales, for instance, the elimination of anti-social behaviour became a political priority from the election of New Labour in 1997 (Carr and Cowan 2006; Flint 2003). ASBOs (civil orders restraining particular types of behaviour with criminal consequences for breach) were used alongside private law measures, to prevent begging and to exclude homeless people from particular areas of cities, shopping malls and transport hubs. At the same time there has been an increased use of more longstanding laws designed to prevent begging. Prosecutions under section 3 of the Vagrancy Act 1824 increased from 1510 in 2006–07 to 2365 in 2015–16 (Cromarty and Strickland 2018). More recently Public Place Protection Orders (PSPOs) have been used in connection with homeless people. Here it is not the individual behaviour which is targeted but the spaces which they occupy. The argument is that it is not rough sleepers but any anti-social behaviour they present which is targeted.

However, research by the national homelessness charity Crisis in 2016 found that 36 per cent (29 out of 81) of local authority respondents had specifically targeted rough sleeping with enforcement measures. A close examination of the PSPO imposed in the city centre of Canterbury in September 2017 supports

[2] *cf* www.routledge.com/Policing-Cities-Urban-Securitization-and-Regulation-in-a-21st-Century/Lippert-Walby/p/book/9780415540339.

these conclusions. The order criminalises any refusal to stop drinking alcohol in that area; swearing, shouting or acting in a manner likely to cause harassment, alarm or distress; persistently begging, with begging defined broadly as including passive as well as active methods to receive alms; urinating or defecating in a public place; and refusing to cease busking or other street entertainment. The presence of homeless people on the High Street has as a result been severely curtailed, but there is no evidence that they have ceased to be homeless (in fact, although there are some disputes over the collection of the data, the street count shows a dramatic increase in rough sleeping in the city). As Liberty points out, 'PSPOs don't alleviate hardship on any level. They are blunt instruments which fast-track so-called "offenders" into the criminal justice system'. Liberty has urged the Government to rethink these powers: 'handing hefty fines to homeless people … is obviously absurd, counterproductive and downright cruel' (quoted in Cromarty and Strikland 2018: 6). In one sense these measures respond to the feelings of insecurity in the domiciled population. However there is a close affinity with the entrepreneurial city. The PSPO in Canterbury is supported by the Business Improvement District, led by businesses which are concerned that the presence of homeless people in the centre of Canterbury, a UNESCO world heritage site and global tourist destination, inhibits retail activity.

In peripheral capitalist Brazil the disciplinary and exclusionary practices are divided among the different levels of government, which also means a division of accountabilities. Legislation is given to municipal powers; police repression comes from State powers; and the federal government outlines general guidelines for street population policy. Many larger cities in Brazil have legislated municipal codes of general ordinances, which call for citizens to have 'good postures and behaviours', many of which make unlawful practices common to homeless people. In Belo Horizonte, an example is law n. 8.616/2003. It prohibits hawkers and requires permits for car-washers, shoe-shine boys and recycled material pickers, which are common economic activities of homeless people. Permits have to be renewed annually at a high fee. The permits also specify the materials which may be carried by the permit holder, tricky for the homeless, since all property used for other purposes and not specified in the permit is commonly confiscated by municipal guards or by the police. The Code also defines hazardous activities, which require additional licensing and insurance. Superficially reasonable, but the banning of the storage of plastic and foam on the grounds of flammability provides an excuse to confiscate plastic used as tents and the small foam mattresses carried by rough sleepers. The codes are zealously enforced against the homeless, but loosely applied, for instance, to the informal construction of fences and obstacles erected to inhibit the homeless from sleeping, sitting or wandering in public places. This is indicative of a second source of discipline and exclusion; one which emanates from the increased protection of private property rights.

Gough points out that in neoliberal cities '[p]rivate property is to be freed from collective rights and obligations, in particular from state interference, though the state is required all the more strongly to protect property from infringement by others' (Gough 2002: 405). So for instance, in England and Wales, squatting in residential properties became for the first time a criminal offence in the Legal Aid, Sentencing and Punishment of Offenders Act 2012 leading to 59 convictions and eight people being imprisoned in 2016 (Squash 2017). Just as important as the criminalising of homeless people, the Act deters vulnerable people from squatting, with potentially lethal effects, as the death of Daniel Gauntlett in 2013 exemplifies (Squash 2013). The Act demonstrates an intriguing relationship between state interventions to protect property and the emergence of property guardianship, a market response to intensified concerns about the vulnerability of property (Hunter and Meers 2018). Here a property guardian company will 'protect' what would otherwise be an empty property on behalf of its owner, by accommodating, for a fee, occupiers. These occupiers are insecure, and can be evicted without formal process, once the owner requires the property again. The residents are forced to behave entrepreneurially, trading the security they would have in the rental market for reduced costs, and 'funky' places to live. This provision of different forms of accommodation does not, however, help many homeless people, who would be excluded because they are not in employment and have no fixed address.

In Brazil, squatting is defined as a minor crime with a relatively low penalty of six months' detention. In practice, however, police enforcement and public prosecutors indict squatters for other crimes in order to increase their penalties. One typical charge is gang membership, which can lead to a six-year prison sentence if associated with the presence of children and possession of weapons. Squatters describe constant police surveillance, and intimidation using tactics such as helicopters flying over at night and dawn and the release of flyers threatening the integrity and safety of families. Criminalisation of the movements themselves is common. Whilst eviction follows due process in theory, this can be circumvented through by-laws which give law enforcement officers extensive discretion, enabling eviction without court orders or without providing due notice.

An interesting feature of the neoliberal city is that it uses entrepreneurial devices to try to rehabilitate those who have fallen outside of employment. So, for instance, the homeless are to be rehabilitated by giving them skills. In England and Wales there is an increasing emphasis on indoor projects as opposed to street services because those projects provide the rehabilitative services required to start the process of getting people into employment. The Big Issue project perhaps best exemplifies this approach to rehabilitation of the homeless. Homeless or vulnerably housed people are able to earn money by selling the Big Issue magazine. However the code of conduct issued to vendors insists that they must avoid all behaviour, such as sitting down, which may confuse what they are doing with begging. Pitches are licensed and it is made clear to those who purchase the magazine that they must take a copy of the magazine to complete the contract and ensure that the price of the magazine is not the equivalent of a charitable donation. In Brazil there is a similar connection between enterprise and street homelessness through associations, government and private companies which, in their own words, aim to promote productive chains that strengthen the economy.[3] In Belo Horizonte, for instance, homeless people are paid to organise parking for restaurant customers, while more formally, an association of homeless individuals has carried out rubbish collection and recycling in the city for many years.[4]

This entrepreneurial spirit extends to the NGOs who help the homeless. They are required to compete for funding, to shape their services according to local and national priorities set by the state, and to ensure that their services meet quality-control standards. More spontaneous projects, such as soup runs, are clamped down upon by the state, not only because they prevent the rehabilitation of the homeless, but because they run the risk of encouraging people to live on the streets (Hunter 2016). Importantly, this is not solely through the hard edge of state power, but engineered through the formalities of regulatory requirements, from insurance to food hygiene, which restrict creative and responsive engagements with the street homeless.

This rhetoric of health and safety can also produce other actions of discipline and exclusion. So for instance in Canterbury, there was an incident which became notorious on Facebook after someone reported that an employee of a local business (Wilko) had hosed down sleeping homeless people near its entrance to force them to move on. The explanation provided by the business was that it was cleaning the area of urine and broken glass. What is significant here is the close relationship between commerce, health and safety, and discipline and exclusion. Enterprise and insecurity appear closely related, and the needs of enterprise for clean streets and safe enclaves become justification for actions against homeless people.

IV. Insecurity and the Future – The Possibilities of 'Ethopolitics'

It is easy to be caught up in the logics of the entrepreneurial and insecure city. Our contention is, however, that it is possible to imagine the city otherwise, and we start with Rose's intervention which is designed to provoke a different reaction to the current despair felt by those interested in a progressive politics. In his analysis of the relationship of freedom and liberty in what he tentatively claims is a post-neoliberalism governmentality developing in a Trump-led world of popular authoritarianism, Rose argues that there is contemporary need for an 'ethopolitical'

[3] asmare.org/trabalho-social.html.

[4] See: www.forbes.com/sites/sap/2012/08/02/recycling-lives-redemption-amid-the-rubbish/#52d3f1e357a8.

perspective. Ethopolitics aims to act upon the ethics of the population, concerned with 'the self-techniques by which human beings should judge themselves and act upon themselves to make themselves better than they are' (Rose 2007, quoted in Rose 2017: 316). In his account, the rise of populist politics is 'ethopolitics with a vengeance' – a mixture of contradictory economic concerns about migration costing society by simultaneously undercutting both welfare and wages, and narratives based on race, framed

> more generally in terms of a conflict of values, between our true people whose identity is threatened by those from outside with different values – not necessarily deemed inferior, but sometimes merely radically distinct from ours – and those who, because they challenge such an identity in the name of the pluralism of values and of cosmopolitanism, are indeed the moral enemy within; enemies of the people (Rose 2017: 317).

The objective of this ethopolitical strategy is to reveal the vulnerability of the population. The argument of the authoritarian populist, as Rose sets it out, is that these dual opponents of the 'true people' – the liberal elite media-political complex and the illegal outsiders – have corrupted the nation and its institutional protections and left the people vulnerable. This is because this combination has disrupted traditional security, meaning that there can no longer be a reliance on systems which kept them safe. But more than this: in another incoherent shift, those systems themselves have been responsible for undermining the key response to this 'pervasive vulnerability' – the 'need to draw upon, celebrate and enhance the collective resilience of our people' (Rose 2017: 317).

Although he does not engage with this scholarship, the populist authoritarian framing of individual and collective vulnerability Rose describes can be seen as an odious mutation of arguments from vulnerability and precariousness developed by Judith Butler (Butler 2004; 2010). Both accounts build from a foundation of socially-wrought vulnerability – we are vulnerable because we live collectively – and both share a critique of any claims to provide absolute security to resist this vulnerability. Both suggest instead that a bottom-up, collective response to this precariousness is critical, and both also engage with the ways in which some are made more or less vulnerable. But it is here that they radically diverge.

The divergence is linked to the question of protection. Rose concludes that post-neoliberal governmentality has dropped freedom as a central tool, and instead resuscitated and re-imagined governance through liberty. Instead of the insistently gentle proddings and putatively autonomous choices which techniques of freedom deploy, governance through liberty reinvigorates the distinction between a world of public rules and exceptions, and a personal space in which individuals are responsible for containing and directing their own conduct. The challenge posed by Rose is how to respond to these shifts, to find progressive ways to re-imagine the new relations he posits between liberty, security and control – 'no longer obliged to try, in our way, to be free, but to hope to live in a controlled world where our vulnerabilities are understood and managed, and where we can experience a kind of security' (Rose 2017: 319).

In contrast, the socially constructed precariousness in Butler's account, as developed by Isabell Lorey (2015), eschews incoherent calls for protection and security. Instead this line of scholarship seeks ways to embrace collective precariousness, with Lorey drawing on examples of care strikes and other subverting techniques by radical social movements of the precariat. For Lorey, the concern with claims of protection and security is chiefly one with the way that such techniques have been used as tools for exclusion and distributing precarity. She argues that the immunisation provided by the welfare state promised protection for some, protecting from the virus of the (racialised) other, and at the same time operating to privatise care along gendered lines.

Lorey's is a compelling account which points to the urgent need – if Rose's analysis is right – to regalvanise feminist criticisms of the public/private divide. However, one of the difficulties Rose calls for scholars to grapple with – the question of protection – is not fully elaborated in Lorey's account. Critical of the excluding nature of state protection, the collective stance of the precariat founded on an acceptance of precariousness necessarily provides a form of protection. One way to reconsider the question of socially constructed vulnerability is therefore to consider how to frame protection without recreating the conditions of precarity which claim to protect some and leave others exposed. A potential way to begin this analysis is to proceed from care, to reframe protection as founded in care and so seek to subvert relations of liberty, security and control. It is for this reason that we focus on the disruptive potential of care, the ways in which care provides the potential for re-imagination of these relationships, and the dismissal of the straw men constructed in the ethopolitics of the populist authoritarians.

And, as literature on care, and this collection demands, it has to be care in a particularity – and our focus is care in the city. We disrupt the ways in which care traditionally creates the radically distinct other by using case studies which simultaneously emphasise the individual context and universally human precariousness. Care, for us in this account, is importantly not downwards – carer/dominant and cared for/vulnerable. Our claim is that finding instances of care in a particularity can enable the disruption of a hierarchical view of care, and our argument is that the recognition of such care opens democratic possibilities. Our case studies also seek to disrupt the notion of the cosmopolitan insiders by drawing attention to their connections – caring, loving, situated – in the spaces and communal life of the state.

V. Alternative Visions of Cities

Many scholars and activists have sought to challenge the city as a fearful, insecure space. From the 'right to the city' movement, to the English city of York's self-declaration as a city of Human Rights, and the 'sanctuary city' movement in the US and the UK, including Sheffield's decision to be a city of sanctuary, these efforts have drawn on themes including rights, hospitality and sanctuary. Our reframing takes inspiration from these endeavours, but instead starts from an examination of the disruptive potential of care. This disruptive potential is evident when care opens up other ways to be in a city, challenging both entrepreneurialism and insecurity and suggesting ways to think about protection without exclusion. One way in which this can operate is through care by the homeless for the city or its inhabitants. Importantly, care here is not solely about the meeting of immediate physical needs, but civic care associated with individuation and citizenship, and for example, can be linked to reading and libraries. In London, the Quaker Mobile Library has operated since the late 1990s. Owned by a national charity – Quaker Homeless Action – the library operates out of a van which is entirely staffed by volunteers, and attends sites around the capital on a weekly basis. The diverse group – from regulars to one-time borrowers – who use the library (the 'readers') do not need to provide any documentation apart from a first name, and are permitted to borrow two books for three weeks at a time. Some of the volunteers are themselves former homeless readers, while regular readers also offer insights and help to volunteers and the newly homeless. Critically,

> [u]nlike most social services, the Mobile Library remains as free from prescription as from proscription: it seeks to fulfil its patrons' desires, not to mould them. Yet the white van delivers more than books, providing occasions to discuss, to recommend, and to exchange opinions along with objects (Price 2015: 694).

The creation of this itinerant space to talk is central to the conception of the library.[5] As Leah Price, Francis Lee Higginson Professor of English Literature at Harvard, notes, 'In this age of eviction, a civic temple may be less useful than a parking space' (Price 2015: 696) – and in cities moulded by globalisation, white vans can become civic temples, resisting narratives of entrepreneurism and insecurity through relationships of care.

In Belo Horizonte, for example, plans to demolish a square and cut down an ancient tree in a middle-class neighbourhood of the city led to protests. A group of homeless individuals in the city built a tree house in the tree, opened a small public library in the tree house and, for two years, persuaded the city authorities to hold off on plans to redevelop the square as a space of commerce but instead used it as a community space. It is to this example we turn, to explore in more detail a case study of the city as a space of care.

VI. Care in the Tree House

The story of the Tree House is an example of how care can be disruptively democratic as it may turn explicit the interdependent relationships that constitute

[5] And see: journals.sagepub.com/doi/abs/10.

a city. The politics of care, developed along the struggle to preserve the Tree House, confronts neoliberalism, but, at the same time, resists the paternalistic logic of welfare politics in which governments and charity, from a position of power, bring care as a ready-made and non-negotiable response to homelessness. In contrast, the Tree House is a space created by homeless people, that is embraced by housed citizens, and that emerged through conflict. This agonistic negotiation is generative; it enables the homeless to rethink their capabilities and change their lives. At the same time, it inverts the logic that some are vulnerable weights to be carried by those who have escaped the fate of vulnerability.

Daniel, a homeless man living in the streets near the Nova Suíça neighbourhood in Belo Horizonte, puts it this way: 'Empathy. If 1% of human beings had empathy and listened to his fellow, globally, we would have tolerance'. The Tree House became a larger public issue for the first time through a Facebook page (@defendoacasadaarvore)[6] on 13 September 2017, after founders Douglas, Greice, Warley and Marlon, received a demolition order issued by City Hall on 11 September 2017.

> [A] local resident came up to us in rage saying that this had become a place of drug use. Yes, we cannot deny this. We tell this man that he has to remember that inside our co[m]fortable middle class houses drug is [sic] also used and destroys families. With homeless people it is no different, they are victims just as the well-brought-up and scented youngsters, with one fundamental difference: those in the street are despised and treated as slag [sic]. The biggest traffic dealers and owners of this Empire occupy high-ranking positions in the Republic's powers, with their helicopters and aircraft filled with drugs,[7] that fly over our heads and go unpunished, giving a voice of command in the public powers. So pointing the accusatory finger at the more fragile part of that link is easy. The man left head down and without arguments to refute what he heard. (Casa da Árvore 1 October 2017)

The Tree House was built over a few weeks around a mango tree in a forgotten square. In the city's development plan, the square was originally designed to be a green area in the neighbourhood, but ended up as an irregular parking lot for cars and fly tipping. Douglas, a former hairdresser, who served some time in jail and began his life on the streets due to drug use, cleaned and recuperated the green areas, collected some of the material found in the litter and built a precarious shelter. The place attracted other homeless people. They collected, cleaned and catalogued books from the litter, organising them by title and genre in shelves around the tree and among plant and flower pots, benches, improvised chairs

[6] Today the Facebook page is @defendoacasadosaber.

[7] He refers to the case of a Minas Gerais senator whose helicopter was found in a minister's hacienda with half a ton of cocaine base paste, calculated to cost US$20 million, in November 2013. The pilot was imprisoned for a few days, and in only two months the helicopter was released by a judge, the pilot was freed and the press stopped covering the case. Nothing happened to the senator and the minister. In fact, they are still in government.

and colourful umbrellas, building something remarkable for the least curious of passers-by. As more people stopped to talk, they were welcomed to sit and read, or to take a book home. Eventually they developed a system, allowing any passer-by interested in one book, to take it free of any obligation, and for those interested in two or more, to exchange them for others.

Local business owners rapidly articulated the sanitary insecurity narrative, complaining that customers were afraid of walking near the square. The quotation above reveals that drug use was an issue. Their entrepreneurial voices were also present in the defence of the commercial value of the neighbourhood, driven by the logic of business, but it is notable that police files show that no complaints were registered during the period of the Tree House.

In contrast, local residents had a memory of the former degradation of the square. They viewed the cleanliness of the space and the curious construction that was erected using the tree branches as an opportunity to interact with the tree's inhabitants by sharing, discussing and reciprocally recommending books. A local TV channel put the story in the news. Very soon this forgotten corner started attracting the interest of people who knew that the west side of the city lacked cultural inputs, of those who were engaged in 'right to the city' movements, of mass media and politicians.

By the time City Hall issued the demolition order, both sides had become organised movements; the businessmen continuing to pressure for the removal of the Tree House and, in response to the order, the four Tree House founders writing a letter to City Hall. This letter explained that they had all abandoned drugs and returned to their homes, and outlined their will to preserve the Tree House as a cultural project that would serve the neighbourhood with a public library and a reference centre for the street population. They also explained their will to take responsibility for its use. The letter was also signed by other homeless people, local carnival groups, people living nearby and civil associations for the street population, for the rights to the city and for cultural movements. Left-wing political parties also supported the continued existence of the Tree House.[8]

On 24 September 2017, a few days after the controversy involving the dump and demolition order, the Tree House caught fire, which destroyed 2,500 books and the mango tree itself. Although no-one was hurt, the four inhabitants lost their personal documents and belongings. In the documentary *The Tree House*,

[8] Carnival blocks that support the Tree House: Pena de Pavão de Krisna, Bloco Bethânia Custosa, Bloco Parque Jardim América, Bloco Unidos do Oeste, Bloco União do Oeste. Cultural movements: Coletivo 1207, Quintal Mimoso, Quintal Escambo Cultural, Espaço Comum Luiz Estrela, Associação Comunitária Cultural e Desportiva da Nova Suíça, Grajaú e Adjacências. Other social movements: Movimento Parque Já and Quilombo dos Luíses. Traditional institutions for the right to the city: National Coordination of Black Institutions, the Catholic organisation for homeless, National Centre for the Defence of Human Rights of People with Street Trajectory, Minas Gerais Front for Drugs and Human Rights, Popular Brigades, a political association for housing policy. Left-wing political parties: Worker's Party Executive, City Councillors Pedro Patrus (Worker's Party), Cida Falabela and Áurea Carolina (both from the Socialism and Liberty Party).

shown in February 2018, a devastated Warley says: 'It took three years to build and ten minutes to destroy' (Alessandra 2018: 48 min 50 sec). In the 'Official Note of Institutions that Support the Tree House Project' (Casa da Árvore 25 September 2017) the signatories expressed their sorrow at the loss of 'one of the most beautiful projects of occupation of public space, created by homeless people'. They highlighted the fact that the project has received hundreds of supporting notes and signatures. They called attention to the climate created by the demolition order, by City Hall's lack of response and its inability to mediate between the supporters of the Tree House and those few voices against it, which contributed to the bad feelings that led to the fire.[9] The note also criticised the limited vision of the response to the underlying and severe social problem of street homelessness and the way governments had reacted with successive disastrous and hygienist public policies.

Supporting groups and a large number of inhabitants of the neighbours in West Belo Horizonte took turns in a vigil around the leafless tree. Colourful umbrellas were hung from the branches in substitution for its green leaves. The place was cleaned up and new books donated, with donors arriving in cars, bicycles and on foot. A post on the Facebook page, on 1 October 2017, tells of a quick and symbolic act one Sunday in favour of the Tree House: some of the participants read parts of the books they have brought; among them, the Federal Constitution of Brazil, from which they read the articles that speak of individual and collective protection of rights (Casa da Árvore 1 October 2017).

A Public Advocate accompanied the Tree House ex-residents, who by then called themselves librarians, to a series of meetings with City Hall representatives and the Deputy Mayor. These culminated in the commitment from the City to design a project by 20 October 2017 for a public library and cultural centre. Some conditions were set by the librarians: that the space remained open, with the least walls possible, that a garden was integrated into the library, that recycled material was used in the construction, that the access remained free, in a way that the space could remain a place of encounter between homeless people and other library users.

On 15 October 2017, National Teacher's Day in Brazil, there was another event noted on Facebook and in the documentary. Teacher Fátima Reis says 'they have given us a space full of books' (Alessandra 2018: 25 min). She observes that generally people have difficulties in having a sense of belonging, but this space is a space for all. Neide Pacheco, a psychologist and activist, says: 'We thank you, Marlon, for your idea' (Alessandra 2018: 26 min). Saulo de Castro Setragni, a hairdresser, reflects: '30 per cent of Brazilians have never bought a book. … This is a new paradigm, a new way to access books … much more evolved' (Alessandra 2018: 32 min 18 sec). Larissa Alberti, an actress and teacher, notes the poetic presence of

[9] The investigations of the causes of the Tree House fire were inconclusive. The police had evidence of criminal intention.

the Tree House, the most beautiful house of the neighbourhood, according to her (Alessandra 2018: 39 min 10 sec).

In an interview given to the local news television, Greice, one of the former inhabitants of the Tree House and the person considered by all to be the 'main librarian', tells her story of involvement with drugs and prostitution and the role of books in her recovery. 'Books are like oxygen to me … I died fifteen years ago, and I am back to life four months ago [sic]' (when she quit drugs after involvement with the Tree House project). She is asked why she thinks someone would want the house burned. She answers: 'We bother [them], for sure, because we took eyes away from shop windows and we directed them to homeless drug addicts. The streets and drugs cannot only be seen as an abyss, but as a resumption' (Casa da Árvore 25 September 2017).

These words reflect the conflicts between the three city imaginaries we have considered. The neoliberal and welfare imaginaries are based on economic development and security, transformed for many into places of financialisation, which shatter relationships with place. A city where illegalities are hierarchically organised, the illegal use of a public square as a parking lot, flouting city regulations, is tolerated; the use of the space for culture and reception of the most vulnerable is criminalised. The 'Official Note' describes this city as a place where 'the mediocrity and the cowardice tried to silence, once again, the birth of culture and popular art' (Casa da Árvore 25 September 2017).

The other imaginary is as a city of care where potential for liberation and self-realisation is made possible by encounter and self, collective management. The Tree House is a place of reception and reference for street populations. But it does not work within the welfare logic of segregation and discipline. It is a place of encounter of many different people, some of whom, at first glance, would seem mutually hostile. They are united under the mango tree solely because of their love for reading books. And this gives us clues as to how those involved manage their vulnerabilities in relation to the city. The homeless find a place of reception and belonging that can help them reconstruct their lives. The citizens of the formal city find a place of security and a sense of how culture can transform their everyday life. The 'Official Note' describes this as a place where 'perplexity and collective indignation with … violence … will be our theoretical framework in the struggle that we will now fight to defend the resurgence of the House' (Casa da Árvore 25 September 2017).

In this unlikely space the sense of rights are built in conflict, in the process of comprehending responsibilities towards the other. This movement 'towards' allows us to change the place of indifference to a new active place in which the consequences of our choices matter. From this perspective, care is not related to a contraposition between reason and emotion. An ethics of care is inseparable from the politics of care. It presupposes respect for rights and a complementarity of voices and points of view, which can only be visualised in conflict and in tension. This tension opens the possibilities of redefining the asymmetries of distribution of power.

Our city of care is as different from a city of dependency and subordination, as it is from the neoliberal city. Both neoliberal and welfare paradigms of care presuppose societal hierarchies in the way public policy is constructed. As Nancy Fraser and Linda Gordon argue, dependency is often stigmatised in industrial societies, where wage labour is seen as a sign of independence (Fraser and Gordon 1994). In such societies the figure of the 'pauper' is considered deviant and its segregation and elimination are naturalised through moral and psychological controls, even in public policy. What this discourse fails to identify is its gender, race and colonialistic biases, which enable it to sustain contradictions – such as those which see as positive the dependency of women and children in the private sphere whilst any dependency in the public and labour spheres are considered highly objectionable.

The Tree House case signals, although in a precarious and subtle way, that citizenship is based on the acknowledgement of interdependency. An ethics of care presupposes the possibility opened to denaturalise political hierarchies. A portion of the letter written by the four homeless founders of the Tree House project to respond to City Hall's demolition order reveals the power of a city of care. They give up using the house as their home, recognise its role in the public sphere and demand the installation of a cultural centre and public library, justifying their action through these words: 'after all, knowledge does not take up space' (Casa da Árvore 27 September 2017). These words can be understood as a disruptive and revolutionary paradox. The paradox is that the Tree House is, in many senses, knowledge that occupies space through the performance of bodies – humans, books, trees. Their presence in that space not only redefines the space and the bodies themselves but, above all, helps redefine vulnerability, politics and care. In this sense, the Tree House promotes an inversion in the politics of care based on the hierarchy between privileged care givers and vulnerable and weightful care takers. In an interdependent paradigm these places are interchangeable. The Tree House shows how care takers become care givers and by changing places make evident the ethopolitics involved in care. In fact the ethopolitics of care is framed by encounter and conflict, by negotiation and democratic deliberation and discussion. In this aspect it has a public dimension attached to the practices of politics and law, and cannot be segregated to the private sphere.

VII. Conclusion

> [O]nly when the state focuses more clearly upon the quality of care offered by the non-statutory sector, rather than seeking simply to dictate who might be 'deserving' of the sector's aid, is Britain's landscape of street homelessness liable to become less uneven and more akin to a meaningful 'landscape of care' (May et al 2005: 728).

May et al's claim is a starting point, but we aim to go much further. Taking Rose's suggestions, we explored the progressive possibilities provided by examples where the imagination of vulnerability and power are put into doubt and are inverted by practice, revealing the possibilities of ethopolitics. The Tree House shows that it is possible and ethically desirable to frame protection from the point of view of those whose vulnerability is usually understood as a justification for inferiority. The inversion of their role as they become those who care and construct a sense for the uses of the city is politically disruptive. It enables us to acknowledge vulnerability as an inevitable human condition and the asymmetrical power relationship fed by paternalistic, authoritarian and bureaucratic structures, as political and ethical choices which are not given but constructed. Acknowledging these points invites us to re-imagine cities as places of care

This chapter is intended as a provocation, on security, liberty and space. In the Tree House, and elsewhere, such as in London's mobile library, protection extends beyond physical protection, to encompass protection of a common space, of a community founded in care. Our claim is twofold: that re-imagining the city as a space of care can have material consequences, and that it can point to ways in which the state could begin to conceive of protection without exclusion. In relation to material consequences, we argue that just as the re-imagination of the city as spaces of entrepreneurialism and insecurity has had material consequences for the spaces and lives of cities, the re-imagination of the city as a space of care has the potential to have an effect on the cities themselves. Further, we argue that foregrounding relations of care, and examining homelessness and civic care in the context of the city, can be a starting point for progressive reframings of the relationship between liberty, security and control. Further work is needed to trace these threads and to develop the themes in our case studies, but as we have sought to demonstrate in this chapter, just as with the cities we live in, they are bursting with possibilities of radically imagining the world otherwise.

References

Alessandra, T (2018) Casa da Árvore Documentário, available online at: www.youtube.com/watch?v=iwoMQR-Nc48.

Brenner, N and Theodore, N (2002) 'Cities and the Geographies of "Actually Existing Neoliberalism"' *Antipode* 34(3).

Butler, J (2009) *Frames of War: When is life grieveable?* (London, Verso).

—— (2004) *Precarious Life: The power of mourning and violence* (London, Verso).

Carr, H and Cowan, D (2006) 'Labelling: Constructing Definitions of Antisocial Behaviour' in J Flint (ed), *Housing, Urban Governance and Anti-Social Behaviour: Principles, Policy and Practice* (Bristol, Policy Press).

Casa da Árvore @defendoacasadaarvore Facebook Page at: www.facebook.com/defendoacasadaarvore.

Cromarty, H and Strickland, P (2018) *Rough Sleepers and Anti-Social Behaviour* (House of Commons Briefing Paper), available online at: researchbriefings.parliament.uk/ResearchBriefing/Summary/CBP-7836.

Flint, J (2003) 'Housing and ethopolitics: constructing identities of active consumption and responsible community' *Economy and Society* 32(4): 611–29.

Fraser, N and Gordon, L (1994) 'A Genealogy of Dependency: Tracing a Keyword of the U.S. Welfare State' *Signs* 19(2): 309–36 (Chicago IL, Chicago University Press).

Gough, J (2002) 'Neoliberalism and Socialisation in the Contemporary City: Opposites, Complements and Instabilities' *Antipode* 34(3).

Harvey, D (1989) 'From Managerialism to Entrepreneurialism: The Transformation in Urban Governance in Late Capitalism' *Geografiska Annaler Series B Human Geography* 71(1).

—— (2005) *A Brief History of Neoliberalism* (Oxford, Oxford University Press).

Hunter C (2016) 'Caring for the homeless: Westminster City Council and anti-homeless bye-laws' in R Harding (ed), *ReValuing Care in Theory, Law and Policy: Cycles and Connections* (Abingdon, Taylor and Francis).

Hunter, C and Meers, J (2018) 'The "Affordable Alternative to Renting": Property Guardians and Legal Dimensions of Housing Precariousness' in H Carr, B Edgeworth and C Hunter (eds), *Law and the Precarious Home* (Oxford, Hart Publishing).

Lorey, I (2015) *State of insecurity: Government of the precarious* (New York, Verso Books).

Macleod, G (2002) 'From Urban Entrepreneurialism to a "Revanchist City"? On the Spatial Injustices of Glasgow's Renaissance' *Antipode* 34(3).

May J, Cloke, P and Johnsen, S (2005) 'Re-phasing Neoliberalism: New Labour and Britain's Crisis of Street Homelessness' *Antipode* 37(4).

Monroe, K (2016) *The Insecure City: Space Power and Mobility in Beirut* (New Brunswick, Rutgers Press).

Price, L (2015) 'Books on the Move' *PMLA* 130(3): 690–96.

Procacci, G (1991) 'Social Economy and the Government of Poverty' in G Burchell, C Gordon and P Miller (eds), *The Foucault Effect: Studies in Governmentality* (Chicago IL, University of Chicago Press).

Rolnik, R (2015) *War of Places: The Colonization of Land and Housing in the Financial Era* (São Paulo, Boitempo).

Rose, N (2017) 'Still "like birds on the wire"? Freedom after neoliberalism' *Economy and Society* 46(3): 303–23.

Sassen, S (2001) *The Global City* (Princeton NJ, Princeton University Press).

Venugopal, R (2015) Neoliberalism as concept *Economy and Society* 44(2): 165–87.

7

Formal and Informal Care in the Public and Private Spheres in England and Australia

BRIAN SLOAN*

I. Introduction: The Conundrum of Space and Formal, Informal, Public and Private Care

Any attempt to distinguish between public and private spheres as spaces of care gives rise to immediate difficulties. This is true not least because it is necessary also to distinguish between formal care, provided pursuant to a contractual or other legal duty, and informal care, provided in the absence of such a duty. For example, while formal social care tends to be associated with public responsibility and the state, in England 'few local authorities are now involved in the direct delivery of care and support services', with most services operated by private, for-profit providers (Kelly 2013: 24).[1] Much formal care takes place in private homes, and such homes and other private property can be appropriated to fund the social care system. Moreover, privacy must be an important value in the context of a care home that might in other respects be characterised as public (Hughes 2004). Conversely, the recognition of, not to mention reliance on, *informal* care (which might legitimately be characterised as a matter of private arrangement, albeit inherently informal) by

* This chapter builds upon research that I undertook while a doctoral student, an Early Career Fellow at CRASSH in Cambridge, and an Academic Visitor at the University of New South Wales. I am grateful for the Fellowship, funding from the Society of Legal Scholars and the Cambridge Humanities Research Grant Scheme and the support of, among others, Kevin Gray, Jens Scherpe, Daniel Joyce, Isabella Alexander and Wendy Schrama. Comments were gratefully received from attendees of seminars at UNSW, the University of Technology, Sydney and the Molengraaff Instituut voor Privaatrecht in Utrecht. The aim has been to state law, policy, financial values, etc, correct as of 25 September 2018.

[1] See also Robertson et al (2014: 19), albeit that most providers in Australia are apparently non-profit. The common theme with Dominey and Gelsthorpe's chapter in this volume (Chapter 3) is noteworthy.

the state arguably gives it a public character, and the social care system on occasion turns informal carers into care workers through mechanisms such as direct payments (Ungerson 2004). There is also an important distinction between public and private *law*, with the former encompassing claims against the state by one or more individuals and the latter encompassing claims by one or more private individuals against another such individual or group. The concepts of public and private therefore cut across the economy of care.

Mindful of these difficulties, this chapter will focus on the relationship between formal (associated with the public sphere) and informal (associated with the private sphere) care in England and Australia, in terms of their legal recognition and funding. It will highlight the fact that, while both formal systems have recently moved towards limiting the liability of care recipients to pay for their formal care (albeit very tentatively in England), several parts of Australia have been much more willing to facilitate the rational recognition of informal caring relationships in *private* law than has been the case in England, with the result that property transfers can be mandated between care recipients (generally via their estates) and informal carers. The chapter will consider whether approaches to the funding of *formal* care can be squared with the recognition of informal care in private law.

II. Formal Care

A. England

Adult social care is the responsibility of local authorities in England. While it lacks a statutory definition, it has been said that it 'supports people of all ages with certain physical, cognitive or age-related conditions in carrying out personal care or domestic routines' (Commission on Funding of Care and Support 2011: 4). It is distinct from health care provided by the National Health Service (NHS), which is designed to 'secure improvement'[2] 'in the physical and mental health of the people of England'[3] and 'in the prevention, diagnosis and treatment of physical and mental illness'.[4] This distinction assumes particular importance as regards the funding of care, but is frequently criticised (Herring 2016: 54).

The charging regimes for health care and social care have been separate since the beginnings of the NHS (Bilton 2014: 14). The National Health Service Act 2006 mandates that '[t]he services provided as part of the health service in England must be free of charge' except where legislation expressly provides otherwise.[5]

[2] National Health Service Act 2006, s 1(1).
[3] National Health Service Act 2006, s 1(1)(a).
[4] National Health Service Act 2006, s 1(1)(b).
[5] National Health Service Act 2006, s 1(4).

By contrast, however, the Dilnot Commission on the Funding of Care and Support (2011: 11) explained that '[v]ery broadly, under [the social care] system, people with assets over £23,250 receive no financial state support and need to fund their own care' and '[t]he level and type of state support for people with assets below this threshold depends on their needs and income'. A care recipient's liability to pay is assessed by a local authority (separately to a needs assessment)[6] using an extremely complex set of regulations to determine the existence of relevant capital and income.[7] Baxter (2016) estimated that in the recent past between 20 and 25 per cent of those receiving care in their own homes, and between 43 and 45 per cent of those doing so in a care home, paid for their own care, as well as predicting future increases in those figures.

The starkness of the funding differences is not, however, reflected in the distinction between the types of care (Spencer-Lane 2015: [1–268]). There is also controversy over NHS Continuing Healthcare:

> [A] package of ongoing care … arranged and funded solely by the [NHS] for individuals outside a hospital setting who have complex ongoing healthcare needs, of a type or quantity such that they … have a 'primary health need' … as a result of disability, accident or illness (Department of Health 2018: [15.33]).[8]

The King's Fund (2014: 3) describes NHS Continuing Healthcare (with its very stringent criteria) as involving an 'all or nothing' assessment, whereby those who pass it receive free care and accommodation.

Mayhew and Smith (2014: 670–71) emphasise that '[a] … system for funding social care … along similar lines to the NHS … would involve a combination of higher taxes, more borrowing and/or redirecting public finances from other priority areas', at a time of a perceived need for austerity and in which local authorities are already struggling to meet demands (Age UK 2016) and the dignity of those who require care is far from guaranteed, whatever the rhetoric surrounding the introduction of the Care Act 2014 (Sloan 2016). Even so, the King's Fund (2014: vi) asserts that pressures in health and social care and the needs of an ageing population 'call for a response that goes well beyond patching up existing services and making the changes set out in the Dilnot report [involving the capping of liability]'. The Fund makes the bold claim that 'higher public spending on health and social care is affordable if it is phased in over a decade' and recommend that it be funded 'through tax and national insurance increases, reallocating funds from other areas of spending, and changes to prescription charges'. For the time being, however, the marked distinction between the funding arrangements for health and social care looks set to stay.

[6] Care Act 2014, ss 9–13.

[7] Care and Support (Charging and Assessment of Resources) Regulations, SI 2014/2672, made under Care Act 2014, ss 14 and 17, inter alia.

[8] See National Health Service Commissioning Board and Clinical Commissioning Groups (Responsibilities and Standing Rules) Regulations SI 2012/2996, Part 6.

The charging and funding regime in the Care Act 2014 was nevertheless 'intended to make charging fairer and more clearly understood by everyone' (Department of Health 2018: [8.2]). Hopkins and Laurie (2015: 112) describe it as 'a significant rebalancing of the individual-state relationship in terms of responsibility for funding … social care, whilst maintaining the underlying model of funding through both individual and state contributions'.

Under the regime that would have been introduced via the Care Act 2014, based somewhat on the Dilnot Commission's proposals but then delayed by the Government until 2020 before being scrapped (BBC News 2017), people with assets of £118,000 (where the person's home is included in the financial assessment; the figure was £27,000 otherwise) would start to receive help with care costs (Department of Health 2015: [9.7]). £17,000 would have been the new lower limit of the means test below which no contribution will be expected from the individual (Department of Health 2015: [9.8]), increased from £14,250.[9]

The lifetime cap on an individual's social care contributions was a central aspect of the Dilnot proposals and the Act.[10] It was expected to be £72,000 for those developing eligible care needs after the age of 25 if it was first introduced in April 2016 (Department of Health 2015: [10.2]), and it would have been adjusted annually to account for inflation.[11] The effect of the cap would have been limited, however. Even before its implementation was delayed, the King's Fund (2014: 3) emphasised that only the cost of meeting *eligible* needs would count towards the cap, which are likely to be critical or substantial and not low or moderate. There was also concern that progress towards the cap could be set below what it costs *an individual* to pay for care (Department of Health 2015: chapter 4) because the local authority could secure cheaper provision itself (Spencer-Lane 2015 [1–317]). It should also be emphasised that the cap would exclude so-called 'general' or 'daily' 'living costs' within a care home, and these were expected to be set at around £12,000 per year (Department of Health 2015: [7.3]; Fernández and Nadash 2016). These limitations on the cap would have left many people paying a considerable sum towards their care even if the cap were brought into effect (Institute and Faculty of Actuaries 2015). For example, the Institute and Faculty of Actuaries (2014) has estimated that those who reached the cap would have spent an average of £140,000 before doing so, and that only around 10 per cent of those who pay for care would ever reach it (Independent Age and Institute and Faculty of Actuaries 2017). As a consequence, it recommends an inclusive £100,000 cap that includes the local authority rate, daily living costs and 'excess' top-up fees based on average care costs.

Aside from the cap, a major area of funding reform within the Care Act relates to the offering of deferred payment agreements (DPAs), allowing the payment of

[9] National Assistance (Assessment of Resources) Regulations SI 1992/2977, r 28(1).
[10] Care Act 2014, s 15.
[11] Care Act 2014, s 16.

social care costs to be deferred (via a secured loan) until a point such as the death of the care recipient or the sale of her home.[12]

The Government hoped that a market in insurance products would develop once the cap came into effect, to help people pay for care (Department of Health 2014). The King's Fund (2014: vi), however, claimed that there were 'no signs' that such a market would develop. Mayhew and Smith (2014: 670) express concern that '[i]f spending by the state and by the individual does not keep pace with need, … the quality and availability of care will suffer unless there are better mechanisms to help people support themselves'.[13] An extra £2 billion for social care was pledged by the Chancellor in 2017, and a further £150 million was announced by his successor the following year, but there are concerns that this remains insufficient to improve the level of care appropriately and cope with increased demand (Campbell 2017; Walker 2018).

The future of the funding of social care remains in doubt following the 2017 general election. In fact, the Conservative manifesto (Conservatives 2017) proposed to remove the 'disregard' preventing a person's home being included in the assessment where she is to receive care in her own home. The objective was said to be increasing fairness in the system while also assisting it to cope with increased demands as a result of the ageing population. This would have meant some people currently receiving free care being expected to pay for it in future, but would have been offset by an increase in the current £23,250 threshold to £100,000 (which local authorities have indicated they are unable to afford: Elgot 2017). The aim was expressed to be to ensure that self-funders would have £100,000 to pass on via inheritance. The cap was not mentioned in the manifesto at all, although the then Prime Minister Theresa May later indignantly asserted that there would be such a cap without specifying what it would be (Asanthana 2017). Following the Conservatives' failure to secure an overall majority in the House of Commons, the Queen's Speech (HM Government 2017) covered social care in a rather 'light touch' manner: all that is really known is that proposals will be brought forward for consultation via a Green Paper, which will apparently not now be published until autumn 2018 (Jarrett 2018). It was announced in December 2017 that the cap planned for 2020 would not be brought forward, albeit that some form of limitation on liability to pay is still apparently planned (BBC News 2017).

The reality is that, pending any further reform, a significant portion of the population in England will have to pay a considerable sum towards their care, not least since the average annual cost of a care home in December 2017 was exceeding £40,000 if nursing care is necessary (Paying for Care). This could have significant implications for any recognition of informal care in private law, discussed in

[12] The DPA prima facie falls due for repayment 90 days after the person's death or on disposal of property on which the local authority has a charge: Department of Health (2018: [9.108]; Care and Support (Deferred Payment) Regulations SI 2014/2671, r 7.

[13] They therefore propose Personal Care Savings Bonds.

the next section. More broadly, it perpetuates a form of discrimination between people with different types of care need, even if that is not actionable, and can produce situations where the system fails fully to meet the needs of a social care recipient in a manner consistent with her dignity, and charges her catastrophically for the privilege of enduring that failure (Sloan 2016). The potential undesirability of the extent of the current 'user pays' principle must, however, be seen in the context of the fact that any reduction in the amount going into the system might prejudice its ability to meet the needs of those who genuinely cannot afford to pay for their care, particularly since a considerable care funding shortfall for the future has already been predicted. The next sub-section analyses the funding of formal social care in Australia.

B. Australia

Australia is dealing with similar demographic issues to England, and an independent report (Tune 2017: 7) has said that 'there is a need for more high-level care at home' and that 'meeting projected future demand will need additional investment by government beyond that currently planned'. There is a broadly similar distinction in Australia as compared to England between health and social care, comprising a 'user pays' principle in respect of social care. The King's Fund (Robertson et al 2014: 17) explains that, '[a]s in England, the Australian social care system is not universal and government assistance focuses on those with low incomes', with '[a] range of services … offered by national and local government'. Again as in England, wealthier people often pay the full cost of their care out of pocket, up to the government-defined limit, and it is difficult to buy private insurance to cover these costs (ibid: 18; Lacey 2014). In contrast to the English emphasis on deferred payment agreements, however, the Australian Government chose not to 'support' a recommendation for 'the introduction of a government-backed scheme to enable consumers to draw on the equity in their home to pay their aged care costs' (Tune 2017: 70).

As regards residential care, 'individuals make a means-tested contribution to their care costs, and pay accommodation costs and daily living expenses themselves', with regulations setting out 'a maximum amount each person can be charged for accommodation, based on their assets, and a maximum daily living charge' (Robertson et al 2014: 17–18). Carney (2014: 23) has said that '[r]esidential aged care is a small but very expensive sub-set of Australian aged care services', and it is significant that 'the majority of aged care funding is provided by government' with just under a quarter provided by consumers (Tune 2017: 89). All care home residents can be expected to pay 'a basic daily fee equivalent to 85 per cent of the basic single age pension' (Aged Care Financing Authority 2017: 18). That is all that is payable for people whose income and assets are below a certain level, but only 18.8 per cent of care home residents were otherwise fully supported in June 2016 and 55.4 per cent were classed as 'non-supported' (ibid: 21). It should also be noted that '[h]ome care for the elderly is provided through the Commonwealth Home Support Program' and that '[s]ubsidies are income-tested and may require copayments from recipients' (Glover).[14]

Significantly for our purposes, Australia has also undertaken a capping process for care via amendments to the Aged Care Act 1997 made by the Aged Care (Living Longer Living Better) Act 2013, making for an interesting comparison. The appropriateness of the comparison continues in the next sub-section, since England and Australia share a common law heritage that combines a default principle of testamentary freedom with the possibility of court applications for discretionary provision out of an estate, albeit that Australian States and Territories recognise care much more explicitly within that system.

It has been said that the aim of the 'living longer, living better' programme embodied in the Australian 2013 Act is 'to build a better, fairer, more sustainable and more nationally consistent aged care system' (Trurong 2013). In the aged care reforms, there is

> a strong emphasis to make it easier for older Australians to stay in their home while they receive care and a removal of the distinction between low and high aged care services, along with a tighter means test to assess home care and residential care fees (ibid).

There are fears that 'part-pensioners and self-funded retirees may end up paying higher fees' (ibid), the latter of which is clearly reflected in England. But in Australia there is now (as of July 2018) both an annual cap of $26,964.71 and a lifetime cap of $64,715.36 (Department of Health (Australia) 2018). Those capping arrangements are applicable to all residents entering into permanent residential aged care on or after 1 July 2014, but there also appears to be an equivalent lifetime cap in the *income*-tested care fee for those receiving care in their own homes and a variable annual cap (Tune 2017: 84). It is significant that the lifetime cap (approximately £35,770.12 on the July 2018 value) is similar to the cap suggested by the Dilnot Commission in England, and superficially much lower than the £72,000 originally suggested by the Government there. Significantly, '[n]either basic daily fees nor accommodation costs are counted towards the annual and lifetime caps' (ibid), displaying similar limitations likely to be applied to any cap likely to be implemented in England. Again similarly to England, only a small percentage of permanent residents (specifically 5–6 per cent) are expected to reach the cap in Australia (ibid).

There is now a combined asset and income test for those in residential care in Australia (Tune 2017: 72). McCullagh (2014: 71) also asserts that 'most ordinary assets are included' in a residential care assessment, 'but not the value of the former home if still occupied by a partner (or certain carers or relatives) when entering care'. Occupation by certain people can cause the home to be disregarded in England (Sloan 2017), although it has been seen that the extent to which it

[14] *cf* Tune (2017: 19) on Victoria and Western Australia.

should be disregarded in relation to domiciliary care has been the subject of much political debate there. In Australia, only income (and not capital assets, except when deemed to be income) are assessed for the purposes of domiciliary care, and Tune (2017: 71) described this as 'appropriate', since the inclusion of the home might jeopardise the care recipient's ability to remain in it and thwart a key purpose of the Act. It seems that the value of the home to be counted in the assessment is largely capped at $165,271.20 (as of July 2018) in Australia where included (Department of Health (Australia) 2018), although Tune (2017: 80) recommended that the full value be included (where it is not excluded by virtue of a 'protected person').

While there are significant similarities between social care in England and Australia, not least that both are subject to a means test and are distinct from health care, more health care appears to be subject to patient contributions in Australia by virtue of the Medicare system.[15] As Carney (2014: 19–20) puts it, 'Australia operates a publicly funded, universal system of medical benefits known as Medicare, principally funded by the federal government', albeit via a levy imposed on taxpayers in a certain income bracket. Medicare 'reimburses medical providers a "scheduled fee" component of medical costs, and funds state and territory governments under a cost-sharing agreement to provide hospitals and other infrastructure'. The percentage of the fee reimbursed varies according to the cost and type of medical treatment.

Conversely, the National Disability Insurance Scheme (NDIS) could be an important source of support in Australia.[16] The scheme, piloted in 2013 by the federal Government in partnership with States, seeks to 'provide more-flexible funding support (not means-tested), allowing greater tailoring of services' (Glover). The aim of the NDIS is to 'provide no-fault insurance cover for Australians who are born with or acquire a severe or profound disability' (Green and Mears 2014: 25). One description is that '[u]nder the NDIS, anyone under the age of 65 and with a disability that is permanent, or likely to become permanent, and significant will be eligible for the NDIS', subject to immigration status (Cebulla and Zhu 2016: 257).[17] Funding for the NDIS was provided by an increase in the Medicare levy (Walsh and Johnson 2013).

Windholz (2014: 89) has said that the NDIS 'revolutionises the provision of services to persons with disabilities', and that '[t]he cornerstone of the scheme … is the provision to persons with disabilities of greater choice and control over the support they receive'. The system appears similar to NHS Continuing Healthcare, albeit on a more generous scale, with an emphasis on personalisation.

It therefore seems that there is an attempt to distinguish age- from disability-related care in Australia, more so than within England. Wark (2015: 93–96)

[15] Health Insurance Act 1973; Minford (2001).
[16] National Disability Insurance Scheme Act 2013.
[17] See further National Disability Insurance Scheme Act 2013, s 22.

asserts that 'the issue of ageing with a disability does not appear to have been appropriately considered in the … NDIS legislation', such that '[t]here remains a divide between aged-care support options predominantly funded by the Commonwealth Government and disability services auspiced through the various states'. He asserts that

> [u]nder the NDIS legislation, individuals with disability who are ageing will be able to maintain their disability support programs or can convert to the mainstream aged-care support model once they reach 65 years of age, but the policy framework indicates that a person must choose one system or the other, as supplementary funding support to address emerging needs associated with ageing is not possible.

He thus claims that '[t]he integration between the social and healthcare systems in the UK and Ireland was better managed than in Australia', although it has been seen that the relationship between the NHS and social care has created significant issues. There are fears that

> [t]he introduction of the … NDIS … with its principle of entitlement to services based on need means that specialist disability services may be more freely available to younger people than to older Australians (those aged 65 or older) with the same disability and need. (National Aged Care Alliance, 2016: 5)

Similarly to the situation in England,

> [t]he different roles and responsibility for medical, ageing and disability related aids and equipment continues to confuse consumers, whose eligibility, access and out-of-pocket costs will differ depending on where they live, their age and which service system they are able to access. (ibid: 28)

Whatever the differences of detail, there are thus a number of common themes within the Australian and English systems: means-tested social care systems in broad contrast to health care systems, with wealthy people expected to contribute significant amounts to their care, credible allegations of discrimination and inequity of provision within the system, and an attempt to personalise services (Glover). The common feature that will form the background of the remainder of this chapter, however, is the sense that there should be some limitation on the amount that any individual should be expected to pay for her formal care, even if this feature is in some doubt in England, and even though Tune (2017: 9) when reviewing the Australian 2013 Act recommended that 'the annual and lifetime caps for fees should be abolished' to 'ensure that consumers contribute to the costs of their care commensurate with both their care needs and relative financial capacity'. He was concerned that '[t]he caps limit the amount that wealthier consumers contribute to their care costs, after which taxpayers effectively subsidise the full cost of their care' (ibid: 84), albeit that in England such arguments have been met with objections relating to the possibility that catastrophic costs will be imposed on some people and that discrimination will operate between those who require different types of care. The next section will consider the recognition of *informal* care in *private* law.

III. Informal Care

A. England

Despite the existence of a social care system, there are around 5.8 million informal carers in England and Wales (Office for National Statistics 2013). Such carers vitally provide support to elderly and disabled people in the absence of a contractual or other legal duty to do so,[18] and the majority of elderly people receiving care in their own homes do so from family members (Pickard 2015). The reasons for this are likely to include the social care system being unable to provide the required support, the costs associated with social care (discussed in the last section), and resistance to leaving one's home and/or 'official' involvement in one's care (Sloan 2013: chapter 1). The Government seems to have accepted that some responsibility for care should, or at least will inevitably, rest with family members (Swinford 2017; Sloan 2015; Conservatives 2017: 60), particularly in the aftermath of the much-anticipated 'Brexit' (Allegretti 2018).

Such carers do have some recognition in public law (Herring 2013), despite the fact that their work may well be located in the 'private' sphere because of its nature. The Care Act 2014, for example, created 'the first ever entitlement to support for carers' (Department of Health 2014a). My previous work, however, has considered the extent to which carers do or should nevertheless have a claim against the property and/or estate of a care recipient in recognition of their efforts and the fiscal and health disadvantages that they suffer (Sloan 2013 and 2015), and an aim of this chapter is to assess whether such a claim is appropriate in light of the possible moves towards limiting liability of care recipients to pay for *formal* care. This will be placed in the context of the wide recognition of caring relationships in Australian private law, addressed in the next sub-section.

Proprietary estoppel is an equitable doctrine that has been used to facilitate claims by informal carers against care recipients or their estates (McFarlane 2014). An estoppel claim arises where:

> The owner of land [or other property], A, in some way leads or allows the claimant, B, to believe that he has or can expect some kind of right or interest over A's [property]. To A's knowledge, B acts to his detriment in that belief. A then refuses B the anticipated right or interest in circumstances that make that refusal unconscionable (HM Land Registry and Law Commission: [5.29]).

Lord Walker (2008: 234) has said that '[i]n modern authorities the [estoppel] claimant's case is usually founded … on [his] personal assistance to the defendant', and there have been a number of successful estoppel claims involving informal

[18] See Herring (2013: ch 2) for a discussion of the difficulties relating to definitions in this context.

carers (Sloan 2013: chapter 2). Claims are often brought after the death of the representor, for example on the basis that the care recipient promised to leave property to the claimant in a will but failed (whether accidentally or deliberately) to do so.

Proprietary estoppel is controversial because of uncertainties surrounding its requirements, and because it circumvents the usual restrictions placed upon a valid contract, a valid disposition of an interest in land and a valid will (ibid; Dixon 2010).[19] It is nevertheless well-established, and does provide a remedy for some carers. That said, the doctrine is limited to the enforcement of promises or expectations somehow generated by the care recipient.[20]

It might be assumed that a remedy could readily be sought by an informal carer on the basis that the care recipient was unjustly enriched by the services provided (Nield 2007). Even so, the possibility of using the principles of unjust enrichment to claim a remedy for caring or other domestic services, such as a quantum meruit calculated according to their reasonable value,[21] remains controversial in England (Sloan 2013: chapter 4).[22] It is relatively well-established that, in England, a successful unjust enrichment claim involves the enrichment of the defendant at the expense of the claimant in particular circumstances rendering the enrichment unjust and where there are no defences.[23]

Even if it can be shown that the care recipient was enriched at his expense (Sloan 2013: chapter 4), the claimant carer must still identify the relevant unjust factor through which restitution of unjust enrichment can be sought.[24] This is not an easy task, and Wells (2007: 69) argues that that 'the courts have not always scrupled to identify the unjust factor present in more recent quantum meruit cases'. Several factors could be relevant (Sloan 2013: 124–28), but a fundamental difficulty faced by the carer who seeks a remedy is that in many situations he can plausibly be described as a 'domestic risk-taker' (Mee 2009: 374).[25] In other words, it could often be said that he voluntarily assumed caring responsibilities without entering a contract, and 'gambled' (Burrows 1988) on the care recipient's

[19] On the advantages of the statutory approach of the Law Reform (Testamentary Promises) Act 1949 in New Zealand, see, eg, Sloan (2013: ch 3).

[20] *cf* Sloan (2013: ch 8).

[21] *cf*, eg, Havelock (2016).

[22] *cf* the antiquated cases on the provision of urgent medical treatment for 'paupers', eg, *Lamb v Bunce* (1815) 4 M & S 275, (1815) 105 ER 836 (KB).

[23] *Banque Financière de la Cité v Parc (Battersea) Ltd* [1999] 1 AC 221 (HL), 227 (Lord Steyn). *cf Investment Trust Companies (In Liquidation) v Revenue and Customs Commissioners* [2012] EWHC 458 (Ch); *cf* Birks (2005) on 'absence of basis' as the justification for an unjust enrichment claim. For a discussion of possible defences to an unjust enrichment claim, see, eg, Mitchell, Mitchell and Watterson (2016: part 6).

[24] See, eg, *Deutsche Morgan Grenfell v Inland Revenue Commissioners* [2006] UKHL 49 [21] (Lord Hoffmann).

[25] For a devastating critique of the language of 'risk-taking' in the law of unjust enrichment, see Wilmot-Smith (2011).

willingness to pay for his services after the event. Virgo (2015: 36–37) considers it a fundamental principle that where a claimant has acted officiously in transferring a benefit, the law of unjust enrichment will not come to his aid.[26]

It can be concluded that a carer is likely to encounter difficulty in utilising the English law of unjust enrichment at present. *Walsh v Singh*,[27] a case involving the property and business affairs of former fiancés, could be illustrative of the current attitude of the English judiciary to the use of unjust enrichment in the domestic context. Without discussing particular unjust factors, Judge Purle QC expressed concern that

> [i]f dashed expectations of a long-term domestic relationship open the door to unjust enrichment claims, a wide range of claims which the concept of unjust enrichment was never meant, and is ill equipped, to deal with will come marching through'.[28]

It may be possible to distinguish care cases from *Walsh v Singh*, but it is conceivable that Judge Purle QC's more general statement will become influential.

Succession law is a possible basis of claim for an informal carer, although the basic principle of English succession law is that that 'an Englishman still remains at liberty at his death to dispose of his own property in whatever way he pleases'.[29] No family member or carer of any sort has an inherent right to provision from an estate. That said, the Inheritance (Provision for Family and Dependants) Act 1975 allows certain people to seek discretionary provision out of the estate (Sloan 2017a: chapter 9). One such category (in section 1(1)(e) of the Act) is a person who was maintained by the deceased, even if he did not have another familial or conjugal relationship with the deceased. Early section 1(1)(e) case law was prejudicial to carers because care was considered 'full valuable consideration' for the carer's maintenance, which eliminated the claim.[30] While amendments to the Act now make clear that 'full valuable consideration' applies only to arrangements of a commercial nature,[31] the category is inherently premised on a requirement that the *deceased* (care recipient in our context) maintained the *claimant* (carer) rather than the other way around.

Adult children[32] and people whom the deceased treated as a 'child of the family' notwithstanding they were not legal children of the deceased[33] are also included among the categories of applicant, albeit that (in common with those who are not spouses or civil partners of the deceased)[34] they must show that 'the

[26] See also, eg, *Deutsche Morgan Grenfell v Inland Revenue Commissioners* [2006] UKHL 49, at [25]–[27] (Lord Hoffmann).

[27] *Walsh v Singh* [2009] EWHC 3219 (Ch).

[28] ibid [67].

[29] *Re Coventry (decd)* [1980] Ch 461, 474 (Oliver J).

[30] Inheritance (Provision for Family and Dependants) Act 1975, original s 1(3); see, eg, *Re Wilkinson (deceased)* [1978] Fam 22.

[31] Inheritance (Provision for Family and Dependants) Act 1975, s 1(3), as amended by the Inheritance and Trustees' Powers Act 2014.

[32] Inheritance (Provision for Family and Dependants) Act 1975, s 1(1)(c).

[33] Inheritance (Provision for Family and Dependants) Act 1975, s 1(1)(d).

[34] *cf* Inheritance (Provision for Family and Dependants) Act 1975, s 1(2)(a)-(aa).

disposition of the deceased's estate effected by his will or the law relating to intestacy, or the combination of his will and that law, is not such as to make reasonable financial provision' for the applicant's *maintenance*.[35] In deciding both whether this is the case and what provision should be made, the court will take into account a wide range of factors.[36]

Of course, many carers will be able to demonstrate a relevant need for maintenance that might justify provision from the former care recipient's estate,[37] and one of the strongest justifications for a private law remedy is that the carer will have suffered disadvantages generating such a need (Sloan 2013: chapter 5). The leading case on the 1975 Act, however, is the Supreme Court's recent decision is *Ilott v The Blue Cross*.[38] It involved a claim by a daughter who had been *estranged* from her mother for some 26 years before the mother's death. The daughter and her family were dependent on state benefits, but had her substantial award reduced back to £50,000 by the Supreme Court. Significantly, Lord Hughes contrasted the facts of the current case with a hypothetical one involving a

> claimant … child of the deceased who had remained exceptionally and confidentially close to her mother throughout, had supported and nurtured her in her old age at some cost in time and money to herself, and … had been promised many times that she would be looked after in the will.[39]

While 'adhering to the concept of maintenance', he opined that 'a judge ought in such circumstances to attach importance to the closeness of the relationship in arriving at his assessment of what reasonable financial provision requires'.[40] That said, he was also anxious that 'care must be taken to avoid making awards under the 1975 Act primarily rewards for good behaviour on the part of the claimant or penalties for bad on the part of the deceased'.[41] The requirement to show a need for maintenance inevitably means that some carers will be unable to secure any provision even if they fall within an eligible category of applicant.

Given that English Law is already content to interfere with testamentary freedom for several reasons and for a wide range of applicants (Herring 2016a), reform in this area should be seriously considered.

In contrast to the wide range of applicants who can claim statutory property or financial provision from an estate, only (at least purported or former) spouses (who can be any combination of genders)[42] or same-sex civil partners,[43] and

[35] Inheritance (Provision for Family and Dependants) Act 1975, ss 1(1), 1(2)(b).
[36] Inheritance (Provision for Family and Dependants) Act 1975, s 3.
[37] See, eg, *Re Jennings* [1994] Ch 286 (CA), 300; *Estate of McGarrell* [1983] 8 NIJB; *Re Callaghan (deceased)* [1985] Fam 1.
[38] *Ilott v The Blue Cross* [2017] UKSC 17, [2018] AC 545. See, generally, Sloan (2019).
[39] [2017] UKSC 17 [35].
[40] ibid.
[41] ibid [47].
[42] See, eg, Matrimonial Causes Act 1973, Part II.
[43] See, eg, Civil Partnership Act 2004, sch 5.

usually minor children (or at least those still in education)[44] can claim similar provision while the defendant is still alive (Sloan 2013: chapter 6). As might be expected, those within the prohibited degrees of relationship (including parents and children) are prevented from entering a valid marriage or civil partnership,[45] notwithstanding the attempt to remove the degrees from the Civil Partnership Bill as it passed through Parliament (Glennon 2005).[46] Moreover, child support plays a very limited role once the child in question reaches 18 (Masson, Bailey-Harris and Probert 2008: [15-032]). The prospects for a caring adult child bringing a successful *inter vivos* statutory claim are therefore very slight and they are essentially non-existent for other non-spouses/civil partners. It should be noted that even conjugal cohabitants are denied such a statutory claim in their own right (Sloan 2015a), and changing this may well be seen as a priority (Law Commission 2002 and 2006).

The focus on conjugality and countervailing failure to prioritise care per se in English family law has been criticised (Herring 2013: chapter 6), and is not consistent with all other jurisdictions (including in Australia, as will be seen in the next sub-section). That said, statutory *inter vivos* claims by carers may not reflect public expectations (Peart 2008),[47] and bring additional difficulties as compared to succession-based claims in light of the care recipient's continued need of her property and the awkwardness that such a claim might cause within a caring relationship (Sloan 2013: 138–39). The recognition of caring relationships in Australia ought now to be considered.

B. Australia

As in England, despite the availability of social care, informal carers play a vital role in Australia. It has been said that '[m]ost aged care is informal, provided by families, friends, communities and volunteers' (Tune 2017: 6), and one study found that 92 per cent of 'people living in their own homes with severe or profound limitations in core activities receive informal care', with '[t]hirty-eight percent receiv[ing] only informal assistance and 54 percent receiv[ing] a combination of informal and formal assistance' (Glover). Conversely, '[a]pproximately 2.3 million people provide some informal care of the aged' and '[i]n 2009, 12 percent of Australians were informal caregivers and around 30 percent of those were the primary caregiver [carer]'.

[44] Child Support Act 1991; Children Act 1989, sch 1.

[45] Matrimonial Causes Act 1973, s 11(a)(i); Civil Partnership Act 2004, s 3(1)(d).

[46] A similar attempt was made while the Marriage (Same Sex Couples) Bill passed through: Hansard, 24 June 2013, Volume 746, Cols 525–547.

[47] *cf* Briggs (2015: 670).

Public state support for carers is available, for example in the form of the 'carer payment' and 'carer allowance' and covering both children and adults.[48] In 2011–12, the federal government 'provided AUD3.18 billion (USD2.07 billion) under the income-tested Carer Payment program, and AUD1.75 billion (USD1.14 billion) through the Carer Allowance (not income-tested, and offered as a supplement for daily care)' (Glover). The Government 'also provides an annual Carer Supplement of AUD480 million (USD313 million) to help with the cost of caring'.

In a number of Australian States and Territories, however, caring relationships are recognised on a similar basis to other adult relationships, such as marital or de facto (ie conjugal cohabitational) ones. This includes recognition in succession law (National Committee on Uniform Succession Laws 2004: 7 fn 42), in contrast to the piecemeal and non-tailored approach of English Law considered above. On Wong's (2009: 53) account, the Australian Capital Territory's Domestic Relationships Act 1994 was 'the first sub-national legislation to shift the focus of domestic relationships from status to interdependency'. It was described as 'representing a movement towards a more fluid concept of relationships governed by redistributive law',[49] including non-couple relationships where care and support was present.[50] Other Australian States and Territories have similarly gone further than England and Wales by specifically recognising the relationship between carer and care recipient on a basis similar to that between conjugal couples (married or unmarried).[51]

The New South Wales concept of a 'close personal relationship', introduced in 1999[52] and now governed by the Succession Act 2006 in the succession law context,[53] would provide something of a solution to the problems currently faced by carers under the English 1975 Act (and private law in general). It is apparently backward- rather than forward-looking, at least as regards eligibility,[54] which means that a 'pure' carer without another relationship with the care recipient is nevertheless likely to fall within the parameters of the category based on what he has done for the deceased in the past.

A 'close personal relationship' exists

> between two adult persons [who are not in a marriage or de facto relationship with each other], whether or not related by family, who are living together, one or each of whom provides the other with domestic support and personal care.[55]

[48] Social Security Act 1991, Part 2.5.
[49] *McKenzie v Storer* [2007] ACTSC 88 [57] (Stone J).
[50] Domestic Relationships Act 1994 Act (ACT), s 3.
[51] See, eg, Relationships Amendment (Caring Relationships) Act 2009 (Vic).
[52] Property (Relationships) Legislation Amendment Act 1999 (NSW).
[53] *cf* Family Provision Act 1982 (NSW), s 6(1)(a)(ii).
[54] *cf* Sloan (2013: section 5.4.10).
[55] Succession Act 2006 (NSW), s 3(3) (as amended).

A claim is precluded, however, if the domestic support or personal care is provided 'for fee or reward' or 'on behalf of another person or an organisation (including a government or government agency, a body corporate or a charitable or benevolent organisation)'.[56] The 'close personal relationship' must exist at the time of death.

One restriction in the amended Succession Act 2006 is that applicants who invoke the 'close personal relationship' provision are not eligible as of right, and must convince the court that 'having regard to all the circumstances of the case (whether past or present) there are factors which warrant the making of the application'.[57] In relation to other claimant categories, the courts require 'good and sufficient grounds for the application'.[58] A significant amount of care should constitute a factor warranting the application, not least because it has been allowed to do so in applications by dependants.[59] Significantly, in *Estate MPS*, there were said to be 'factors warranting' an application despite the fact that the 'care' provided was held to be 'inappropriate and inadequate',[60] which arguably raises issues concerning what might be called the 'dark side' of care.

Interestingly, the court is permitted to have regard to the same list of factors when determining whether an applicant is an eligible person as when it is exercising its discretion on determining the relief to be granted.[61] This discretionary approach appears open-ended.[62]

The 'close personal relationship' is composed of a number of elements. Notwithstanding the fact that the deceased and the applicant must have been 'living together', in *Hayes v Marquis* the Court of Appeal of New South Wales has accepted that the parties to a close personal relationship do not have to do so on a full-time basis.[63] McColl JA suggested that the common residence requirement might be 'somewhat more attenuated' for the purposes of a close personal relationship than for a de facto relationship between cohabitants.[64] This is significant, since it is not strictly necessary even for de facto partners to share a household to qualify for provision in New South Wales. That said, Einstein J considered it important that the parties regard the place they live together as 'their home', even if family or work commitments sometimes required them to leave it.[65] Moreover, the 'domestic support' requirement was said to underline the notion of a shared household.[66]

[56] Succession Act 2006 (NSW), s 3(4). A carer's pension is not a relevant fee or reward: *Woodland v Rodriguez* [2004] NSWSC 1167.
[57] Succession Act 2006 (NSW), s 59(1)(b).
[58] *O'Shaughnessy v Mantle* (1986) 7 NSWLR 142, 146 (Young J).
[59] *Blackley v Proctor* [2001] NSWSC 537; *Barlevy v Nadolski* [2011] NSWSC 129 [199] (Slattery J).
[60] *Estate MPS, deceased* [2017] NSWSC 482 [107] (Lindsay J).
[61] Succession Act 2006 (NSW), s 60(1)(a).
[62] *cf* Victorian Law Reform Commission (2013: ch 6).
[63] *Hayes v Marquis* [2008] NSWCA 10 [78].
[64] ibid [79].
[65] ibid [166].
[66] ibid [76] (McColl JA).

In *Dridi v Filmore*, it was confirmed that the domestic support and personal care requirements were cumulative, increasing the sense in which the legislation recognises care per se.[67] There is, however, an inevitable overlap between the concepts. In *Hayes*, the phrase 'domestic support' was not held to 'occasion any particular questions of ambiguity'.[68] The Attorney General, in the debates leading to the passing of the 1999 reforms, opined that such support consisted of 'attending to the household shopping, cleaning, laundry and like activities'.[69]

The 'personal care' requirement, crucial for present purposes, has been a source of greater difficulty. The Supreme Court of New South Wales originally interpreted 'personal care' to mean 'assistance with mobility, personal hygiene and physical comfort', with the result that emotional support in itself was insufficient.[70] The effect of this, according to Graycar and Millbank (2007: 149), was to turn the concept into 'one addressing only (unpaid) live-in caregivers'. The Law Reform Commission (2006: [3.10]) proclaimed that: 'The "personal care" element is not easy to satisfy.' In one case, the performance of housework and the transporting of the deceased to medical appointments was not sufficient to constitute 'personal care'.[71] In another, '[t]he fact that the appellant provided … support for weekly periods over … 15 months did not constitute the relationship as one that involved the closeness or intimacy necessary for a close personal relationship'.[72] It is clear that a certain amount of domestic support and care is needed before the statute is engaged. In the opinion of McColl JA in *Hayes*, 'if two adults lived together full-time and one provided domestic support and personal care to the other only once or twice a year, it would be difficult to say that a close personal relationship had been established'.[73]

A carer who provides a significant level of care is unlikely to have any difficulty in satisfying the 'domestic support' and 'personal care' criteria provided he can demonstrate a sufficiently shared household. Moreover, the courts have shown themselves to be willing to infer that care has taken place.[74]

The Succession Act 2006 (taking up the mantle of the previous Family Provision Act 1982) is an important example of how family provision law can specifically address scenarios involving care in order to provide a remedy for informal carers. Nevertheless, although the category apparently prevents a gap in the legislation, the New South Wales Law Reform Commission (2006) reports that few cases have been brought by people in 'close personal relationships' and that such claims tend to be presented as falling within another category. This would not, however, detract

[67] *Dridi v Filmore* [2001] NSWSC 319 [104] (Master Macready).
[68] *Hayes v Marquis* [2008] NSWCA 10 [167] (Einstein J).
[69] New South Wales Legislative Council, Parliamentary Debates, (Hansard) 13 May 1999, 228.
[70] *Dridi v Filmore* [2001] NSWSC 319 [108] (Master Macready). It was accepted, however, that such activities would 'include an element of emotional support'.
[71] *Bogan v Macorig* [2004] NSWSC 993.
[72] *Amprimo v Wynn* [2015] NSWCA 286 [79] (Meagher JA).
[73] *Hayes v Marquis* [2008] NSWCA 10 [84].
[74] *Hughes v Charlton* [2008] NSWSC 467 [55].

from the justice served by such a provision if it were introduced in England. This is particularly true given the problems caused by the 'maintenance' point associated with dependency discussed above, and by the focus on conjugality and living in the same household in the case of cohabitants. In the previous edition of his book, Kerridge (2009: [8–79]) hints at the possible need to recognise carers specifically when he argues that a cohabitant of the deceased is in a privileged position as compared to a sibling who provides care, although he points out that such a sibling will often be provided for under the intestacy rules.

In the New South Wales context, the 'close personal relationship' category has sometimes proved vital in cases where an applicant has been unable to bring himself within one of the other categories, and it has been said it is not possible for the same two people to be in both a de facto relationship and a 'close personal relationship' simultaneously.[75] In *Hughes v Charlton*, for example, 'the evidence point[ed] to the [applicant] being a housekeeper for the deceased', and the applicant was therefore eligible only as a result of the 'close personal relationship' category.[76] Admittedly, difficult definitional problems would have to be addressed, as illustrated by the New South Wales experience itself (Head 2011). Nevertheless, that is an inevitable feature of discretionary schemes regulating informal relationships and should not preclude an attempt at reform in England.

On a more principled level, the advent of a 'carer' category in England could be met with the objection that it would effectively introduce almost diametrically opposite categories of applicant into the 1975 Act. This allegation is justified to an extent, since one category would be based on the fact that the applicant was dependent on the deceased, and another is effectively based on the fact that the *deceased* was dependent on the *applicant* (albeit in a different sense). Nevertheless, the New South Wales legislature was apparently content to place both categories in its Act. It is worth noting that in the case of 'close personal relationships' the care recipient is equally eligible to bring a claim on the estate of the carer.[77] This reflects the reality of interdependence that is often present between the parties to such relationships, and Herring (2007) points out that it can be difficult to determine which party is the carer and which the care recipient.[78] The categories of the dependant and the party to a close personal relationship may be more consistent with each other than they first appear.

Moreover, given the repugnance expressed by some commentators about the idea that a slothful individual is more likely to succeed under the 1975 Act than an industrious one, the introduction of an opposing category could nevertheless be a positive development.

[75] *Thompson v The Public Trustee of New South Wales* [2010] NSWSC 1137 [69] (Hallen AsJ).

[76] [2008] NSWSC 467 [47] (Macready AsJ). See also *Smith v Daniels* [2010] NSWSC 604.

[77] See, eg, *Woodland v Rodriguez* [2004] NSWSC 1167.

[78] *cf* Wells (2007a: 319), who argues that 'the provision of caring services will frequently be a one-sided arrangement'.

A 'carer' category could also shift the emphasis away from maintenance and future need. Since there is not always a direct connection between work done in the past and the present need for maintenance, the new category could be more about remuneration. This echoes the emphasis on desert present in some of Fineman's (2004) writings.[79] If the sole aim of statutory family provision is to allow the continuation of maintenance, a new category is not necessarily consistent with it. On the other hand, if the aim of such statutes could be reformulated as the encouragement and fostering of domestic support in general, a 'carer' category would simply extend this aim to include the provision of such support before death.

Unfortunately, the English Law Commission (2011: [6.92]) purposely rejected the inclusion of carers as a specific category of family provision applicant in their recent report on intestacy and family provision. It argued that outside cases of carers who were maintained by the deceased (who would be able to apply under the existing legislation), there are difficulties in 'identifying precisely who was to benefit and why'. Examples of problems given by the Commission are the level of care required (and how much entitlement it would bring), and the correct approach where another family member or friend was prevented from caring by the applicant. These are significant issues, but it is not clear that the relevant amount of care is any more difficult a question than the extent to which the deceased maintained an applicant or treated him as a child of the family (already crucial aspects of English family provision law). Moreover, the quantum of provision is separated from eligibility throughout the rest of the Act, and it is surprising that the Law Commission conflated the two matters as regards carers. Given that New South Wales and other jurisdictions have found methods of including carers within family provision, it is regrettable that the Commission did not explicitly adopt a comparative approach when swiftly rejecting the specific inclusion of carers.

As well as bringing a family provision claim, parties to 'close personal relationships' in New South Wales can secure orders to redistribute property if the relationship breaks down while both parties are still alive.[80] In spite of these *inter vivos* remedies, according to the Law Reform Commission (2006: [3.22]),

> [i]n most cases, such relationships are likely to end with the death of the person being cared for, in which case the person who has taken care of the other may have recourse against the estate if they feel they were not adequately provided for.

Hayes v Marquis involved an *inter vivos* claim in which the parties were held to be in a 'close personal relationship'. Nevertheless, it is significant that the relationship later met the criteria for a 'de facto' relationship.[81]

[79] *cf* Fineman (2008).

[80] Property (Relationships) Act 1984 (NSW); See New South Wales Law Commission (2006: [3.26]–[3.35]) for discussion.

[81] See also *Burgess v Moss* [2010] NSWCA 139.

The apparent rarity of *inter vivos* claims in genuine care situations, even where such claims are possible, adds weight to the appropriateness of family provision law in providing a remedy for the carer. The specific advantages of succession law cannot be applied to *inter vivos* provision, not least because the care recipient still has need of her property and the parties do not necessarily expect their property to be regulated in such a way while they are still alive. An approach based on family provision is therefore a preferable remedy, even if an *inter vivos* solution has the potential advantage of remedying the detriment suffered by the carer at an earlier stage.

The Relationships Act 2003 (Tasmania) provides an alternative model with its concept of 'caring relationships'.[82] These are defined using similar terms to the New South Wales 'close personal relationships', but with a non-exhaustive checklist to aid in determining whether a 'caring relationship' exists.[83] The Act similarly enables those in caring relationships to apply for property adjustment and maintenance on the breakdown of their relationships.[84]

Caring relationships can be registered in Tasmania.[85] Registration is conclusive as regards the existence of the relationship,[86] eliminating the need to resort to the checklist. The registration of a relationship also permits access to a wider range of benefits than if it is unregistered, and still more benefits remain reserved for registered couples in a conjugal relationship (Graycar and Millbank 2007). Independent legal advice is required before registration can occur,[87] and it must relate to both 'the effect of the registration … on the rights of the parties'[88] and 'the advantages and disadvantages, at the time that the advice was provided, to the party of registering a deed of relationship'.[89] A considerable limitation is that the parties will not be able to register unless each of them can declare that he/she is unmarried and not a party to a 'significant' (ie de facto conjugal) relationship or another 'caring' relationship, whether registered or unregistered.[90]

In the first three years of the operation of the Tasmanian Act, no 'caring relationships' were registered (Graycar and Millbank 2007), and although Rundle (2011) records four such registrations by 2011, the Tasmanian registry of births, marriages and deaths reported no more by October 2017.[91] Graycar and Millbank (2007: 150–53) suggest that the limited take-up could indicate the redundancy of the provisions, and claim that there is 'no empirical evidence to demonstrate an unmet legal need for any broadly-based recognition of

[82] Relationships Act 2003 (Tas), s 5.
[83] Relationships Act 2003 (Tas), s 5(5).
[84] Relationships Act 2003 (Tas), part 5.
[85] Relationships Act 2003 (Tas), s 11.
[86] Relationships Act 2003 (Tas), s 5(4).
[87] Relationships Act 2003 (Tas), s 11(3).
[88] Relationships Act 2003 (Tas), 11(3)(a).
[89] Relationships Act 2003 (Tas), s 11(3)(b). See Rundle (2011) for criticism.
[90] Relationships Act 2003 (Tas), s 11(2)(a).
[91] Personal correspondence with the author.

non-couple relationships'. On the other hand, they also admit that lack of public information could be a factor, and many of the general problems with opt-in schemes for unmarried cohabitants are likely to apply in this context (Law Commission 2007; Scherpe 2005) alongside the inherent informality of large numbers of caring relationships.

The Tasmanian experience did not prevent Victoria from enacting a similar registration scheme in 2009.[92] New South Wales, on the other hand, appears to have excluded 'close personal relationships' from its registration scheme for couples[93] in spite of the Law Reform Commission's (2006) recommendations.

In any case, exclusive registration-based schemes for the recognition of carer relationships compound the general difficulties with *inter vivos* remedies (Sloan 2013: section 5.2; Glennon 2005: 144–45).[94] It may therefore be the case that recognition for particular purposes, such as family provision law, is preferable. Whatever the particular model adopted, it seems tolerably clear that the recognition of care in private law is much more rational and tailored in Australia than it is in England.

IV. Synthesis and Conclusion

This chapter has sought to consider the recognition and funding of formal care (broadly associated with the public sphere) and informal care (broadly associated with the private sphere) in England and Australia. It is noteworthy that both England and Australia have considered a capping process on formal care (albeit that the process is apparently complete in Australia but remains controversial there and has a particularly uncertain future in England as of September 2018), but that New South Wales (for example) is much more rational in its recognition of caring relationships, and that this was the case long before the capping process undertaken in the 2013 Act.

The scope for any successful private law claim could be increased by the needs as well as resources of a care recipient in a manner that I have suggested is undesirable in the case of formal care. That said, a distinction could perhaps be made with regard to informal care where it concerns a genuine caring *relationship*, whereby care is not merely a service provided by the state (funded by the anonymous taxpayer) to an individual but part of the ubiquitous exchanges involved in everyday life. The argument might run that if we are content to mandate transfers between private individuals consequent on relationships, particularly where one of the parties has died, care would be an

[92] Relationships Amendment (Caring Relationships) Act 2009 (Vic), amending Relationships Act 2008 (Vic).

[93] Relationships Register Act 2010 (NSW).

[94] See Rundle (2011) for a general discussion of registration schemes.

appropriate principle upon which to base such transfers (Sloan 2013). This would fit with Herring's (2013; also Chapter nine this volume) advocacy of a relational approach to care. It could also be said that the mere fact that liability to pay for formal care might be *limited* does not mean that there should be no liability to pay for it at all, and that appropriating the unpaid labour of a devoted carer is not always a legitimate means of avoiding paying for one's care. That said, it is important that private transfers of property are not seen as an excuse for the state to abdicate its responsibilities to address the conundrum of care and provide adequately for the needs of its citizens (Sloan 2015).

References

Age UK (2016) '1.2m older people don't get the social care they need', available online at: www.ageuk.org.uk/latest-news/archive/12m-older-people-dont-get-the-social-care-they-need/ (accessed 25 September 2017).

Aged Care Financing Authority (2017) 'Report to inform the 2016–17 review of amendments to the Aged Care Act 1997'.

Allegretti, A (2018) 'Women may have to quit jobs to fill care roles post-Brexit, report warns', *Sky News* (6 August 2018), available online at: news.sky.com/story/women-may-have-to-quit-jobs-to-fill-care-roles-post-brexit-report-warns-11463021 (accessed 25 September 2018).

Asthana, A (2017) 'Theresa May will not reveal social care cap before general election', *The Guardian* (28 May 2017), available online at: www.theguardian.com/society/2017/may/28/theresa-may-will-not-reveal-social-care-cap-before-general-election (accessed 25 September 2018).

Baxter, K (2016) 'Self-funders and social care: findings from a scoping review' *Research, Policy and Planning* 31: 179.

BBC News (2017) '£72,500 social care cap to be scrapped, MPs told' (7 December 2017), available online at: www.bbc.co.uk/news/uk-politics-42266076 (accessed 25 September 2018).

Bilton, K (2014) 'Care Arrangements: Who Cares? Who Pays?' *Bulletin of the Social Work History Network* 1: 14.

Birks, P (2005) *Unjust Enrichment*, 2nd edn (Oxford, Clarendon Press).

Briggs, M (2015) 'Rethinking Relationships' *Victoria University of Wellington Law Review* 46: 649.

Burrows, A (1988) 'Free Acceptance and the Law of Restitution' *Law Quarterly Review* 104: 576.

Campbell, D (2017) 'Hammond's budget bows to demands for social care cash injection', *The Guardian* (8 March 2017), available online at: www.theguardian.com/uk-news/2017/mar/08/hammonds-budget-bows-to-demands-for-social-care-cash-injection (accessed 25 September 2018).

Carney, T (2014) 'Where Now Australia's Welfare Stare?' Sydney Law School Research Paper No 14/89.

Cebulla, A and Zhu, R (2016) 'Disability, and social and economic inclusion: who is in and out of the Australian National Disability Insurance Scheme?' *Scandinavian Journal of Disability Research* 256.

Commission on Funding of Care and Support (2011) *Fairer Care Funding.*

Conservatives (2017) 'Our Manifesto', available online at: www.conservatives.com/manifesto (accessed 25 September 2018).

Department of Health (2015) *The Care Act 2014: Consultation on Draft Regulations and Guidance to Implement the Cap on Care Costs and Policy Proposals for a New Appeals System for Care and Support.*

—— (2014) *Review of Care Products – Key Messages.*

—— (2014a) *Factsheet 2.*

—— (2018) 'Care and Support Statutory Guidance', available online at: www.gov.uk/guidance/care-and-support-statutory-guidance (accessed 25 September 2018).

Department of Health (Australia) (2018) 'Schedule of Fees and Charges: From 1 July 2018', available online at: agedcare.health.gov.au/sites/g/files/net1426/f/documents/06_2018/schedule_of_fees_and_charges_for_residential_and_home_care.pdf (accessed 25 September 2018).

Dixon, M (2010) 'Confining and Defining Proprietary Estoppel: The Role of Unconscionability' *Legal Studies* 30: 408.

Elgot, J (2017) 'We cannot afford to fund "dementia tax" proposals, councils warn', *The Guardian* (17 October 2017), available online at: www.theguardian.com/society/2017/oct/17/we-cannot-afford-to-fund-dementia-tax-proposals-councils-warn (accessed 25 September 2018).

Fernández, J-L and Nadash, P (2016) 'The Long-term Care Financing Problem' in C Gori et al (eds), *Long-term Care Reforms in OECD Countries: Successes and Failures* (Bristol, Policy Press).

Fineman, MA (2004) *The Autonomy Myth: A Theory of Dependency* (New York, New Press).

—— (2008) 'The Vulnerable Subject: Anchoring Equality in the Human Condition' *Yale Journal of Law and Feminism* 20: 1.

Full Fact (2017) 'The adult social care spending gap', available online at: fullfact.org/health/adult-social-care-spending-gap/ (accessed 25 September 2018).

Glover, L 'The Australian Health Care System' (Commonwealth Fund), available online at: international.commonwealthfund.org/countries/australia/ (accessed 25 September 2018).

Graycar, R and Millbank, J (2007) 'From Functional Family to Spinster Sisters: Australia's Distinctive Path to Relationship Recognition' *Washington University Journal of Law and Policy* 24: 121.

Green J and Mears, J (2014) 'The Implementation of the NDIS: Who Wins, Who Loses?' *Cosmopolitan Civil Societies Journal* 6(2): 3915.

Havelock, R (2016) 'A Taxonomic Approach to Quantum Meruit' *Law Quarterly Review* 132: 470.

Glennon, L (2005) 'Displacing the Conjugal Family in Legal Policy – A Progressive Move?' *Child & Family Law Quarterly* 17: 141.

Head, A (2011) 'The Legal Recognition of Close Personal Relationships in New South Wales – A Case for Reform' *Flinders Law Journal* 13: 53.

HM Government (2017) 'The Queen's Speech and Associated Background Briefing, on the Occasion of the Opening Of Parliament On Wednesday 21 June 2017' (Crown).

HM Land Registry and Law Commission (2001), *Land Registration for the Twenty-First Century: A Conveyancing Revolution* (Law Com No 271).

Herring, J (2007) 'Where are the Carers in Healthcare Law and Ethics?' *Legal Studies* 27: 51.

—— (2013) *Caring and the Law* (Oxford, Hart Publishing).

—— (2016) *Medical Law and Ethics*, 6th edn (Oxford, Oxford University Press).

—— (2016a) 'Will-Substitutes and the Claims of Family Members and Carers' in A Braun and A Röthel (eds), *Passing Wealth on Death: Will-Substitutes in Comparative Perspective* (Oxford, Hart Publishing).

Hopkins, N and Laurie, E (2015) 'Social Citizenship, Housing Wealth and the Cost of Social Care: Is the Care Act 2014 "Fair"?' *Modern Law Review* 78: 112.

Hughes, M (2004) 'Privacy in Aged Care' *Australian Journal of Ageing* 23: 110.

Independent Age and Institute and Faculty of Actuaries (2017) *Will The Cap Fit?*

Institute and Faculty of Actuaries (2014) *How Pensions Can Help Meet Consumer Needs under the new Social Care Regime.*

—— (2015) *How Financial Products Can Work Alongside the Care Act 2014 to Help People Pay for Care: An Overview.*

Jarrett, T (2018) 'Social care: forthcoming Green Paper on older people and parallel programme (England)' (House of Commons Library Briefing Paper Number 8002).

Kelly, D (2013) 'Editorial: Reflecting on the Implications of the Care Act 2014 for Care Providers' *Journal of Care Services Management* 7: 74.

Kerridge, R (2009) *Parry and Kerridge: The Law of Succession*, 12th edn (London, Sweet & Maxwell).

King's Fund (2014) *A New Settlement for Health and Social Care: Final Report.*

Lacey, W (2014) 'Neglectful to the Point of Cruelty? Elder Abuse and the Rights of Older Persons in Australia' *Sydney Law Review* 36: 99.

Law Commission (2002) *Sharing Homes: A Discussion Paper* (Law Com No 278).
—— (2006) *Cohabitation: The Financial Consequences of Relationship Breakdown. A Consultation Paper*, (Law Com No 179).
—— (2007) *Cohabitation: The Financial Consequences of Relationship Breakdown* (Law Com No 307).
—— (2011) *Intestacy and Family Provision Claims on Death* (Law Com No 331).
Masson, J, Bailey-Harris, R and Probert, R (2008) *Cretney's Principles of Family Law*, 8th edn (London, Sweet & Maxwell).
Mayhew, L and Smith, D (2014) 'Personal Care Savings Bonds: A New Way of Saving Towards Social Care in Later Life' *Geneva Papers* 39: 668.
McCullagh, R (2014) 'Aged Care Reforms: The Residents' Perspective' *LSJ: Law Society of NSW Journal* 4: 70.
McFarlane, B (2014) *The Law of Proprietary Estoppel* (Oxford, Oxford University Press).
Mee, J (2009) 'The Limits of Proprietary Estoppel: *Thorner v Major*' *Child & Family Law Quarterly* 21: 374.
Minford, M (2001) 'The Boundaries Between Health and Social Care for Older People in Developed Countries' (Nuffield Trust).
Mitchell, C, Mitchell, P and Watterson, S (2016) *Goff & Jones: The Law of Unjust Enrichment*, 9th edn (London, Sweet & Maxwell).
National Aged Care Alliance (2016) 'Improving the Interface Between the Aged Care and Disability Sectors'.
National Committee on Uniform Succession Laws (2004) *Family Provision: Supplementary Report to the Standing Committee of Attorneys General* (Queensland Law Reform Commission Report No 58, Brisbane).
New South Wales Law Reform Commission (2006) *Relationships* (Report No 113).
Nield, S (2007) 'Testamentary Promises: A Test Bed for Legal Frameworks of Unpaid Caregiving' *Northern Ireland Legal Quarterly* 58: 287.
Office for National Statistics (2013) 'More than 1 in 10 Providing Unpaid Care as Numbers Rise to 5.8 Million', *BBC News*, 15 February 2013: https://www.bbc.co.uk/news/health-21471544.
Paying for Care, 'Care home fees', available online at: www.payingforcare.org/care-home-fees (accessed 19 December 2017).
Peart, N (2008) '*De Facto* Relationships (or Maybe Not) in New Zealand' *International Family Law* 130.
Pickard, L (2015) 'A growing care gap? The supply of unpaid care for older people by their adult children in England to 2032' *Ageing and Society* 35: 96.
Robertson, R et al (2014) *The social care and health systems of nine countries* (King's Fund).
Rundle, O (2011) 'An Examination of Relationship Registration Schemes in Australia' *Australian Journal of Family Law* 25: 121.
Scherpe, JM (2005) 'The Legal Status of Cohabitants – Requirements for Legal Recognition' in K Boele-Woelki (ed), *Common Core and Better Law in European Family Law* (Antwerp, Intersentia).
Sloan, B (2013) *Informal Carers and Private Law* (Oxford, Hart Publishing).
—— (2015) 'Informal Care and Private Law: Governance or a Failure Thereof?' *Canadian Journal of Comparative and Contemporary Law* 1: 275.
—— (2015a) 'Keeping up with the Jones Case: Establishing Constructive Trusts in "Sole Legal Owner" Scenarios' *Legal Studies* 35: 226.
—— (2016) 'Adult Social Care and Property Rights' *Oxford Journal of Legal Studies* 36: 428.
—— (2017) 'Charges for Charges: Home Sales under the Care Act 2014' in H Conway and R Hickey (eds), *Modern Studies in Property Law: Volume 9* (Oxford, Hart Publishing).
—— (2017a) *Borkowski's Law of Succession*, 3rd edn (Oxford, Oxford University Press).
—— (2019) '*Ilott v The Blue Cross* (2017): Testing the limits of testamentary freedom' in B Sloan (ed), *Landmark Cases in Succession Law* (Oxford, Hart Publishing, 2019).
Spencer-Lane, T (2015) *Care Act Manual*, 2nd edn (London, Sweet & Maxwell).

Swinford, S (2017) 'Parents responsible for care of their elderly mothers and fathers as much as their own children, minister says', *Daily Telegraph* (31 January 2017), available online at: www.telegraph.co.uk/news/2017/01/31/parents-responsible-care-elderlymothers-fathers-much-children/ (accessed 25 September 2018).
Trurong, W (2013) 'Aged care reform: complex changes to residential aged care' *IOOF TechConnect Technical bulletin*, Summer.
Tune, D (2017) 'Legislated Review of Aged Care 2017' (Commonwealth of Australia).
Ungerson, C (2004) 'Whose Empowerment and Independence? A Cross-National Perspective on "Cash for Care" Schemes' *Ageing and Society* 24: 189.
Victorian Law Reform Commission (2013) *Succession Laws: Report.*
Virgo, G (2015) *Principles of the Law of Restitution*, 3rd edn (Oxford, Oxford University Press).
Walker, P (2018) 'Councils give cautious welcome to extra £150m for social care', *The Guardian* (6 February 2018), available online at: www.theguardian.com/society/2018/feb/06/councils-cautious-welcome-150m-social-care-funding-uk (accessed 25 September 2018).
Walker, R (2008) 'Which Side "Ought to Win"? – Discretion and Certainty in Property Law' *Singapore Journal of Legal Studies* 229.
Walsh, J and Johnson, S (2013) 'Development and Principles of the National Disability Insurance Scheme' *Australian Economic Review* 46: 327.
Wark, S (2015) 'Ageing, end-of-life care, and the National Disability Insurance Scheme: What can we learn from overseas?' *Journal of Intellectual & Developmental Disability* 40: 92.
Wells, R (2007) 'Testamentary Promises and Unjust Enrichment' *Restitution Law Review* 15: 37.
—— (2007a) 'Testamentary Promises: A New Approach' (PhD thesis, King's College London).
Wilmot-Smith, F (2011) 'Replacing Risk-Taking Reasoning' *Law Quarterly Review* 127: 610.
Windholz, E (2014) 'NDIS Beware: Pink Batts Below!' *Alternative Law Journal* 39: 89.
Wong, S (2009) 'Caring and Sharing: Interdependence as a Basis for Property Redistribution' in A Bottomley and S Wong (eds), *Changing Contours of Domestic Life, Family and Law: Caring and Sharing* (Oxford, Hart Publishing).

8

Care and the Workplace: The Dutch Approach to Part-time Work, Flexible Working Arrangements and Leave

SUSANNE BURRI[1]

I. Introduction

The Dutch socio-economic context in relation to work and care is quite unique given the predominance of part-time work. Both women and men work part-time much more often than in other EU countries. Some forms of part-time work allow workers with care responsibilities to reconcile work and care, and this is the main reason why many women reduce their working time, in particular after the birth of their child. Dutch statutory law offers workers strong rights to adjust their overall working time, scheduled working hours and/or workplace, in addition to diverse forms of leave, such as parental and carers' leave.[2] In the light of the recently adopted EU directive on work-life balance,[3] the Dutch experience with workers' rights to flexible working patterns and carers' leave is utterly relevant. After a sketch of some characteristics of part-time work, this chapter provides a thorough description of the statutory rights for flexible working arrangements and relevant case law. A picture of statutory leave for parents and carers and the take-up of leave in practice follows. The scope of the chapter is limited to rights of workers in employment and the obligations of employers to grant flexible working arrangements and leave. At the core of this chapter are thus the relationships between private parties and how far these are influenced by public policies and

[1] Dr Susanne Burri is Associate Professor at the School of Law of Utrecht University and senior expert for gender equality law of the European network of legal experts in gender equality and non-discrimination. See for more information: www.uu.nl/staff/SDBurri/0 and www.equalitylaw.eu/.

[2] Dutch legislation is available online at: www.wetten.nl.

[3] Directive (EU) 2019/1158 of the European Parliament and of the Council of 20 June 2019 on work-life balance for parents and carers and repealing Council Directive 2010/18/EU, [2019] OJ, L188/79.

statutory legislation. It ends with a discussion of the Dutch approach in the light of the EU work-life balance directive.

A concluding observation is that the Dutch approach is characterised by a structural and constant occurrence of part-time work, even further facilitated by increasing possibilities for workers to realise flexible working arrangements according to their needs. These individual strategies entail disadvantages for the workers concerned, in particular a loss of income, which seem to be taken for granted by women in particular. In addition, the gender imbalance in care responsibilities persists, probably also related to gender stereotyping of the respective roles of men and women in work and care. The take-up of leave is relatively low and when leave is unpaid, it offers a rather short-term solution to workers, which does not fit with long-term care responsibilities for children and/or ill or disabled relatives. Working part-time for a longer period seems then a better option for individual workers. However, as long as structural policies result in the absence of accessible and affordable childcare facilities, tax incentives and suitable organisation of (professional) care for (chronically) ill or disabled people, gender gaps will probably persist.

II. Part-time Work in the Netherlands

A. Labour Market Participation of Men and Women

The net labour participation rate in the Netherlands of both men (82 per cent in 2015) and women (71 per cent in 2015)[4] is relatively high, compared to, for example, Southern and Eastern European countries.[5] Labour market participation has steadily increased; the net female labour participation rate has increased more than the male rate and the gender employment gap has decreased since 2005 (Dirven and Portegijs 2016: 63). The increase is significant for women with a partner, living in a single household with (young) children. Women without a partner, living with children have a much lower rate of participation in the labour market (61 per cent in 2015).[6]

[4] Dirven and Portegijs (2016: 57) with a summary in English, available at: www.scp.nl/Publicaties/Alle_publicaties/Publicaties_2016/Emancipatiemonitor_2016. These figures include all persons employed for at least one hour a week.

[5] See Eurostat (2016), available at: ec.europa.eu/eurostat/statistics-explained/index.php/File:Employment_rate,_age_group_20_%E2%80%93_64,_2016_(%25)_YB17.png.

[6] For women with children 0-3 years old, from 70% in 2005 to 78% in 2015; for women with children 4–11 years old from 71% in 2005 to 79% in 2015; and for women with children 12–17 years old from 73% in 2005 to 79% in 2015. The employment rate of men with children remained stable (Dirven and Portegijs 2016: 63).

B. Some Characteristics of Part-time Work

Part-time work is a central feature of employment in the Netherlands, in particular for women.[7] In 2015, 73 per cent of women in employment and 21 per cent of men had a part-time job in the Netherlands (Dirven and Portegijs 2016: 66). Across the EU, the averages are 32 per cent and 8 per cent respectively (Braken and Merens 2016: 251). Dutch women worked mostly either in part-time jobs of 20–27 hours a week or full-time (35 hours or more). Less than a quarter worked a maximum of 20 hours a week. Men more often worked full-time (79 per cent) or had a job of 28–34 hours a week. Only 7 per cent of the men in employment worked less than 20 hours a week (Dirven and Portegijs 2016: 66).

C. Working Time and Care Responsibilities

Typically, women reduce their average working time between the ages of 25 and 35 years, and barely increase it again thereafter. A majority of couples with minor children work in a so-called *one and a half model* (58 per cent): the man works full-time and the woman part-time. The breadwinner model has become less predominant, as this model applied to 25 per cent of the couples in 2005 and 18 per cent 10 years later. Having both parents working full-time is even less usual, as only 10 per cent of couples with children worked full-time in 2015 (Roeters and Alejandro Perez 2016: 90). The reduction in working time of women mainly takes place just after the birth of the first child (Roeters and Alejandro Perez 2016: 94). Mothers with a partner worked in 2015, on average 24–26 hours a week; fathers with a partner, 40 hours a week. The main reason for working part-time for women is the care of children or others and household tasks (57 per cent). This is also an important reason for men with a part-time job (27 per cent). A significant proportion of both women (20 per cent) and men (26 per cent) work part-time because they cannot work more hours with their employer (Dirven and Portegijs 2016: 75). More women than men would like to change their working hours (on average two hours more if the pay also increases); when their children are older, mothers also wish to work more hours (Dirven and Portegijs 2016: 72).

D. Taking into Account Care Responsibilities when Determining Working Hours

According to the Working Time Act (*Arbeidstijdenwet*, hereafter: *ATW*), one of the general obligations of the employer is to take into account – as far as can be

[7] See on part-time work in the Netherlands for example: Plantenga (1996), Visser (2002).

reasonably expected – the personal circumstances of the worker in its policy on working time and rest periods.[8] In addition, the employer has to take into account personal responsibilities of the worker outside work, which include care for children and dependent family members, as far as can be reasonably expected.[9] Specific provisions apply in case of pregnancy, breastfeeding and after the end of parental leave. A worker has, for example, the right to request a change in their working hours schedule for a period of a year or for another agreed period after the end of the parental leave.[10] However, the Act on Flexible Working now provides even stronger rights (see below).

E. Some Consequences of Part-time Work

It is clear that part-time work is an individual decision that involves costs for the worker. To mention only a few: it entails a reduced income, as well as less social security and pension contributions – which are partially paid by the employer – and this impacts social security and pension benefits. In many functions, working part-time means fewer career prospects, fewer training facilities offered by the employer, less pay, and loss of (for example) overtime supplements or extras for inconvenient hours, or other additional pay elements such as a lease car.[11] In 2015, most employers (79 per cent) felt responsible for facilitating the reconciliation of work and care. However, only 58 per cent of the employers considered that part-time work should be possible at all levels in the organisation.[12] The possibilities to work part-time might thus be limited in practice in some organisations.

The Dutch policies on emancipation aim at higher labour market participation by women and, in more recent years, longer working hours for women.[13] The reasons put forward are the use of the capacities and skills of women, but also economic independence. However, only 54 per cent of the women and 74 per cent of the men aged between 20–64 years were economically independent in 2015, which amounts to a net income of more than €1000 per month (Herbers (CBS) and Brakel (CBS) 2016: 158).[14] This means that 46 per cent of women do not even have such minimum income.

The above figures show that part-time work is still widely chosen, in particular by women, in relation to care responsibilities, even if part-time work entails disadvantages.

[8] Article 4:1(1) *ATW*.

[9] Article 4:1a *ATW*.

[10] Article 4:1b *ATW*.

[11] See the literature mentioned in n 7 above and Burri (2000).

[12] Echteld and Voogd-Hameling (2017), available at: digitaal.scp.nl/arbeidsmarktinkaart-werkgevers 2017/faciliteren-balans-werk-en-zorg/.

[13] See: www.rijksoverheid.nl/onderwerpen/vrouwenemancipatie.

[14] According to the definition used in Statistics Netherlands, a person having a net income from employment or self-employment of at least 70% of the statutory net minimum income, which amounts to €992.12 per month in 2018: www.st-ab.nl/bijstandsnorm.htm.

Part-time work is also rather common for men (including fathers) in the Netherlands. However, this has little impact on their involvement in unpaid care (Cloïn 2013: 63–64). Women spend weekly twice as much time caring for children as men (11.5 hours compared to 5.9 hours). When caring for children combined with other activities such as domestic tasks is taken into account (without the presence of other persons to help), women spend indirectly an additional 8.6 hours and men 2.9 hours a week on the care of children. An equal share of unpaid care between men and women is thus still not achieved.

F. Act on Equal Treatment Regardless of Working Time

Since 1996, a specific law prohibits differences in employment terms based on working time, unless such differences are objectively justified (*Wet verbod van onderscheid op grond van arbeidsduur*).[15] The points of departure in this law are the differentiation of working time – the full-timer is not always the point of reference – and high-quality part-time work. The employer (whether in the private or public sector) is prohibited from differentiating between employees on the basis of working time, in the conditions under which a contract is concluded, continued, or terminated, unless the difference is objectively justified. The aim has to be legitimate and the means of achieving that aim have to be appropriate and necessary. The test applied is thus the same as in case of indirect sex discrimination.[16]

Since 2000, the opportunities for workers to adjust their working time have been enhanced. The possibilities to have flexible working hours, flexible working schedules and/or to use remote working arrangements are since 2016 even greater.

III. Flexible Work Arrangements[17]

A. Debates and Legislation on Adjustment of Working Time

The social partners at a national level played a key role in developing flexible working arrangements in the Netherlands. In 1993, a national agreement was concluded in the bipartite Labour Foundation (*Stichting van de Arbeid*), (Stichting van de Arbeid 1993). This Foundation issued a recommendation to the social partners aiming at including provisions in collective agreements to facilitate greater differentiation of working time and to enhance facilities to work part-time. In particular, employers would have to accept a worker's request to reduce or

[15] *Stb.* 1996, 391, in force since 1 November 1996. This prohibition is also included in the Civil Code in Article 7:648 CC.

[16] See further Burri (2000).

[17] See also Burri (2018).

increase his or her working time, unless a serious business reason would prevent granting such demand. However, only a few collective agreements implemented the recommendation of the Labour Foundation.[18] But since 1994, most Dutch public servants have the right to reduce their working hours, unless the serious interests of the service would preclude it.

The adjustment of working time has been a matter of political debate in the Netherlands concerning employment strategies and equal opportunities since the beginning of the 1990s.[19] Four legislative proposals have been discussed. The main question at stake was how to meet, on the one hand, the interests of workers who would like to adjust their working time and hours to personal needs without losing their employment or facing worse working conditions; and on the other hand, the interests of employers who might be confronted with problems of continuity of the work or production, flexibility in working schedules and the workforce. Eventually, the government's proposal was adopted and in 2000, the Working Time Adjustment Act (*Wet aanpassing arbeidsduur, WAA*) entered into force.[20] The starting point of this legislation is that the flexibility of working hours can meet both the needs of companies and workers. The 2000 Working Time Adjustment Act granted employees a restricted statutory right to reduce or extend their individual working time, resulting in a change to their employment contract. This statutory right to adjust working hours has been framed according to the recommendation of the Labour Foundation published in 1993. This illustrates the significant role the Dutch social partners play in this area of social law. The Working Time Adjustment Act has been amended twice, in 2015 and 2016, but a worker's working time adjustment rights have remained essentially the same.

B. The 2000 Working Time Adjustment Act

The aim of this Act was twofold: an increase of the number of persons participating in the labour market as well as facilitating the reconciliation of work, family and private life.[21] The Act applied to all employers in the public and private sector, except those with fewer than 10 employees. The employee had to be employed by his/her employer at least for a year before such request could be made. The provision on the *extension* of working time was not imperative; derogations were allowed in collective agreements. However, no derogations were permitted regarding the right to *reduce* working time. The employer was obliged to grant the requested change in working time unless this was precluded by weighty work-related reasons which would lead to serious problems. If the request was granted, the employer determined the weekly working hours in conformity with the wishes

[18] In 1998, in only 14 conventions was a provision similar to the recommendation included: Arbeidsinspectie (1999).

[19] See further, Burri, Opitz and Veldman (2003).

[20] *Stb.* 2000, 114, 115, in force since 1 July 2000. See Kuip and Verhulp (2000), Wolff (2000).

[21] *Kamerstukken II* 1998/99, 26358, 3, p. 7.

of the employee. The distribution of working hours could be amended in cases where the employer had such an interest, but the wishes of the worker would only have to give way to that interest where deemed reasonable. The interest of the worker had thus more weight as regards the reduction or increase in working time, while the employer had more influence on the schedule of working hours. The Dutch legislator wanted in such a way to find a balance between the workers' and the employers' interests. A worker could only file a new working time adjustment request two years after a previous demand had been accepted or refused, in order to avoid repeated working time changes for the employer.

In 2003, this legislation was subject to an evaluation, which was positive and did not result in any amendment of this Act.[22] In practice, an adjustment of working time mostly follows an agreement between the worker and the employer without any reference to this Act. However, according to the government, the Act offers a framework within which such request has to be granted.[23]

In 2015, some amendments were made to the Act on procedural aspects in order to facilitate requests by workers. One such amendment allows a temporary change in working time. A working time adjustment can now be requested for variable periods and changing working times. The adjustment is thus not necessarily structural anymore, offering even more flexibility to workers both in the public and private sectors.[24]

C. Case Law on Adjustment of Working Time

There is little case law on the interpretation of the right to adjust working time. This fits in the Dutch legal culture, as, generally speaking, there is little litigation on working conditions during the employment relationship. The majority of employment cases concern dismissal.

In most cases the reasons put forward by employers for refusing a working time change are subject to judicial review. Between 1 January 2005 and 1 January 2015, only 47 cases were published (Bevers 2016). Of these 47 cases, 27 concerned a reduction of working time and in 24 of these 27 cases, the reasons put forward by the employers were subject to judicial review. In nine judgments the courts considered the reasons put forward by the employer in fact to be weighty business or service reasons leading to serious problems as defined by law. In 15 cases, the courts decided that the arguments provided by the employer to justify a refusal were *not* such weighty reasons. When a worker had taken parental leave and

[22] MuConsult, *Onderzoek ten behoeve van evaluatie Waa en Woa. Eindrapport*. Amersfoort: MuConsult 2003 (with a summary in English), available at: docplayer.nl/14453238-Onderzoek-ten-behoeve-van-de-evaluatie-waa-en-woa.html.

[23] *Kamerstukken II* 2003/04, 29501, 1, p. 1.

[24] *Wet modernisering verlof en arbeidstijden, Stb.* 2014, 565, in force since 1 January 2015 and amended since 1 April 2016. See Heeger-Hertter and Veldman (2016) and Bevers (2016).

requested a reduction of the working time at the end of the leave, such request had often to be granted.[25]

During the period under review, only five cases concerned a demand to increase the working time. In three of these cases, the reasons put forward by the employer were considered by the courts to be weighty business or service reasons leading to serious problems; in two judgments, this was not the case.

D. The Act on Flexible Working

The Act on Flexible Working (*Wet flexibel werken, WFW*) replaced and partially modified the Working Time Adjustment Act.[26] Workers and civil servants have (since the *WFW* entered into force on 1 January 2016) not only the right to adjust their working time, but also their working hours and place of work. The *WFW* is aimed, just like its predecessor, at facilitating the reconciliation of work, private and family life.

(i) Scope

The Act applies to workers with an employment contract in the civil or public sector, even if the work is carried out abroad.[27] In Dutch law, a temporary agency worker has an employment contract with the temporary work agency and can therefore not invoke the rights of the *WFW* vis-à-vis the undertakings where the work is carried out. A person who has reached the pensionable age is explicitly excluded from the personal scope of the *WFW*.[28]

The Act does not apply to undertakings employing fewer than 10 workers, but these employers have to draw up an internal regulation concerning the right to adjust working time.[29] Workers working in these undertakings have thus no specific statutory right to adjust their working hours and/or place of work.

(ii) Procedural Requirements

Article 2 is the main provision of the *WFW* and stipulates that a worker employed for at least 26 weeks before the presumed date of change can request an adjustment of working time, working hours or place of work. The worker does not have to stipulate any reason for his/her demand. Such request might involve variable

[25] See for example *Ktr.* Nijmegen, 18 July 2001, *JAR* 2001/192 and *Ktr.*'s-Hertogenbosch, 7 January 2003, *JAR* 2003, p. 64.

[26] *Stb.* 2015, 245, 376 & 464. See Andel (2017) and Verhulp (2016).

[27] Article 1 (a) and (b) *WFW*; *Kamerstukken II* 1998/99 26358, 5, p. 20. Specific provisions apply to the military: *Stb.* 2000, 344 and Article 2 (2) *WFW*.

[28] Article 1a *WFW*. The aim of this provision is to avoid increases of working time of older persons which would decrease employment possibilities of younger workers.

[29] Article 2(16) *WFW*.

periods or differences in the extent of the change, allowing all kinds of temporary adjustments.[30] A worker working for 40 hours a week on five days can, for example, ask for a reduction of working time of eight hours a week for a period of one year and for working hours on Monday to Thursday from 7 am to 3 pm. Such changes can thus also concern scheduled working hours and the workplace, allowing remote work. The rights provided in the *WFW* are therefore much more flexible than under the Working Time Adjustment Act, and broader, as they also encompass adjustments of working hours and workplace, in addition to working time.

If a worker desires frequent and/or short adjustments, it might be advisable to take one or more periods of long-term leave (see section IV below). An adjustment of working time, working hours and/or workplace results in a change of the employment contract and this might have consequences for some rights, for example those linked to holidays or pensions.[31] Frequent changes might in addition lead to organisational problems for the employer.

The seniority required before a demand can be submitted is now shorter and in specific circumstances, a request can be filed even before the period of 26 weeks has ended.[32] If the worker is on leave, the period on leave counts as well for determining the period of 26 weeks, as the decisive criterion is the duration of the employment relationship. Periods of work interrupted for less than six months are put together, as well as periods of work for different employers who might be considered each other's successors.

The request has to be filed in writing at least two months before the intended adjustment, save in exceptional circumstances. This term is also shorter since the entry into force of the *WFW*. In the request, the intended date of the change, the desired adjustments and the (weekly) working time schedule have to be specified. The worker can ask once again for an adjustment of the working time, working hours or workplace no less than a year after the employer has granted or refused the demand, save in exceptional circumstances.[33] This period between two requests is now also shorter. The worker will have eventually to clarify that there are exceptional circumstances at stake, which justify an even shorter period than a year between two requests and the employer will have to consider such request as a 'good employer'.[34]

The employer has to consult the worker on the request in order to find a solution which suits both parties.[35] If the demand lacks some details, for example the desired date of the change, the worker is given the opportunity to fulfil the legal

[30] Article 2(1) *WFW*.
[31] This point has been highlighted by Heeger-Hertter and Veldman (2016: 3).
[32] Article 2(1) *WFW* and *Kamerstukken II* 2014/15, 32889, 20.
[33] Article 2(3) *WFW*.
[34] This concept (Article 7: 611 Civil Code) can be applied to different situations, for example in relation to working time issues. See for example *Ktr.* Alkmaar 10 February 2017, *AR*, 2017-0268. A refusal of such request has to meet the requirements mentioned in Article 2(5)–(11); *Kamerstukken II* 1998/99, 26358, 5, p. 9 et *Handelingen I* 1999/2000, p. 16-634.
[35] Article 2(4) *WFW*; *Kamerstukken II* 1998/99, 26358, 3, p. 16.

procedural requirements. The worker can also amend the request if the consultation shows that some wishes of the worker will not be fulfilled.

(iii) Reasons for Not Granting a Request

The employer has to grant a request to adjust the working time or the working hours as regards the date and the extent of the change, unless weighty business or service reasons leading to serious problems prevent this.[36] A few examples of such serious reasons for refusing a *reduction* of working time are specified in the Act: serious problems for the organisation with regard to filling the hours that become vacant, to ensure safety, or to schedule the organisation's work. In the case of an *extension* of working time, serious business reasons would be at stake if this would lead to serious financial or organisational problems, if there is a shortage of available work, or due to an insufficient personnel budget.[37] Since the entry into force of the Act on Flexible Working, only one case has been published concerning a rightly refused increase of working time.[38]

The *WFL* now also specifies some weighty business or service reasons leading to serious problems that might justify a rejection of a change of working hours (*werktijd*). The non-exhaustive list includes safety reasons, work schedules or financial or organisational problems.[39] This right for workers is now much stronger because before the *WFL* entered into force, a worker could only invoke the general obligation of the employer in the Working Time Act (*ATW*) to consider his/her personal circumstances when establishing the (undertaking's) working time schedules (see II D). Under the Working Time Adjustment Act a change of the employee's working hours schedule could only be requested in relation to a working time adjustment, and could be amended if the employer had such an interest that the wishes of the worker reasonably had to give way. However, in the *WFW* the employer still has the right to amend the spread of the working hours (*spreiding van de uren*) if the wish of the worker has to give way to the interest of the employer.[40] It is not yet clear how the rights of the worker on adjustment of the working hours (*werktijd*) and the employers' rights on the spread of the hours (*spreiding van de uren*) relate to each other. This might be important in practice as workers with care responsibilities often need specific working hours in order to fit schedules of, for example, available child-care facilities or other persons providing care.

A change of the workplace can be refused more easily than a request on adjustment of working time or working hours, as the employer only has to consider such a request and inform the worker in the event of refusal of the application.[41]

[36] Article 2(5) *WFW*.
[37] Article 2 (9) and (10) *WFW*.
[38] Ktr Amsterdam 1 February 2017, AR 2017-0158, ECLI:NL:RBAMS:2017:771. The cut-off date is 1 January 2018.
[39] Article 2(11) *WFW*.
[40] Article 2(7) *WFW*.
[41] Article 2(6) *WFW*.

(iv) The Employer's Decision

The employer has to give his decision on the request in writing. If the employer does not grant the request, or if the employer adjusts the working time, the working hours or the workplace, or adjusts the working hours schedule inconsistently with the wishes of the worker, the reasons have to be provided in writing.[42]

If the employer has not taken a decision within a month before the intended date of the requested adjustment, the working time, working hours or workplace are adapted in line with the wishes of the worker.[43]

The employer has now the option to revise his decision if serious business or service reasons occur after the decision has been taken. Such a possibility did not exist in the Working Time Adjustment Act. In addition, the employer has to consult the worker before modifying his decision and inform the worker in writing of the change, mentioning the reasons.[44]

(v) Limited Obligations

The *WFW* allows for either a decrease or increase of working time. There is no obligation for the employer to make arrangements to fill in the vacant hours in the case of a decrease of working time. This might lead to a higher workload on the worker if the tasks the worker has to perform are not adapted to the reduction of the working time and/or some duties of the worker are not taken over by another worker.

An increase of the working time can only be requested for the employee's own function. For example, a teacher can demand more teaching hours in his/her teaching field. Sometimes, it will be difficult to clearly define which tasks correspond to a certain function. The description in the employment contract of the duties belonging to the function will provide an indication, as well as the tasks performed in practice. The employer has the obligation as a 'good employer' to offer hours to the worker corresponding to the worker's function and might follow an internal procedure to fill in the vacancy.[45]

(vi) Derogations

The Act offers the possibility to derogate on some points by collective agreement or other civil service regulations for a maximum period of five years, which may be renewed. However, no derogations by collective agreement are permitted as far as the right to *reduce* working time is concerned. Employers with fewer than 10 workers, who have to draw up their own regulation on working time, may nevertheless give fewer rights to workers in this respect than those offered by the

[42] Article 8 *WFW*.
[43] Article 2(12) *WFW*.
[44] Article 2(13 and 14) *WFW*.
[45] *Handelingen II* 1998/99, p. 5891.

statutory legislation. The *WFW* does not specify any further requirement for these employers.

Derogations are possible by collective agreement – or if no collective agreement or civil service regulation applies – by written agreement between the employer and the Works Council regarding the increase of working time, the working hours or the workplace.[46] This possibility illustrates the role social partners play in drafting specific regulations at sector or undertakings' level, allowing the specificities of the sector and interests of employers to be taken into account.

(vii) Protection against Victimisation

The worker is protected against victimisation. The employer cannot terminate an employment contract or decide not to prolong a fixed-term contract due to the fact that an employee has requested an adjustment of working time, working hours or workplace.[47] This protection does not cover other forms of unfavourable treatment. However, the prohibition of direct and indirect discrimination, for example on the ground of sex, might be applicable to other forms of victimisation if the treatment in question is related to pregnancy and/or maternity or if many more women than men would be disadvantaged due to a request of an adjustment of working time, working hours and/or workplace.

An evaluation of the *WFW* has to take place five years after the entry into force of this Act, and should therefore take place in 2021.[48] To the author's knowledge, there is no information yet available on the use in practice of the *WFL*. Conclusions on the current possibilities to request a temporary reduction or increase of working time, adjustment of working hours and/or workplace can therefore not yet be drawn.

Dutch legislation offers diverse forms of leave to workers. Research is available on the use in practice of this leave. Leave exists in relation to pregnancy and maternity, care for children, but also care for others in case of illness. The next section offers a short overview of the main categories of leave under Dutch legislation and their take-up. Note that the leave described here can be extended and, in some cases, amended by collective agreement, an issue which is not extensively addressed in this chapter.

IV. Leave in the Work and Care Act

The Work and Care Act (*Wet Arbeid en Zorg, WAZO*)[49] since 2001 has contained the most important categories of statutory leave and has been amended a few

[46] Article 2(15) and (17) *WFW*.
[47] Article 3 *WFW*.
[48] Article 5 *WFW*.
[49] *Stb.* 2001, 567.

times since then. This Act aims, just as the Flexible Working Act does, to facilitate the reconciliation of work, private and family life. It applies to workers with an employment contract and civil servants. Some rights apply to other groups; self-employed women have, for example, the right to a benefit in case of pregnancy and maternity.[50]

The *WAZO* allows derogations disadvantaging workers by collective agreement or civil service regulations on some aspects of some leave. If no collective agreement or civil service regulation applies, derogations are possible if the employer and the Works Council reach a (written) agreement. No derogations are allowed to pregnancy and maternity leave, which is a compulsory category of leave for female workers and is also the longest paid leave.

A. Pregnancy, Maternity and Adoption Leave

The statutory pregnancy and maternity leave is 16 weeks, fully paid up to a maximum of a gross daily salary of €209.26 (since 1 January 2018). The benefit is paid from the Unemployment Fund. The right to take this leave exists six weeks before the expected birth date until 10 weeks after the birth. A minimum of four weeks of leave has to be taken before the expected birth date. Flexibility is possible here as well: the female worker has the right, after six weeks of maternity leave, to take the maternity leave in different periods during a period of 30 weeks. Such flexible leave has to be requested and the employer has to grant the leave, except if serious business or service reasons prevent this.[51]

There exists a right to paid adoption leave of a maximum of six weeks, which can also be taken in case of employees providing foster care.[52]

B. Paternity and Parental Leave

The Act on Work and Care provided for paid paternity leave, after the birth of a child, of two days leave for the husband, registered partner, cohabiting partner or person who has acknowledged the child. In addition, three days of unpaid parental leave following the paid paternity leave could not be refused by the employer.[53] A governmental proposal (*WIEG*) to extend the paternity leave has now been adopted.[54] The paid paternity leave is, since 1 July 2019, five days fully paid, and will be extended from 1 July 2020 with five additional weeks of 'birth leave' paid at 70 per cent of the worker's salary.

[50] Article 3:8 *WAZO*.

[51] Article 3:1 *WAZO*. If the mother dies in childbirth or during maternity leave, her partner is entitled to the remaining paid leave: Article 3:1a *WAZO*.

[52] Article 3:2 *WAZO*.

[53] Articles 4:2 and 6:5(4) *WAZO*.

[54] Staatsblad 2018, 451.

The *WAZO* also provides for an individual statutory right to unpaid parental leave of 26 times the weekly working time. Parental leave can now be full-time or part-time leave and can also be divided into different periods. The employer has no option to refuse the parental leave, but can reject the desired way of taking the leave – for instance as regards the proposed weekly working hours – by invoking serious business or service reasons.[55] A worker has a right to parental leave for his/her child until the child is eight years old and for any child he/she takes care of on a regular basis and who lives at the same address. Parental leave is only paid leave if the employer or a collective agreement provides for (partially) paid parental leave, which is more often the case in the public, than in the private sector.

C. Carers' Leave

Employees with caring responsibilities have the opportunity to take three different kinds of leave in different situations: emergency leave, short-term leave and/or long-term leave.

The group of persons in need of care for whom the employee is entitled to short-term and/or long-term leave is broad. It encompasses the husband or wife, registered partner or life partner cohabiting with the employee; his/her child or child of the husband or wife, registered partner or life partner cohabiting with the employee; a foster child living at the same address as the employee; a relative in the first and second degree; a person (not being an employee of the carer) living at the same address as the employee and a person with whom the employee has social relations, as far as the care is directly linked to this relation and reasonably should be provided by the employee.[56]

(i) Emergency and Time-Off Leave

Fully paid time-off leave for *force majeure* is possible during a short and reasonable period, which is not further specified, but mostly amounts to one or two days. This leave exists in case of unexpected or very special personal circumstances. Such personal circumstances include a spouse or partner (whether registered or not) giving birth, attendance of medical visits which are urgent, unplanned or cannot be scheduled outside working hours, or the sudden illness of a child, partner or a person belonging to the group described above.[57]

(ii) Short-Term Carers' Leave

This leave, of a maximum of twice the weekly working time in each period of 12 months, enables the employee to provide the necessary care in case of illness

[55] Articles 6:1, 6:2, 6:4 and 6:5 *WAZO*.
[56] Article 5:1 *WAZO*.
[57] Article 4:1 *WAZO*.

of a person belonging to the group described above. An employee working 20 hours a week has thus the right to take short-term leave of 40 working hours in a year.

The requirement of 'necessary care' means that there is not only a need for care of a person, but also that the employee has to provide care to this person which cannot be given in another way. This implies that short-term leave is not possible for someone who is hospitalised. There is then no need of care because the sick person is already receiving (professional) care. The leave must be reported as soon as possible, stating the reasons. It is conditional, as the employer has the right to refuse the requested leave due to serious business reasons which reasonably prevail over the interests of the employee. The employee is entitled to 70 per cent of his/her salary during the leave, which must amount to at least the statutory minimum pay[58] and has to be paid by the employer.[59]

(iii) Long-Term Carers' Leave

This unpaid leave can be taken for a maximum of six times the weekly working time of the employee in each period of 12 months, in order to take care of a person suffering from a life-threatening illness or for the necessary care of an ill person or a person needing care. There are no legal requirements as to where care has to be given. Long-term leave can thus be taken regardless of whether the sick person stays at home or not. This leave must be notified at least two weeks in advance, giving reasons. It is also conditional, as the employer has the right to refuse the requested leave due to serious business reasons which reasonably prevail over the interests of the employee.[60] The long-term leave will be curtailed if the person in need of care dies or no longer requires care. The leave ends on the day following the day such circumstance has occurred.

D. Low Take-up of Leave

Research shows that the take-up of carers' and parental leave is low.[61] This is in particular true for the short-term and long-term carers' leave. In 2009, less than one per cent of workers took leave to take care of an ill child for example, often by taking a day off. Short-term or long-term carers' leave was taken in 2009 again only by one per cent of workers, both men and women. The allocated carers' leave – even the long-term leave – is relatively short if taken full-time or only applicable to

[58] Since 1 January 2018 the monthly statutory minimum wage amounts to €1,578 for employees of at least 23 years old, working full-time.

[59] Articles 5:1–5:4 *WAZO*.

[60] Articles 5:10–5:14 *WAZO*.

[61] SCP, Meester and Keuzekamp (2011) (with a summary in English), available at: www.scp.nl/.

a small number of working hours if taken part-time. For this reason, seven per cent of persons in need of leave do not take the leave (SCP, Meester and Keuzekamp 2011: 31). Especially long-term leave might thus fall short if employees have to face situations in which care has to be provided for a long period of time or when care has to be provided to more than one person. Aspects relating to the organisation of the work play a more prominent role in decisions of employees not to take up care leave than financial considerations. Asked about the reasons for non-use of the leave schemes, 39 per cent of employees indicated that their workload does not make it possible or that they do not want to burden colleagues (SCP, Meester and Keuzekamp 2011: 31; Burri and Heeger-Hertter 2015: 116-17; van Echtelt 2016).

Parental leave was taken more often in 2009: 10 per cent of parents with a child younger than eight years took parental leave. However, more mothers than fathers did so (12 per cent compared to six per cent). The main reasons given for not taking parental leave were financial reasons, expected disadvantages to their career, and organisational problems.[62]

It is clear that using the available statutory leave is unpopular in the Netherlands, and it is working part-time – in particular having a high proportion of women in society working part-time – that has become the de facto solution. Leave provides rather incidental solutions and when care is needed for the long-term, for example for childcare, more structural arrangements such as part-time work seem more convenient. This having been said, one of the reasons for the low take-up of parental leave, for example, might be that this leave is unpaid in many sectors or only partially paid in others (for example in the public sector). However, the option of working part-time certainly also entails disadvantages (see II E), in particular in the long-term in the form of sacrificing wages, limiting career prospects and lesser pension rights for example. In the Dutch context, these disadvantages are not often broadly debated in public, but seem to be taken for granted, in particular by women in relation to care responsibilities. This is rather striking, as the very short paternity leave allowance and discussions on longer paid paternity leave are part of the public debate, in particular after the publication of the EU proposal on work-life balance.[63] The same is true for the integration of diverse leave after the birth of a child.[64]

[62] SCP, *Weinig gebruik van verlof voor zorg en ouderschap*, Persbericht, The Hague, 8 November 2011, available at: www.scp.nl/Publicaties/Alle_publicaties/Publicaties_2011/Verlof_vragen.

[63] COM(2017) 253.

[64] See for example: *Volkskrant* 30 June 2017; *NRC* 22 February 2018, p 11 and *NRC*, 25 February 2018, pp E16-17.

The Social and Economic Council of the Netherlands has, for example, recently published an advisory report on the reconciliation of work, study and care in the future (SER 2017), available at: www.ser.nl/nl/publicaties/adviezen/2010-2019/2016/werkzame-combinatie.aspx, as well as an advisory opinion on leave after the birth of a child, in particular the *WIEG* proposal (see Section 4.2) and parental leave: SER, Advies 2018/01 *Optimalisering verlof na geboorte kind*, The Hague: SER 2018, available at: www.ser.nl/nl/publicaties/adviezen/2010-2019/2018/verlof-geboorte-kind.aspx.

V. Dutch Legislation in the Light of the EU Directive on Work-life Balance

The EU directive on work-life balance for parents and carers was adopted in July 2019[65] and should be transposed into national law by 2 August 2022.[66] The European Commission's proposal for this directive was published in April 2017 in the framework of the European Social Pillar.[67] This directive should in particular contribute to a more equal sharing of caring responsibilities between men and women and equal treatment policies should address gender stereotypes.[68] Two new types of leave are introduced at EU level: paid paternity leave of 10 days for fathers,[69] to be taken on the occasion of the birth of a child; and unpaid carers' leave of five days per year.[70] The carers' leave is meant for workers who provide personal care or support to a relative, or to a person who lives in the same household as the worker, and who is in need of significant care or support for a serious medical reason.[71] In addition, the existing parental leave would be amended: the individual right to take parental leave of at least four months, to be taken up until the child reaches eight years,[72] will be non-transferable between the parents for two months.[73] During these two months, the worker will be entitled to a payment or allowance to be defined by the Member State or the social partners.[74] The paternity leave should be paid at least at the level of sick pay.[75] The directive also includes stronger rights for flexible work arrangements for parents with children up to at least eight years and for carers. These flexible arrangements may be subject to a reasonable limitation.[76] Workers may request to adjust their working patterns, including through the use of remote working arrangements, flexible working schedules, or reduced working hours.[77] Employers have to consider such requests within a reasonable period of time and provide reasons for a refusal or

[65] Directive (EU) 2019/1158 of the European Parliament and of the Council of 20 June 2019 on work-life balance for parents and carers and repealing Council Directive 2010/18/EU, [2019] OJ, L188/79.

[66] Article 20(1). The transposition period as regards the payment or allowance corresponding to the last two weeks of parental leave ends two years later on 2 August 2024 (Article 20(2)).

[67] Proposal for a Directive of the European Parliament and of the Council on work-life balance for parents and carers and repealing Council Directive 2010/18/EU, COM(2017) 253. See for a discussion of the proposal, Carracciolo di Torrella (2017) and Burri (2018).

[68] Preamble, recital 11.

[69] Or equivalent second parents, where and insofar as recognised by national law and has to be granted irrespective of the marital or family status: Article 4(1) and (2).

[70] Article 6.

[71] Article 3(1)(c).

[72] The age has to be specified by each Member State or by collective agreement, up to the age of eight: Article 5(1).

[73] Article 5, which also addresses issues as notice, required length of service, postponement of the leave etc.

[74] Article 8(1) and (3).

[75] Article 8(1) and (2).

[76] Article 9(1).

[77] Article 3(1)(f).

postponement of the request. If the changes are of limited duration, the worker has the right to return to the original working pattern at the end of the agreed period.[78]

The transposition of this directive into Dutch law implies necessary changes to the paternity leave as provided in the Dutch Act on Work and Care.[79] With the adoption of the *WIEG*, the minimum requirement of 10 days leave paid at the level of sick pay will be met by 1 July 2020, and in fact (unlike the EU proposal) the paid leave will be six weeks in total.[80] The existing carers' leave in the *WAZO* does not have to be amended. The Dutch rights to adjust working time, working hours and/or the workplace are much more far-reaching than required by the EU directive.

The Dutch provisions on parental leave have to be amended, as regards the payment or allowance during the two non-transferable months of the parental leave. This requires a significant change of the current Dutch provisions and it is therefore not surprising that the Dutch government was not in favour of such (partially) paid parental leave.[81]

VI. Some Conclusions

There are roughly three different strategies that workers with care responsibilities follow in the Netherlands: a reduction of working time by working part-time; making use of flexible work arrangements, including remote working; and taking up leave. These strategies are often combined in an individual situation. Most of these options are temporary and often linked to specific individual (family) situations. Leave might be required at some time for caring for children and later in a career for care of a dependent spouse, friend or neighbour, for example. These strategies imply that care can be provided outside the workplace; the space of care will probably be the home of the worker. The described options might facilitate providing informal kinds of care by individuals. However, it should be noted that part-time work is not always possible in all organisations; the same is true for remote working for instance. In addition, available and affordable childcare facilities, tax incentives and the organisation of (professional) care for (chronically) ill or disabled people (for example) also play a role in facilitating the reconciliation of work and care. Compared in particular to the described possibilities to take up leave, childcare and tax incentives, etc usually offer more long-term and structural opportunities to reconcile work and care responsibilities. Such policies involve

[78] Article 9(3).
[79] Legislation valid on 11 October 2019.
[80] *Stb.* 2018, 451.
[81] *Fiche 1: Mededling en richtlijn betreffende betreffende evenwicht werk en privéleven voor ouders en mantelzorgers*, available at: www.google.nl/search?q=Fiche+1+COM+2017+(253)&sourceid=ie7&rls=com.microsoft:nl-NL:IE-Address&ie=&oe=&gfe_rd=cr&dcr=0&ei=l627WurcJIeAgAaCjrDgBQ&gws_rd=ssl and *Kamerstukken I*, 2017-2018 21 501-31.

mainly state involvement in the Netherlands, predominantly in the form of available subsidies for (private) organisations and funding of municipalities. These aspects have not been addressed in this chapter, but the possibilities to work part-time, adjust one's working time, working hours and the workplace, as well as leave, should be considered in this wider context. The same is true for the rise of flexible employment relations – fixed-term work contracts, on-call work, personal entrepreneurship – which increasingly characterises the Dutch employment market, an issue which has not been considered here either. Working part-time, flexible work arrangements and leave are in principle available, but certainly not all workers will be able to realise their wishes. Depending on the form of their employment relationship, their specific employment context, as well as organisational and cultural issues and their income, etc, many workers might not be willing or able to make use of the legal facilities offered. In addition, gender stereotyping of the respective roles of men and women in work and care might hamper the taking up of leave and/or flexible working arrangements by men, including part-time work.

The predominance of part-time work in the Dutch labour market is clearly gendered, as many more women work part-time than men, and as a consequence, also often suffer disadvantages related to part-time work such as a reduced income, less social security and pension contributions and entitlements. The predominance of female part-time employment thus contributes to the gender income and the gender pension gap. Economic independence is still not realised for many women, even at the level of a minimum income. Only one out of two women is economically independent in the Netherlands, meaning that they have an income of at least 70 per cent of the statutory net minimum income. Part-time work often also involves lesser career prospects. Women more than men are confronted with such risks related to part-time work.

In addition, part-time work does not contribute to a gender-balanced division of care and household responsibilities at home. Women spend on average twice as much time on unpaid work (including care) as men. As women more often reduce their working time, in particular when they become parents than fathers do, this might reinforce gender stereotypes regarding the caring roles of women and men.

There is a broad range of opportunities to adjust working time available in the Netherlands. Workers have had a statutory right to adjust their working time – either in the form of a reduction or an increase – since 2000. The Flexible Working Act has offered workers since 2016 even stronger rights, as workers can now even temporarily adjust their working time in a flexible way, in accordance with their needs. The requirement for the employer who refuses to grant a request to provide weighty business reasons leading to serious problems for the undertaking, is strict. The worker now has in addition the right to adjust their working hours and the same strict requirement applies in case of a refusal of such a demand by the employer. However, employers can reject requests for a change in workplace more easily. The starting points of this legislation are the individual, private needs of the worker, which have to be accommodated by the employer within the legislative framework. The role of the state is principally limited to legislating and its responsibilities as employer in the public sector.

It has to be seen how these rights allowing even greater flexibility for workers will be used in practice. There is little case law on adjustment of working time up to now. It would seem that in the part-time work context, workers and their employers often agree on changes of working time. An evaluation of the Working Time Act of 2000 shows that the application of the right to adjust working time in practice has been rather unproblematic, even if organisational problems might hamper such adjustments in some functions, organisations and sectors to a larger extent than in others.

The rights of workers to flexible working arrangements are much more far-reaching in Dutch statutory law than those in the EU work-life balance directive, which only requires that the employer has to consider requests and provide reasons in case of a refusal. The Dutch approach to flexible working offers thus more possibilities to meet the individual needs of workers with care responsibilities than are provided by the EU directive.

The same is true for the statutory carers' rights, in particular short-term and long-term care leave, which provide even more rights than the EU directive. However, with the exception of pregnancy and maternity leave, Dutch statutory leave for parents is still either short or unpaid. Parental leave is not yet paid leave (even if some collective agreements provide for partially paid parental leave, in particular in the public sector). The same is true for long-term care leave. Budgetary restrictions apply currently to professional care institutions and much more care, for example for partially disabled or elderly people, has to be provided by family members, friends or neighbours (Burri and Heeger-Hertter 2015). It can be expected that such forms of care will be provided more often by women than men, given the still existing traditional gender roles in relation to care in the Netherlands and the high female part-time work rate. Whether the enhanced opportunities for flexible working arrangements, the extended paid paternity leave and the future partially-paid parental leave (after the transposition of the EU work-life directive into Dutch law) will contribute to a more balanced gender division of work and care in the Netherlands remains to be seen. As long as coherent work-life balance policies – dealing with the most relevant matters with which workers with care responsibilities are confronted – are not structurally addressed, the costs of reconciling work and care will mainly rest on women. This is not to say that the Dutch policies amount merely to window-dressing. They reflect a step-by-step process towards more possibilities for a better work-life balance, even if there is still much more needed in order to address persistent gender gaps in particular in employment, care, income and pensions.

References

Arbeidsinspectie (1999) *Deeltijdarbeid in cao's* (The Hague, Ministerie van SZW).

Bevers, E (2016) 'De Wet modernisering regelingen voor verlof en arbeidstijden: noodzakelijk en nuttig?' *Tijdschrift voor de Arbeidsrechtpraktijk (TAP)* 2015/2: 60.

Burri, S (2000) *Tijd delen. Deeltijd, gelijkheid en gender in Europees- en nationaalrechtelijk perspectief* (Deventer, Kluwer, Utrecht dissertation).

—— (2018) 'Articuler vie professionnelle, familiale et privée aux Pays-Bas: quelle flexibilité pour les salariés ?', *Revue du droit comparé et de la sécurité sociale*, 2018/1: 32.

—— (2018) 'The EU Proposal on Work-Life Balance and its Potential Impact in the Netherlands', in: J Pircht & K Koldinská (eds), *Labour Law and Social Protection in a Globalized World. Changing Realities in Selected Areas of Law and Policy,* Bulletin of Comparative Labour Relations 103 (Alphen aan den Rijn, the Netherlands, Kluwer Law International BV, 2018) 305–323.

Burri, S and Heeger-Hertter, S (2015) 'Zorg voor de werknemer-mantelzorger: Een vergelijking van verlofregelingen in het Europese, Duitse en Nederlandse recht' in K Boele-Woelki and SD Burri (eds), *De rol van de staat in familierelaties: meer of minder?* (The Hague, Boom Juridische Uitgevers).

Burri, S, Opitz, H and Veldman, A (2003) 'Work family Policies on Working Time put into Practice. A Comparison of Dutch and German Case Law on Working Time Adjustment' *International Journal of Comparative Labour Law and Industrial Relations* 19: 321.

Carracciolo di Torrella, E (2017) 'An Emerging Right to Care in the EU: a "New Start to Support Work-Life Balance for Parents and Carers"' *ERA Forum* 18: 187–98.

Cloïn M (ed) (2013) *Met het oog op de tijd. Een blik op de tijdsbesteding van Nederlanders* (The Hague, SCP).

Dirven, H (CBS) and Portegijs, W (SCP) (2016) 'Arbeid', in W Portegijs (SCP) and M van den Brakel (CBS) (eds), *Emancipatiemonitor 2016* (The Hague, SCP and CBS).

Eurostat (2016) Statistics Explained *File: Employment rate, age group 20–64, 2016.*

Heeger-Hertter, S and Veldman, A (2016) '"Het nieuwe werken" in nieuwe wetgeving. Flexibilisering van verlof, werktijd en arbeidsplaats' *Arbeidsrecht* 2015/28.

Herbers, D (CBS) and van den Brakel, M (CBS) et al (2016) 'Inkomen en economische zelfstandigheid' in W Portegijs (SCP) and M van den Brakel (CBS) (eds), *Emancipatiemonitor 2016* (The Hague, SCP and CBS).

Kuip, S and Verhulp, E (2000) *Wet aanpassing arbeidsduur* (The Hague, SDU Uitgevers).

Plantenga, J (1996) 'For Women Only? The Rise of Part-time Work in the Netherlands' *Social Politics: International Studies in Gender, State & Society* 3(1).

Portegijs, W (SCP) and van den Brakel, M (CBS) (eds) (2016) *Emancipatiemonitor 2016* (The Hague, SCP and CBS).

Roeters, A and Alejandro Perez et al (2016) 'De combinatie van betaalde arbeid en zorgtaken' in W Portegijs (SCP) and M van den Brakel (CBS) (eds), *Emancipatiemonitor 2016* (The Hague, SCP and CBS).

SCP (the Netherlands Institute for Social Research) (2011) Meester, E and Keuzenkamp, S, *Verlof vragen. De behoefte aan en het gebruik van verlofregelingen* (The Hague, SCP).

SER (*Sociaal-Economische Raad*) (2017) *Een werkende combinatie. Advies over het combineren van werken, leren en zorgen in de toekomst* (The Hague, SER).

—— (2018) Advies 2018/01 *Optimalisering verlof na geboorte kind* (The Hague, SER).

Stichting van de Arbeid (1993) *Overwegingen en aanbevelingen ter bevordering van deeltijdarbeid en differentiatie in arbeidsduurpatronen* (The Hague, Stichting van de Arbeid).

van Andel, H (2017) 'Van (wet) aanpassing arbeidsduur naar (wet) flexibel werken' *Arbeidsrecht* 2017/14.

van den Brakel, M (CBS) and Merens, A (SCP) (2016) 'Emancipatie in Europees perspectief' in CBS and SCP, W Portegijs (SCP) and M van den Brakel (CBS) (eds) *Emancipatiemonitor 2016* (The Hague, SCP and CBS).

van Echtelt, P et al (2016) *Aanbod van arbeid 2016. Werken, zorgen en leren op een flexibele arbeidsmarkt* (The Hague, SCP).

van Echtelt, P and de Voogd-Hameling, M (SCP) (2017) *Arbeidsmarkt in kaart Werkgevers 2017, Faciliteren balans werk en zorg.*

Verhulp, E (2016) 'Wet flexibel werken' in JM van Slooten, MSA Vegter and E Verhulp (eds), *Tekst en commentaar, Arbeidsrecht* (Wolters Kluwer).

Visser, J (2002) 'The first part-time economy in the world: a model to be followed?' *Journal of European Social Policy* 12(1): 23.

Wolff, D de (2000) *Wet aanpassing arbeidsduur* Actualiteiten Sociaal Recht (Deventer, Kluwer).

9

Ethics of Care and Disability Rights: Complementary or Contradictory?

JONATHAN HERRING

I. Introduction

Sometimes academic debates can produce strange bedfellows. Infamously radical feminists can find themselves arguing to similar effect as conservative moralists in relation to pornography or prostitution. But they can also produce strange disagreements. One such is the subject of this chapter. It involves a tension between supporters of ethics of care and supporters of disability rights. It might be thought such well-minded souls would be very much seeking similar agendas. However, as this chapter[1] will highlight, there can undoubtedly be tensions between the promotion of care by supporters of ethics of care; and the promotion of disability rights.

This chapter will explore this debate and argue that it can be resolved once care is understood in a relational way. Care should not be seen as something that is done by one person to another. Instead we should consider caring relationships, whereby both parties are contributing to each other and respect each other. Indeed, it is in the nature of caring relationships that the boundaries between the parties become blurred. The line between who is carer and who is cared for; who is disabled and who is able-bodied break down. This approach can find convergence between disability rights and carers' rights advocates.

This chapter will have three sections. Section II will offer a brief summary of the central themes of ethics of care. Section III will then set out the critiques of the ethic from a disability rights perspective. The final section will argue that ethics of care can be adapted in a way to meet the disability critique.

[1] Which builds on Herring 2013 and 2014.

II. Ethics of Care

There is a substantial and rich literature on ethics of care[2] and it is not possible to do more than provide a very brief overview here. At its core is the claim that caring should be the most highly valued activity in society. A central role of any state is to ensure the essential needs of its citizens are met, and care is required to meet those needs. Caring is often invisible in public policy and ethics, when it should be at the heart of it.

Joan Tronto (1993: 12) explains that ethics of care is

> a set of moral sensibilities, issues and practices that arise from taking seriously the fact that care is a central aspect of human existence … a species activity that includes everything that we do to maintain, continue and repair our 'world' so that we can live in it as well as possible. That world includes our bodies, ourselves and our environment, all of which we seek to interweave in a complex, life-sustaining web.

As this quotation indicates, ethics of care cannot be reduced to simply the ethics of personal relations as some have suggested (Rachels 2012: 12). Its application can have profound impact on political thought, international relations and core concepts of legal rights and responsibilities (Held 2006; Engster 2007).

The central themes of ethics of care are as follows:

A. Care is Part of Being Human

We all have needs, and caring for others in meeting these needs and having our needs met by the care of others is a universal experience. Wendy Holloway (2006: 2) argues that 'care is the psychological equivalent to our need to breathe unpolluted air'. There will be few, if any, stages during anyone's life when they are not in caring relationships. As Eva Feder Kittay, Bruce Gennings and Angela Wassuna (2005: 426) put it:

> People do not spring up from the soil like mushrooms. People produce people. People need to be cared for and nurtured throughout their lives by other people, at some times more urgently and more completely than at other times.

Not only is care essential, it should be accepted as a moral good. Care should be treasured and valued as a good part of life. As Robin West (2002: 89) explains:

> Caregiving labour (and its fruits) is the central adventure of a lifetime; it is what gives life its point, provides it with meaning, and returns to those who give it some measure of security and emotional sustenance. For even more of us, whether or not we like it and

[2] See eg Gilligan 1987; Tronto 1993; Sevenhuijsen 1998; Groenhout 2004; Held 2006; Engster 2007; Bridgeman 2009; Herring 2013; Barnes, Brannelly, Ward and Ward 2015; Harding, Fletcher and Beasley 2016; and Harding 2017.

> regardless of how we regard it, caregiving labour, for children and the aged, is the work we will do that creates the relationships, families, and communities within which our lives are made pleasurable and connected to something larger than ourselves.

Care is the outworking of that most core moral value: love. It involves achieving a primary good: meeting the needs of others.[8]

B. Emotions are Ethically Significant

The law has traditionally been rather sceptical of emotions. It has preferred the idea of law to be governed by rationale and rule-following, rather than turning on the whims of emotions. Emotions cannot be assessed by empirical evidence and cannot be trusted. As a result emotions are largely ignored, or even treated with suspicion. The love which goes on caring and caring, and the grief, disappointment, frustration, anger and despair, which are all part of life, find no place (Herring 2017). Ethics of care, by contrast, regards emotions as offering important moral insights. For care work, values such as trust, empathy, compassion and sensitivity are key. If a legal intervention undermines such emotional values the intervention will be ineffective.

C. Intermingled Interests

Ethics of care is based on the belief that people are relational. People understand themselves in terms of their relationships. They do not seek to promote only their own interests, not because they are 'selfless', but because their interests are tied up with the interests of others. They cannot seek to promote their own interests with no attention paid to others. If good things happen to those they are in a positive relationship with then that is good for them (Downie and Llewellyn 2011).

Ethics of care, therefore, takes a particular view of the nature of the self; one that is constructed through and finds its meanings in relation to others (Foster and Herring 2017). Supporters of ethics of care do not need entirely to reject the notion of an individual self, but simply recognise that its identity and nature can only be appreciated through relation to others. In relationships of caring and dependency, interests become intermingled. We do not break down into 'me' and 'you'. As Virgina Held (2015: 145) puts it:

> Care should not be understood as self-sacrifice. Egoism versus altruism is the wrong way to interpret the issues. Yes, the interests of care giver and care receiver will sometimes conflict, but for the most part we do not pit our own interests against those of others in this context. We want what will be good for both or all of us together. We want our children and others we care for to do well along with ourselves, and for the relations between us to be good ones. If we are the recipients of care we want our care givers to do well along with us.

D. The Importance of Responsibilities

Ethics of care emphasises the importance of responsibilities within caring relationships (Collins 2015). Indeed many ethics of care supporters suggest that responsibilities should be the primary ethical tool, with rights playing a subordinate role. The classic liberal perspective is that one is 'born free' and that any responsibilities one takes on must be in some sense voluntarily assumed. However, for the ethics of care approach, with its starting point being that people are relational, then the supposition is that there will be responsibilities for others. We are born into relationships which carry responsibilities with them. So, the central legal or ethical question on a given issue should not be 'do I have a right to do X?'; the question should be 'what is my proper obligation within the context of this relationship?' (Held 2006). Under this vision, rights primarily exist to enable people to carry out their responsibilities (Herring 2017). And the role of the law should primarily be to encourage and enable people to fulfil their responsibilities to each other, rather than enforce their rights.

E. The Importance of Non-Abstraction

One of the key aspects of care ethics is that an ethical analysis must start with the context and concrete reality of the particular situations and the individuals and their relationships and characteristics. It rejects the stance of many mainstream ethical approaches, which seek to develop general rules that apply across all cases. Ethics of care argues that what might work for one group of people in one situation, will not work in another. What will be caring will depend on the particular individuals and the obligations they have. What will meet a person's needs cannot be generalised.

F. Gender and an Ethics of Care

Carol Gilligan is the leading pioneer of ethics of care thinking. In her 1980s writing she developed her approach as a response to the writing of Lawrence Kohlberg, who had argued that universalised and principled thinking was the highest and most sophisticated moral analysis. Kohlberg found that a greater percentage of boys in his samples scored more highly than girls. Gilligan's response to this was that the girls were speaking in a 'different voice'; ethics of care, as opposed to ethics of justice. Although she has sometimes been interpreted as suggesting that the ethics of care reflects a feminine voice, it seems her writing does not support the view that by that she means that women are more likely to adopt it than men. Certainly nowadays few ethics of care supporters claim it represents a particularly female way of ethical analysis.

Nevertheless the ethic has attracted considerable support among feminists, although it has supporters who do not explicitly adopt a feminist approach (eg Slote 2007). Its support among feminists can in part be explained by the fact that women undertake a significantly greater proportion of care work in contrast with men, and the political, social and ethic neglect of this work results in disadvantages for women.

Having provided a very brief overview of an ethics of care, we can turn to the disability critique of it.

III. The Disability Critique

Ethics of care has received a strong challenge from some disability theorists (Williams 2002). To understand the nature of the challenge it is necessary to briefly discuss the hotly-debated issue of the nature of disability. As is well known, this commonly involves considering two contrasting models of disability: the individual model and the social model (Shakespeare 2006).

Under the individual model a disability is a difference in a person's body or mind that causes them to have impaired functioning, when compared to a 'normal person'. Under this model the cause of any disadvantage flowing from disability is the limited function the individual is thought to suffer from. The appropriate response to disability is to eliminate disability, by curing it or (more controversially) preventing disabled people from being born the first place. If this is not possible we should attempt to mitigate the disadvantages flowing from disability by providing what services we can (Radcliffe Richards 2002).

Under the social model, by contrast, the problems flowing from disability are due to society's failure to provide the necessary services to ensure no difficulties flow from the difference in function or psychology. So, if someone cannot reach the first floor of a building, this is better explained by the fact there is no appropriate provision for them to reach the first floor. No one can reach the first floor of a building without some kind of accommodation. The provision of stairs, say, will enable some but not others to reach the first floor. The social model argues that society chooses to provide accommodations for some limitations people face (be it shops, transport, sewerage, etc), but not for others. Those limitations which society does not meet are labelled as disability. The Union of Physically Impaired Against Segregation (UPIAS 1975), adopting the social model, defined disability in the following way:

> Disability is something imposed on top of our impairments by the way we are unnecessarily isolated and excluded from full participation in society. Disabled people are therefore an oppressed group in society. To understand this it is necessary to grasp the distinction between the physical impairment and the social situation, called 'disability', of people with such impairment. Thus, we define impairment as lacking part of or all of a limb, or having a defective limb, organ or mechanism of the body; and disability as the disadvantage or restriction of activity caused by a contemporary social organization which takes no or little account of people who have physical impairments and thus excludes them from participation in the mainstream of social activities. Physical disability is therefore a particular form of social oppression.

Some commentators argue that we can combine the two theories to explain that some disadvantages are a result of a physical impairment, but others result from a failure to make social provision. Myrian Winance (2016: 101) suggests we can

> separate the deficiency (an individual biological characteristic) from the disability (a social reality, a position of exclusion defined in relation to the balance of power between people). … Disability is a social difference piled on top of a natural specificity.

This debate between the social and individual models of disability is complex and has become intense. This chapter is not the place to explore all the issues properly. However, enough has been said here to understand the criticisms of ethics of care launched by those writing from a disability studies perspective.

A. Care and the Social Model of Disability

The disability critique claims that the standard presentation of care plays into the individual model of disability. By presenting care as the meeting of needs, this appears to locate the 'problem' in the body of the disabled person, which is met by the care. In particular it assumes a norm for bodies, and disabled bodies are those departing from this norm, and so requiring care from an 'able bodied person' which can bring them back to the norm.

This becomes all the more problematic given that much writing on care, and particularly the organisations promoting the interests of carers, highlight the burdens and disadvantages that care work brings. This impliedly paints the disabled person as the cause of carers' disadvantage. To give one example, in their survey of the literature on caregivers, of those with Alzheimer's disease Daniel Kaufer et al (2005) explain:

> Family and friends provide nearly three quarters of all care for patients with Alzheimer's disease. This informal care results in significant burden to caregivers. Caregiver burden is the set of physical, psychological or emotional, social, and financial problems that family members may experience when caring for impaired older adults. Caregivers of Alzheimer's disease patients report higher rates of physical symptoms, mortality, depression, and fatigue, as well as adverse effects on employment compared with those who are not caregivers for Alzheimer's disease patients.

Unintentionally it can imply that disability is 'a problem', for which carers pay the cost of solving.

B. Care and Power

In the ethics of care literature, care can be presented in idealised terms. It is assumed to be an inevitable good, but this can overlook the 'dark side of care' (Fine 2007: 4). The ethics of care literature certainly acknowledges that there can be abuse within caring relationships. However, what is less acknowledged is the 'paternalistic edge' that regularly accompanies care (Shakespeare 2001: chapter 2). Jenny Morris (1997: 54) has also argued that care itself is a form of oppression against disabled people:

> The only way to empower disabled people is to throw off the ideology of caring which is a form of oppression and an expression of prejudice. Empowerment means choice and control; it means that someone has the power to exert choice and therefore maximise control in their lives (always recognising that there are limits to how much control any of us have over what happens in our lives). Care – in the second half of the twentieth century – has come to mean not caring about someone but caring for in the sense of taking responsibility for. People who are said to need caring for are assumed to be unable to exert choice and control. One cannot, therefore, have care and empowerment, for it is the ideology and the practice of caring which has led to the perception of disabled people as powerless.

To similar effect, Richard Woods (quoted in Shakespeare 2001: 63) contends:

> Disabled people have never demanded or asked for care! We have sought independent living, which means being able to achieve maximum independence and control over our own lives. The concept of care seems to many disabled people a tool through which others are able to dominate and manage our lives.

What these quotes capture is the way that 'caring for another' can readily amount to an exercise of power. The 'carer' identifies the need of the 'cared for' and then decides how to meet it. The carer is the active person, the 'cared for' is passive (Weicht 2010). Zygmunt Bauman (1993: 11) warns that 'the impulse to care for the other, when taken to its extreme, leads to the annihilation of the autonomy of the other, to domination and oppression'.

There are horrific examples of this, as Christine Kelly (2011: 565) writes:

> In the name of 'caring for' individuals or society at large, disabled people have been subjected to multiple forms of oppression, including forced sterilization, painful and ineffective physical 'therapies', physical and emotional abuse, and of course, institutionalization.

But, the concerns are not restricted to such dramatic examples. Julia Twigg (2000a: 180) has researched older people's experiences of being bathed and that highlights this quite clearly:

> One person, strong and able, stands above and over another who is frail and physically vulnerable, forced to rely on their strength and goodwill. Being naked in the face of someone who is not, contains a powerful dynamic of domination and vulnerability, and it is often used in situations of interrogation and torture as a means of subjugating the individual.

This way that care silences and dominates disabled people, of course, reinforces the range of ways disabled people are within society more broadly disadvantaged and marginalised (Silvers 1995).

C. From Care to Assistance

Many writing from a disability studies perspective have argued that we need to shift away from the notion of care, and towards attendant services. The Centre for Independent Living in Toronto (2010) defines these:

> Attendant Services are physical assistance with routine activities of daily living as directed by the consumer. The consumer is responsible for the decisions and training involved in his/her own assistance.
>
> Attendant services include: bathing and washing, transferring, toileting, dressing, skin care, essential communications, meal preparation.
>
> Attendant services do NOT include: professional services such as nursing care, physiotherapy, occupational therapy, respite care, physician services, 'care' or taking responsibility for the person with a disability.

The shift in terminology from carer to attendant or assistance makes it clear that the disabled person is the one who directs the services. Rather than being the passive recipient of care, they control, direct and utilise the service to achieve independence. This understanding, it is said, promotes empowerment, choice and control.

This shift in terminology could be welcomed by carers' groups too. The language of being an assistant or attendant makes it clear that it is a job that is being done. One of the downsides of the language of care is that it can promote the selfless, dedicating loving carer who is devoted to the person needing care. That can put it outside the scope of financial reward or recognition. This is well captured by the quote of Gordon Brown (2007: 16) who argues:

> It is far more a matter of love than of duty – caring that expresses itself in the priceless gift of sustained and dedicated support for people close to them ... Every one of the carers I have met is an inspiration and refutes a widespread cynicism that in today's society, selfishness matters more than services to others.

Having looked at the disability critique of care we can return to consider whether or not ethics of care can respond to these challenges.

IV. Responses of Care Ethics

In light of these points it is not surprising that there appears a tension between a feminist ethics of care and disability activists (Beckett 2007). It must be a cause of some embarrassment to the ethics of care literature that most attention has been on those 'giving care'. Much is written in the care literature on the social isolation of carers; the personal and economic disadvantage of carers; and the lack of recognition that carers are given in society. This is all welcome and important, but in making such points those 'receiving' the care and the disadvantages they face, have also been ignored. Further, there is the possibility that the abuse of care gets overlooked in the care literature.

However, I do not think the disability critique requires an abandonment of ethics of care. Clare Beckett (2007: 360) correctly identifies the key issue: 'to what extent are disempowering factors and inequality inherent in conceptualizing care?' The answer to that question is, I suggest, a significant extent. However, that shows us that what ethics of care should be seeking to promote is not care as an abstract concept, but rather caring relationships. This point needs developing.

A. Caring Relationships, Not Carers

It is certainly true that in terms of political engagement and charities concerned with care, the emphasis has been on the carer's perspective. There have been calls for carers' rights and a charter for carers. These can be combined with attempts to determine the economic value of care work. All of this can be seen as focusing on the task performed by one person to another (Held 2006: 26). This can be echoed in the academic literature. Diemut Bubeck (1995: 129) argues care involves

> the meeting of needs of one person by another where face-to-face interaction between care and cared for is a crucial element of overall activity, and where the need is of such a nature that it cannot possibly be met by the person in need herself.

However, in *Caring and the Law*, I argued that rather than promoting 'care' we should promote caring relationships (Herring 2013: chapter 2). My hope was that in using this terminology the contributions of both parties would be recognised. We should recognise that traditional division between carer and cared for fails to capture the dynamic of a caring relationship. We are all givers and receivers of care. What we do is not understood as an 'activity' but as a part of a relationship. The relationship gives what is done meaning and value. It is important, too, to realise that most caring is 'embedded in long-term dyadic relationships' such as partner, parent or child (Larkin and Milne 2014: 26). These are relationships marked by a shared life course and history. They are fluid and complex and need to be understood in their relational context.

Such relationships will change over time so that pigeonholing the parties into categories of carer and care receiver become artificial. As Clare Beckett (2007: 362) puts it: 'to be caring or cared for are not positions, attributes or roles that are necessarily oppositional or dualistic in practice, but are part of the weave of any social relationship'.

The importance of seeing caring relationships, rather than an activity, as the heart of ethics of care, will be explored further below.

B. Over-emphasising Autonomy

A core idea within the personal assistant model is that the disabled person directs what is done. Judy Heumann (cited Stoddard 1978), one of the founders of the

Independent Living Movement, wrote: 'To us, independence does not mean doing things physically alone. It means being able to make independent decisions. It is a mind process not contingent upon a normal body.'

However, such an approach assumes an ability to make decisions and direct the services. It can only be plausible for some people with disability, perhaps the most articulate and vocal. For the profoundly disabled and those with intellectual challenges the responsibility of directing their care may be an impossibility or a burden.

The seeking of independent decision-making is not what most people want. Most people when making decisions of any significance will consult with friends and others. Decisions, particularly those which affect others, are typically made together. It is not surprising therefore that many people making caring decisions discuss the issues with their family members, carers and friends (Glendinning, Mitchell and Brooks 2016). A dialogue about the best way to arrange care is empowering (Keyes, Webber and Beveridge 2015). This language of making caring decisions jointly ensures that care is not provided uni-directionally and ensures the disabled person is not left to make the decision in an isolated environment. The writing on relational autonomy highlights how decision-making is best understood in the context of the rich and complex social connections people have (Herring 2015). The personal assistant model of care fails to capture the way autonomy needs to be understood as relational. It is through having deep caring relationships that our autonomy flourishes, not having assistants we can direct.

C. Care is Not Just an Activity

Eva Kittay (2011: 51–52) is concerned that the view of carers as personal assistants involves the 'denigration of care' and it makes the work and value of carers invisible. There is a danger, she suggests of 'creating one oppression in the effort to alleviate another'. She describes as an important part of caring 'a positive, affective bond and investment in another's well-being'. That is a mark of both parties to the relationship and is more than the performance of a task. Without that attitude the tasks will not be good care.

In good caring relationships the parties do not treat each other as objects but rather recognise each other as fellow human beings. Robin Dillon (1992: 128) captures this with the word 'attention' and argues:

> The term 'care' denotes here an epistemic attitude, understood as a moral ideal of attention: a commitment to attend, with intensely focused perception to all aspects of the irreducible particularity of individual human persons in their concrete contexts.

This is important because good caring involves the parties recognising that each other are unique individuals. That requires empathy and anticipation. Joan Tronto (1993: 15), for example, has been clear that a central part of care is responsiveness: consideration of the position of others as they see it and responding in the way they want it. It is not the doing of the job (as the term personal assistant might suggest) but working together at a task. It involves talking through and reaching a consensual solution. Importantly, this means not just seeing a person with a particular condition and providing the solution to the task, but treating the person as a whole. There must be awareness of how the other person is experiencing the care. This involves interaction and engagement with the individual. Obviously, care provided with no thought to the response of the person receiving it is in danger of objectifying the person receiving the care (Lindemann 2003). The relational model of care highlights how good care is a two-way interaction.

D. Interdependence

Whether the language of 'carer and cared for' or 'disabled person and personal assistant' is used this creates a false image that the interests of the parties can be separated. This is false at several levels.

First, often 'carers' are themselves receiving care. Notably in the UK 27 per cent of carers were found in one study to be themselves recipients of benefits on account of their disability (NHS Information Centre 2015). Thus, it is more accurate to acknowledge the networks of care that we live in, rather than dividing us up into providers and recipients of care. There is yet further significance in focusing on relationships of care. The discrimination against those seen as having a disability or infirmity can operate as a disadvantage to those in a relationship with them. Negative attitudes about disability are reflected in negative attitudes about care. As Bill Hughes and his colleagues (2005: 265) put it:

> [T]he parties involved in the caring relationship are perpetually invalidated because the value of care is measured against the autonomous adult male who neither requires nor delivers care. To be a carer or cared for – male or female, disabled or non-disabled in either role – is to be found wanting, to be other in relation to the masculine subject of modernity, to be reduced to 'the other of the same'. Those who give and receive care are marginalized, 'used and wasted' bodies, existing, by and large, on the margins of what counts as the truly human community.

Secondly, in caring relationships the interaction is typically far more complex than one party giving and one party receiving care. Kelly Fritsch (2011: 2) has provided a powerful practical example of how in caring relationships individual identities become merged. In her sensitive analysis of the use of carers or attendants to facilitate and enable sexual encounters for disabled people she shows how the line between bodies in these cases is complex. The carer and the cared for

> experience a leaking of their identities, a mingling of their sexualities, and multiple intimate slippages of selves as the attendant participates in the daily work of feeding, bathing, shopping, facilitating sex, and numerous other activities. In the interaction between a disabled person and an attendant, both bodies extend into one another, displacing the limits of their assumedly contained sovereign selves. … The emphasis, then, is placed not on what you can do for me but rather what we can create together.

Caring relationships are therefore far more complex than the carer/cared for; disabled person/personal assistant models will allow. As Twigg (2000: 392) writes, care is better seen as a co-production: 'It is in the dynamics of the care encounter that the nature of what is produced is defined; production and consumption collapse into one another. … [U]sers and workers are co-producers of care.'

It might be claimed that this is idealised in cases where a person has a profound disability (Simplican 2016). But that is not the experience of those caring for such people. Eva Feder Kittay's daughter, Sesha, has cerebral palsy and has profound physical and intellectual impairment. However Feder Kittay (2002: 100) writes that Sesha possesses:

> [T]he most important faculties of all. The capacities for love and for happiness. These allow those of us who care for her, who love her, who have been entrusted with her well-being to form deep and abiding attachments to her. Sesha's coin and currency is love. That is what she wishes to receive and that is what she reciprocates in spades.

E. The Nature of the Self

Many of the issues discussed to date relate to our understanding of the norm for bodies and selves. Much modern legal and ethical thought is premised on the norm of an autonomous, self-contained self. This is problematic for disability, as Myrian Winance (2016: 102) writes:

> The difference between disabled people and able-bodied people lies in the fact that, for the latter, their 'standard' body matches the construction standards of the heterogeneous networks that make up our society; it is therefore easier for them to acquire the status of autonomous and independent subject. Disabled people, for their part, must face many gaps and therefore have a harder time making themselves into autonomous subjects.

My concern with the personal attendant model of care is that it seeks to adopt the autonomous subject model as the ideal (Fineman 2008). Ethics of care offers a powerful alternative. It is based on the assumption that we are all profoundly dependent on others for our physical and psychological well-being. Part of our vulnerability leads from our embodiment. We like to present our bodies as self-contained and secure structures. In fact, our bodies are leaky and in a constant state of flux (Herring and Chau 2007). Our bodies are insecure and vulnerable. Our society has built up a wide range of structures and forms of assistance which disguise our vulnerability. Indeed, we are forced by a wide range of societal pressures to disguise or mitigate our vulnerability so that we can behave in an acceptable way in the public realm. In a powerful article, Kate Lindemann (2003: 502) contrasts the emphasis that is paid to the accommodations for disabled people to minimise the impact of their disability, with the lack of appreciation of the similar accommodations for the able bodied:

> Colleagues, professional staff members, and other adults are unconscious of the numerous accommodations that society provides to make their work and life style possible.

> ATM's, extended hours in banks, shopping centres and medical offices, EZpass, newspaper kiosks, and elevators are all accommodations that make contemporary working life possible. There are entire industries devoted to accommodating the needs of adult working people. Fast food, office lunch delivery, day time child care, respite care, car washing, personal care attendants, interpreters, house cleaning, and yard and lawn services are all occupations that provide services that make it possible for adults to hold full time jobs.

We thus highlight the facilities used to deal with the vulnerabilities of others, while overlooking the accommodations 'we' need to deal with our vulnerabilities. Further, we readily class those who need care from others as vulnerable, without seeing the vulnerability that caring creates for the carer (Herring 2017).

The significance of the failure to acknowledge our common vulnerability is that, as Martha Fineman (2008: 24) argues, we lose sight of the power and privilege that is used by some to disguise theirs:

> When we only study the poor, the rich remain hidden and their advantages remain relatively unexamined, nestled in secure and private spaces, where there is no need for them or the state to justify or explain why they deserve the privilege of state protection. We need to excavate these privileged lives. While sometimes this will be a difficult and complex undertaking, there are certainly abundant records and instruments of privilege all around us that can be accessed relatively easily. These archives are located in corporate boardrooms and in the rules setting up or limiting state and national regulatory regimes. They can be gleaned from tax and probate codes, history books, literature, political theories, and of course, from the language and logic of the law.

There generates an important uniting force between care ethics and disability studies. The model of independence, with linked themes of self-sufficiency and the importance of economic productivity, can be used to side-line all in caring relationships. Downgrading care works to the disadvantage of disabled people. Downgrading disabled people impacts on those in relationships with them.

Winance, Damamme and Fillion (2015: 163) argue that ethics of care promotes a new understanding of the self as 'fundamentally relational, that is elaborated and evolves by and in care relationships'. Such a model will challenge the assumption about the normal body and what is productive citizenship, which is harmful for both the valuing of disability and care. As Rosemarie Garland-Thomson (2002: 2) argues:

> [D]isability is perhaps the essential characteristic of being human. The body is dynamic, constantly interactive with history and environment. We evolve into disability. Our bodies need care; we all need assistance to live. An equality model of feminist theory sometimes prizes individualistic autonomy as the key to women's liberation. A feminist disability theory, however, suggests that we are better off learning to individually and collectively accommodate bodily limits and evolutions than trying to eliminate or deny them.

Vulnerability and dependence are not only inevitable parts of humanity; they are to be greatly welcomed. They are virtues, not vices. Self-reliance has become a dominant theme in social policy. Be it lone parents or care in the community, autonomy and independence have become key policy goals. But this ignores the fact that as humans we are interdependent. No one can be truly independent. Hence, the aspiration of the UK Government (2012: 18) on care is utterly misguided: 'Our vision is one that promotes people's independence and wellbeing by enabling them to prevent or postpone the need for care and support'.

The anti-vulnerability narrative tends to promote disablist approaches to the issue. As many writers from disability studies have written, there is great pressure on disabled people to be perceived as being independent and lacking vulnerability. Success for a person with a disability is measured by the extent to which they may be able to be (or present themselves as being) independent and autonomous – in short, to be 'normal'. As Jayne Clapton (2003: 540) puts it:

> Such a construction, which privileges a particular understanding of personhood, assumes a prototypical disembodied person – that is, typically a male characterized by independence and the presence of rationality and reason; or in other words, that which constitutes, in the philosophical sense, 'normal'.

We need to recognise the benefits of vulnerability. Janine Wiles (2011: 575) writes:

> Vulnerability is often seen as fragility or weakness, but it may also be conceptualised as openness, susceptibility, and receptiveness. Ideas about vulnerability as inherent to the self and as formative might be usefully applied to the experiences of older care recipients. To experience and acknowledge one's vulnerability may be a process of renegotiation of one's sense of embodied self and relationships to people and places.

Our universal disability reflects how Martha Fineman (2008: 1) describes vulnerability as a 'universal, inevitable, enduring aspect of the human condition'. We are all limited by our bodies in different ways by what we can and cannot do. At different points in our lives, our bodies restrict us in different ways. In one sense at birth, we are all profoundly disabled and dependent on others. Even those in the 'prime of health' are dependent on others for services; from public transport, to the supply of energy, to the provision of food. We all have a range of limitations and need others and our community to meet our needs (Garland-Thomson 2011).

I am not seeking to suggest that are we are all vulnerable or disabled in the same way. We all have our unique weaknesses and strengths. Indeed our weaknesses can be strengths in some contexts, and weaknesses in others. However, we should emphasise the vulnerability we all have, the care we all receive and the care we all give. These caring relationships, however, cause disadvantages and we need to ensure that our social provision and legal responses ensure a fair distribution of the costs of caring relationships.

Following up on this last point, by way of example, much of the law is based on the assumption that we are competent, detached, independent people who are entitled to have our rights of self-determination and autonomy fiercely protected (Herring 2013). Legal rights and rules operate to draw boundaries around ourselves and protect us from interference from others. However, ethics of care would emphasise that the reality is that we are ignorant, vulnerable, interdependent individuals, whose strength and reality is not in our autonomy, but our relationships with others (Meyer 2004). The law should start with a norm of interlocking, mutually dependent relationships, rather than an individualised vision of rights.

More positive things can be said about vulnerability than that it is simply an inevitable part of the human condition. Our mutual vulnerability requires us to reach out to others to offer and receive help from them. The virtues of beneficence and compassion are encouraged and necessary. We have to become open to others and our own and others' needs. A recognition of our mutual vulnerability leads to empathy and understanding. It creates intimacy and trust. It compels us to focus on interactive, co-operative solutions to the issues we address. It encourages creativity in finding new ways of overcoming our human limitations and requires a desire to accept others as they are.

Vulnerability is essential to relationships. In entering a relationship with others this creates an understanding of trust, the assumptions of responsibility, and obligations of care. These things create a vulnerability: we are in danger of not meeting our obligations; we are at risk of others not meeting theirs to us. Our trust might be misplaced. The opening up of our natures creates a risk we will be taken advantage of, that private information will be used to harm us, and the risk of grief and loss. Yet relationships are good and beneficial. Indeed they may well be described as one of the basic goods. Relationships, intimacy, care; all of these things in their nature render us vulnerable. Exclusion of the other to achieve invulnerability is an anathema to relationships.

Feder Kittay (2011: 621) is 'not given to sentimentality' but still she writes of her disabled daughter Sesha:

> Sometimes I wonder if Sesha is a special being sent to us from elsewhere, for there is an impossible-to-articulate sweetness, graciousness, and emotional openness about her – qualities we rarely find in others. On any conventional definition of health, Sesha would be found unhealthy, but does not her sweetness, graciousness and openness demonstrate a rare health? We elevate the capacity for logic, rational thought and autonomy over the capacity for wonder, gentleness and warmth, but perhaps the first set of qualities make for a better person than the other.

We need not hide and be embarrassing by our precarious, leaky independent bodies. We need not to pretend to know it all, be hyper-rational and driven by our high-order values. We need not claim to be self-sufficient, able to survive without government handouts or the help of others. Our destiny and sense of purpose is not found in ourselves. We are not people of autonomy but people of dependence. We are created for and with one another. We can say 'I am because we are' (Feder Kittay 2013). We are fragile, fearful, broken; but that is as we should be.

V. Conclusion

This chapter has explored the disability studies critique of ethics of care. With some justification, that critique has complained that the writing on care has focused on 'carers' and has not considered the position of those 'cared for'. Nor has it acknowledged the paternalism and power that can mark care. However, these concerns do not undermine care ethics. They require us to emphasise that we should seek to promote caring relationships, not just carers. The emphasis on caring relationships acknowledges that it is a huge simplification to separate people into 'carers' and 'cared for'. In fact in the caring relationships we are all in there is a merging of interests and selves. Vulnerabilities, care and identities become mutual and interdependent. We need to break down the division between the 'carer' and the 'cared for', between the 'disabled' and the 'able-bodied'. The chapter argues that ethics of care recognises the harms of the idealised, autonomous, contained self that has done much to set back the interests of everyone including disabled people. By recognising our mutuality and interdependence and the dependency of everyone on services, a better vision for ethical and legal analysis is provided.

References

Barnes, M, Brannelly, T, Ward, L and Ward, N (eds) (2015) *Ethics of Care: Critical Advances in International Perspective* (Bristol, Policy Press).

Bauman, Z (1993) *Postmodern Ethics* (Abingdon, Blackwell).

Beckett, C (2007) 'Women, Disability, Care: Good Neighbours or Uneasy Bedfellows?' *Critical Social Policy* 27: 360.

Bridgeman, J (2009) *Parental Responsibility, Young Children and Healthcare Law* (Cambridge, Cambridge University Press).

Brown, G (2007) 'Why we must all care' in *Daily Mail*, 21 February 2007: 16.

Bubeck, D (1995) *Care, Gender and Justice* (Oxford, Oxford University Press).

Centre for Independent Living in Toronto (2010), cited in C Kelly 'Re/Moving Care from the Ontario Direct Funding Program: Altering Conversations among Disability and Feminist Scholars' (2014) *Social Politics* 21: 124, 126.

Clapton, J (2003) 'Tragedy and Catastrophe: Contentious Discourses of Ethics and Disability' *Journal of Intellectual Disability Research* 47: 540.

Collins, S (2015) *The Core of Care Ethics* (London, Palgrave).

Dillon, R (1992) 'Respect and Care' *Canadian Journal of Philosophy* 22: 105.

Downie, J and Llewellyn, J (2011) *Being Relational* (Vancouver BC, University of British Columbia Press).

Engster, D (2007) *The Heart of Justice. Care Ethics and Political Theory* (Oxford, Oxford University Press).

Feder Kittay, E (2002) 'Not my way Sesha your way' in C Mui and J Murphy (eds), *Gender Struggles: Practical Approaches to Contemporary Feminism* (London, Rowman & Littlefield).

—— (2011) 'The Ethics of Care, Dependence, and Disability' *Ratio Juris* 24: 49.

Feder Kittay, E, Jennings, B, and Wassuna, A (2005) 'Dependency, Difference and the Global Ethic of Longterm Care' *Journal of Political Philosophy* 13: 433.

Fine, M (2007) *A Caring Society?* (Palgrave).

Fineman, M (2008) 'The Vulnerable Subject: Anchoring Equality in the Human Condition' *Yale Journal of Law and Feminism* 20: 1.

Foster, C and Herring, J (2017) *Identity, Personhood and the Law* (Berlin, Springer).

Fritsch, K (2011) 'Intimate Assemblages: Disability, Intercorporeality, and the Labour of Attendant Care' *Critical Disabilities Discourse* 1: 2.

Garland-Thomson, R (2002) 'Integrating Disability, Transforming Feminist Theory' *Feminist Disability Studies* 14: 1.
—— (2011) 'Misfits: A Feminist Materialist Disability Concept' *Hypatia* 26: 591.
Gilligan, C (1987) 'Moral Orientation and Moral Development' in E Feder Kittay and D Meyers (eds), *Women and Moral Theory* (London, Rowman & Littlefield).
Glendinning, C, Mitchell, W and Brooks, J (2016) 'Ambiguity in practice? Carers' roles in personalised social care in England' *Sexualities* 19: 959.
Groenhout, R (2004) *Connected Lives: Human Nature and an Ethics of Care* (London, Rowman & Littlefield).
Harding, R (2017) *Duties to Care* (Cambridge, Cambridge University Press).
Harding, R, Fletcher, R and Beasley, C (eds) (2016) *Revaluing Care in Theory, Law and Policy* (Abingdon, Routledge).
Held, V (2006) *The Ethics of Care* (Oxford, Oxford University Press).
—— (2015) 'Care and Human Rights' in R Cruft, M Liao and M Renzo (eds), *Philosophical Foundations of Human Rights* (Oxford, Oxford University Press).
Her Majesty's Government (2012) *Caring for Our Future* (London, The Stationery Office).
Herring, J (2013) *Caring and the Law* (Oxford, Hart Publishing).
—— (2014) 'The Disability Critique of Care' *Elder Law Journal* 8: 2.
—— (2015) *Relational Autonomy and Family Law* (Berlin, Springer).
—— (2017) 'Compassion, Ethic of Care and Legal Rights' *International Journal of Law in Context* 13: 158.
Herring, J and Chau, P-L (2007) 'My Body, Your Body, Our Bodies' *Medical Law Review* 15: 54.
Holloway, W (2006) 'Introducing the Capacity to Care' in W Hollway (ed), *The Capacity to Care: Gender and Ethical Subjectivity* (Abingdon, Routledge).
Hughes, B (2005) 'Love's Labours Lost? Feminism, the Disabled People's Movement and an Ethic of Care' *Sociology* 39: 259.
Kaufer, D, Borson, S, Kershaw, P and Sadik, K (2005) 'Reduction of Caregiver Burden in Alzheimer's Disease by Treatment with Galantamine' *CNS Spectrums* 10: 481.
Kelly, C (2011) 'Making "Care" Accessible: Personal Assistance for Disabled People and the Politics of Language' *Critical Social Policy* 31: 562.
Keyes, S, Webber S and Beveridge, K (2015) 'Empowerment through Care' *European Journal of Disabilities Research* 9: 236.
Larkin, M and Milne, A (2014) 'Carers and Empowerment in the UK: A Critical Reflection' *Social Policy and Society* 13: 25.
Lindemann, K (2003) 'The Ethics of Receiving' *Theoretical Medicine and Bioethics* 24: 501.
Meyer, C (2004) 'Cruel Choices: Autonomy and Critical Care Decision-Making' *Bioethics* 18: 104.
Morris, J (1997) 'Care or Empowerment: A disability rights perspective' *Social Policy & Administration* 31: 54.
NHS Information Centre (2015) *Survey of Carers in Households* (NHS).
Rachels, J (2012) *The Elements of Moral Philosophy*, 7th edn (New York, McGraw-Hill Education).
Radcliffe Richards, J (2002) 'How Not to End Disability' *San Diego Law Review* 39: 693.
Sevenhuijsen, S (1998) *Citizenship and the Ethics of Care* (Abingdon, Routledge).
Shakespeare, T (2001) *Help* (London, Venture Press).
—— (2006) *Disability Rights and Wrongs* (Abingdon, Routledge).
Silvers, A (1995) 'Reconciling Equality to Difference: Caring (f)or Justice for People with Disabilities' *Hypatia* 10: 30.
Simplican, C (2016) 'Care, Disability, and Violence: Theorizing Complex Dependency in Eva Kittay and Judith Butler' *Hypatia* 30: 217.
Slote, M (2007) *The Ethics of Care and Empathy* (Abingdon, Routledge).
Stoddard, S (1978) 'Independent living: Concepts and Programs' *American Rehabilitation* 3: 2.
Tronto, J (1993) *Moral Boundaries* (Abingdon, Routledge).
Twigg, J (2000) 'Carework as a Form of Bodywork' *Ageing and Society* 20: 389.

—— (2000a) *Bathing – the Body and Community Care* (London, Routledge).
Union of Physically Impaired Against Segregation (1975) *Fundamental Principles of Disability* (New York, UPIAS).
Weicht, B (2010) 'Embracing Dependency: Rethinking (In)Dependence in the Discourse of Care' *Sociological Review* 58: 205.
West, R (2002) 'The Right to Care' in E Feder Kittay and E Feder (eds), *The Subject of Care: Feminist Perspectives on Dependency* (London, Rowman & Littlefield).
Wiles, J (2011) 'Reflections on being a Recipient of Care: Vexing the Concept of Vulnerability' *Social and Cultural Geography* 12: 573.
Williams, F (2002) 'The Presence of Feminism in the Future of Welfare' *Economy and Society* 31: 502.
Winance, M (2016) 'Rethinking Disability: Lessons from the Past, Questions for the Future' *European Journal of Disability Research* 10: 99.
Winance, M, Damamme, A and Fillion, E (2015) 'Thinking the Aid and Care Relationship from the Standpoint of Disability: Stakes and Ambiguities' *European Journal of Disability Research* 9: 163.

10

Kinship Care

PERVEEZ MODY

In a ground-breaking paper first published in 2001, John Borneman argued that anthropology's desire to identify a 'regulative ideal for humanity' had caused it to 'repress care' in favour of those aspects of social life that bore upon collective reproduction, such as marriage (2001: 31). He argued that anthropologists should instead privilege what he called 'caring and being cared for' as 'processes of non-coercive, voluntary affiliation'. Caring relationships for Borneman were both vitally important but also optative (ie a matter of design rather than fate) and for this reason, preferable as a focus for anthropological study to more 'traditional' forms of 'given' kinship. One significant risk of Borneman's line of argument that sought to supplant a theory of kinship with 'care', was that anthropologists might actively diminish the importance of kinship ties and in so doing, also diminish the importance of ties that oblige people into particular shapes of relatedness and forms of action, focusing instead upon the malleability of ties that were constructed (and the obligations that are in turn 'chosen' rather than given).

At around the same time as Borneman's validation of care, a movement was sweeping through anthropology, giving birth to what came to be known as 'new kinship studies' (Weston 1991; Carsten 2001; Sahlins 2013). This invigoration of the anthropological study of kinship presented itself as concerned with those processual aspects of relationships that manifest as subjective, agentive and largely celebratory of possibilities for combination, choice and freedom. New kinship studies sought to supplant the already much-maligned term 'kinship' with all its heavy baggage and replace it with the lighter and more mobile notion of 'relatedness'. Intimacies and relationships were the building blocks of new kinship studies that sought to understand the processes through which relatedness 'congealed' together, indexed by processes of human relationality shorn free of biological connectedness.

The means by which both Borneman and 'new kinship studies' constructed their critiques of kinship, generates a shared ground in which their putative alternatives ('care', 'relationality') reject the narrow constraints of meanings ascribed to kinship (now more or less designated as a 'traditional' anthropological construct) and instead follow relationships that are socially constructed through processes of making and varying forms of materialisation (McKinnon 2016). However, this emphasis on relationality and the element of choice in creating relationships appears somewhat distant from many kinship constraints, in large swathes of the world, that continue to exercise themselves upon those whose lives are dominated and defined by being kin and are not shaped by 'non-coercive, voluntary' choices. In a recent and important intervention in the debate on kinship, Kuper says:

> [K]inship matters. It provides the only social security system that most people in the world can rely on. It delivers the daily bread, emotional support, favours, role models and a sense of identity. Wherever ethnographers travel they find that parents and children live together, expect to love one another, and hope that they can call on more distant relatives to help them out. So kinship is a universal, vital principle of social life.

Kuper strongly rejects the characterisation of kinship as mere symbolic system, or worse still, as a symbolic discourse that pays little attention to 'the messy day to day business of family life'.

This chapter is deeply concerned with the symbolic discourses that deal with what people 'ought' or indeed 'want' to do and the consequences this has on the ways in which they conceive and enact care. My work on the phenomenon known as 'forced marriage' has caused me to argue elsewhere that many South Asian parents who coerce their children into marriages against their will, did so because they nevertheless believed that arranging their children's' marriage suitably (in their terms) was a profound act of parental care – their children would be grateful in the long run for the prudence and maturity of decisions that they were unable to make themselves because they did not fully understand the things their parents knew mattered (eg status in the community, ritual rank, financial stability, kinship – see Mody 2015). This is an important anthropological insight, because it helps us understand why many South Asian parents condemn 'forced marriages' in the abstract but fail to put themselves into the same picture – from where they stand, what they are doing is characterised as both responsible and caring. An abdication of the responsibility to 'settle' your children properly through arranging an appropriate marriage is conversely, a profound act of neglect and irresponsibility.

While this is a starting point for my work on 'forced marriages' it isn't sufficient by any means for an understanding of the phenomenon. Many of the young people I worked with had indeed been coerced and forced in ways that had damaged them profoundly. Nevertheless, working with informants to obtain their perspectives, in some cases over a period of many years, has allowed me to see the ways in which both kinship and care are negotiated and navigated by individuals who have been forced, and by their families and wider kin. This chapter is also concerned with the mess and detritus of everyday life when the familial and kinship scripts collapse due to events that spiral out of control, to reveal much greater complexity in terms of how people navigate ideals and practices of care for those they call family. To get to the heart of Kuper's critique of new kinship studies, kinship matters because kinship is universally a locus not just of 'choice', as new kinship studies has it, but also of its very opposite – that is, constraint and obligation alongside love, intimacy, choice and care. In this regard, I characterise kinship as a space of care but also and equally, as a space in which constraint, coercion and choice mutually inform and interact with each other as a sort of working-out of kinship relations.

Borneman's exhortations about the importance of opening up our analytics to everyday practices of care are vitally important, alongside Kuper's warning not to so speedily dismiss the obligations of kinship but instead pay heed to the ways in which they are configured, embedded, endure and flourish. I will argue that these paired concerns compete with but also complement each other, inviting us to shine more critical light upon the interaction and co-constitution of kinship and care. This chapter therefore explores the ways in which the obligations of kinship care (now conjoined) are described, called upon or dismissed by informants who have themselves experienced what they have called 'forced marriages' at the hands of their own families. In looking at 'kinship care' as a dialectic in need of suitable ethnographic inquiry, I will explore the ways in which kinship and caring endeavours intersect to forge new spaces through which relations are managed, navigated and recovered in uniquely interesting ways.

I. State Care Versus Kinship Care in 'Forced Marriage'

To the legal mind, 'forced marriages' are those in which either (or both) parties to the marriage do not give their full and free consent, and so the marriage can be annulled. The difficulty of applying this legal clarity to British South Asian marital forms arises in the first instance in the identification of 'the parties' to a marriage and to the agency the law attributes to the party as an individual. Underlying the consent of the individual in a typical arranged marriage is the social/cultural conceptualisation of the 'two parties' to a marriage as the two families who arrange and consent to it (not merely the marrying individuals). It is the active desire of these collectivities that is widely understood to 'cause' marriages to happen (Dumont, 1998; Ballard 2011) as well as to sustain the marriage through time. Rituals of South Asian marriages across diverse caste or ethno-religious groups often express the active agency of the kinship groups involved in the marital rituals through presenting the agency of the bride, groom (and couple) as merely dutifully acquiescing to their parents' wishes (Gell 1994). At the level of policy however, successive Governments in the UK (Labour, then Conservative and Liberal Democrat, and then Conservative) have based their policy responses to 'forced marriage' as 'epistemologically predicated on a desire to modernise minority communities that is, in turn, based on a concept of cultural *othering*' (Anita and Gill 2011: 48). The result is that the complex features of the phenomenon and differential experiences of immigration, life in the UK, education, work, race, class, gender and so on have been largely subsumed in the public sphere, within an indistinct notion of 'cultural factors'.

In a striking departure from highly essentialised and ossified academic accounts of British South Asians, Simeran Gell (1994) has shown in her work that the transformations in marriage amongst British South Asians lie less in the realm of dowry payments and gifts, and more in terms of how communities have sought to internalise the complex experience of immigration in their new motherland. She fixes upon an intriguing 'two marriage sequence' that she finds is widespread amongst her informants in Bedford and argues that this demonstrates that British South Asian marital forms do not emphasise 'consent' but instead performatively bring into being what they seek to enact – here, the experience of earlier generations who experienced immigration and encountered state suspicion and surveillance around the nature of arranged marital unions between putative strangers. This ran counter to Euro-American presumptions and prejudices of love between two heterosexual individuals being the only acceptable basis for marriage; such that many immigration cases were bolstered by elaborate (but fabricated) 'love letters' between betrothed couples to demonstrate the authenticity of the union in the only terms in which it could be understood. Gell shows that British South Asians in the 1990s in Bedford re-enacted this history by sequencing their marital rituals: first a Registry marriage in 'English style' and half a year or-so later, a religious marriage in a community-based space like a temple with 'Indian style' of dress, comportment, food and sociality. It was only after the second sequence that the couple cohabited and consummated their union. The marital rituals of Registry office civil marriages that preceded the 'religious marriages' amongst Jat Sikhs revealed that second-generation British South Asians sought to use their marriages as an opportunity to 'smile at the state'; incorporating its logics of civil marriage legitimation and authorisation so that their own 'alien' cultural forms (arranged marriages consecrated ritually in a temple or Gurudwara) could be made available for suitable audit and could be satisfactorily incorporated as legitimate marital unions recognisable to both state and the wider society of white work colleagues, neighbours and friends.

This work fits well with Charles Piot's more recent argument about the American visa lottery in Togo where he argues that 'situational kinship' (of the sort generated by the bureaucratic protocols of the USA's green card 'diversity lottery' process) generates new 'faux real marriages' as well as new family configurations, with lottery winners maximising the opportunities for additional US immigration (and bank-rolling of expensive *in situ* costs) by temporarily marrying another spouse for the purpose of immigration, with an anticipated later divorce and remarriage (back again) to their old spouses so that they may bring over to the US two families with any children, instead of one (2010). In a similar vein, Gell's work on the situational kinship of Jat Sikhs in Bedford constitutes an important backdrop to my work on the rituals surrounding 'forced marriage', as both these works engage anthropologically in the space between the law and everyday kinship.

An increasing level of publicity in relation to the rights of immigrant communities (eg the right to consent to a marriage) and women's rights – made notorious in a series of high-profile cases of so-called 'honour killings', 'runaway marriages' and 'forced marriages' – has meant that the British government (like numerous governments across Europe) recognised a sufficient public mandate to pass the Forced Marriage (Civil Protection) Act 2007. This law provides two of the three possible policy responses to such marriages (Phillips and Dustin 2004): 'regulation' (ie protection afforded to all British individuals under human rights law in the realm of marriage) and 'exit' (ie the means of individuals leaving coercive cultural situations). The third policy option posited by Phillips and Dustin, that of 'dialogue' (engaging with community members, seeking to communicate, and to better understand the range of meanings and contexts in which such marriages take place) has been treated warily, since it opens up the state to the possibility of manipulation by gatekeepers and to allegations of homogenising diverse groups (Shariff 2012: 550).

Underlying the clarity of a law designed to criminalise force in marriage, lies an anthropologically complex set of marital practices amongst ethno-religious, regional, caste and national groups from a vast, diverse and ever transforming sub-continent. Here, some definitions prove helpful, with 'love marriages' being characterised in the South Asian community as self-arranged marriages driven by desire or love that frequently take place across more carefully guarded social boundaries of class, caste, community, linguistic or ethno-religious group. The term is also often used to describe chosen marriages that are opposed by parents or kin. 'Arranged marriages' – by contrast are arranged by the couple's families and these characteristically conform to notions of caste, ethno-religious and class endogamy (including amongst Muslims, for whom the *biradari* or clan serves as an endogamous group). In instances described popularly as 'love-cum-arranged' marriage, parents may agree to endorse publicly the love-choice of their child through domesticating acts of arrangement (for instance, throwing a public reception to signal their support of the marriage choice) thus drawing marriages that were initiated through coupling and love into a culturally acceptable repertoire of parental consent and arrangement. It is now well documented that the terms 'love-marriage' and 'arranged marriage' refer to a spectrum of marital behaviour that involves varying degrees of parental management as well as varying powers of veto and consent on the part of the marrying individuals (Charlsey and Shaw 2006a; Mody 2008; Grillo 2015). What emerges is that when it is desirable for love to flow in the direction of ideal marital kin, parents may even turn a blind eye to emotional closeness or even facilitate intimacies between affines in the hope that these may culminate in bonds that bolster the possibilities of successful arranged marriage (Charsley and Shaw 2006b). By contrast, in 'forced marriages', the discovery of inappropriate romantic love by the parents or community can often serve as a precursor to kinship force.

I use the term 'forced marriage' in quotation marks to signal that in this work, I recognise the multiple, moralised (and conflicting) meanings the term has come to carry in popular British discourse, and to hold in abeyance the question of whether or not each of these marital acts constitutes a 'forced marriage' in a legal sense or even in the same sort of way – indeed, for many of my informants (as we shall see), the force of their parents in marital choosing was so often anticipated as to be entirely unremarked upon. My informants frequently wished this to remain so, with the 'force' remaining well below the public gaze, and certainly beneath the regulatory mechanisms of the law and the state.[1]

Some community members that I have worked with support the government strategy in criminalising parental coercion in their children's marriages, whilst others vociferously disagree, arguing that the new law has alienated those whose marital practices it sought to engage, pushing the problem under the carpet rather than bringing about change. Certainly, anthropologists working on British South Asian kinship in the UK report that discussions about forced marriages are now a part of family debates in which various marriages are assessed and evaluated on the basis of assessments about familial involvement in matters of love and arrangement (see Grillo 2015: 59–91). Furthermore, it is clear that these are times of change in which 'ideas of the rights of women (and children) have gone global, permeating legal and social templates across the world' (Grillo 2015: 82). Whether or not this will cause the sort of moral revolution that the philosopher Kwame Appiah seeks is another matter though. Speaking about honour crimes – specifically, the crime of 'honour killing' where male relatives seek to protect the honour of the patrilineage by killing female members of their families or communities in order to restore honour (2010: 137–172) – Appiah seeks to understand what, if anything, might lead to the cessation of such culturally validated practices. Historicising the phenomenon in the context of other moral revolutions (his examples concern the end of duelling, foot-binding and slavery) Appiah argues that 'honour killing will only perish when it is seen as dishonourable' (ibid: 172). In a similar vein, some activists believe that the UK government's failure to engage British communities in genuine and open dialogue has made it more difficult to imagine the sort of moral consensus that might bring an end to 'forced marriage' because the current consensus has focused on external regulation rather than internal social transformation and change. In a similar vein, the new law is surprisingly silent on familial coercion that seeks to prevent unsuitable marriages – a rife phenomenon – whilst having rather a lot to say about arranging 'forced' ones (Grillo 2015: 82).

The extant law, then, is designed to enforce the state's intolerance of families coercing their children into marriage, and to prevent such marriages in the first place by creating civil remedies directed against those using force for this purpose. The law is described as making provision for 'protecting individuals against being forced to enter into marriage without their free and full consent and for protecting individuals who have been forced to enter into marriage without such consent'. Under this law, to 'force' is defined in section 63A(6) as to 'coerce by threats or other psychological means'. By this definition, physical and emotional threats designed to coerce can attract civil redress in the shape of 'Protection Orders'. Furthermore, the violation of

[1] Indeed, the recent legislation on 'forced marriage', particularly criminalisation, has been notable for languishing on the English statutes, with most agencies working on the issue reporting that children don't want to prosecute and in so doing risk criminalising their parents.

a Forced Marriage Protection Order or indeed, using any form of coercion for the purpose of causing someone to enter into a marriage is now a criminal offence in England and Wales (note – a separate law pertains to Scotland) under Part 10 of the Anti-social Behaviour, Crime and Policing Act 2014. Anthropologists studying the law and responding to the UK government's consultation prior to criminalisation sought to locate these marriages within the wider context and argued that criminalisation would do nothing short of destroying those that were so affected. Ballard and Shariff for instance, argued that few young British South Asian women had been brought up to contemplate leaving behind the familial ties of 'interpersonal reciprocities' that they had been brought up with, even if they were encouraged by well-wishers to do so when all else failed (Grillo 2015: 84).

Conversely, outside of academic discourse, the media and political discourse on 'forced marriage' has raised claims that the British state has been 'soft' on 'minorities' due to misplaced notions of multiculturalism, with calls for a more 'muscular liberalism' needed to stand up to 'forced marriage' which has been most unhelpfully linked to 'radicalisation and terrorism' as part of the same problem (Shariff 2012, 555). The anthropological response has been to better understand the ways in which notions of kinship bear upon 'forced marriage' – and in this work, on the ways in which care does too.

A documentary film on 'forced marriage' (*Unholy Matrimony*)[2] designed to explain the phenomenon to British viewers reveals the cultural construction of 'forced marriage' in the UK rather well when one elderly British South Asian respondent explains:

> Because as a parent, I want to teach your [sic] children your own culture, your own values, your own traditions, and nowadays the girls and children they don't want to learn those things, and it's an easy way to escape from the home, to say: 'Oh, my mother is forcing me to marry'. So there will be a breakage of families. So let them sort out their own problem. You have to see where you have to intervene. One or two cases, yes, are genuine cases, where they are really forcing; majority of them, they just make it up!

This characterisation of dubious or 'fake forced marriage' allegations was a common theme I encountered in numerous community discussions about the new law. At a government-organised 'road show' to discuss 'forced marriages', a female community leader despaired when she said: 'Young people in Bradford are having [secret] affairs; they don't tell their parents about it and then, when their parents try and arrange their marriages, they claim they are being forced!' The allegation here is that 'forced marriage' becomes a convenient (and lethal) kinship instrument in the hands of the young to challenge the moral authority of elders with the threat of the law.

In fact, my own work found a surprising lack of engagement with the law amongst those who were saying they had married against their own will. This is a picture observed by other anthropologists who have written about

[2] www.fco.gov.uk (accessed on 11 October 2012).

'forced marriages' (eg Grillo 2015). Fauzia Shariff, who worked at the precursor to the Forced Marriage Unit (known as the 'Community Liaison Unit' or 'CLU') found that even where the Home Office was being contacted to conduct urgent rescues abroad in cases of reported 'forced marriage', the victims frequently insisted on no mention being made about the 'forced marriage' or that they had been in touch (2012). Furthermore, she argues that 'once back in the UK many of those who the unit helped were reluctant to cut off ties with their families and frequently faced a total absence of any meaningful alternative social support network' (2012: 553). My own ethnographic research with those who had experienced 'forced marriages' thoroughly confirmed this picture, with many – if not most – of the young people I worked with choosing not to bring the fact of the 'forced marriage' to the attention of the authorities for fear of making a difficult situation with their families far worse.

In my own work, some of my informants were in touch with and received support from the police and the British Government's Community Liaison Unit (latterly, the Forced Marriage Unit or 'FMU'), whilst others never did. Interestingly, for those informants who have gone on to have children from these forced unions, the encounter with UK state authorities for protection has sometimes been followed by what are colloquially known as legal 'care proceedings' complete with their detailed assessments of the 'fitness' of one or both parents to care for their children. The characterisation of 'care' is thus a deeply political and highly contested one in which the intentions and processes that are designed to support those who have experienced a 'forced marriage' may never be used, or may indeed, be found to be turned against someone who has experienced a 'forced marriage'. Instead, what many of my informants found helpful were the friends, family members and varied British South Asian NGOs who sought to provide personalised and culturally pertinent forms of empathy, advice, counselling and support. In the next section of this chapter, I will look at the lives of two informants who had 'forced marriages', both of whom I met at very different stages of my research and moreover, at very different stages of their own post-marital lives. Farida had three very young children whilst Kavya was now separated from the husband who had been forced upon her and was caring for her two teenage children, having just left a refuge and been provided by the state with a house of her own. Their narratives show the multiple ways in which kinship care can be conceived, experienced and navigated by those who have experienced what they describe as a 'forced marriage'.

II. Farida

On a cold spring morning in East London, I met Farida, a mum with three toddlers under the age of five at a local community centre. As we spoke, she stood on the perimeter of the building looking out onto the dull grey London sky above the adjacent car park. Drawing sharply on a cigarette and blowing smoke into the morning air, her children played behind her noisily. I was struck by the figure she presented. Dressed in *hijab* her back was intentionally positioned squarely to the space in which the children ran around. Dragging on her cigarette she appeared to be defiant. The smoking (in such near proximity to children playing) was already visibly annoying other parents whose gaze flitted upon us, heavy with barely-restrained disapproval. A couple of them loudly, and to my mind pointedly, supervised the play of their toddlers behind us, drawing further attention to Farida's turned back and to the deficit of parental supervision it appeared to implicitly represent.

Farida was an East London girl with a strong Newham accent. The three children with her were born, she said, of a marriage arranged by her parents into which she had been forced. When she had reached marriageable age, her parents goaded her to marry a man of their choosing from Pakistan. She disliked the man and protested against the marriage vociferously but could not stop it. She had been a plucky and rebellious teenager and didn't have many supporters or allies in her family. Her parents prevailed, the marriage went ahead and the new husband was abusive and unkind and now lived with her in London. Her parents defended her against his frequent violence by stepping in, providing refuge, protesting on behalf of their daughter and mediating when the arguments became unbearable, but they nevertheless insisted on Farida staying in the marriage and putting up with him. In her description, by way of a sop, they bought her a flat close to their own home so that they could help her out and support the marriage. Farida's three children also lived with her, but she said that her parents took care of them most of the time. She said that she had made her parents pay for the damage they had done to her life. She ensured that she set them the terms on which she would now live the life that they had chosen for her. She described a trade-off in which she would dress to keep up the social pretence of her being a good wife, but her parents in turn had to allow her the freedoms she demanded in exchange for her continuing public forbearance toward the fact of her marriage. Most especially, she said in language peppered with expletives, her parents gave her spending money and her mother was bringing up the children, providing them with most of their childcare. In her words, her parents had landed her in this mess and so she expected them to bear the full consequences of it.

My previous work on love-marriage in India meant that I was very familiar with the phenomenon of parental coercion at the time of arrangement, though it was never described in Delhi as 'forced marriage' – this was a peculiarly English lexicon encountered in the print media in the UK in the late 1990s to describe a phenomenon in which parents of mostly South Asian backgrounds in Britain were seen to be insisting on their children marrying spouses of their own choosing, despite the child's stated desire not to do so. In 1997 an account of a young couple hit the newsstands – the eponymous tale of Jack and Zena shed light on the lengths that South Asian families were willing to go to track down young women who married of their own will, sparking a public discussion about arranged marriages (Briggs and Briggs 1997). Farida's situation struck me as notable because at the time I met her the UK government was engaging in a large public consultation about the need or desirability for a law prohibiting 'forced marriage' in the UK. From the discussions I had with her, it was clear that she felt very strongly about how she wished to handle what had happened to her. She made clear to me that she had very little interest in taking the matter of her marriage to any police or seeking any redress from British law courts. She pointedly said that everyone already knew about her 'forced marriage' and so, what was the point in telling them again. Indeed, while my concern for her well-being was not unwelcome, she also made clear to me that she would continue to seek redress and respite from her kin and her family, where the consequences of actions could be made to matter. Farida did this by demanding financial support and kinship care from her parents on her own terms, almost by way of recompense for the abuse and injury they had inflicted upon her through the painful 'marriage'. Since she had not wished to inhabit the role of this man's wife, she felt little moral obligation to play the part of respectable wife or loving mother to the children born of the union. Her parents on the other hand, had materialised these children through their act of wilful coercion upon their daughter, and it was here that she felt that she could exact the full extent of their parental obligation to provide money and care. Farida characterised childcare – for her children – and parental care – *from* her parents – as her entitlement; since her parents had foisted the marriage upon her, she saw no role in seeking to reciprocate any care towards them other than by remaining dependent upon them – dependence being a fine corollary of the care they had shown through their arrangement (cf Kittay 1998). Her parents now inhabited the personhood and role of grandparents claimed for themselves, by themselves. Much as the state sought to protect, Farida preferred direct action and continuing dependence by extracting kinship obligations that she demanded from her parents as a right.

III. Coercing Care Back into Kinship: Kavya

When I first met Kavya, she explained to me the hardest bit about her life after her 'forced marriage' was the loneliness and lack of family once she left her husband and sought recourse from the state. The refuges that she and her children were put in were uncomfortable places to be, with co-habitants who were frequently in states of crises and breakdown and whose children had varying behaviour that could bear negatively upon the well-being of her own. She described how alienating it was to live in such intimacy with non-South Asians who didn't share the same attitude to cooking and feeding or the social expectations and cultural values of other '*desis*' (South Asians). The secrecy required of people living in such refuges meant that she also could not easily sustain the everyday sociality that those who lived in their own homes could afford, so she could never invite non-refuge people back to hers; nor could she take lifts from people who offered to drop her home. She had to constantly protect the refuge address so as to ensure the secrecy of its location, and she explained how even taxi rides returning home had to be made cautiously, so that the area's (mostly South Asian) taxi drivers didn't come to associate particular properties with a transient and vulnerable female population. The picture Kavya painted was one of enormous loneliness and was described in terms of social abandonment. Fortunately, however, she met a group of South Asian women in a similar situation to herself (an NGO that catered to survivors of forced marriages) and this had provided important opportunities for creating a support network for herself and a space of care in which she was able to share her experiences and gain love and support from those around her.

Kavya introduced me to a close friend of hers, a young woman from Hull named Mariam who she explained had also suffered a 'forced marriage'. Kavya said that Mariam and she were very close, and I noticed over the course of the day we spent together in Kavya's home that the younger Mariam called Kavya 'mum'. Mariam also spent time chatting to Kavya's children who clearly appreciated her youthful exuberance. Kavya said that friends like Mariam constituted her 'new family', so even though she was now living in a part of the country where she had no one to call her own, Mariam was always a phone-call away. She pointedly said that they sent each other birthday and *Diwali* festive cards, shared the children's half-term and school holidays together and spoke to each other regularly over the phone because they understood how isolating it was for *desis* to live in Britain without the everyday interactions, sociality and intimacies of wider kin networks.

Almost exactly a year after I had first met Mariam, Kavya said one day that Mariam had fallen out with a third common friend (who had also had a 'forced marriage') because of a misunderstanding. Upon hearing my sympathies, Kavya revealed that her relationship with Mariam had also gone sour. Mariam had spent time supporting Kavya during a very difficult legal battle over the children's residence with her former ('forced') husband and at this time, Mariam had become close to a married male friend of Kavya who had also provided Kavya support and solidarity through her ordeal of court proceedings and care hearings. Kavya was hurt that during her time of crisis, Mariam was busy 'experimenting with other relationships' despite an engagement to another man. She said to me indignantly: 'She used to call me "mum"!' Kavya felt that she had been used by Mariam to gain access to her male friend with whom she had now taken up. She declared to me: 'I have deleted him! I have deleted her!' The contact list on her phone represented the full extent of her maternal excision. Deleting the name of her 'daughter' Mariam and the male friend from her contacts also deleted them from her life.

What does it mean to 'delete' your 'daughter' (even a newly made one) from your life? In some ways, Kavya re-enacted the classic South Asian declaration of the social death of children enacted through verbal utterances when they have behaved in ways that offend the family's morality and honour. In lines reminiscent of many a Bollywood script, a disapproving parent utters the dreaded words: 'I have no child, my child has died'. Such declarations of social death carry a grim warning and an explicit threat to the continued kinship and legal existence of the offending offspring (see Mody 2008: 156–160). Over the many years that I have known Kavya, I have seen how much she has had to struggle to create a structure of support around herself due to the circumstances that preceded (and followed in the wake of) her 'forced marriage' and the consequent breakdown of familial and kinship relations. Such 'deletion' of someone she called her daughter (following soon after her own estrangement with her parents, family and wider kin network due to her 'forced marriage') revealed that the reversals inherent in the kinship that is given are also incumbent on that which is made. Whilst 'deletion' implies erasure, it also marks the withholding of care through distance and an inattentiveness; a demonstration of the cold communication that signifies an absence of presence and care.

Kavya's family situation was by her own reckoning unusual in that her experience of home was one that was peppered with very violent physical abuse. She had grown up in a wealthy but traditional North Indian household in Durban, South Africa where she fell in love with another Indian but not from her own community. She decided to elope with him and, knowing full well that her parents would not accept her love-marriage, she left a note for her parents, ran away from home to live with him and married her boyfriend. When her family caught up with them some days later, they had the police with them, and she was packed off in a car across the border into Zimbabwe until they were able to retrieve her passport from her husband and put her on a plane to India. Here she was to remain with her mother at her grandparents' home where she lived under watchful surveillance for two years, initially in a heavily curtailed state but slowly with the ability to go out of her room, cook, go to the temple and meet people. During this time, she realised that the relationship with her husband would never be accepted and she began to concede defeat. Worn down into subservience through her isolation from everything she knew and all her friends and loved ones, she became ready to play the part of a suitable and marriageable bride for which she found herself being prepared.

Kavya soon learnt that the kindly family friends who they met and spent time with were to be her future in-laws; she was due to be married to their son who was working temporarily in the UK. Resigned to her fate, she was married to him on a visit he made to India. During this period, her father also brought her to the UK and applied on her behalf for 'indefinite leave to remain' on the basis of his own grandfather's right of abode – thus facilitating her future (second) husband's citizenship in England. After marriage, the couple moved to Manchester where he worked as a taxi driver and where she had two children. It was a deeply unhappy time because soon the kind façade that she had found appealing and agreeable slipped away, unearthing an unpleasant and violent man. Even though Kavya tried hard to make things work her husband's incessant drinking and continual violence made her life miserable. Soon after the second child was born, she realised she was unable to bear the unhappy marriage and severe domestic violence any further.

She began to call the police to report the violence. Her husband in turn was aggressive to her because he accused her of having been married before – a fact that had been shared with him openly prior to the marriage. Eventually, the husband threw her out and she went to live in a refuge with the children until she suffered a breakdown and he was granted residence of the children. She contested the residence order on the basis of the 'forced marriage', abuse and violence she had suffered and eventually got the children back, and in the process, sought out her mother's support as she had now moved to the UK herself and set up home in Bath, where she was bringing up Kavya's younger siblings. Kavya's renewed contact with her parents was meant to bolster her legal case to show the state that she was in a good position as a single mother to provide a stable network of 'kinship care' for her children.

During the stressful legal proceedings in which Kavya was told that her husband alleged that she was being violent to her children, her husband had taken up with another woman and continued, by Kavya's account, to poison the minds of the children. Even though her mother was aware of the new woman in his home she urged Kavya to 'patch things up with him' for the sake of the children. A few years down the line however, it was very obvious to everyone including her parents that Kavya had suffered enough at the hands of this man. In 2012 she was diagnosed with post-traumatic stress disorder (PTSD) and began receiving counselling and support for this. She also had periods when she was extremely unwell and needed extensive investigations and surgical medical procedures. At around this time, she had just been back to South Africa to see her grandmother, who was ailing, and to show her wider community her two children who were now teenagers. She described this to me as a trip in which she hoped to 'make her peace' with her family:

> My mum has been really supportive and has gone out of her way. She understands. My dad was so proud of me when I was there, showing off my children to my grandmother, saying: 'See how good their manners are. See how tall the children are'. It was strange to see him literally showing them off to everyone. When we left, my dad started crying and my son asked him – '*Dada*, why are you crying?' He couldn't speak. I also had tears in my eyes. There was so much that needed talking about. My dad was saying, move away from your ex-husband, move into a new marriage that will help to keep him away from the children. I told my dad, 'Look, just respect my life and help me to move forward with the children. Marriage is not a solution; there are other ways to help me. You can finance me and the kids rather than putting money into a marriage!' He has been talking to my mum about helping me out. At the end of the day, I still love them, they are my parents.

Despite the persistent childhood violence that Kavya had said she suffered at the hands of her strict and disciplining mother and the terrible marital orchestrations of her father, it seemed incredible to me that she had once again sought out her family to provide her and her children with the kinship support structure they craved. Interestingly, whilst she was able to reconcile and reunite with her parents, her relationship with the 'family she chose' – the friends like Mariam – was even more fraught and painful; as she put it poignantly, Mariam was like a daughter to her and used to call her 'mum'. It was also striking that her upset with Mariam was based on a matter of moral propriety – in just the same way in which her own mother had effectively 'deleted' her desires and her love-marriage from her kinship consciousness, Kavya had inadvertently done exactly the same.

After having heard about the importance of the emotional and everyday support that the network of women who had experienced a 'forced marriage' had once provided to Kavya, it struck me how that network of care appeared to have also collapsed in the years that followed. Kavya says that when her children were taken from her due to her husband's allegations about her capacity to care for them she got back in touch with the women's organisation that had once supported her and asked them if they would write a report to the court on her behalf. She was assured of their support but says she never heard back. When she went back to visit the town where they had all lived together and asked to meet up with those she had once known so well, she said that they were all 'suddenly very busy'. She felt heavily let down by them, and alone.

Whilst it is undoubtedly the case that Kavya is the one who has borne in her body and mind the extreme effects of her parentally 'forced marriage', she also pointed out to me that when her grandfather heard about the extent of the cruelty of her ('forced') husband and the eventual breakdown of that marriage he said to all his remaining unmarried grandchildren that they would need to find their own spouses, as nobody in his family would be arranging marriages for the children ever again. Consequently, Kavya's younger sister married her long-term Bengali boyfriend at the late age of 34. She had been living with her boyfriend during her studies in the US and she announced to her family in Durban that the time of the marriage had been arranged and they should come if they could. Kavya said that her father felt enormously shocked to have had his daughter serve him her wedding notice in this way. Sensing that he may react unreasonably, Kavya's maternal uncles went over to him and threatened him, warning that he shouldn't dare do to her what he had done to Kavya. At the time, Kavya was living with her mother in England, and whilst her mother and brother flew out hastily for the wedding, Kavya wasn't informed of the impending marriage or invited to attend the festivities. It is hard to say why this happened other than to note that at least in the eyes of some of her relatives, there was a recognition that Kavya's experience should never be allowed to be repeated again; and that even though she bore the brunt of it all, her 'forced marriage' had in fact thoroughly damaged the entire family.

IV. Transforming Kinship Care

Evelyn Nakano Glenn defines caring as 'the relationships and activities involved in maintaining people on a daily basis and intergenerationally' (2010: 5). The marital arrangements that parents engineer for their children sit along a temporal continuum of kinship care, but they are care (in their own terms) nevertheless – even if they are experienced by their own children as a painful form of intimate coercion. The predominant assumption is that the older generation regard their children as innocent of the true nature of marriage and because of this they can't possibly be trusted to make good decisions based on their values that privilege the immediacy of gratification, love and desire over less ephemeral and more enduring values such as obligation and care and the sublimation of the self towards the values of the group. However, this is a rather static image of what is going on in British families of South Asian origin, where the facts of migration invite a reconsideration of the past and the future and what works for whom. As Kavya's family shows, they have lost their stomach for both 'forced' and arranged marriages, with her grandfather urging all marrying offspring to make their own arrangements, thank you very much. In describing the subjectivities at play for my informants, I have sought to show the importance of recognising the complex ways in which narratives of care (and demands for it) are marshalled to the cause of kinship values, but also change them.

We can't say where precisely care resides because it is manifestly inter-subjective. While Farida deals with her 'forced marriage' by demanding her parents care for their grandchildren, Kavya must mend her path so that it takes her closer to her own mother, whose support she both craves and needs. Reflecting on the obligations she has towards her own children, Kavya said to me:

> I want to do something so that my kids can have support as they grow up, maturing into their own persons … [so] I will help them understand that they are the product of a forced marriage. I cannot trust my father to give them a good insight into this.

Kavya sees that she must help her own children to understand their past and that her own kinship care consists of ensuring that they understand what happened to their mother within the context of their own affections for their grandparents. And in just the same way that care goes on through generations, the individual also sits on a continuum of regulation between a socialising community (or kinship group) and the state with its laws. An anthropological perspective on 'forced marriage' provides us with the analytic purchase that allows us to see care and coercion in the same act.

On one occasion when I met Kavya she had just returned from seeing her parents in Bath. She looked drained and said it had been an emotional visit. Worrying that they must have been talking about her 'forced marriage' with retributions flying about how it was continuing to affect her daily life, I asked what happened. With a pained expression on her face she said: 'I had an argument with my dad. He was having a drink. He has liver problems and heart problems …' she trailed off.

As I have tried to show, studying 'forced marriage' after the fact of such a marriage (in some of my cases, many years after the fact) can allow us anthropologically significant insights into the meanings of care in ways that might not be evident when studying such marriages as a snap-shot of what happened and 'who did what to whom'. The long passage of time allows us to better see the ways in which these marriages sit within the ebb and flow of intergenerational familial relations that are utterly transformed and re-shaped as an outcome of 'forced marriages', which become 'kinship events' with kinship and caring consequences.

The forms of kinship that I have examined (in the shape of an analysis of forced marriages over a period of time) shed helpful light on kin-making as a process that continues over time and is closely tied to the intersubjective relations between all those involved. In the ethnographic cases of Farida and Kavya that I have presented here, the sort of uncomfortable compromises that characterise kinship care recurred as a theme, with discussions about their 'forced marriages' providing opportunities to examine how my informants have created spaces of refuge and care through the uncertainty and confusion raised by frequently loving acts of one sort or another that they recognise as simultaneously coercive to themselves. What I hope to have shown is that spaces of care emerge for my informants through their ownership and more thoroughgoing and critical appraisal of what was given to them as kinship care. This takes account of care as an act of kinship (as above) and kinship made evident as acts of care.

A study of kinship care through an exploration of the effects of 'forced marriages' reveals transformations of relationships and cares that are more dynamic (and surprising) than generally acknowledged in anthropological accounts of either kinship or care. The significance of 'kinship care' in this context is that it questions the characterisation of both kinship and care as morally positive (or at best, morally neutral) concepts. I have argued here that the ethnographic evidence allows a much more nuanced analysis of the ways in which my informants recognise and re-shape the coercion that was given to them into forms (even demands) of care that allow them to manage, re-articulate and transform kinship care to suit their own ends.

References

Adams, C (2017) 'Towards a Philosophy of Care through Caregiving' *Critical Inquiry* 43.

Appiah, K (2010) *The Honour Code: How Moral Revolutions Happen* (London, Norton).

Borneman, J (2001) 'Caring and Being Cared For: Displacing Marriage, Kinship, Gender, and Sexuality' in J Faubion (ed), *The Ethics of Kinship* (Oxford, Rowman & Littlefield).

Briggs, J and Briggs, Z (1997) *Runaways: A true Story of Love & Danger* (London, Vista).

Charsley, K and Shaw, A (2006a) 'Introduction: South Asian Transnational Marriages in Comparative Perspective' *Global Networks* 6(4): 331–44.

—— (2006b) 'Rishtas: adding emotion to strategy in understanding British Pakistani transnational marriages' *Global Networks* 6(4): 405–21.

Dumont, L (1998) [1970] *Homo Hierarchicus: The Caste System and Its Implications* (New Delhi, Oxford University Press).

Garcia, A (2010) *The Pastoral Clinic: Addiction and Dispossession along the Rio Grande* (Berkeley CA, University of California Press).

Gell, S (1994) 'Legality & Ethnicity: Marriage among the South Asians of Bedford' *Critique of Anthropology* 14(4): 355–92.
Grillo, R (2015) *Muslim Families, Politics and the Law: A Legal Industry in Multicultural Britain* (London, Routledge).
Kittay, E (1998) 'Welfare, Dependency, and a Public Ethic of Care' *Social Justice* 25(1): 123–45.
Kuper, A (2018) 'We need to Talk about Kinship' in *Anthropology of this Century*, available online at: aotcpress.com/author/adam-kuper/ (accessed 4 February 2019).
Mody, P (2015) 'Forced Marriage: Rites and Rights' in J Miles, P Mody, and R Probert (eds), *Marriage Rites and Rights* (Oxford, Hart Publishing).
Phillips, A and Dustin, M (2004) 'UK Initiatives on Forced Marriage: Regulation, dialogue and exit' *Political Studies* 52: 531–51.
Piot, C (2010) *Nostalgia for the Future: West Africa after the Cold War* (Chicago IL, University of Chicago Press).
Shariff, F (2012) 'Towards a Transformative Paradigm in the UK Response to Forced Marriage: Excavating Community Engagement and Subjectivising Agency' *Social and Legal Studies* 21(4): 549–65.
Thelen, T (2015) 'Care as social organisation: Creating, maintaining and dissolving significant relations' *Anthropological Theory* 15(4): 497–515.

11

Home and Away: Mobility and Care in Botswana's Time of AIDS

KOREEN M REECE

Matlo go sha mabapi.

Neighbouring houses burn together.

I seldom slept in. It was usually impossible. Most days, there were cars starting, children hollering, buckets banging, and chickens screeching from early in the morning. But on this particular Saturday morning, one of my first weekends in the field, my sleep went uninterrupted until the gathering heat set the corrugated iron roof ticking as it stretched, sometime past nine o'clock. I woke in what was otherwise an uncanny silence.

I emerged from my room, stretching and perplexed, into the *lelwapa*, or courtyard. There was no-one there. It was not yet mid-morning, but the stoop had been swept, and the tea boiled and drunk, its dregs left in cups scattered across a table by the fire.

It was no small feat for the yard to be so thoroughly unpeopled. Four generations were intermittently in residence, from the elderly couple who had founded the household, through their seven children, 11 grandchildren, and one great-grandchild, for a total of 21 (plus me). Typically, the house was teeming: with children playing or cooking, people sitting and chatting in the *lelwapa*, the men tinkering with vehicles in the yard, the women sweeping or mopping or laundering. But today it was empty.

The yard was expansive, focused around a huddle of structures at its centre, which in turn gravitated around a square, paved courtyard behind a low wall – the *lelwapa* in which I stood. Two of the structures were houses: the rectangular two-and-a-half-roomed house, in which I stayed, stood perpendicular to its predecessor, a larger six-room building. In front of the larger house, and across from the smaller one, stood the *isong* or outdoor kitchen, also partly enclosed in a low brick wall and covered by a roof of corrugated iron.

I tapped on the door across from mine, where one of the adult sisters stayed with her son, but found it locked. I stuck my head in the door of the main house, only to find the TV blinking fitfully to an empty sitting room. The three adult brothers who lived at home each had rooms opening off this room, but were often away in the daytime. The kitchen at the back of the house, too, was empty.

Wandering towards the *isong*, I finally noticed two enormous, cast-iron, three-legged pots steaming over a low fire. The whole family spent a lot of time in the small, ramshackle *isong*; food was cooked and served there, and we all warmed bathwater, made tea, or tended the fire and sat around talking there. But given a cooking project as big as this, someone – probably the grandmother, whom we all called Mma – had to be around. The door to her room, which she shared with several of her grandchildren, opened directly off the stoop, and was slightly ajar.

Just then, the old woman came bustling out, wrapping a heavy wool blanket around her waist. I greeted her with some relief, asking where everybody was. 'They've gone out. I'm going out to check someone', she said, without further explanation. My Setswana was still too childlike for her to bother with long sentences. 'Watch these pots. Look, like this', she added, lifting the heavy lid from one with a wire loop. It was full of broth and bones, a toothy cow jaw and socketed skull having floated to the surface. She hefted a long stick with a short fork at one end into the pot and showed me how to lift and stir. The smell of boiled marrow and rancid flesh was overpowering. 'I'm coming', she added – as Batswana usually say when they are going. And with that, she left me alone with the stinking, bubbling cow heads.

The yard in which I was left with this curious culinary task stood in a village in southeastern Botswana, less than an hour's drive from the capital city. It was a yard I had known for well over a decade, from the time I had arrived in the village to volunteer with an orphan care project set up in response to the ongoing AIDS crisis. When I returned to conduct fieldwork for my PhD, I had planned to visit for a couple of weeks; instead, I stayed, and the yard became home. Life there forced me to rethink my understanding of what makes a place home, in both its familiar and fraught dynamics; and from that perspective, to rethink family, intervention, and the epidemic itself.

Botswana is often described as 'Africa's miracle', thanks to its diamond-driven success in state-led development since independence from Britain in 1966. But despite its relative wealth and stability, the country has been facing one of the world's worst epidemics of HIV and AIDS for over 30 years. An exemplary track record, combined with sustained political leadership and state investment, has generated substantial international funding and support for Botswana's AIDS response, producing many of the world's best practices in addressing the epidemic – including the free provision of antiretroviral treatment nationwide. These initiatives have saved and extended lives, but have proven less effective in curbing the spread of HIV. Roughly a quarter of the population is HIV-positive, and the rate of new infections has changed little in the past decade. Those who are not infected invariably have been affected – by the illness and loss of family, friends and colleagues, and by the unpredictable changes HIV and AIDS have brought to social life.

Throughout Botswana's epidemic, HIV and AIDS have been cast as crises: a crisis of national survival, a moral crisis, an economic crisis, a cultural crisis.

These discourses have shifted as responses to the epidemic have progressed; but the dominant and most persistent framing of the epidemic has been as a crisis of the family. Envisioning a 'lost generation' of sick, dying, or dead adults – their elderly parents left with the burden of their orphaned children – government and non-governmental organisations alike have cast AIDS as a crisis of kinship, social reproduction, and above all, of care, requiring the intervention of specialist agencies and the state. This inexorable logic has motivated a vast range of responses from within Botswana and around the world, from major foreign government and philanthropic funding initiatives to community-based projects focusing on home-based care or orphan care. In this sense, Botswana's epidemic provides a field in which local and global logics, ethics, economies and practices of care have been tested, contested, and negotiated for decades – making it an apt context from which to consider the question of care broadly and comparatively.

The epidemiology of HIV and AIDS has focused on spatiality from the outset, and on the pathological dimensions of mobility in particular. The rapid progression of HIV has been traced along transport and migration routes, its transmission linked with imperatives to move away from home for work or other opportunities, and to return home for care, or to die (see, eg Dilger et al 2012; Dilger 2006, 2010; Farmer 1992; Klaits 2010: 40–45; Thornton 2008: 74–76). In many ways, these are contemporary reformulations of long-standing concerns: during the colonial era, the anthropologist Isaac Schapera framed labour migration from Botswana to neighbouring South Africa in similarly devastating terms, warning of the 'disintegrating tendencies of frequent separation' (1940: 178) and suggesting that 'home life … does not really exist' (1940: 173). In both cases, mobility is understood simultaneously to create and reflect social crisis, specifically in the form of family breakdown – an understanding that fits neatly with the broader logic of the AIDS narrative above.

In this chapter, I want to challenge some of these assumptions about mobility, crisis, and care by looking at the way everyday care is spatialised in the Tswana home. As careless as it may seem to leave an anthropologist in charge of cooking one's cow heads, I want to suggest that the Saturday disappearances described above speak less to an absence than to an expected return – less to an apparent abdication of responsibilities of care, and more to fulfilling a multitude of them across time and space, all as perpetual and immediate as a boiling pot on the fire, or as the need to cook, feed, and eat. The empty yard invites us to rethink what constitutes a space of care, to reconsider how that space is produced, used and occupied, and thereby reconceptualise what care is, does, and makes. Clues to these questions lie in the yard I have described: in the access enjoyed or denied and the work undertaken in each of its spaces; and in the multiplicity of its structures, the distinctions and connections made between them. Further clues lie in the places to which the family had dispersed that Saturday morning, to which I return below. While these spatialities may be specific to the Tswana home, they also offer ways of de-familiarising and refining ideas about care that are suitable to quite different contexts – including those described elsewhere in this volume.

In the sections that follow, I examine the ways that spaces of care are produced and experienced by Tswana families. First, I describe the scattered, multiple places that constitute the Tswana *gae*, or home. Specifically, I consider the practices of movement, staying, and work that characterise and integrate those places over time, constituting them into a space of care. These spatial dynamics and practices require careful management, and frequently produce *dikgang* (singular *kgang*): risks, conflicts, and crises, including illness. In the second section, I explore these *dikgang*, and the unexpected ways in which they reinforce the kinship roles and responsibilities patterned by the spatialities of the *gae*. From this perspective, care and crisis prove deeply intertwined and unexpectedly generative, each reproducing the other as well as the families they define. Finally, I compare these insights to the spatialities that characterise governmental and non-governmental (NGO) programmes of 'supplemental care' launched in response to AIDS, the ways they both echo and invert kin spatialities, and the new 'crises of care' they may pose for Tswana families.

I. *Ko Gae*: House and Home

It was already early evening by the time people started to filter back into the yard. Mma had generalised in her description of their whereabouts, which proved to be far-flung.

Three of Mma's adult sons and a couple of their nephews had gone to the cattle-post (*moraka*), a three-hour walk from the village along rough, sandy roads. No-one lived at the *moraka*, though there was a thatched hut and large kraal there. The cattle roamed widely in search of water and good grazing in the area, the lands they covered being shared and unfenced; the work of finding the herd, watering them, and checking their health was onerous, particularly in the dry months. Two of the brothers returned at nightfall, but the rest stayed out for the weekend, as they often did thereafter.

Meanwhile, one of the adult daughters, her two girls and three nephews had all gone out to *masimo* – the lands – where Ntate,[1] the grandfather of the family, lived most of the time. *Masimo*, too, was well over an hour's walk, in almost the opposite direction from the cattle-post. It was a more developed site than the *moraka*, having been the family's primary residence before they built in the village. Two dilapidated rondavels faced on to a rough *lelwapa*, and a covered cooking area was tucked against a stout barbed-wire fence, anchored by thick upright logs dug in around the perimeter. The layout was roughly similar to that of the village residence. The farmland itself was perhaps a 10-minute walk away, across a dry riverbed; it generated much of the family's maize and beans for the year, plus some

[1] 'Ntate' is a generic Setswana term for 'father', as 'Mma' is for 'mother'.

to sell. Two of the children found their ways home well after dark, while the others stayed out to help look after the goats.

The rest of the family had had obligations to attend to elsewhere. Another of the adult daughters had gone to attend a funeral early that morning, and had stayed to help with the cooking, serving, and clean-up of lunch, returning in time to relieve me of my cow head-stirring duty. Yet another had left slightly later to make it to a neighbouring village for a planning meeting, held in anticipation of an upcoming wedding. As for Mma, she returned as evening began to close in, having been to see a relative who had been taken sick on the other side of the village.

Over the months I spent living with the family, this weekly family migration proved to be typical – though it was not unchanging. Not everyone left the yard every Saturday, nor did the same people go to the same places. Men and women alike might stay at home to spend a morning doing their laundry; children might stay home to study, or play; women might put their efforts into cleaning the house and yard instead. Depending on whose they were, funerals, weddings, or parties might become the focus of the weekend's journeys, residence and work. But there were distinct gendered and generational patterns to these weekly movements. *Moraka*, for example, was a place the men usually went. In principle, everyone was welcome, but the women and girls in the yard seldom tagged along. The family's eldest son went there weekly without fail, and was not expected to go anywhere else. *Masimo*, on the other hand, was the purview of the elders and the women. In fact, the family owned two *masimo*, the second several hours away by bus and foot. Ntate was resident in the nearby *masimo*, and Mma in the distant one, for most of my year with the family. The family's eldest daughter spent much of her time at the closest farmlands, and it was more common for the children, both boys and girls, to help at *masimo*.[2] The ways in which these movements were mobilised were also tied to familial roles: parents calling and sending their children and grandchildren – even when the latter have become adults, and often over long distances – both established and responded to claims each had upon the other, in turn reproducing the hierarchies and reciprocities of their relationships (Klaits 2010: 107, 119).

There was, of course, a seasonal aspect to these movements as well (not dissimilar to that described in Schapera 1940: 27). In months of drought (including most of the winter), the eldest son and any available brothers would be out at *moraka* daily, taking nutritional supplements to the cattle and ensuring the weaker ones had not become bogged down in the viscous mud surrounding their dried-up watering holes. Similarly, throughout the growing year – from times for sowing,

[2] Owning lands and cattle-posts was common in the area I studied (cf Morton 2007: 165), and not necessarily a sign of special wealth. Virtually every family I knew in the village had both lands and cattle-posts, as did friends and colleagues elsewhere in the country; and those that didn't, enjoyed – in principle at least – the government-assured right to acquire them free, much as individuals have a right to free residential land in their home districts.

through weeding and harvest – everyone would be expected to help at *masimo* as often as possible.[3] The children were frequently called by Mma to join her at the lands for the duration of their school holidays; during quieter periods, parents would send out their children on their behalf. A weekend on which no-one went either to the lands or the cattle-post was vanishingly rare; movement out and back was as constant as the work was unrelenting, and everyone routinely undertook both. As a result, the family were often apart, separated and brought together in shifting patterns depending on age, gender, and the work of the season, and the people they stayed and worked with shifted too. In other words, it was not simply through staying together in the village *lelwapa* that the family experienced kinship, but through staying and working with different groups of kin at the lands and cattle-post, and through being sent and called between all three places as well.

The *lelwapa*, or courtyard, was the lodestone of these migrations, the gravitational centre and heart of the *gae*, and the space in which the bulk of shared family life unfolded. Perhaps unsurprisingly, '*lelwapa*' also signifies 'family' in Setswana. *Go aga lelwapa*, to build a *lelwapa*, is both to build a house and to build a family. The terms that describe family, in other words, are explicitly spatialised; and they are explicitly located in (or in relation to) the *lelwapa*. And indeed, the *lelwapa* plays an important role in a variety of events and everyday practices that define, constitute and delimit family as well. It is not only the space where family members eat, socialise and sometimes sleep, but where important discussions are held, where visitors are welcomed and fed, where marriage negotiations are conducted, and around the edges of which parties and weddings are celebrated or funerals observed – even, in some cases, where people are buried. It is also a space in which grain is dried, laundry washed, games played and homework finished, and in which long hours are spent braiding hair, gossiping, or simply sitting together. The *lelwapa* is simultaneously public and private, and marks the overlap in those two categories: it is at the heart of the compound, but also in full view of the street; it hosts both the formal greeting of visitors and everyday acts of personal and household hygiene; disagreements internal to the family are settled there, but with dimensions of formality and display that encourage shame; and so on. Crucially, it is a space *in between* – in between the houses and other places of the yard, in between the family and its visitors or passers-by, in between the lands and cattle-post. And it is this in-betweenness, I suggest, that makes the *lelwapa* a particularly potent place in the *gae*: it marks a crossroads, through and from which the family's movement is continuously sustained and directed.

[3] Comaroff and Comaroff (1991) describe colonial-era patterns of movement in which '[l]eaving their houses, women moved out seasonally to the fields, bringing back the harvest, while men moved daily inward to the ward and chiefly courts … spelling out the connection between the communal centre and the domestic periphery' (1991: 137). Significant social change since the colonial era – including new obligations of waged labour and school attendance, among others – has no doubt affected these patterns; but at the same time, this description elides the long-standing movement of men and boys to the peripheral cattle-posts, for example, and downplays different generational habits of movement as well, which may suggest greater continuity with contemporary practices than expected.

The kin-making dimensions of these practices of movement, staying, calling and sending were linked closely to the reasons for that movement: namely, obligations to contribute to the family's care. Frederick Klaits (2010; see also Livingston 2003, 2005) contends that for the Tswana, care, or *tlhokomelo*, is expressed through the provision of specific things and work. The Tswana explicitly prioritise food and cooking, cattle and their care, money and its management, among a range of other specific care-things and care-work. Klaits links these to an exhaustive list of 'housing activities' – including 'nursing, visiting, staying, calling, hearing, obeying, drinking, bathing, praying, asking, singing, healing, procreating, confining, hiding, marrying, moving, consoling, mourning, and burying' (2010: 31–32) – the provision or refusal of which builds sentiments of love, care, jealousy or scorn over time (Klaits 2010: 31–33, chapter two). Care, understood thus, is emplaced ('housed'), but also produces space ('houses'). But while people provide care for friends, neighbours, and more distant kin – of the sort Mma and her daughters had undertaken in attending funerals, weddings, and sick relatives – I would argue that these contributions of care differ significantly from those undertaken for close kin, and that those differences are also spatialised. The care offered by participating in wedding planning or a funeral is tied to less-frequent movement than that characterising the *gae*, and often to unique or bounded events more than continuous practice. The comparative infrequency of movement, staying, calling or sending effectively marks progressively distant gradations of relatedness – much as specific expectations and contributions of care differentiate kin roles by gender and generation, as we have seen above. Movement, in other words, is not only a key practice of care used to mark out specific spaces of care, but also a means of identifying, ordering, and delimiting relatedness.

The movement undertaken between *lelwapa*, *moraka*, and *masimo*, its temporalities, and the care-work undertaken in each place, together integrate those distant places into a specifically familial space of care – and simultaneously map out the specific roles and responsibilities of family members. The frequency of movement between these places, and its regularity, sets the *gae* apart. There are no other places between which all (or most) members of a family customarily move, much less at such a distance, as often as weekly or in season-specific cycles. The paths between all three places are well-worn, and the journeys back and forth frequent enough to take on an almost continuous, perpetual quality. This sense of constancy is enhanced by the fact that family members frequently stay at either *masimo* or *moraka* for short, long, and occasionally semi-permanent stretches of time. Lands and cattle-posts, like yards in the village, are often known by the names of the people who stay there. And staying, with its associated ease of coming and going (both near each place, and back and forth to the others), is very rare for anyone but people who identify as family members.

The *gae*, then, is a divided, multiplicitous, scattered, and yet bounded place, defined and integrated by the movement, staying, and care-work of kin. Regardless of the other places in which one might work, live, or build, the *gae* is the only place in which one nevertheless remains, and to which one is inevitably drawn back. And yet, it is not changeless. As we have seen, there may well be more than one *masimo* or *moraka*; they are usually far removed from each other, and from the *lelwapa*; they may be used consistently, infrequently, or perhaps not at all; and indeed, they may be swapped, sold, acquired or given away with relative ease. They are also constantly being built and rebuilt (see also Morton 2007). In this sense, the *gae* is not only multiple, but mutable. The continuous movement of kin between and among the spaces of the *gae*, to work and stay, therefore becomes critical to sustaining and integrating them through change, and over time. And this movement simultaneously binds people and places together, and keeps them apart – articulating a tension between closeness and distance that defines not only the *gae*, but the Tswana family itself.

This tension becomes even clearer in light of the ways *gae* are connected and reproduced. By custom, a Motswana has only one *gae*: either one's parents' home (including their *lelwapa*, *masimo* and *moraka*); or, in the case of a married woman, her husband's parents' home. In practice, however, even married women often speak of their parents' home as *ko gae*, emphasising its connotation with one's place of origin. When Mma took us to visit the yard in which she grew up – now uninhabited – she explained simply, '*Ke ko gae*', this is home. Mma's identification with two *gae* suggests the ways in which the movement of women in particular serves to connect *gae* with each other, while also distinguishing them (married women are strongly discouraged from returning to their natal homes except in dire circumstances). Of course, when two people marry and found their own *lelwapa*, acquire their own *masimo* and *moraka*, they are establishing a new *gae* – not their own, but their children's. As this process may unfold over a very long time, they continue to bear responsibility for assisting with their parents' *gae*, moving among, staying and working in its spaces, and sending their children along the same paths. In this way, rather than simply splitting or fragmenting, the *gae* slowly but surely multiplies and expands.

What are the ramifications of this scattered, multiplying spatiality, the continuous movement it requires and the tensions it generates, for the Tswana family?

II. Going Up and Down: Mending Ntate's Ways

It was early evening, and Ntate had come in from the lands unexpectedly. He sat on the low wooden chair he favoured, in the corner of the *lelwapa*. He'd hung his hat on the back of the chair, had pulled off his shoes and socks, and was rubbing one foot absent-mindedly. His feet and ankles were swollen, thick and round – unsurprising, I supposed, for a man in his mid-seventies having just walked several miles in the heat. Then he stretched back into the hard chair, and spent the rest of the evening calling and sending the boys on various errands, or upbraiding them for some overlooked chore.

He was still home for a number of days thereafter, which was decidedly unusual. He was seldom at home for longer than a day and a night, maybe two, generally at the beginning of the month when he'd come to collect his meagre pension from the post office. Otherwise he was almost always at the lands. It was an arrangement that suited everyone, as he had a cantankerous streak and a penchant for provoking disputes. But for the time being, one of his sons had been sent out in his place, and he remained in the village.

Things had been particularly bad with Ntate for several months before my return to the field. First, Mma had discovered that he had taken up with the neighbour, a woman who had been widowed the year before. As well as being neighbours in the village, they were neighbours at *masimo*; even their children, who had acquired residential plots elsewhere in the village, were neighbours. While his wife was tending several acres at the family's other farm, a considerable distance away, the old man stayed at the lands near the village, and became more and more unwisely entangled. He diverted dribs and drabs of money and part of his harvest to the widow and her family, and he began to opt out of settling disputes or engaging in ongoing issues at home. In the most dramatic incident, shortly before my arrival, he had unilaterally decided to sell most of the family's donkeys and give the money to the widow. His wife suffered much of this ignominious treatment stoically, muttering and occasionally attempting to talk sense into him. When she found out about the donkeys, however, she rebuked her husband roundly in front of their children, and began speaking openly of her contempt for his behaviour. The situation had become a serious *kgang*, or issue, at home.

Ntate's ill-advised liaison had created several awkward situations for his children and grandchildren as well. Some months before my return, he had been in the neighbour's yard, and had heard one of the children there complain of being insulted by one of the children from his own yard. Immediately he had summoned the accused child from home, and his eldest grandchild Boipelo as well, asking the latter to act as mediator in resolving the dispute. She had been appalled – and was still appalled, judging from the incredulity with which she recounted these tales to me. 'Imagine! Calling his own children to *someone else's yard*! And what did he want me to do there?'

Adults in Botswana are generally free to discipline the children of their friends, neighbours, or even strangers, and will do so without compunction. I often saw children respond to such discipline with humility and respect. But such situations only really arise in public places, or in the disciplining adult's own yard. By calling his grandchildren into the neighbour's yard, Ntate was behaving as if he was *of* that yard, had taken on its *dikgang*, and had assumed the role of disciplinarian there. Indeed, it was as if he had decided to take the neighbour's children as his own, and treat his own children as if they were simply neighbours. This swapping of places, roles and allegiances was distasteful and hurtful in its own right; but what made it ridiculous to Boipelo was that, having adopted this new position, the old man could not engineer a reconciliation without relying upon his original position and the claims to which it entitled him. By calling both the accused child and Boipelo in as the mediator, in other words, he was calling himself out, emphasising his inability to mete out discipline among his experimentally-assumed kin by having to rely on his established kin to pull it off. The physical distance from family created by his living at the lands made room for an upending and rearrangement of relationships; but at the same time, those rearrangements had their limits. To the extent they could not bring about a total break from his family, his connection to and reliance upon them was reasserted.

As his feet swelled up, Ntate's behaviour began to change. The change was out of necessity more than choice: he couldn't walk without pain. And so, for a short time, he stayed at home, did not go to the lands, and made only brief visits out of the yard. Before long, he went to visit his *ngaka*, or traditional healer, and was advised that his feet were swelling up because of his inappropriate dalliances – and that they would continue to do so until he stopped. No-one I spoke to made any claims about the causality at work, but during the colonial era, Schapera (1940: 195) recorded the attribution of various such afflictions to liaisons with widows whose blood was still 'hot' – a marker of dangerous sexuality due to their closeness to death. Ntate's children had a clear sense of the justice in the situation. He had been 'going up and down', as Batswana say (often in English) when describing suspicious habits of movement. He had been moving in ways he shouldn't – ways that were hurtful to his family; an illness that curtailed his movement and forced him to behave appropriately had therefore afflicted him.

Perhaps a week after this diagnosis, Ntate was back out at the lands, his feet improving. And it seemed he had given up on his extra-marital fling: while he would continue to distress and confound his family in other ways, there were no more complaints of ongoing improprieties with the neighbour. On the rare occasion when they both found themselves at home from the lands, he and his wife would sit up late with their heads together by the fire, sharing news, apparently reconciled.

Ntate's dalliances created a particularly difficult *kgang* for his family, but not an altogether unusual one. The imperatives of movement among the places of the *gae*, and the close links between those imperatives and the specific roles and responsibilities of kin, meant that mobility was subject to close scrutiny and concern. Children and young people might be beaten for 'going up and down', and it was a phrase often used to express disapproval about adults' behaviour as well. We might be inclined to assume that the ultimate source of these *dikgang* is the scatteredness of the *gae* itself, the continuous movement it involves, and the distances it creates. Certainly these factors provided the opportunity for Ntate's transgressions, and the familial conflicts they sparked. But Ntate's indiscretions were not met with attempts to collapse or erase those distances. He was not called to stay at home at any point, and neither his wife nor anyone else in his family moved to stay with him. Nor was he excluded or cut off from his family's usual visits to work and help. Rather – after the temporary immobility of his illness – his relative distance was carefully reasserted. The necessity of maintaining distance suggests that intimacy and proximity, too, present risks of *dikgang* which distance helps ameliorate. The spatialities of the *gae*, in other words, are not so much about ensuring closeness, as ensuring the appropriate balance between closeness and distance, and an appropriate ordering of people and places. It was not Ntate's movement, distance, or absence as such that were at issue, so much as the fact he was moving in the wrong ways, in the wrong directions, at the wrong times, for the wrong purposes. Mending Ntate's health involved mending his ways, in the sense both of his behaviour and the paths he took.

The family's response to the appropriateness of Ntate's illness – which affected his ability to move freely across the distances and between the places that defined his role, as well as his capacity to transgress them – seems to suggest that *dikgang* produce illness as a matter of course; and that the management of illness ought also, ultimately, to involve the management of *dikgang* (see also Livingston 2005: 10). Schapera (1940) notes that illness – especially affecting small children – was frequently traced either to the neglect of ancestors, or to conflict between specific family members (usually elders and their offspring), which had to be mediated and resolved for the illness to be cured. Klaits (2010: introduction), too, describes scorn as the refusal or abrogation of responsibilities of care, and links the sentiment it communicates to the production of illness. In both cases, the resolution involves, in part, providing care to the ill. Illness both indicates *dikgang* and provides an immediate means of addressing them. Families often express a preference for looking after ill family members at home, in part to discharge any outstanding responsibilities or debts of care to them, and also to expiate any *dikgang* that may remain. AIDS, of course, may be understood in similar terms: as indicative of familial strife, and a refusal or failure of care. But understood in the context of everyday care, these become familiar problems, rather than devastating new ones. Tensions inherent in expectations and practices of care inevitably produce *dikgang*, even unto the point of illness; and those *dikgang* require specific, different sorts of care to be addressed. Care, in other words, is an ongoing object of crisis for the Tswana, and the crisis it produces generates and sustains care in turn. If AIDS marks a 'crisis of care', Tswana families may be unexpectedly well-equipped to deal with it.

As the AIDS epidemic has unfolded worldwide, rather different narratives have framed its origins and effects, generating rather different responses on the part of governments, NGOs, donors, and other agencies. The family, however, remains a central site of concern and intervention. While there are many agencies and programmes that seek to intervene in families, focusing on everything from poverty alleviation to community development, here I focus on those oriented towards care for people infected and affected by HIV and AIDS. The Tswana assess the government and NGOs in terms of their capacity to provide care, and the spatial dynamics of these programmes closely mirror those of Tswana families, creating a powerful link between the community organisation and the home. But I suggest that important differences in practice disrupt and invert kin spatialities, and expose families to *dikgang* that they may be less well equipped to absorb.

III. The Geographies of Intervention: Supplemental Care

Mpho sat on the hard, narrow bench in front of the social worker's office, waiting. It was only quarter past seven in the morning, but she was not alone: three other women, their heads scarved and their waists wrapped in woollen blankets, sat quietly with her on the shaded stoop. The Social and Community Development (S&CD) office shared a small two-room council building with the Water Affairs office, in the corner of the village near the highway. At this hour, the doors and burglar gates were still locked tight. One could never tell whether one would get to see any government official on any given day, but showing up before they started work was usually the best bet.

Mpho was one of our neighbours, and in her late fifties. She had recently lost her eldest daughter, Kedi, who had left behind three daughters of her own: one already an adult, the others 13 and nine years old respectively. Mpho had been raising Kedi's girls since shortly after each was born, while their mother worked in the city. When Kedi had first returned to stay in the village, already quite ill, a friend had visited and encouraged the family to register with the local home-based care – an NGO perhaps 15 minutes' walk from their home, near the heart of the village. After some hesitation, Kedi had agreed.

After registering her, volunteers at the home-based care had accompanied Kedi to register with the local social worker – at the very office in front of which Mpho now sat – so she could receive the government food basket designated for people living with HIV. They had also taken responsibility for driving Kedi back and forth to town to pick up her free antiretrovirals, as well as trips to doctors and clinics outside the village – trips that would otherwise have been expensive and exhausting to make by public transport. They visited the house frequently during Kedi's illness, mostly sitting and praying with her and talking with Mpho. Occasionally either Kedi or Mpho might be invited to workshops or events at the home-based care building, or in nearby towns.

After Kedi's death, the volunteers had encouraged Mpho to return to the social worker and register her two youngest granddaughters as orphans, so that the family might receive the government food basket, and help with the costs of school fees, transport, and uniforms as well. Mpho had first come to the social worker's office – perhaps a half-hour's walk from home – the week before, but hadn't realised she would need her daughter's death certificate to complete her granddaughters' registration. Retrieving this certificate had involved a trip to the hospital in the largest village in the district, almost an hour away by bus and combi – easily a day's project, including the waiting involved.

Today, Mpho was luckier. The social worker was in at seven-thirty, and saw her quickly, registering the girls in a large ruled notebook and opening client files for them, with assurances that they would begin receiving their food basket from the end of that month. Mpho was then directed to yet another agency: the local orphan care NGO. It was another half-hour's walk away.

She set out along the dusty pathways in the gathering heat. She had heard mixed reports about the local orphan care NGO, and the children registered there were earning a reputation for being spoiled and disobedient. But the NGO fed the children lunch and a small afternoon meal; it was a place for them to go after school, and they were often sent home with schoolbags, clothing, or shoes. The project occupied an enormous plot, close to the dam at the centre of the village.

It comprised several buildings – classrooms, offices, a hall and kitchen among others, making it almost as large as the nearby schools – and had large open spaces for play and gardening, all encircled by a high, barbed-wire fence. Occasionally children who were not orphans clung to the fence, watching their friends or relatives playing or eating inside, sometimes in the company of foreign volunteers. Mpho entered the gates with some hesitation, and was quickly ushered into the office next to them. There a secretary took her granddaughters' details, told her briefly about the services provided, and asked that she send along the girls the next day to be shown around. Mpho herself was shown back out of the gates, and would only enter again later that year when specially invited for a Christmas event.

Over the months that followed, there were still other registrations. Another NGO based nearby, a Christian organisation that ran counselling camps a couple of times a year, had been sent by the social worker to sign up the girls. And then Mpho had been called to a meeting at the school to be briefed about another organisation that took Standard Seven students out on therapeutic wilderness retreats to the far north. Soon Mpho began to complain that the girls were never at home: they would come home late from the orphan care centre; on weekends there would be events and trips; on major school holidays they were often out on camps. Sometimes she wasn't altogether sure *where* they were. When she tried to call them, send them for things, or take them along to the lands, they began to refuse and to argue.

In Mpho's registration journeys, certain consistencies between the spatialities of intervention programmes and of kinship emerge. Like the places of the *gae*, places of intervention are multiple, and often distant from one another. They require and enable movement, which client and agency staff or volunteers undertake together, often daily, or frequently enough to be almost continuous and perpetual. Each place might be understood as a place where care is undertaken; indeed, government and non-governmental agencies alike frequently described their programmes as forms of 'supplemental care', designed to augment the care provided by families. While it would be difficult to say these agencies are altogether 'integrated', there are a dizzying number of coordinating committees at village, district, and national level that work to connect and coordinate them (with greater and lesser success). Staff and volunteers frequently move between posts in government, NGOs, and donor agencies, and share a variety of professional and social links with others in their field that bind organisations together. And these agencies call and send clients, and have clients called from and sent to them, including by those clients' parents. They occasionally rankle clients' elders by calling and sending them, too, and by being difficult to call and send in turn, but the hierarchies which this calling and sending spatialise fit a kin logic. Intervention spatialities are thus, in many ways, similar enough to kin spatialities to link the two. And it is the links and echoes between familial spaces of care and supplemental spaces of care that make the disruptive potential of interventions so potent.

This potential becomes clearest in the distinctions made in the spatialities of supplemental care. Clients, for example, seldom stay with the agencies in which they are registered, and certainly not with any regularity or for any length of time. Residential orphan care has been scrupulously avoided in Botswana (though many social workers and NGO staff have recently begun to suggest this should change). The care-work undertaken under the auspices of each agency, though similar to the care-work undertaken in the *gae*, is not contributed jointly by client and agency, but only by the latter on the part of the former; and only in very loose terms might it be seen to contribute to a prosperity they share.

NGOs and government offices alike also establish – and destabilise – boundaries in unique ways. Like every yard, shop, or business, both government offices and NGOs were marked off with fences and gates, some of them quite intimidating. But more than these, they created bureaucratic boundaries: one could not access them without appropriate referrals, without proof of claims (in appropriate paperwork), without registering, without waiting and often being turned back. Even once these requirements had been met, access was controlled: Mpho was not allowed in past the office of the orphan care centre, except for invitation-only special events; she would not be taken along on the children's retreat camps, nor see the offices of the NGOs that ran them; and she had minimal access even to the building of the home-based care project. Her granddaughters, in turn, may have found it difficult to approach the social worker's office without Mpho present, though their access to these other spaces was unfettered. Boundaries to each of these agencies, then, created differential claims of access to care that distinguished Mpho from her granddaughters.

Of course, homes also have boundaries: fence-lines mark the edges of yards, low walls distinguish the *lelwapa*, and the walls of the house set out spaces of sleeping, bathing, and intimacy. And each boundary works to exclude specific groups: suitors may not pass beyond the yard's fence; visitors must announce themselves when entering the *lelwapa*, and will not usually pass beyond it; and the interior spaces of the house are reserved for immediate family, close friends and occasionally neighbours' children, with the bedrooms of adults generally off-limits even to these. Limiting access to different spaces is a key means of ordering relationships; and the limits agencies impose on the families of clients have profound implications for both the relationship of the family to the organisation, and for relationships within the family as well. Where one member of the family can enter, as a client, and the others cannot, familial patterns of authority and responsibility are effectively suspended, and family relationships rendered meaningless. In this sense, we might see the boundary-making work of NGOs and government offices – like others of their spatial practices – as a process of creating an alternative, family-like space and set of allegiances by creating alternative sorts of boundaries.

But perhaps most importantly, the patterns of movement undertaken by agencies differ sharply from those undertaken by kin. As we have seen, kin move between the spaces of the *gae*, in a constant coming and going that inevitably gravitates back to the *lelwapa*. Mpho's movements to, among and from the various agencies founded to support her family also mimicked this sort of mobility. But where movement in the *gae* is cyclical, and essentially centripetal, the organisations described produce and require centrifugal movement. NGOs that take children out on therapy retreats are an obvious example of this tendency; but home-based care trips to clinics and workshops, or social worker subsidies for transport to school, also demonstrate the same pattern. Referrals onwards and outwards, constantly expanding a client's responsibilities for movement, add an onerous strain – and rarely take in the *lelwapa* of clients at all. This apparent avoidance distinguishes government and NGOs not only from kin, but from neighbours, friends and colleagues, for whom visiting is a key expression of care. It was not uncommon for people to reflect disparagingly on social workers – and for social workers themselves to express frustration – in these terms, complaining about being stuck in their offices or away at workshops when they should be moving around the village. To some extent, the types and directions of movement agencies undertake are reminiscent of the problematic aimlessness of 'going up and down': they involve moving away from the *lelwapa*, partly as a means of establishing and entrenching an alternate base. (Notably – regardless of the prohibitive costs involved – non-governmental agencies right across Botswana were quite insistent about building their own centres, rather than working through existing facilities or in an exclusively home-based manner.) Distance is continuously reproduced and extended, and becomes a defining spatial characteristic of the relationship between agencies, clients, and their families. And, of course, it serves to throw the careful compromise Tswana families seek between closeness and distance off-balance.

This potential for disruption was already emerging in Mpho's story above. Children or teenagers returning home from the orphan care centre frequently accompanied their friends 'halfway', stopping to hang about by the train tracks, or going off for illicit meetings, not returning until after dark. The centre, already shut, took no responsibility for these situations (and could hardly track 70 children across the village in any case). Arguments between the adults at home and the children dallying en route – about missed chores, unwashed school uniforms, missed meals, and their undesirable goings up and down – were frequent. Children resisted and avoided these demands, spending even more time away, adeptly deploying the sheer variety of possible excuses to do so (Dahl 2009). They developed a reputation in the village for being children who didn't listen (*ga ba utlwe*), who were disrespectful and contrary, even for frequenting bars (and being otherwise 'out of place'); and they were beaten at school and at home accordingly. A cycle of worsening tension and conflict, of serious *dikgang*, emerged. While this situation presents perhaps an extreme example – going well beyond the *dikgang* that other programmes generated – it is nonetheless illustrative of the risks such interventions present, by the proliferation of 'in between' spaces, in competition with the anchoring 'in-betweenness' of the *lelwapa*, that their fragmentation creates. The *dikgang* arising were borne primarily by clients and families, rather than the centre or any other organisation. But unlike Ntate's illness, they presented no obvious means of management. The new risks they represented, I suggest, were not simply a matter of people being in the wrong places and the wrong times; they were linked to a spatiality of care that competed with and disrupted that of the family.

If these risks are compounded enough to generate all-out conflict, the agencies I have been describing do have one alternative open to them. Home visits – by social workers and the orphan care project in particular – were rare, but they tended to be reserved for interventions: the confrontation of problems, reported either from within or outside the family, undertaken inside the family yard. Often these took the shape of formal discussions, though in worst-case scenarios they could involve more serious accusations, the calling of authorities, and, for social workers, the removal of children. Interventions are, I suggest, the most powerful means of disrupting kinship spatialities, because they turn the spatial dynamics of *dikgang* inside out. As we have seen, conflict within families is usually dealt with in a two-stage process, depending on its severity: first, by calling anyone involved in the *kgang* and key mediators *in*to the yard; and second, by taking the issue *out* of the yard, generally by going to figures like *dingaka* (traditional doctors), the *kgosi* (chief) at the village customary court, and so on. In interventions, the issue is brought *in*to the yard by people from outside of it; and in worst-case scenarios, family members are taken *out*. The spatial practices of the agencies described create a further inversion as well: while government and NGO spaces are difficult to access and gradually acquire exclusivity, the space of the home becomes fully accessible, and incontrovertibly public. While interventions of this sort were extremely rare in my fieldsite, both NGOs and social workers had established an open claim to them; and this claim was in itself sufficient to pose a threat, against which the family's management of space, care, and *dikgang* alike had to be insulated.

IV. Conclusion

In reflecting on the emplacement of sentiment, Klaits (2010) offers a helpful interpretation of the double meaning implicit in the Tswana greeting, *O kae*? (where/how are you?): '*where you are* affects *how you are*, both in terms of your relationships to others, and … your physical well-being' (2010: 120). To this observation, I would add that the questions which usually follow – *O tswa kae? O a kae?* (where are you from? where are you going?) – suggest not only the Tswana proclivity for constant movement, but a sort of short-hand assessment of relationships to home and family, of which staying and movement are taken to be emblematic. As we have seen, both are subject to constant change and significant uncertainty, and perpetually produce *dikgang* – the management of which requires careful balances to be struck between closeness and distance, mobility and presence. The reminder that neighbouring houses burn together – as the proverb quoted at the outset of this chapter provides – is both an injunction for those who live close together to help one another, because they are often afflicted by the same challenges, and also a subtler suggestion, that keeping a little distance between houses may be safest. This balancing act, in turn, ensures both the coherence of family over time, and room for change.

Of course, AIDS – an epidemic in which movement, closeness and distance have taken on pathological potential – might be understood as just this sort of *kgang*. In turn, the long-standing practices of managing space among kin to enable and produce care might be better-suited to addressing the epidemic than popularly assumed. However, to the extent that governmental and non-governmental responses to the epidemic have misread the dangers in kinship spatialities – and therefore introduced new spatial logics and practices that invert and transgress them – that coping potential may have been sharply undermined, and a much more damaging 'crisis of care' inadvertently produced in its place.

References

Comaroff, JL and Comaroff, J (1991) *Of Revelation and Revolution* (Chicago IL, University of Chicago Press).

Dahl, B (2009) 'Left Behind? Orphaned Children, Humanitarian Aid, and the Politics of Kinship, Culture, and Caregiving during Botswana's AIDS Crisis' (Unpublished PhD thesis, University of Chicago).

Dilger, H (2010) '"My Relatives are Running Away from Me!": Kinship and Care in the Wake of Structural Adjustment, Privatisation, and HIV/AIDS in Tanzania' in H Dilger and U Luig (eds), *Morality, Hope and Grief: Anthropologies of AIDS in Africa* (Oxford, Berghahn Books).

—— (2006) 'The Power of AIDS: Kinship, Mobility and the Valuing of Social and Ritual Relationships in Tanzania' *African Journal of AIDS Research* 5(2): 109–21.

Dilger, H, Kane, A and Langwick, SA (eds) (2012) *Medicine, Mobility and Power in Global Africa: Transnational Health and Healing* (Bloomington IN, Indiana University Press).

Farmer, P (1992) *AIDS and Accusation: Haiti and the Geography of Blame* (London, University of California Press).

Klaits, F (2010) *Death in a Church of Life: Moral Passion During Botswana's Time of AIDS* (London, University of California Press).

Livingston, J (2005) *Debility and the Moral Imagination in Botswana* (Indianapolis IN, Indiana University Press).

—— (2003) 'Reconfiguring Old Age: Elderly Women and Concerns over Care in Southeastern Botswana' *Medical Anthropology* 22: 205–31.

Morton, C (2007) 'Remembering the House: Memory and Materiality in Northern Botswana' *Journal of Material Culture* 12(2): 157–79.

Schapera, I (1940) *Married Life in an African Tribe* (London, Faber and Faber Ltd).

Thornton, RJ (2008) *Unimagined Community: Sex, Networks and AIDS in Uganda and South Africa* (Berkeley CA, University of California Press).

12

Witnessing, Containing, Holding? The German Social Welfare State (*Sozialstaat*) and People in Flight

JOHN BORNEMAN

The UNHRC estimates an unprecedented 68.5 million people are currently in flight from their homes, of which 25.4 million are designated refugees, including 3.1 million asylum seekers (2019). A growing number of these have arrived in Europe, reaching its apogee in 2015, where they expect the more advanced welfare states to extend to them some of the cradle-to-grave care they offer to their own citizens. Some of this care, informed by an historically achieved ethos and readily granted in the Cold War period, has indeed been forthcoming. But this current extension of care to refugees and migrants (the two categories are difficult to disentangle) has led to a mobilisation of anti-immigrant sentiment within Europe, creating acute cultural and political challenges, unsettling collective identifications, undermining traditional party systems, and destabilising the project of European integration.

In this chapter, I address this worldwide crisis in care for people in flight by building on work I began over 20 years ago. In 1996, at a conference on kinship at Rice University, Texas, I chose to think about kinship through the concept of care, the potentiality of which rests on its qualities as both a virtue and a critical descriptive tool (Borneman 2001). I was inspired by Tzvetan Todorov's (1996: 103) claim that, among the three 'ordinary virtues' – of dignity, care, and life of the mind – caring is the 'morally superior act'. In caring, he writes, 'the "I" addresses itself to one or several individual you's – in other words, to particular human beings with whom there has been established a relationship of reciprocity, a possibility of a reversal of roles'. In what follows, I first follow the arc of the refugee crisis as I have experienced it in my own relation, as an anthropologist, to Syrian refugees. I ask whether witnessing is sufficient, specifically when working with refugees, if the holding environments of our research subjects have collapsed? Focusing on Todorov's insight – that reciprocity is an integral part of care as a 'morally superior act' – I suggest care for refugees also entails, at an individual level, serving as a container for their anxieties and, at an institutional level, facilitating a holding environment in their places of exile. Finally, I discuss the relation of refugees to the specific type of holding environment of the German welfare state (*Sozialstaat*), and what the relation of care to reciprocity means in this setting.

In one way, I share with much of the general public a similar relation to refugees, characterised, first of all, by an unavoidable, coercive witnessing. News of the plight of refugees reaches across the planet daily, bombarding us with an endless flow of heart-breaking digital images and tragic stories that often exhaust our ability to remain alert to their presence. I would like to distinguish this level of witnessing from care, which makes specific demands on the listener for reciprocity that might enable a transformation of what has been witnessed. I have felt the demand for reciprocity as a call, very personally, having worked ethnographically between 1999 and 2008 in Aleppo, Syria (Borneman 2007). The city became one of the centres of the Bashar Al-Asad regime's war against its own people, and has been destroyed. Citizen participation in the Arab Spring of 2011 has been brutally penalised, especially in Syria: 6.5 million have been internally displaced, 25 per cent now live in exile, 500,000 have been killed, 2 million wounded (UNHRC 2018). I have felt both called to immediate action on behalf of those people I came to know well, and yet frequently paralysed by an inability to address the crisis in a mode appropriate to the scale of misery at hand.

I. On Containing, Holding, Metabolising

Witnessing, for anthropologists, usually entails listening to our interlocutors and documenting their experience. My prior research had prepared me to witness and document, in that sense, but not to contain traumatic dislocations and facilitate the creation of a holding space following the uprising against the government in 2011. Containing and holding are intimately connected yet distinct concepts that are sufficiently ambiguous – neither too specific nor too general – to lend themselves to a wide range of associations.[1] This makes them highly useful to ethnographic fieldwork, where different relationships and diverse sociocultural contexts compel a certain elasticity in the translation of general analytic terms into specific socio-linguistic, experiential registers. As I have written elsewhere, if fieldwork is not to be 'a monadic exercise of information exchange or retrieval, subject to archival contextualization', we must also learn from and respond to the demands to serve as 'a container for the emotions of our interlocutors'. The psychoanalyst Wilfred Bion (1957) coined this concept, theorising how a 'container' helps us come to terms with our disturbing lived experiences. He called these experiences

[1] Holding, as I am using it with regard to adult refugees, is an ontological concept concerned primarily with sustaining a sense of continuity of self over time. This is significant, since through radical displacement people in flight experience a rupture in their sense of self. The dynamic of containment is not about what is being thought but how one thinks, concerned primarily with the 'the processing (dreaming) of thoughts derived from lived emotional experience' (Ogden 2004: 1362).

'the contained', and argued that precisely because they brought forth associations difficult to think and dream with, another being was required to serve as a container for them (Borneman 2014: 442–43). Needless to say, in fieldwork with refugees, anthropologists studying the experience of flight and resettlement face potentially all-consuming demands for containment.

The refugee experience begins with a rupture in one's own holding environment, impelling flight. This rupture removes one from familiar referents, in particular from place, and most often from kin and family. The self is experienced as the opposite of held: as fragmented, discontinuous, disintegrated. The psychoanalyst and paediatrician Donald Winnicott formulated the concept 'holding environment' to describe the conditions of good mothering.[2] A 'good enough mother' provides an adequate emotional space for her child to feel secure, to grow up, and eventually to care for itself and for others. Writing in the 1950s, Winnicott sought to demystify the work of mothering, arguing against the increasingly detailed demands made on the care for infants and children. He insisted that mothering was in fact a form of 'ordinary loving care', a minimal set of conditions necessary to lay the foundation of mental health (Winnicott 1973: 44, 1957: 32). The ordinary loving care of an infant entails attentive holding, which includes bathing, feeding, and putting to sleep. Caregivers who are asked to contain and mirror the affective states infants display may experience these states as overwhelming, or they may simply misrecognise and mistranslate what in fact the infant desires. Infants, on the other hand, learn how to calibrate their reactions to the outside world through this mirroring. The point is that infants only come to understand their desires through the adult's translation, in a context in which they feel held, physically and mentally. Winnicott understands holding both literally, as in putting you between my arms, and in all figurative extensions of this physical act, such as attentive listening and creating a feeling of security.

Empirically and figuratively, the entire digestive system of children is forced to react to what they are given by adults and the outside world, involving a continual development in the ability to metabolise. As Bion wrote (1957), a healthy relationship between caregiver and receiver is one of mutual metabolism. Through attentive holding, the adult must detoxify and contain the thoughts of the child, while the child is asked to respond to the same demand to detoxify, but of the thoughts of the adult. In this communicative process, what is projected into us by each other is modified, and a relationship of ordinary loving care may develop. For our purposes here, adequate holding is essential to facilitate the digestion of foreign elements, which could be other people, food, feelings, or thoughts. Adequate holding creates a sense of security so that disparate experiences may be integrated into the self. The opposite of integration would be splitting (such as into a good and bad),

[2] In social science and administrative circles today, the term 'best practices' does work similar to what 'good enough' did for Winnicott. The difference is that 'best practices' allows for the vision of a technical ranking, as in the business world, while 'good enough' does not rank but sets a minimal standard that also implies a moral rather than technical evaluation (good versus bad).

dissociation (separating out certain emotional experiences so they cannot be linked to the self), or psychotic rejection. Ultimately, holding enables development of the capacity to empathise, to exercise imagination in play, to show curiosity. Challenges to the digestive system continue throughout life. And the need to be held – attentive loving care – extends beyond the family into other relationships, such as the ethnographic encounter, as well as to integrative institutions, such as the school and workplace, and to the local community within a welfare state.

II. Containment and Holding in the Syrian Refugee Crisis

The attempt to crush the 2011 Syrian uprising created the refugee crisis. I joined Facebook the year before to keep in touch with Syrian friends I had met during fieldwork there. They were suddenly highly mobile. In less than a year after the uprising, a hopeful revolution had turned sour (Borneman 2019: 23–38). Friends reported being tortured by the regime, and witnessed the state turn into a killing machine. And the state targeted not only those protesting against the regime but also civilians who might in some way support the uprising, and uninvolved others to shock their acquaintances into compliance.

One shoe salesman I know, Musab, disappeared and then, six months later, sent me an email explaining his absence, writing, simply, 'I was in prison'. Musab has a very elementary education. His father deserted the family early in his childhood, and this abandonment shaped his life in many ways. He had never before been in the least politically engaged. I asked no further about his imprisonment for fear of offering evidence to the government, which of course keeps tabs on Facebook and telephone communication, to fabricate a not infrequent charge of collusion with a foreign power. I reasoned that young men with more formal education could at least to some degree calculate the risk they were taking in communicating with me. But Musab is of humble origins, with little education and no connections, family or otherwise, who might have intervened on his behalf if he became suspect through me. In an effort to scare everyone into political passivity, there were many arbitrary arrests and disappearances, with routine use of torture to inflict intentional cruelty. In 2012, several young men I know well who were completing military service defected from the army and fled to Turkey. They feared having to shoot at fellow citizens, or feared that they themselves would be shot on fabricated grounds of suspected treason.

My witnessing at this time was complicated both by an inability to communicate with my interlocutors other than in the depthless mode of the electronic, and by the increasingly urgent, even existential demands of containment made on me. Communication took place in a virtual reality: I was presented with scenes through visual media as if I were there. This position was no different from that of other viewers of television news or readers of newspapers. It was not that of a fieldworker. I shared with other informed listeners and readers a coercive witnessing of the suffering of those in flight but with no means to address or, possibly, transform those scenes. We could all witness a repetitive nightmare from a certain distance, often without even talking to a single refugee, and we could direct our anger at government policies, at both the Syrian government's repressions and the Western governments' refusal to help. Given this distance, I was challenged to verify competing stories through electronic message exchange and my reading of media accounts alone. At the uprising's start, all of my close friends – Sunnis, Kurds, and Alewites – announced they were in favour of reforms, but not all joined the uprising. Outside militia quickly entered the scene and engaged in their own atrocities, forcing complicity in crimes, compromising any virtuous position of resistance. My own distance from Syrian lives did not necessarily limit the demand of containment, but it did constrain how I could understand or respond to emotions deposited in me.

At the same time, the range of representations that the refugees themselves produced seemed to accurately represent the enormous scale of their numbingly repetitive experience of horror. Especially on Facebook, Syrians themselves were able to document events as they unfolded, circulate photos, videos and texts in live time. Suddenly, they could and were representing themselves, sharing with us their hopes and their suffering, not only in Arabic but also in English and French, often in simultaneous translations. Their representations went quickly viral, enlarging the community of witnesses to a global audience. The need for me to document on-site happenings would have been redundant or superfluous.

In December 2012, I travelled to Istanbul to meet with men who had deserted the army. Syria has an all-male conscript army, and I knew some of these soldiers as boys. I thought their experience might provide me with a specific window into the changing nature of the violence of the Syrian regime and the resistance to it, and to its eventual collapse (Borneman 2012a, 2012b). Each story about the way of and the reasons for desertion was so unique, however, that it seemed to disaggregate rather than reflect a particular Syrian experience (Borneman 2019). The fugitives formed no coherent group outside the fact of their refusal to further serve in the military. The location of exile further disaggregated their Syrian identities while constituting them merely as a digitally-connected swarm (Han 2017). Their only other collective relation to each other was in their massing for ineffectual protests in front of the Syrian embassy. They did inform me of collective problems within the military, and of the effects of desertion on entire families, many of which fled into exile after being targeted due to a son who had deserted. But my witnessing, and telling of these stories, could not even approach the scale of their collective disintegration and its temporal disjunctures.

In Istanbul, after I introduced myself to one young media activist from Damascus, he opened his computer and insisted I look at the photos of his body after torture: over-extended wrists, cigarette burns, abrasions over the whole body. What was I supposed to do with this communication? He intended to return and continue his documentary work in Syria. I learned from one of the leaders of the resistance in Homs, a city tightly encircled by the regime and subject to its most aggressive assault at the time, that since late autumn starving residents had been eating their cats. I also met with a few young men whose bitter disappointment at the corruption of the American-Saudi-supported Free Syrian Army led them to express support for the Islamic State in Syria (ISIS) to build a Caliphate – on the grounds it was less corrupt than the others. I learned that deserters did not share a political orientation; many had escaped for very personal reasons of endangerment; nearly all had no idea about what a future in Turkey might hold for them – all were still hoping for a quick collapse of the regime and return to their homes. As we know, in the intervening eight years, the regime has not collapsed, and nearly all refugees remain in exile.

In the end, I could bear witness only to individual cases, one of which I wrote up and delivered as a talk in 2013 in Bochum, Germany. The audience asked few questions and appeared uninvolved. I gave a general talk at Princeton, where the audience pushed me to propose a resolution of the conflict; I had no idea. In the face of what had become a quagmire in Syria, I was humbled as an intellectual. I did not publish anything of this research, fearing then that any individualised stories of this sort might circulate back into Syria and endanger the families of my interlocutors. Over the next three years, I invested considerable time in helping those people I might be able to help, given my own knowledge and networks, to find a refuge in the West. I found programmes in universities to which they might apply in France, England, Scotland, Germany, Sweden, Switzerland, and the US. I rewrote and edited many, many personal statements and applications. I wrote perhaps a hundred recommendations. I paid for application fees, visa renewals, and counterfeit passports. No one had a credit card, even if they might be able to afford the fees, and all universities, even those with special programmes for Syrian refugees, demanded payment of application fees by credit card. I sent money via Western Union for emergency support to individuals in exile. I wrote letters in support of asylum claims. Ultimately, my support has been meagre, involving only select individuals. For most Syrians, for those who remained and those who fled, a crisis of displacement endures.

By 2014, rumours seem to have circulated that I was doing research on Syrian refugees; many journalists contacted me for interviews, including the BBC and NPR (interviews that were ultimately not aired, one displaced by a story on Egypt, the other by a story on Israel); *The New York Times* asked me to write an editorial (which they did not publish); anthropologists wanted my contacts (which I shared). And I have been asked to review many articles for journals, without having already published on these topics myself. I am ambivalent about these interactions. I never wanted to be an expert on refugees, much as my interlocutors had never dreamed of becoming refugees. We were both in unchosen locations. I concluded that what we call the media, with its diverse global circuits of information exchange, including the anthropological, were not usually looking for expertise but rather input that might help expand their brands and markets. That the uprising, the revolution, the civil war, arrested me said nothing about how to engage these events with attentive loving care for the participants. Without a PR firm or access to some network to place op-eds or interviews, what I was learning remained very local, personal, without larger effects.

To give our interlocutors voice and find ways to tell their stories has been the preferred activity entailed in the witnessing of many anthropologists. The argument is that we mediate and regurgitate raw stories to make them digestible for our own publics. This was also the primary location of the contributors to the influential volume in medical anthropology on 'social suffering' edited by Arthur Kleinman, Veena Das, and Margaret Lock (1997). They sought above all to place the individual voice in its social context, as a product of the social and as an urgent appeal to the social to address social suffering, despite uncertain outcomes and effects. Kleinman and Kleinman (1996: 1–24) specifically explore the moral conundrums faced when telling stories of others' suffering, including the problems of addressing different audiences and the danger of appropriating the suffering of the other for one's own purposes. While there is a compelling moral justification for giving voice to suffering – to study and document 'The Weight of the World', as a group of scholars in France under Pierre Bourdieu et al (1999) called it – the effects of witnessing in this way have processual and scalar dimensions that deserve more critical attention.

As to process, in 2011, the voice of Syrians whom I knew changed with shifts in *Stimmung* (public mood) (Borneman and Ghassem-Fachandi 2017a). Initially, it was not one of suffering but of optimistic aspiration, joyful about the possibilities of change. Within months, suffering quickly entered the picture; within two years, it dominated. With regard to scale, the Syrian crisis quickly made local voices of suffering into global issues. The proliferation of social media enabled direct access to voice for most of my interlocutors. The experience of a city, country, region could be easily shared in simultaneous time across the globe.

Dissatisfied with witnessing after-the-fact and from a distance, retelling, in retrospect, refugee stories that the refugees themselves were already sharing on social media, I sensed I had to narrow the distance to my interlocutors and go to the places to which they were fleeing. In face-to-face interaction in these new destinations, the issue of containment arose even more precisely and acutely, redefining my anthropological obligation as not merely witnessing but also containing the emotional experience of their flight and displacements. Many anthropologists working in other parts of the world on other subjects suddenly also felt called upon to represent Syrian refugees. What increasingly unsettled me about their projects was not that they presented themselves as witnesses to the refugee crisis, but that they did so before actually doing much of any research, before they knew much of anything or had critically examined what refugees needed from them. Certainly, they felt arrested by events. This arrest positioned us all as cosmopolitan 'spectators of calamities', Susan Sontag's apt phrase in *Regarding the Pain of Others*; it offered us a steady diet of 'the pleasure of flinching' (2003: 18, 41) at daily photos of the brutality of war. Engagement for most scholars was mediated through these images alone, through reading representations from a distance. Such engagement with and through media alone does not position us – as viewers, readers and listeners – to respond to the demands of containment and holding that are obvious to anyone who works face-to-face with actual refugees. I could not help feeling that, however well intended, many scholars and reporters were making careers off the suffering of others: precisely what Kleinman and Kleinman had warned against. As Sontag wrote, 'To designate a hell is not, of course, to tell us anything about how to extract people from that hell, how to moderate hell's flames' (2003: 114).

By 2015, I had come to the conclusion that, at this moment in time, attempts to represent the suffering of refugees, despite our best intentions, were often misplaced, precisely because such representational work offered no clue on how to moderate hell's flames. For one thing, there is the uncomfortable fact that one creates aliveness for oneself by getting people in flight to speak of their near-death experiences; for another, the request to retell the trauma of flight can be more an act of cruelty than of giving voice, as only under certain conditions might creating a representation through witnessing this recall make possible a re-symbolisation of the original experience. And that is one way in which academics might contribute to the transformation of their hell: re-symbolisation. It is perhaps the only factor over which refugees have considerable control. But without establishing a personal relationship with a refugee, where one not only bears witness to what is said but also struggles to contain what has been conveyed and mirrors this back to the speaker in a less toxic form, one may in fact make them feel used by simply collecting their stories, doing more harm than good.

Given the fragmentation of self that all refugees necessarily experience in exile, and the dissociation required to act as if the new environment can sustain the same integration of self as the old one, I sensed that my witnessing must focus on the new environment in which refugees land. I should listen for possibilities of self-integration. In June 2015, I began a project in Germany on what Europeans call 'social integration'. That year, 1.143 million foreigners entered Germany, 45 per cent of whom came from other EU countries; 442,000 applied for asylum, of whom 298,000 are Syrians (BAMF 2018). In 2016, I asked my partner, Parvis Ghassem-Fachandi, a German citizen and professor of anthropology at Rutgers University, to join me in a research project on incorporation of refugees in Germany.

We began working primarily with men between the ages of about 21 and 35, who constitute about 75 per cent of all refugees to Germany. Our initial contacts were young men who I had met in Aleppo in 2004, most of whom were still children at that time. In their new surroundings, they experienced a general disorientation. Upon arrival, they were assigned residence in different parts of Germany, based on the availability of lodging and a complex formula that distributed migrants to different regions to prevent a conglomeration in districts considered to be problematically densely settled with foreigners.

I initially visited a '*Containerdorf*' (container village), as they are called, north of Berlin, quickly assembled at the cost of 20,000 euros per resident. This one housed over 150 people from seven countries who spoke 10 different languages.

There was no lingua franca within the house; several translators were hired to visit once a week to ask about major problems. The federal distribution scheme ignored the wishes of most migrants, who had specific destinations in mind and did not want to be divided from friends. Given the choice of place, there is in fact a strong tendency for migrants from cities to move to other cities, or to move to areas with concentrations of people who share the same origin or mother-tongue or religion. One problem with being assigned to small towns and rural areas has been that those places in Germany are often depopulated, with few younger residents to interact with, and no history of dealing with cultural difference, especially not with Muslims or Arab groups. This is generally true of the former East Germany, where during the Cold War, residents had minimal experience with migrants other than with other displaced Germans from the Eastern territories after the Second World War. A considerable number of residents themselves in fact came from families displaced at the end of the war. These factors increased the incentive for refugees to move from places initially assigned to large cities like Berlin, where the information quickly spread that in the Neukölln district people had created an 'Arab street' – die Arabische Strasse – a term even Arab children reference in German. That street, people told me, had the shops and restaurants, the smells and sounds, of Damascus. However, people who moved to Berlin without proper legal steps risked losing social welfare, as legality and benefits were dependent on the approval not of federal but regional administrators.

Making the initial experience less welcoming was the opacity of the administrative rules regulating legal status, jobs, and mobility, which refugees experienced differently from person to person and by place. The resettlement centres were rarely equipped to facilitate language learning or to enable meeting Germans, two wishes of many new arrivals, and two of the conditions most facilitating integration. Refugees I knew felt increasingly estranged from 'Germany' after the initial enthusiasm and contact with volunteers had waned. Most volunteers found the obstacles to integrating the refugees more formidable than expected, and wanted to return to the lives they had lived before the events of 2015. In any event, the formal help refugees were offered was eventually replaced by interactions with bureaucracies. On the rare occasions they met Germans privately, it tended to be the elderly who had time for them. The lingua franca in discussion was usually a broken English. We sought in our fieldwork to bring Syrians closer to Germany as an experiential site, to facilitate access to Germans and things people in Berlin do that Syrians also might enjoy. Meanwhile, some Germans and permanent residents were also doing the same thing as we were, including establishing a formal legal relationship of guardianship (*Patenschaften*) with adolescent refugees.

In 2016–17, Parvis and I spent 15 months in Berlin where we met nearly daily with individuals or small groups of Syrian refugees. After about 10 months of many informal gatherings, I asked one young man when he was going to tell me more of his experiences in Syrian jails and of his early experience in exile working with the resistance. He said, tartly, 'No, I don't want to tell you'. The time to recount memories of the past would have to be chosen by him, not dictated by my fieldwork schedule. I had known him as a 10-year-old in Aleppo, and I knew his entire family. We had established a level of trust that made me confident enough to make this request. In fact, he had already confided in me some of his experiences in prisons in Syria, and how he had become politicised, embraced radical Islamist ideology and then turned cynical about how politics actually worked. He experienced the death of friends and new acquaintances up close, and had himself come close to death several times. In Germany, he often had difficulty sleeping, not uncommon among refugees generally; he told me of waking up from nightmares. Once he surprised me by asking for a referral to a therapist, something I had offered months before. Such help is available in Berlin, though much of the time a translator is needed, and the therapist herself must pay for this work. After I established a contact for him, and she reached out to him, he decided he no longer needed the therapy. 'All I need is a friend', he said. 'You need a professional', I replied, 'someone anonymous'. We left it at that.

In the final analysis, our acts of listening substitute not for the missing external observer but the missing internal observer in our subjects. One of our goals must be to facilitate an internal conversation that is not taking place due to the erasure produced by the traumatic experiences of war and flight. Our subjects can and must have this conversation with themselves, with their own internal objects, if they are to come to symbolise their own experiences. They must re-establish links with what has become unspeakable. We cannot force this conversation, but we can facilitate it. That entailed, for myself and my partner, being prepared to serve as containers and to make the refugees aware of their new holding environment. Our refugee subjects needed not only our listening but also our stability, our money, and our time. We secured a few people's safety; we enabled a few to study in the West; we found others apartments. And we acted as friends who were familiar with German living and eager to introduce them to aspects of German life in which they might want to take part. What I say does not negate the absolute imperative of committed listening, nor do I want to minimise the suffering of others. But I would like to add to listening containing and holding, and here scale up from the anthropologist to parallels with and within the welfare state, and to care for refugees in this setting.

III. Care and the Welfare State

Since Otto von Bismarck developed the model of the *Sozialstaat* (social state) in 1870, what in English is simply dubbed the 'welfare state', it has been adapted and extended throughout northern Europe. During the Cold War, it was elaborated most by the socialist states of Eastern Europe. The welfare state is a type of holding environment that has been constructed for those who belong to a nation, a particular kind of abstract community – what Benedict Anderson (1983) analysed as deep horizontal membership – that is based on imagined connections of kinship and civil religion, initially extending to citizens only. In the post-WWII period, care in welfare states was extended further, not only to national citizens but also to other kinds of residents, and accompanied by an expansion of the kinds of care provided by the state for particularly vulnerable or dependent citizens (children, the elderly, the disabled, etc). TS Marshall (1950) theorised this expansion as an evolution from civil to political to social rights. The dominant anthropological perspective over the last several decades has been to pluralise the concept of citizenship, thereby critical of any attempt to delimit the term while remaining within a legal rights framework (Caglar 2014; Ong 1996).

Following the end of World War II, the huge flows of people across the European continent led to the regulation of refugees in the 1951 UN Refugee Convention, with Additional Protocols signed since by most states in the world. This means that people in flight from their homes have a claim, theoretically based in these international legal accords, to either 'subsidiary protection' or 'refugee status' (asylum). That is, they have the right to make a legal appeal to stay in the country they have fled to.[3] Those who flee to European welfare states can claim access not only to certain legal rights but also to an ethos of care, which rests on the assumption of both being cared for (social support within the confines of the customs of the host countries) and being able to care for oneself (eg access to employment, education, mobility and some government programmes). My focus here will be on this ethos of care, a concept of care I stretch from its domestic origins – what Clifford Geertz (1963) called 'primordial attachments', among kin, family, neighbourhood, clan, or tribe – to take in care for non-citizens, strangers with whom one's attachments, if they exist, are not based on a history of a lived relationship.[4] Even though states may be legally bound by treaties regulating care for refugees, the ethos of care for strangers is never limited to institutional, normative, or ethical obligations that define legal rights. There are, rather, elements of the incalculable, spontaneous, and unstructured that appeal to an ethos that grows out of an encounter with people in flight. These include, within European welfare states, what is not part of United Nation treaties: namely an expectation of reciprocity on the part of citizens and permanent residents in their civil societies. This encounter with an expectation of reciprocity shapes the life of a refugee in the social welfare state, and, as well, reshapes the life of citizens and residents in these states through the incorporation (or expulsion) of foreigners. Since my contribution here is more synchronic than historical, I will in the remainder of this chapter discuss the current challenges that the new arrivals present to the holding environment of the German welfare state, specifically how they make claims on the state and society and how Germans respond to them.

[3] Within Europe, the Dublin Protocol stipulates that migrants entering Europe be processed in places they enter, on the periphery. On 24 August 2015, the German Federal Office for Migration and Refugees (BAMF) ratified an order suspending the Protocol, declaring that all Syrian asylum-seekers were welcome to remain in Germany, irrespective of which EU country they had first entered.

[4] James Ferguson (2015) develops the idea of 'the commons' to talk about redistribution without being burdened by particular historical claims. While I agree that historical claims are only one of many legitimating parameters for redistribution, I doubt very much that they can ever be bypassed.

IV. The Collapse of Holding Environments and Imaginable Futures

The collapse of the holding environment in Syria is part of a general pattern of disintegration of 'structure', or, to use an older term, 'social organisation', in many countries of the former Third World or global South. There are many essential elements in an account of this collapse, but, for our purposes, it is important to emphasise that at a certain point the collapse of holding environments leads to the search for new ones rather than an attempt to repair the environment in which one lives. This simple statement of cause and effect is often lost in the attempt to explain the complexities of disintegration. The disintegration of structure always grows out of unsustainable relationships. European countries tend to frame the current refugee flow as a crisis coming from elsewhere, and it results largely from grievous failures and flaws in the authoritarian political and cultural systems in the MENA region (Middle East/North Africa), extending to Africa and South Asia. Nonetheless, imperial Europe initially drew these polities, in the MENA region, through colonisation and creating new boundaries following the collapse of Ottoman rule and World War I. With the rise of independence movements, European countries then largely disavowed responsibility for the relationships they had formed, while structuring a separation whereby former colonies would remain in many ways dependent – as sites of resources, cheap and often skilled labour when needed, consumers for European products, and as fields in which to experiment with forms of surveillance, military technology, and medical products, among a long list of importations from the West.

At the same time, European complicity does not absolve former colonies from their culpability in the current flight. Today the most stable Arab political systems of the MENA region, with controlled emigration, are authoritarian monarchies, for example, Jordan, Oman, Saudi Arabia, and Morocco (although there is also a large exodus from Morocco). The other systems are all variations on authoritarian-military rule: highly corrupt, exploitative of local populations, with large security forces. Only Tunisia among these states has been able to sustain the democratisation wave of the Arab Spring that began in 2011. As a democratic oasis surrounded by authoritarian, unstable states, its stability should not to be taken-for-granted. It is itself unsettled by becoming a major transit space for refugee flows from North and sub-Saharan Africa.

In general, the authoritarian systems that replaced colonial rule have been unable to generate sustainable economies and legitimate political orders and are unlikely to be able to do so in the near future. They seek stability through violence directed against their own populations. Given these hostile environments, the flight of people to Europe from this region will continue in the foreseeable future. Europe's attempt to stem this flow of refugees by means of financial aid to these systems will itself serve increasingly as an important prop to these uncaring, abusive structures. In 1983 Aristide Zolberg analysed how the formation of new states generated refugee flows. Today it is the dissolution of social organisation in these 'new' states that is doing the same thing, with another important difference; that the flow is now imagined with global aspirations and the means to carry those out, and most of the refugees from Africa to Asia aspire to land in Europe.

Who is fleeing, and why? The displaced, dispossessed, and discontented, the persecuted, the poor and the well-to-do, many second- or third-generation descendants of colonial subjects; people of all ages, though most are young men. While a significant number of the refugees and migrants may be fleeing persecution, many are simply fleeing the lack of a future. The colonial past is not what unites them (Brückner et al: 2016). What they have in common is a very limited future in their places of origin. Futures in Europe may, tragically, also be very limited, but, in any event, they are imaginable, whereas home has become a place of no return.

The timing of the arrival in Europe of people in flight from elsewhere is not propitious given the breakdown of political party systems, the waning of social solidarities, and the economic uncertainty that European countries are themselves experiencing. All of these seemingly intractable problems aggravate internal cleavages and are easily attributed to outside agents, facilitating the mobilisation of Islamophobia, anti-EU, and anti-immigrant sentiment. All states within the European Union have increased restrictions on the extension of their holding environments to the new arrivals, even those like Germany and Sweden that were initially more welcoming. In fact, the pressure grows to build fortress Europe, accelerate deportations, and make the conditions of detention more onerous (Stolke 1995). That is in part because at the same time as European citizens are asked to be hosts, many find their own living standards and social welfare benefits have shrunk in the new economies of the post-Cold War order. After the collapse of European and Eurasian communist systems in 1989, neoliberal reforms, even in states with the most advanced systems of collective national cradle-to-grave care, have to varying degrees curtailed state provisions, though not nearly as dramatically as in states that already had only minimal welfare provisions.

Of special empirical and symbolic importance in Germany was the attempt to introduce more flexibility in labour markets (identified with the Harz IV reforms of 2005), which curtailed long-term unemployment benefits. Although dramatically affecting the internal dynamics of class structure, especially the nonworking poor, these reforms were less neoliberal in intent than they were responses to the logic of a global economy in which Germany, like the other northern European welfare states, is positioned in the high end of a competitive export market. In this global competition, refugees and migrants enter Germany as competitors to local residents, who are already threatened by automation and the use of artificial intelligence in labour reorganisation (Borneman 2017).

There are other unanticipated consequences of the end of the Cold War. Before its end, no major political party argued against upholding the 1951

Refugee Convention, or against human rights generally. Today, as citizen fears of immigration – specifically Muslim immigration – grow, established parties defend refugees and migrants with great peril. My concentration on refugees from Syria and other predominantly Muslim countries highlights the major phantasmatic issue for Europeans in this particular flight. There is, on the one hand, the association of Islam with criminality and terrorism (Cesari 2010). Whatever negative stereotypes Europeans had of Muslim immigrants in the 1950s through 1980s, these earlier immigrations did not lend themselves to the same scale of political abuse or use. Today opposing Muslims is a singular issue used to mobilise support for elections. On the other hand, there is the fear that an ongoing demographic change – as the number of Muslim descendants increases relative to the number of Christian descendants – will accelerate the dissolution of syncretic national-religious cultural traditions. By 2050, Muslims are expected to increase from their 2015 number of 4.6 percent of Europe's population to either 7.4 per cent (if no new migration occurs) or 14 per cent (with high migration levels); in Germany, specifically, by 2050, Muslims may make up 20 per cent of the population (with high migration levels) (PEW.forum.org 2017).[5]

Among the new arrivals in Europe, as part of a migration that continues but in reduced numbers from its peak in 2015, Syrians are also the largest and have become the preferred group of refugees. Why do Germans identify more strongly with Syrians than with other national populations who share similar experiences of violence and displacement, such as Iraqis and Afghanis? First, the war in Syria has received more consistent attention than other conflicts, especially since the Islamic State joined the Bashar al-Asad regime in targeting the civilian population. Second, Germans are identifying with an image of urban Syrians that mirrors their own self-image. There is also some truth to the claim that most Syrians are 'whiter' than many other populations in flight; German racial identification with them may be largely unconscious but it is stronger. Third, many Syrian refugees are highly educated youths from middle-class backgrounds, making it easier for Germans, who are also highly educated and largely middle class, to feel it is possible to integrate them into German society. They are seen as more likely to learn and adjust to the German system of education and career advancement than other refugees. In conversations with language teachers, people working in administrative capacities, and others who come into contact with middle-class refugees, Syrians are seen as model migrants in terms of public civility, capacity for language acquisition (many already speaking Arabic, English, Turkish, and French), willingness to

[5] The phantasmatic challenges of incorporation are even more difficult to address than are the empirical ones. All of my Syrian interlocutors report that Germans see them as 'Muslim' before they see their other dimensions of personhood. This is especially important when it comes to dating and friendship, where men report being reduced to a one-dimensional 'Muslim friend' or 'token Muslim' sex partner.

learn German, and experience with a cosmopolitan multiculturalism at home that prepared them to adapt to the behavioural expectations of tolerance in Germany.

V. Asylum Claims in Germany

The right to asylum is the only fundamental right accorded to foreign nationals in Germany, on the basis of the constitution and of obligations under international law arising from the 1951 UN Refugee Convention. In accordance with Article 16a of the Basic Law of the Federal Republic of Germany, it extends to political persecutees the protection of human dignity guaranteed to German citizens in Article 1 of the Basic Law. In principle, courts consider only state persecution and the need for subsidiary protection in general emergency situations. The formal grounds for asylum are restricted to justified fear of persecution because of race, religion, nationality, political conviction, or membership of a specific social group, and in circumstances where one is unable to call on the protection of one's country of origin or does not wish to take it up because of this fear. If one enters Germany via a safe third country, one is not entitled to asylum but required to return to that third country. Yet the granting of asylum or of temporary protected status is not automatic, and reasoning is not always restricted to formal grounds. Judges and lawmakers are increasingly cognisant of factors other than persecution that drive flight, such as environmental catastrophe or economic unsustainability.

In the last several years, Germany has processed more asylum claims and granted more asylum requests than all other 27 EU countries combined. Of the 722,000 claims in 2016, 36.9 per cent were from Syrians (by far the largest single group); in the first six months of 2017, the number of Syrian claims as a percentage of the whole declined, to 23.4 per cent. Of the number of claims by all asylum seekers, in 2016, 36.8 per cent received asylum, and 22 per cent, subsidiary protection. In the first six months of 2017, these numbers dropped to 20.9 per cent and 17.1 per cent, with 40 per cent rejected and the other applicants remaining in limbo (BAMF: 2017). Many of those rejected successfully appeal the decision, and currently some 600,000 individuals whose asylum claims were rejected are still living in Germany, with 80 per cent of those already in residence for at least six years. In 2017, 80,000 migrants were deported, with 27,900 voluntarily leaving. As of February 2018, Germany offers 3000 Euros to individuals who agree to return after asylum claims are rejected (ProAsyl 2018).

There is in fact a ban on deportation of Syrians. They are threatened with deportation only when they have committed a crime in Europe or have already been rejected for asylum. The most controversial deportations within Germany are those to Afghanistan, which has been officially reclassified as 'safe' even though the country remains in a lethal civil war between competing groups. Citizen groups like ProAsyl and religious institutions have offered help and sanctuary to some of those marked for deportation; through 2017, pilots have refused to fly on 222 organised deportations. Yet, despite the increase in the number of actual deportations, many of those marked for deportation are successfully resisting, with the help of members of German civil society, the churches, pilots, and the courts.[6]

Because the right of asylum is coupled with extensive promises of care, citizens of welfare states like Germany may still recognise that right as an obligation while also wanting to restrict asylum claims legally (eg, set a numerical limit, introduce more severe vetting, increase deportations, reduce levels of support) so as to limit the benefits of membership in a system of care designed and intended largely for citizens. When legal claims for protection of foreigners are balanced against social claims for care by citizens, care-giving becomes a voluntary gift, not an obligation, to foreigners. The internal logic of welfare states is that care operates within a closed membership system: all able citizens work (or try to) and then make contributions from earnings to the general fund. This fund is then redistributed for social ends, including for extra care to those who need it most. There is no internal logic within welfare states that mandates such care to non-citizens, even when they are victims of political persecution. There are benefits deemed 'natural', like support for mothers and children, and benefits deemed 'primordial', like support for kin or co-ethnics as in members of the *Volk*, that are linked to necessities for group reproduction. But the extension of citizen benefits to select categories of foreigners, including those seeking or granted asylum, lacks these justifications. The one argument that ties reciprocity to acceptance of migrants is that of the sustainability of labour supply necessary for group survival, but since all refugees or immigrants are not equally likely to fit into the job structure of Germany this argument is difficult to sustain at such a general level. Only certain categories of highly-skilled labour are needed and most migrants are unprepared or unable to fulfil this need. The argument for the obligation to grant asylum and care to refugees must ultimately proceed out of a humanitarian logic.

[6] New legislation in 2017 directs that decisions to deport be made individually on the basis of a balance of interests, weighing factors such as the situation in country of origin, or the interests of Germany to no longer be responsible for a particular refugee. If refugees have been sentenced to prison for a year, for example, they lose their refugee status. Of special concern are crimes against life, against a person's physical integrity, against sexual self-determination, against property (robbery or theft), or attacks on the police; in these cases, deportation would proceed independently of the severity of the custodial sentence or probation. Under the new law, for major crimes, asylum seekers would first serve their sentence in Germany and subsequently be deported. For lesser offences, and if the sentence is suspended, the deportation can be carried out immediately. These restrictions are currently being challenged in court, with the expectation of lengthy appeals following each court's decision. Legal grounds for resisting deportation include illness, loss of documents, and questioning the classification of the country to which the individual is to be deported as 'safe'. An EU-led fast-track assessment system is now operating at the European Union's external borders and offers asylum seekers a quick and credible assessment of their claims.

VI. The German Holding Environment and *Rechtssicherheit*

What makes Germany particularly attractive as a holding environment for refugees is its political stability, security, and wealth, which, taken together, frame the possibility for an expansive ethos of care (Bertoli et al 2013; Münkler and Münkler 2016). The major challenge in constructing this environment is that the same space must function as a holding environment for people in flight and for settled residents. It must facilitate a sense of 'mutual belonging' of groups who make different demands on the social and have different visions of their futures. Chancellor Angela Merkel's audacious decision, on 4 September 2015, to open German borders and accept the thousands of migrants and refugees, destabilised Germans' visions of their futures. A *Willkommenskultur* (welcoming culture), generated by civil society itself, met the sudden initial challenge of incorporating millions of foreigners. But the new arrivals simultaneously awakened a xenophobic sentiment that fed on fears of Muslims, migrants, and terrorists. Counterbalancing xenophilic reactions, xenophobic sentiment found a voice in the politics in a new party, the Alternative for Germany (AfD), which, deploying a *völkisch* concept of the people, rose from zero to 20 per cent of the vote in the 2016 elections. Merkel herself has been Janus-faced on this issue: exclaiming on 31 August 2015, '*Wir schaffen das!*' (We can do it!), as if it were irrelevant what she had concluded five years earlier, on 16 October 2010, '*Der Ansatz für Multikulti ist gescheitert, absolut gescheitert!*' – namely that this thing called multiculturalism had 'absolutely failed' (*Spiegel* 2010).[7]

Anxieties about the stranger work both ways. Once inside Germany, refugees confront a tradition of expecting *Dankbarkeit* (gratitude) from foreigners. Instead of showing demonstrable thankfulness for the generosity extended to them, refugees often instead frame their current lives in terms of problems in obtaining rights, overcoming bureaucratic obstacles, gaining access to educational or retraining programmes, finding employment or housing, or the impossibility of family reunification. While most Germans disapprove of xenophobic attacks on foreigners, they often also counter this fear by pointing to actual attacks by foreigners on them, a point I will elaborate more below. Refugees generally have a difficult time meeting Germans outside of bureaucratic settings, partly because Germans tend to be shy, hesitant, and awkward in initial encounters, but also because many social situations include alcohol and a sexual openness which frightens people raised in more chaste settings.

Germans, by contrast, are engaged in a separate set of debates about how to balance changes in their own welfare (ie increased inequality, cut backs on

[7] *Spiegel Online*, Samstag, 16 October 2010; www.spiegel.de/politik/deutschland/integration-merkel-erklaert-multikulti-fuer-gescheitert-a-723532.html, accessed 16 September 2016. *BBC News*, 'Merkel says German multicultural society has failed': https://www.bbc.co.uk/news/world-europe-11559451.

social support) with obligations to refugees. Their own histories of migration, assimilation, and immigration shadow these debates. Between 1944 and 1961, after Germany ceded territory and property to Poland, Czechoslovakia, and the Soviet Union, more than 12 million Germans were eventually expelled or fled to the West (Bauerkampfer 2008). They comprised a refugee population that initially made up 20 to 25 per cent of all people in the territory of what in 1949 became two German states. Today, even for those two or three generations removed from the actual experience of flight, the current refugee crisis provokes discomforting memories, revealed in both unconscious references and in everyday conversations.

Yet, the major frames used for talking about immigration have long been informed by numbers and negative phantasms of the foreign 'other', with little reflection on how such abstractions relate to one's own experience. A long history of refusal to acknowledge the large number and place of immigrants already living in Germany – a stubborn insistence on being a country of emigration and not immigration – has never helped residents adjust to a multicultural reality (Göztürk et al 2007). Current debates on immigration in public and private raise the dual fears of imported terrorism and of *Überfremdung* (being overwhelmed by foreigners), with the concurrent difficulty of sustaining the tradition (or dream) of a *Volksgeist* (spirit of the people) and *Kulturnation*.

When the impossibility of assimilation (of mostly Muslim migrants) is acknowledged, appeals are made to different models of incorporation. A more conservative model is integration through a *Leitkultur* (a leading, dominant culture) with Christian roots and traditions; a more progressive one proposes the teaching of democratic values and openness to the outside, such as the Enlightenment tradition of emancipation movements. While the German way of life is changing, there are still many shared, fairly non-partisan frameworks that tend to exclude, such as *Gemütlichkeit* (cosiness) in public settings and shared pride in what German society has achieved (or tries to achieve) in sports, politics, or economics. Many Muslims from the Middle East, in particular, have from childhood been taught to question some German norms, such as full equal rights for women, homosexual marriage, secularity in the European version of the separation of Church and State, freedom to criticise the sacred, distancing from the anti-Semitism of the past – all of which are embodied in customs and conventions.

Alongside these debates, proposals to integrate the new immigrants are informed by the experience with *Gastarbeiter* (the majority from Turkey) invited to work in West Germany in the 1960s and 1970s. The *Vertragsarbeiter* (contract workers) imported from socialist-friendly regimes to East Germany in the same period are less recognised in public debates; all except a few, mostly Vietnamese, who were present when the Wall came down, were sent back after their contracts expired. It is generally recognised that labour migrants to both Germanies were necessary to fill certain jobs in the booming economy of the Cold War, and that they contributed essentially to the growth of both economies. In a similar way, the new arrivals today, it is hoped, will fill imminent labour shortages and contribute to paying state pensions as the population ages (Bertoli et al 2013). More critically, most recent guest workers have not returned but stayed, contrary to initial expectations, and most have brought some of their kin. Legal reform after 2000 liberalised access to citizenship through naturalisation, officially recognising the permanent presence of Turks and Kurds in Germany. In 2005 the government introduced formal integration courses for both non-nationals and ethnic Germans (Green 2013). In contrast to prior assumptions regarding the guest workers, it is assumed that most Syrian refugees will stay, at least for a considerable period of time, and for this reason the German government offers immediate support and many integration programmes to supplement private initiatives for refugees (Karakayali and Kleist 2016).[8] This is an implicit if not always spoken acknowledgment of one of the great errors of past experience with migration: that not providing a path to integration for Turks and Kurds led to the construction of a 'parallel society' (*Parallelgesellschaft*), whose members identify more with their country of origin than with Germany (Ceylan 2010). New integration initiatives assume neither the return of all new arrivals nor the uniformity of assimilation.

These positive integration measures are intended to make reciprocity possible. They assume that the new arrivals will work and begin to care *for* Germans much as they are now being cared for *by* Germans. But these measures have also provoked a backlash of sorts. Ethnic Germans from East-Central Europe and the former USSR and other immigrants over the last 50 years accuse the government of favouritism, as they did not receive this level of care. Irrespective of how events unfold, reciprocity on any larger scale will be delayed by decades. Even for Syrians, it can take two or three years before asylum or protective status is granted, before a refugee has a legal right to language training or employment. Some young men I know have learned German on their own using free internet programmes on their smartphones, and only reluctantly then completed official language courses. It took until 2017 to build a large enough infrastructural capacity for language classes for all who qualified to take them, and thus only in the autumn of 2017 were most refugees from 2015 qualified to enter the universities and labour apprenticeship programmes (for which intermediate German is required). Still, many refugees did not and do not want to enter formal educational programmes, making it likely that they will be either permanently underemployed or remain wards of the state. Germans are well aware of these developments and of the specific ways in which they vary by neighbourhood, village, and region.

[8] New legal measures were passed in late summer 2016, requiring migrants and refugees to 'integrate' in return for being allowed to live and work in the country. They entail acquiring language competence and passing an integration course. If asylum seekers reject these new measures, they face cuts to their support. The stated goal of these laws was to make it easier for asylum seekers to gain access to the German labour market, including to new low-paid workfare jobs. The government also suspended for three years a law that required employers to give preference to German or EU job applicants over asylum seekers.

The fear that the generosity extended to strangers will be extracted from the state benefits that flow to citizens comes up frequently in conversations. Many citizens from the former East, who still lag behind the West economically, fear this signals the end of efforts to achieve equality following German re-unification. So as not to provoke this fear, West Germans have never expressed to me publicly, in the presence of East Germans, what they do express privately: a desire to eliminate the 'solidarity contribution' which is automatically deducted from the pay-checks of all West Germans.

Resistance to integration, and to the granting of asylum, came into focus after the explosive 2015/16 New Year's Eve sexual assault in Cologne on young German women involving roughly 1000 foreign men, mostly of Arab origin. The relevant police protocols created a temporal delay in reporting that fostered public frustration and indignation, which quickly turned into a more explicit suspicion: that officials were trying to hide or obfuscate the ethnic origin of perpetrators, and that the government wanted to protect refugees and asylum seekers from German collective anger (Amjahid et al 2016). Each of the many subsequent publicised attacks by migrants in European cities, regardless of nationality of the victim, has reinforced a singular public perception: that the Cologne attack was as an inevitable outcome of the unregulated influx of refugees into Germany. The indifference that characterised the public mood before this series of events turned into ambivalence, and has ultimately led to a waning of xenophilia and increased xenophobia (Borneman and Ghassem-Fachandi 2017a, 2017b).

People today regularly question the scholarly frame that assumed asylum to be an unconditional right. Likewise, in public forums a frequent argument is that the extension of care to refugees was a gift bestowed on non-nationals that should now be withdrawn. Additional attacks by foreigners have since shaken local communities, especially small ones, which are accustomed to an extremely secure environment. Although sex crimes and crimes against property by foreigners are less frequent than such crimes by other Germans, they are given much more publicity when new migrants are involved. In the publicity surrounding such events, the difference between refugees and other new arrivals tends to be effaced, and a generalised anxiety of the foreign arises (Borneman and Ghassem-Fachandi 2017c).

One of the most significant reasons for the Cologne (and other) attacks is that migrant dependency produces aggressive feelings that are often turned against their German hosts, even against those who extend a welcome and care for them. Germans are asked to contain the often-violent projective identifications of migrants and mirror them back in a harmless, modified form. German officials, teachers, employees at asylum shelters, and staff at refugee homes also have to reckon with the heightened aggression between migrants who sometimes seek to harm those from other groups. A modification in mirroring works only if what Germans accrue in self-esteem outweighs both the tasks of containment and their fears of being taken advantage of. That is often not the case.

One way these anxieties are addressed is through increased support for more legal regulation. This confident production of legal regulations is not an approach specific to democratic, Western societies – socialist regimes issued endless regulations, as do Islamist governments. The difference is that citizens in Europe, especially those in northern welfare states, have more trust in their governments, and hence often believe these regulations will have the intended effects. In point of fact, the problem addressed is the sense of loss of *Rechtssicherheit*, legal security or certainty premised on the concepts of compliance and predictability. The influx of new arrivals in 2015, followed by the Cologne sex assault and subsequent violent crimes against Germans committed by foreigners, undermined a sense of legal certainty. A public debate about sex crimes followed, resulting in new legislation that made it easier to prosecute suspects of sexual violence and eased the deportation rules for refugees convicted of sex-related offences.[9] Linking sexual assault generally to foreigners may further stigmatise refugees, turning German public opinion against them.

In this current mood, when neither many German citizens and permanent residents nor refugees feel adequately cared for, the goal of a mutual belonging depends on creating relational visions of the future that are sufficiently elastic and expansive while coming close to the reality that contemporary Germany actually offers. Above all, a sense of mutual appreciation and affirmation of self-worth is a prerequisite for feeling alive and desired, without which care becomes mechanical and one-sided rather than envisioned as reciprocal. We can in our own work of containment contribute to this sense.

Conceptualising our own relation to refugees as containers, and welfare states as holding environments, adds a critical psychological dimension to what is often framed as political economic exchange, governmentality (ways of getting people to behave or making people governable), or pastoral care (emotional or spiritual support). It directs us instead to the inter-subjective and interactive dimensions of everyday care that entail incorporation into a community, in this case a welfare state. Psychological tensions of holding manifest themselves in the experiences of digestion of the foreign, and in expectations of inclusion or autonomy. Because of the temporal delay of opportunities for reciprocity between the new arrivals and citizens, the likelihood of disappointment and withdrawal is high. I would hope that if we track the challenges of metabolising and digesting the strange and foreign, as refugees and citizens encounter each other in the holding environment of a European welfare state, we might be able to anticipate, and critically evaluate, whether the care given or received will create the possibility of a reversal of roles and thus rise to the level of a morally superior virtue.

[9] The new legislation specifies 'no means no' *(Nein heißt Nein)* as a 'basic principle' *(Grundsatz)*, meaning that it is now criminal when a perpetrator ignores the 'discernible contrary will' of his victim. It sharpens punishments for anyone convicted of sexual assault regardless of nationality (now up to five years' imprisonment for sexual intimidation/coercion and rape), and makes it possible to prosecute all members of a group when a sex crime originates in a group.

References

Amjahid, M (2016) 'Sylvesternacht in Köln: Was geschah wirklich?' *Zeitmagazin* 27/2016 (28 June 2016, available online at: www.zeit.de/zeit-magazin/2016/27/silvesternacht-koeln-fluechtlingsdebatte-aufklaerung.

Anderson, B (1983) *Imagined Communities: Reflections on the Origins and Spread of Nationalism* (New York, Verso).

BAMF (2018) *Aktuellen Zahlen zu Asyl* (7/2018) (Berlin, Bundesamt für Migration und Flüchtlinge), available online at: www.bamf.de/SharedDocs/Anlagen/DE/Publikationen/Flyer/flyer-schluesselzahlen-asyl-halbjahr-2018.html.

Bertoli, S Brückner, H and Moraga, J (2013) *The European Crisis and Migration to Germany: Expectations and the Diversion of Migration Flows* (Berlin, BAMF).

Bion, W (1957) 'Attacks on Linking' *International Journal of Psycho-Analysis* 40: 308–15.

Borneman, J (2001) 'Caring and To Be Cared For: Displacing Marriage, Kinship, Gender, and Sexuality' in J Faubion (ed), *The Ethics of Kinship* (Lanham MD, Rowman and Littlefield).

—— (2007) *Syrian Episodes: Sons, Fathers, and an Anthropologist in Aleppo* (Princeton NJ, Princeton University Press).

—— (2012a) 'Und nach den Tyrannen? Macht, Verwandtschaft und Gemeinschaft in der Arabellion' *La Lettre International* 98: 33–48 (translated by M Zillinger and D Saracino).

—— (2012b) 'Border Regimes, the Circulation of Violence and the Neo-authoritarian Turn' in T Wilson and H Donan (eds), *A Companion to Border Studies* (New York, Wiley).

—— (2014) 'Containment in Interlocution-based Fieldwork Encounters: Thought, Theory, and Transformative Thinking' *Anthropological Theory* 14(4): 442–61.

—— (2017) 'Afterword: Further Questions about the Global Care Chain' *Ethics and Social Welfare* 11(3): 296–303.

—— (2019) 'The Syrian Revolution: The political subject' in M Steffen (ed), *Crowds: Ethnographic Encounters* (New York, Berghahn Books).

Borneman, J and Ghassem-Fachandi, P (2017a) 'The concept of *Stimmung*: From indifference to xenophobia in Germany's refugee crisis' *HAU: Journal of Ethnographic Theory* 7(3): 105–35.

—— (2017b) 'Do Germans smell like a rose? Phagia, philia, phobia' Response to comments from H Bude, C Hann and H Cabot on 'The Concept of Stimmung. From indifference to xenophobia in Germany's refugee crisis' *HAU Journal of Ethnographic Theory* 7(3): 153–57.

—— (2017c) 'Syrian Refugees in Germany: Erotic Conflict and Foreigner Integration' *Studies in Humanities and Social Sciences XXII*(1): 20–47 (Shimla India, Indian Institute of Advanced Studies).

Bourdieu, P et al (1999). *The Weight of the World: Social Suffering in Contemporary Society* (Stanford CA, Stanford University Press).

Brückner, H and Fendel, T et al (2016) 'Geflüchtete Menschen in Deutschland: Warum sie kommen, was sie mitbringen und welche Erfahrung sie machen' *IAB-Kurzbericht* 15/2016 (Nurnberg, IAB).

Caglar, A (2015) 'Citizenship, Anthropology of' in JD Wright (ed), *International Encyclopedia of the Social & Behavioural Sciences*, 2nd edn, vol 3 (Oxford, Elsevier).

Cesari, J (ed) (2010) *Muslims in the West after 9/11* (New York, Routledge).

Ceylan, R (2010) 'Muslims in Germany: Religious and Political Challenges and Perspectives in the Diaspora' in American Institute for Contemporary German Studies (ed), *The Many Sides of Muslim Integration: An American-German Comparison* (Washington DC, AICGS).

Ferguson, J (2015) *Give a Man a Fish: Reflections on the New Politics of Distribution* (Durham NC, Duke University Press).

Geertz, C (1963) 'The integrative revolution: primordial sentiments and politics in the new states' in C Geertz (ed), *Old societies and new states: the quest for modernity in Asia and Africa* (New York, The Free Press).

Göztürk, D, Gramling, D and Kaes, A (eds) (2007) *Germany in Transit; Nation and Migration, 1955–2005* (Berkeley CA, University of California Press).

Green, S (2013) 'Germany: A Changing Country of Immigration' *German Politics* 22(3): 333–51.

Han, B-C (2017) *In the Swarm: Digital Prospects* (Cambridge MA, MIT Press).

Karakayali, S and Kleist, JO (2016) *Strukturen und Motive der ehrenamtlichen Flüchtlichlingsarbeit (EFA) in Deutschland* (Humboldt University, Berliner Institut für empirische Integrations- und Migrationsforschung).

Kleinman, A and Kleinman, J (1996) 'The Appeal of Experience; The Dismay of Images: Cultural Appropriations of Suffering in Our Times' *Daedulus* 125(1): 1–23.

Kleinman, A, Das, V and Lock, M (eds) (1997) *Social Suffering* (Berkeley CA, University of California Press).

Marshall, TH (1950) *Citizenship and Social Class and Other Essays* (Cambridge, Cambridge University Press).

Münkler, H and Münkler, M (2016) *Die Neuen Deutschen. Ein Land vor seiner Zukunft* (Reinbek, Rowohlt Verlag).

Pew.forum.org. (2017) 'Europe's growing Muslim Population', available online at: www.pewforum.org/2017/11/29/europes-growing-muslim-population/ (accessed 10 January 2018).

Ogden, T (2004) 'On containing and holding, being and dreaming' *International Journal of Psychoanalysis* 85(6): 1349–64.

Ong, A (1996) 'Cultural Citizenship as Subject-Making: Immigrants Negotiate Racial and Cultural Boundaries in the United States' *Current Anthropology* 37(5): 737–62.

ProAsyl (2018) 'Schutzquoten: Eine Statistik gegen die Frustration', available online at: www.proasyl.de/news/hohe-schutzquoten-eine-statistik-gegen-die-frustration/ (accessed 26 January 2018).

Sontag, S (2003) *Regarding the Pain of Others* (New York, Farrar, Straus, and Giroux).

Spiegel Staff (2010) 'Merkel erklärt Multikulti für gescheitert' *Spiegel Online*, 16 October 2010, available online at: www.spiegel.de/politik/deutschland/integration-merkel-erklaert-multikulti-fuer-gescheitert-a-723532.html (accessed 16 September 2016).

Stolke, V (1995) 'Talking culture: new rhetorics of exclusion in Europe' *Current Anthropology* 36: 1–24.

Todorov, T (1996) *Facing the Extreme: Moral Life in the Concentration Camps* (New York, Metropolitan Books).

UNHRC (2018) *Syrian Emergency*, available online at: www.unhcr.org/syria-emergency.html (accessed 3 May 2018).

—— (2019) *Figures at a glance*, available online at: www.unhcr.org/figures-at-a-glance.html (accessed 16 April 2019).

Winnicott, DW (1973) *The Child, the Family, and the Outside World* (Middlesex, Penguin Books).

—— (1957) *The Child and the Family: First Relationships* (New York, Routledge).

Zolberg, A (1983) 'The formation of new states as a refugee-generating process' *American Academy of Politics and Social Science* 467: 24–38.

13

The Ability of Place: Digital Topographies of the Virtual Human on Ethnographia Island[1]

TOM BOELLSTORFF

I. Prologue: Around Ethnographia Island

Let's fly together around Ethnographia Island a bit, shall we? We can fly because this island exists only in Second Life, a virtual world. We can do it together because no matter where you and I are in the physical world, if logged on we're copresent here. Let's start at my office. I like its curvy walls and high ceilings, its views of the island and the digital ocean lapping upon its shores. I built it myself. That lovely modern chair by my desk (Figure 1)? Far beyond my ability, I bought it from a home furnishings designer.

Here, next to my building, Jeanie has a crystal ballroom, complete with dance floor and sofas upstairs for relaxing. True to its name, crystals are scattered about. Jeanie, who is blind, enjoys their soft tinkling sounds. Next door, Megan has built a gigantic picnic bench. Silhouettes of adults speak gibberish as they tower over a girl sitting on the ground (Figure 2).

We feel small and overlooked – a taste of what Megan, who is Deaf, felt on family outings as a child. A little past Megan's build, Paula's structure rises 30 virtual meters into the sky; I stand on its roof, silhouetted by the setting sun. The building is composed of stacked squares, with a glass room in the centre of each square. The walls of the room on the ground floor are opaque; inside there's a chair

[1] I thank my Second Life interlocutors for their generosity, patience, and truly extraordinary insights. I thank my co-investigator, Donna Z Davis, for her camaraderie and intellectual support. I thank Faye Ginsburg and Rayna Rapp for their encouragement, and for organising the 2018 Wenner-Gren workshop 'Disability Worlds', where I presented a draft of this chapter. My thanks to Danilyn Rutherford, Laurie Obbink, and all participants at that remarkable event for their insights and support. This chapter was further developed at the 'Spaces of Care' workshop at the University of Cambridge. My thanks to Loraine Gelsthorpe, Perveez Mody, Brian Sloan, and all participants at that stimulating event for their comments and suggestions, which further improved this chapter. A documentary about this project, *Our Digital Selves* (Bernhard Drax, director, 74 mins, 2018), is available at: youtu.be/GQw02-me0W4.

Figure 1 Inside my office
Source: All pictures taken by the author.

Figure 2 Megan's picnic bench
Source: All pictures taken by the author.

for your avatar to sit in blackness. As you move up, floor by floor, the walls of each room are more transparent, until on the roof, a chair sits in the open, with unobstructed views across the island.

More than 30 people have parcels of land on Ethnographia Island: so many other stories. But explaining Paula's building must wait; I just got a message that Jeanie is DJ-ing at a club on another island, and we want to go dance away to her tunes.

II. Disability, Mediation, Place

In exploring the ethnographic materials from which the Prologue draws, I employ an analysis informed by the critique of 'inspiration porn', the tokenistic use of disability experience to comfort able-bodied persons and thereby shore up ableism (Rousso 2013). Given this critique it is understandable that some researchers are 'uncomfortable with scholarly insistence that people with disabilities teach us something' (Kulick and Rydström 2015: 16). But a complementary danger is isolating disability experience, as if it offers nothing beyond disability itself.

My path out of this impasse of inspiration versus isolation builds on a time-tested anthropological truism: particular ways of life speak to general questions of human being. In its classic mode, this meant studying 'among a community of perhaps four or five hundred people' (Rivers 1913: 7; see Redfield 1955) while addressing enduring topics like religion or kinship. At first glance Ethnographia Island might resemble these little communities of classic ethnography, and the impression is not entirely mistaken. The internet may make possible 'mass' communication and 'big' data, but much online sociality is constituted of smaller groupings. Those groupings, networked and translocal, differ from the classic communities of ethnographic inquiry – but they share features too, not least because those earlier communities were networked and translocal in their own right.

In this chapter I move outward from a specific online community to address broad questions related to digital place. The conceit is not that disabled persons are poster children for virtual worlds.[2] The point is rather that the experiences and insights of my interlocutors have wide implications, reflecting how disability 'is a category anyone might enter through aging or in a heartbeat, challenging lifelong presumptions of stable identities and normativity' (Ginsburg and Rapp 2013: 55).

Questions of digital embodiment have long fascinated scholars of the online (eg, Damer 1998; Hillis 1999). While I share this interest, this chapter originates in the realisation that embodiment always involves emplacement: 'just as we are always with a body, so, being bodily, we are always within a place as well' (Casey 1997: 214). What are the implications of digital places for embodiment?

[2] I employ 'disabled persons' rather than 'people with disabilities.' Both phrases are commonly employed and neither is perfect, but I find person-first language less effective (see Sinclair 2013; Titchkosky 2001; Broderick and Ne'eman 2008).

Given the centrality of 'place' to this chapter, before proceeding further I need to distinguish it from 'media'. It is absolutely true that from Facebook and Twitter to the global ecosystem of webpages and email, a key form of the digital has been mediation – communication between places that are distant from each other. The very word 'internet' denotes this, and it harks back to the first generation of technologies named with the Greek prefix of distance, *tēle*: television, telephone, telegram, telegraph. Traditionally the implied distance was miles apart, even halfway around the world. You would not telephone someone sitting beside you, nor listen to someone playing piano on the radio if the piano was in your home. But proximal mediation is now a powerful phenomenon. We need theories for Bluetooth socialities, for the mediation of the nearby.

But while 'media' is polysemous, it is not all-encompassing. At the risk of pointing out the obvious, not everything in the physical world is media. 'Offline' and 'media' are not synonyms. *But 'online' and 'media' are not synonyms either.* Since the 1970s – and arguably, a century before that – digital places have existed alongside digital media.[3] Some digital places, which include virtual worlds, are comparatively open-ended: for instance, Minecraft or Second Life. Others are structured more as games: for instance, World of Warcraft or Fortnite. Regardless, as emphasised by Richard Bartle (co-creator in 1978 of MUD, the first publicly accessible virtual world), digital places

> are not games. Even the ones written to *be* games aren't games. People can play games *in* them, sure, and they can be set up to that end, but this merely makes them venues. The Pasadena Rose Bowl is a stadium, not a game (Bartle 2004: 475).

Paraphrasing Bartle: digital places are not media. Even the ones written to *be* media aren't media. In the burgeoning literature on digital culture, work on media tends to overshadow work on places: from communications and media studies perspectives, digital places often seem narrow and unimportant. This can lead to digital places being analysed as if they were digital media, with confusing results.

In saying all this I do not mean to detract one iota from the rich body of media studies scholarship, which is vital for the study of digital places (not least because many digital places have media inside them, or about them). I am simply saying that digital media and digital place cannot be conflated. For disability, the consequences of digital media understandably involve mediation, particularly with regard to mobility and access (eg Chib and Jiang 2014; see Ginsburg 2012). If you cannot drive in a place with limited public transportation, going online can offer important possibilities for information, advocacy, and support. If you have a caregiver, going online can offer opportunities for independent socialisation (Anderberg and Jönsson 2005).

[3] Telephone conversations, which date to the 1870s, can be seen as taking place in '*the place between* the phones' (Sterling 1992: xi).

But how does disability intersect with digital place? If four people leave their physical homes to meet in the physical home of a fifth person, that fifth locale does not 'mediate' their interactions in the same way that a shared newspaper subscription would. So how do online places shape disability experience, in ways distinct from mediation?[4] How does this speak to cultural questions of place in the most fundamental sense? Such questions motivate this chapter. To investigate them, I first clarify my fieldsite and approach. The main body of my argument then moves through three sections that explore themes of landscape, interface, building, proximity, and collaboration. These themes respond to digital embodiment not in terms of appearance but engaged relationships to digital place, recalling cultural geography's attention to 'the articulation of social relations which necessarily have a spatial form in their interactions with one another' (Massey 1994: 120). Such work now includes 'theoretical and empirical exploration of the digital as a particular geographical domain with its own logics and structures' (Ash, Kitchin, and Leszczynski 2016: 8). By the penultimate section of this chapter I will advance a notion of digital topography in response to the digital as a geographical domain of disability experience, and in the conclusion, use this notion to rethink prosthetic metaphors regarding relationships between ability and technology.

III. Sites and Methods

This chapter is based on a collaborative, multi-year study of disability and virtual worlds.[5] For this chapter I draw exclusively on data gathered from Second Life; I got to know disability communities in this virtual world by building on 14 years of prior research (eg Boellstorff 2015; 2019). Owned and managed by the company Linden Lab, Second Life is an open-ended virtual world with about 600,000 active residents during the time of research. You could access Second Life from any computer with an internet connection by downloading free software known as a viewer. An official viewer was available on the Linden Lab website. Several 'third-party' viewers existed as well, usually produced by volunteers; the most popular such viewer was Firestorm. Another, Radegast, had fewer features but was popular with some disabled persons (particularly those with visual impairments) because it allowed one to render one's virtual environment as text that could be magnified or spoken through a screen-reading program. Viewers were thus interfaces, analogous to browsers like Chrome, Firefox, or Safari, distinct from the servers which contained the virtual world itself.

Second Life avatars were highly customisable: not just clothing and jewellery, but any gender or race, a few inches to a hundred feet tall or more, an animal or

[4] For the sake of variety, in this chapter I treat 'digital,' 'online,' and 'virtual' as rough synonyms.

[5] My collaborator, Donna Z. Davis, and I received support from the National Science Foundation, Cultural Anthropology and Science, Technology, and Society Programs [Grants 1459219 and 1459374].

object, even a ball of light. Moreover, avatars can be changed at will, and it was common to have multiple avatars with distinct identities, like having two email accounts. Because of this, determining the precise population of Second Life was difficult. Most Second Life residents lived physically in the United States and Europe, but some lived in South America, Asia, and Australia. More than half of my interlocutors were female, a pattern common in open-ended virtual worlds (Pearce, Blackburn, and Symborski 2015: 15).

The world of Second Life was composed of areas of virtual land (called simulators or 'sims'), 256 by 256 virtual meters in size. At the time of writing 23,342 of these sims constituted Second Life: 6,806 of them made up a series of continents, and the remainder were islands composed of one or more sims.[6] Second Life's economy was based on land. Accounts (and thus avatars) were free, but to build one had to own land (for a monthly fee), rent land, or be part of a group that owned land. Objects (including items worn on avatar bodies like clothing and jewellery) could be given away or sold for Linden Dollars, an inworld currency exchangeable with US dollars. Second Life was thus predicated on user-generated content, a common online economic model (eg Facebook, Instagram, YouTube; see Ondrejka 2004).

During research I met several interlocutors in the physical world, but they are not privileged in this analysis. The disabilities of my interlocutors reflected the diversity of disability more generally and included visual and auditory impairment, limb loss, autism, post-traumatic stress disorder, epilepsy, cerebral palsy, multiple sclerosis, and the effects of cancer, Parkinson's Disease, strokes, and other illnesses. Of course, many of the conditions in question were not straightforwardly considered 'disabilities', but diverse forms of ability that manifest as disability in ableist social contexts.

My methodology, building from earlier work (see Boellstorff et al 2012), involved regular participant observation with my interlocutors in various Second Life locales. These included personal places like homes and places specifically for the disability community (places which often act to create forms of online disability community). It also included a range of places where my interlocutors socialised with other Second Life residents who were not disabled or whose disability status was not known – beaches, shopping malls, dance clubs, book discussion groups, role-playing regions with medieval forests or post-apocalyptic deserts, you name it. I conducted 42 in-depth interviews as of the time of writing, with many additional shorter interviews; these were drawn from about 50 individuals with whom I was deeply engaged for this study (and a larger group of about 150, encountered during participant observation). My co-researcher and I also held 75 focus group meetings.

[6] See www.gridsurvey.com (the quoted numbers are from 24 December 2017).

For three years of the research, grant support allowed my co-researcher and I to purchase two sims that we joined to create Ethnographia Island (Figure 3).[7]

Figure 3 Looking across Ethnographia Island
Source: All pictures taken by the author.

Thirty disabled persons received parcels of virtual land on which they could build anything that expressed their experience of disability and virtual worlds. These 30 persons were chosen on a first-come, first-served basis. Their disability status was based on self-identification as disabled.[8] A few parcels on Ethnographia Island were also set aside for collaborative building projects. John Law, in his call to 'remake social science … [to] catch some of the realities we are currently missing' (2004: 2), concluded 'the argument is no longer that methods discover and depict

[7] Ethnographia Island's name comes from the office I created and named 'Ethnographia' when beginning Second Life research in 2003. There have been other projects in Second Life providing temporary land to disabled artists (eg uwainsl.blogspot.com/2013/09/the-freedom-project-initiative-by-uwa.html). Many disability groups in Second Life (for instance, Virtual Ability and Dreams) have owned land and used that land for socialising, for support meetings, for individual residences, and even building competitions. This meant that many disabled persons who participated in Ethnographia Island were already familiar with the idea of disability groups having places in Second Life.

[8] One reason for this is that not all disabilities are officially recognised, and such official definitions vary globally. My co-researcher and I met some of these disabled persons in the physical world, and some of them were also active in disability communities in Second Life, but we did not ask for medical records or any other official proof of disability status. Ethnography always involves an element of trust in this regard. Most ethnographers of disability in the physical world do not ask for proof of disability status either, and, for instance, in my earlier research on *gay* and *lesbi* Indonesians, I never asked interlocutors to somehow prove their same-sex desires and practices (Boellstorff 2005).

realities. Instead, it is that they participate in the enactment of those realities' (ibid: 45). In this case the research design included a fieldsite – Ethnographia Island – that literally came into existence in the research context.[9]

IV. Landscapes and Interfaces

Violet, an Ethnographia Island resident, invited me to sit with her in a quiet meadow:

> Violet: I'm struggling with something, to the point of an anxiety attack
>
> Tom: Oh gosh, what's wrong?
>
> Violet: Remember how we're supposed to restrict sounds to our parcel? It's Saul and Lydia's builds. There's a visual side to the sounds thing.
>
> Tom: Are their builds blocking your view?
>
> Violet: Not blocking, it's like they're screaming. Maybe they could put a screen around them? It's my PTSD [Post-Traumatic Stress Disorder], my disability.
>
> Tom: Let's think about this together.
>
> Violet: I know they don't mean it.

Issues of sound had arisen on the island before. As noted in the Prologue, Jeanie used auditory effects in her ballroom. I once placed a lighthouse adjacent to the ballroom without realising the interference its ambient sounds produced (unlike a physical lighthouse, the sounds could be simply turned off). I first misunderstood Violet's concern as analogous – blocking a view – but the issue was actually the negative impact of bright colours and flashing lights. Other residents shared the concerns, which were familiar to inworld disability communities with regard to, for instance, PTSD and epilepsy.

This virtual world problem, and its eventual solution, links up to anthropological scholarship addressing 'worlds' of disability experience and sociality (Ginsburg and Rapp 2013), including interfacing objects like wheelchairs, motorcycles, doorways, and ramps (Kohrman 1999; Phillips 2010). This scholarship reflects anthropological understandings of place as 'inhabited and appropriated through the attribution of personal and group meanings, feelings, sensory perceptions and understandings' (Low 2017: 32). One form of ableism involves unequal access to,

[9] Some might see a similarity between Ethnographia Island and the Modernity Project at Vicos, where a group of anthropologists from Cornell University took ownership of a hacienda in Peru between 1951 and 1962 as an applied social science experiment (Stein 2003). Projects like this, however, are not analogous. Ethnographia Island allowed for specific forms of data to be collected, but did not exist for the entire period of fieldwork. Many participants did not have parcels on the island; those who did were already active elsewhere in Second Life. For no one was Ethnographia Island the sole or even primary site of inworld sociality. A better parallel would be participatory visual and digital methods (Gubrium and Harper 2013).

and participation in, such inhabitation and appropriation of place (Titchkosky 2011); interfacing objects are one response to that inequality. This is one reason why 'a focus on disability makes it easier to understand that embodiment and social location are one and the same' (Siebers 2013: 283). Social location can now take the form of virtual social location: what are the implications for embodiment?

This issue of visually triggering objects relates to topics of building and proximity addressed later in this chapter. Here, I use it to launch an exploration of interface, turning to something that might seem unrelated, even trivial: 'third-party' viewers. I noted in the previous section that many disabled persons preferred Radegast to the more popular and full-featured Firestorm viewer. Now consider this conversation between myself and two avatars, Ruby and Diamond, who in the physical world are one visually impaired person, Molly:

> Diamond: See, Ruby is my main avatar, and I used to move her from Radegast into Firestorm when I wanted her to do something like dance with a partner [because dancing is difficult in Radegast]. And then, one day I tried that and my avatar became a cloud. And nobody could figure out why.

Molly eventually learned that viewer incompatibilities were damaging Ruby to the point that:

> Diamond: If I wanted to be able to speak, I'd have to create another avatar that would live in Radegast. Only in Radegast. Ever. And that Ruby could never set foot in Radegast. Ever. Because then she couldn't come back. So I created my voice, I created Diamond.

Molly's challenge might seem unrelated to Violet's. Yet despite obvious differences between visual triggers and visual impairment, both involve interfaces between the physical and digital. The literature on people having multiple avatars often emphasises role-playing, but for Molly multiple embodiments responded to the affordances of interface. Ruby and Diamond would, for instance, go shopping together in Second Life, with Molly accessing Diamond (for speaking) through Radegast and Ruby (for making purchases) through Firestorm. Yet this took a surprising turn:

> Diamond: At first, manipulating Diamond was like playing with paper dolls. Diamond's job was to talk for Ruby. And then something happened. And I'm going to sound really silly, and I don't apologize for it, you'll just have to believe it. She became her own person. Diamond kind of took on her own personality. So I kind of think of her somewhere between a staff member, a maid, and a baby sister for Ruby.

Despite these unexpected consequences of her workaround, Molly saw her solution as suboptimal. This is why she participated in a set of focus groups together with the volunteer programmers behind the Firestorm viewer, who were passionately interested in access. Molly's struggles with speech and text were not unique: the most desired feature from the more than 40 participants in the focus groups was better voice-to-text and text-to-voice functions (to benefit those with auditory and visual impairments, limited hand movement, or less than two hands). Another desired feature – responding directly to the issues that had appeared on Ethnographia Island and elsewhere – was the option to hide bright flashing colours and lights. Other suggestions related to the landscape. For instance, Radegast could translate a virtual landscape into text, but only as a list of objects. As one person noted, 'this list does not tell you in which direction the object is located. It is just a vague list'. Furthermore, if creators did not properly title their objects, visually impaired people could not identify them: a screen reader would simply say 'object'.

These concerns about interface reflect broader imbrications of interface and digital place in everyday disability experience. One virtual morning, Hazel invited me to sit with her on a wooden deck looking out over the unending Second Life ocean, next to a harmless volcano whose churning lava never escaped the cauldron high above our heads. Like many autistic persons, Hazel preferred text chat: no tone of voice or facial expressions, and one could edit a statement before sharing it. Hazel once said these benefits were the 'same with email', and I responded: 'What is distinct about digital places?' She had once told me that she liked to have clear lines of sight in her physical home (doors kept open, no stacking of taller objects in front of shorter ones, etc). Could a digital place like Second Life work in the same manner – in a way that, say, email or Facebook could not?

> Hazel: Yes indeed, what a wonderful area of thought. This spot here is an example of my 'line of sight' need. I can see all around, and nothing can creep up, hidden by buildings etc. In that way, my Second Life interface is very 'safe' for me.
>
> Tom: Right.
>
> Hazel: And I always use the chat window … Encapsulated in its own box, with a black background. Not distracting. Boxes and boundaries and borders – very important to me.

Hazel here describes a dynamic I encountered with a range of interlocutors: since digital place can only be accessed through interfaces, they embody, in a sense, digital selfhood. We might consider Hazel's use of chat windows, or Molly's inworld existence as Ruby and Diamond, in terms of 'interface embodiment.' In fact, right after mentioning chat windows Hazel added that some of her disabled friends in Second Life were also communicating using Discord, a web-based chat platform. I noted that both Second Life and Discord employed text chat, so why did Second Life hold particular value?

> Hazel: I must say I am not as comfortable with Discord as I am with chatting in Second Life. Discord is not a 'place' so the geography is lost … There is no view, no perspective … If I cannot see safely, I start to feel panicky … So 'safety sight' works both for the text and the space – I need to see the text to think and speak. And I need to have my line of sight to breathe and feel safe.

Hazel's words regarding disability, safety, and 'line of sight' reminded me of Paula's build on Ethnographia Island, mentioned in the introduction – a tower with walls becoming more transparent on higher floors. Paula explained it as follows:

> Paula: A series of four floors. I have used the floors to represent my feeling and how I have seen the world for many years. Floor 1: A completely black room from the inside.

> A place where I mostly feel safe and calm. Floor 2: A room where I can see those on the other side of the wall. The place where I spend most of my time. I very rarely interact with people, but I can if I wish to. Floor 3: A room where I am able to see and interact with those on the other side of the wall. The place 'I can live in', but it is not always comfortable for me. Floor 4: A room where there is little to no wall between me and others in the world. I have not come to this place in either my physical life or my Second Life. Now just what does this have to do with my living in Second Life? Well my Second Life is much the same as my physical life. The same four floors are always there, but in Second Life I feel more free to venture out of my dark room and explore, talk, and do things!

Hazel did not know about Paula's structure, so I showed it to her:

> Hazel: Really interesting build. I have the feeling that it is all about control. What I can control and what I can't. Even my issue with voice and text has that element. See your thoughts and build on what you see … you can't do that with voice.

Hazel's use of lines of sight and Paula's build both recall notions of 'landscape', a way of seeing dominant in the Western tradition and which is important to the experience of digital place more generally (Boellstorff 2015; see Cosgrove 1998; Crary 1990, 1999; Friedberg 2006; Healy 1997; Hillis 1999). Indeed, the problem with which I opened this section – builds with bright colours and flashing colours – is a problem of landscape as well. Since Paula's build is close to Violet's, we might as well return to this issue. Ethnographia Island residents, working in close virtual quarters, helped come up with several solutions. We moved some builds hundreds of meters in the virtual air. We also built a curtain 60 virtual meters tall, which screened off some parcels. Saul and Lydia moved their builds 'behind the curtain'; they could no longer be seen unless visited intentionally.

How might we consider this curtain a digitally material 'interface?' And what questions might this discussion raise beyond digital disability? What are our interfaces in the physical world: the 'viewers' that perpetuate ableist constructions of place, and those which disabled persons use to reconfigure and challenge those ableist lifeworlds?

V. Building and Being-Inworld

The discussion thus far already reveals how Second Life is not just a place: it is a place that is built. In virtual worlds predicated on user-generated content, many residents build at least occasionally; arranging and modifying the creations of others (for instance, when furnishing a home) is often considered a kind of building. What does this tell us about placemaking, embodiment, and ability?

Let us join some Ethnographia Island residents on a tour of what Phoebe termed her 'Build Biography'. After leaving a successful career due to disability, Phoebe discovered Second Life, which 'made all the difference in the world'. She wanted to show how:

> Phoebe: Second Life helped me to construct a new, 'many-faceted identity' which now includes being an artist, a builder, a business owner, a teacher, and a philanthropist.

> I decided to … tell my story using a kind of gallery or museum type exhibit … I've also written out notecards (60 in all), which tell the fuller story behind what is being shown on each sign. The notecards also make the installation accessible to anyone who uses a screen reader, or language translator.

This first area described how she became a builder: 'I found building to be like a meditative process for me. I could lose myself in it, getting into something like a "flow state"'. The next area showed how she started making sculpture and seeing herself as an artist. She then led us to a third area, the 'Black Tunnel':

> Phoebe: This part represents a period from 2011 to 2014 … It became very difficult for me to leave the security of my home in the physical world. I felt like I had invisible glass walls around me. A very strange sensation. And in Second Life, I quit all of my public activities, slashed my friends list, stopped building even, and kept almost totally to myself.
>
> Paula: Nods … I understand that.
>
> Phoebe: Yeah Paula, quite a bit like the rooms in your build, come to think of it.
>
> Paula: nods.

Phoebe then brought us to 'a demonstration that I've created, of something that I was experiencing a lot during that time':

> Phoebe: There's a teleporter (the blue sphere here), which goes up to an Emotional Flashbacks Demonstration, which is on a platform in the sky. I built it here to give people an idea of what it's like when a person who has PTSD from chronic trauma (versus a one-time event) has flashbacks.

We tried the demonstration, placed in the sky to take account of the concerns with visually triggering objects discussed earlier. It featured an invisible trap door causing one's avatar to fall without warning to a room below. As we moved through the demonstration, Phoebe said:

> Phoebe: I love this so much about Second Life, that it has this 'immersive experience' aspect. As we all know, it's not just 'show' and 'tell', like the 2D internet, it is also 'be' and 'do'. What we have here isn't mere information delivery. What we have are experiences. Put another way, 'There is a "here" here'.

I can think of no clearer explanation of how digital place and digital media are distinct. Phoebe closed her tour by stating

> Second Life has given me a way to feel once again like I am a contributing member of society. It has helped me reconstruct my sense of identity, in the wake of becoming disabled … The purpose of my build here is to tell my whole story about that.

I could devote this chapter to Phoebe's 'Build Biography', or other Ethnographia Island builds just as fascinating. But even this brief tour highlights implications of digital place for theories of physical-world placemaking (Lefebvre 1991), theories to which anthropologists have long contributed. For instance, in her classic ethnography *The Fame of Gawa*, Nancy Munn noted

> The point of departure for this study is the notion of a lived world that is not only the arena of action, but is actually constructed by action and the more complex cultural practices of which any given type of action is a part (Munn 1986: 8).

Munn's pivotal 'notion of a lived world' originated in the phenomenological philosophy of Husserl, where what orients experience is not the body as 'a thing in objective space, but as a system of possible actions, a virtual body with its phenomenal "place" defined by its task and situation. My body is wherever there is something to be done' (Merleau-Ponty 1962: 250; see Habermas 1987). Husserl himself distinguished between the physical body (*Korper*) and the living body (*Leib*), identifying the 'living body' as 'the only one which is actually given [to me as such] in perception' (Husserl 1970: 107). Avatars are digital 'living bodies', defined through actions and situated tasks. Perception and experience through avatars challenge notions of embodiment predicated on kinesthetic experience, as well as arguably ableist configurations of sensation (Serres 2008).

A novel method of what I term 'participant building' on Ethnographia Island complemented participant observation, providing opportunities to articulate relationships between digital living bodies and digital lived worlds. An example: next to Phoebe's 'Build Biography', Claire's parcel had a series of objects including a tyre swing that was not quite connected to the tree above it. Leading other island residents on a tour, she noted she had only entered Second Life three months before getting the parcel. She described how building the tyre swing helped her understand that a moving object often should not be attached to a stationary one:

> Claire: It was an experiment for me ... I needed to understand animation in Second Life ... I needed to understand how things fit together when they weren't logical to me. Because to me, the swing had to be attached to the tree, and it's not attached to anything because if it is, the pivot [animation] doesn't work ... I literally couldn't wrap my mind around it.

Next to the tyre swing was a tall building crowned by two large books, that formed a house:

> Claire: The bookcases of my mind ... the reality is that when I was little, I couldn't communicate well with others ... so I retreated to books. Books were my life and soul, my food, my blood, my air, they were my everything.

Claire had chronicled a physical-world history of disability, but also a virtual-world history of learning to build. And the experience of building had helped her socialise offline: 'because of this I've moved into restarting things in my physical life. So this is a huge thing'.

This interplay between digital body and digital place recalls Heidegger's phenomenological understanding of 'dwelling' as central to what it means 'to be a human being' (2001: 145). Dwelling, for Heidegger, was a form of action – he noted that the Old German and Old English word *buan* meant 'to build' and 'to dwell'. It is thus intrinsic to being-in-the-world (1962), a notion I have reframed as 'being-inworld' now that virtual worlds make more than one world possible

(Boellstorff 2011). Construing being-inworld as 'building-inworld' allows for considering how ableism is manifest in a phenomenology of placemaking: 'Any body that is excluded from making a contribution to the construction of the social world cannot find a home in it' (Paterson and Hughes 1999: 604; see Petrick 2015; Saerberg 2015; Salamon 2007). This reflects how in the physical world, disability exclusion takes forms of 'misfit', how 'the particularities of embodiment interact with the environment in its broadest sense … a particular aspect of world-making' (Garland-Thomson 2011: 591). Digital misfit should be avoidable in virtual worlds, given the possibilities of different interfaces and reworked relationships to materiality, but because ableism is a cultural logic continually expressed as technological barriers, ability-diverse digital cultures are neither automatic nor inevitable.

VI. Proximity, Collaboration, Digital Topography

While leading us on the tour discussed above, Claire paused to say

> I have learned from each builder that I've seen here. Each one of you. I have walked your plots. Trust me, you may not have seen me, you may have not been around when I did it, but I did it.

From the ethnographic materials above, we see many cases of disabled persons engaged in social relations with others through digital place and placemaking, even when the others were not online at the time. For instance, Claire noted how when she walked those plots of other disabled builders and learned from them, they were often 'not around when she did it'. Furthermore, the specifics of her digital embodiment were not pivotal: her learning did not depend on looking like a young woman, an old man, or a fuzzy rabbit.

This demonstrates a broader and often-overlooked aspect of digital place: when persons move through a digital landscape, their embodied status creates emplaced social relations distinct from avatar appearance or copresence. One's avatar embodiment would not directly affect the experience of Paula's tower: the experience comes from moving through its levels and experiencing the interplay of visibility, height, and security. Someone could move through Phoebe's 'build biography', experiencing the installations and reading the notecards without Phoebe being online. For these social relations, appearance is not fundamental: *they are mediated by the fact of embodiment in digital place as such*. Such social relations of place recall the ontological notion of 'media' as mode of transmission: '"In the middle" of absence and presence, farness and nearness, being and soul, there exists no nothing any more, but a mediatic relation' (Kittler 2009: 26). An important area for further research is to consider how these mediatic relations of digital place are similar and different to, say, reading someone's Facebook page when they are not online.

It is to highlight this aspect of digital place that I have not described or included images of my interlocutors' avatars. This is not to downplay the importance of specific avatar embodiments, or of verbal and non-verbal avatar communication (Tanenbaum, El-Nasr and Nixon 2014). Rather, my focus in this chapter is on how disability experience elucidates a lesser-discussed aspect of digital embodiment: presence in digital lifeworlds. Unlike digital media, which entail connection across distance, digital places thus foreground questions of proximity: they allow for copresence (not just communication) even in cases where the persons in question are physically distant.

In thinking through the emplacement of self in landscapes of digital place, I find it useful to develop a notion of digital topography.[10] Geography references *geo*, the physical world, but topography references any *topos*, 'place'. Whereas, say, all websites are 'equidistant', digital places exist on a topography where some things are closer or farther. The concern over visually triggering objects discussed earlier reflects this. (Compare: an article on cnn.com with visually triggering images does not impinge on nbc.com.) The fact that Ethnographia Island was composed of nearly adjacent parcels foregrounded these issues of proximity – as a problem, or sometimes a resource, as in Claire's statement about exploration, or when Paula and Phoebe realised their builds responded to similar life challenges. Of course, proximity was relevant across Second Life: for instance, disability groups using virtual land for activities involving copresence (a disco) or not (a water slide on the beach). Any disabled person in Second Life moved across landscapes of digital place, many not designed with disability in mind.

Although Claire's statement indicates that embodiment in digital place need not involve copresence, she did deliver it while leading a tour. We are often with others in digital places, and that copresence can involve highly valued forms of collaboration (Boellstorff 2019). In Second Life (as in the physical world), this could take place with other disabled residents, able-bodied residents, or those who did not reveal their disability status. The range of possible activities was also wide: a support group, playing games, relaxing by a virtual campfire. It could also include placemaking. For example, Phoebe offered to help Jeanie create her build. Jeanie's transcript of their conversation included the following:

> Phoebe: Hey, Jeanie! What are you wanting to make?
>
> Jeanie: I want to make a ballroom, if you can make it out of crystal pieces.
>
> Phoebe: Wow, crystal ballroom! I think I can help with a crystal ballroom. Can you build at all?
>
> Jeanie: No, I can't with Radegast, and it's very visual. I can't see, in RL.
>
> Phoebe: Yes, I didn't know what's possible though. I just wasn't sure if there are any kind of descriptive assistive devices.
>
> Jeanie: I'm not sure if there are any.

[10] A notion of cultural topography has been used by intelligence analysts; I do not draw on this work (eg Johnson and Berrett 2011). The only use of 'cultural topography' of which I am aware is Ferguson's analysis of wealth in Lesotho (1992).

Phoebe: You can tell me whatever layout you picture in your mind, and whatever look. Have you ever been sighted? May I ask that?

Jeanie: No, I've been blind all of my life.

Phoebe: How do you imagine a ballroom to be? I would love to know an exact description of what you have in your mind, if you would like to do that.

Jeanie: I was thinking of the ballroom to be like a music room, the walls and floor could be crystal, and the door could be glass, but I want it to be a relaxing atmosphere, the floor could be marble. And the upper ceiling could be like the sky outside with stars and sunlight.

Phoebe: Do you have a sense of colors for these things?

Jeanie: No, I don't.

Phoebe: Warm versus cool 'feel.' Blue and green are 'cool,' red and orange are 'warm.'

Jeanie: Ah. I would like the ballroom to be red.

Collaboration could also involve larger groups, and Ethnographia Island provided opportunities to explore this through participant building. Since Second Life's founding, residents have held a birthday celebration with the support of Linden Lab, which provided temporary islands for builds created by individuals and communities. During the first year of Ethnographia Island the Second Life birthday celebration's theme was 'the shared adventure'. A subset of Ethnographia Island residents decided to build an exhibit, and we set aside a plot of land on the island to prepare it. The design, with colours inspired by Vincent van Gogh's 'Starry Night', featured a meandering pathway between square blocks (Figures 4 and 5).

Figure 4 The birthday celebration build
Source: All pictures taken by the author.

Figure 5 The birthday celebration build
Source: All pictures taken by the author.

A text written by residents explained:

> What is Ethnographia Island?
>
> There are a number of parcels on the island where capability-diverse people like you and me are spending time expressing themselves. Many are making statements directly related to disability and how it affects our lives. Some are giving a direct line to their perspective – of themselves and of their worlds (physical and virtual). Some are interactive. Some are static. Some are playful. Some are serious. All of them are full of heart. All of them take you to a place of exploration.

Each resident had an installation with an image of their build; when clicked, the image provided an explanatory notecard. Claire's notecard stated:

> A newcomer to Second Life, Claire has used her studio parcel to learn how to build, code, have fun, and express being capability diverse … Second Life, in particular Ethnographia Island, provides a means of expression – both creative and mundane. No matter how you perceive yourself, whether that's 'capability diverse' or 'able-bodied' … That makes you and I similar.

A few days before the birthday celebration was to begin, residents moved the exhibit to the assigned location: they were pleased this was directly southeast of the celebration's 'Welcome Area'. Northeast lay an exhibit about Bhutan; north and east, installations of photographs taken inworld. Southwest was a collaborative build by a well-known residential community. Visitors could move through the landscape to find our exhibit, and walking through it, encounter a series of reflections on disability and digital place. To consider, as Claire put it, capability-diverse possibilities for creativity and expression.

VII. A Prosthetic Conclusion

This analysis of disability and digital place has focused on landscape, interface, building, proximity, and collaboration. I came to these topics from ethnographic engagements, but they are in no way limited to this fieldsite, to virtual worlds, even to disability. Recalling my desire to avoid isolating disability experience, I conclude by turning to something associated with both disability and the digital: the prosthetic metaphor. The prosthetic metaphor has served as a key trope for conceptualising the relationship between technology and the human (Bateson 1972); a version of the metaphor that has emerged in recent decades is the cyborg (Balsamo 1996; Haraway 1991). However, the prosthetic metaphor is 'insufficient to analyze … the questions of body-technology boundaries' (Jain 1999: 47) when based on an ableism that 'turns on the problem of the "wholeness" of the body and thus cannot but invoke the questions of whose bodies are whole and how this wholeness is culturally determined and recognized' (ibid).

Some uses of the prosthetic metaphor do presume a teleology of fusion – technology augmenting flawed flesh to make it whole. This teleology of wholeness or fusion resonates with the idea that dualisms of any kind are bad: Cartesian impositions dividing up a world of blurring and flow. With regard to disability studies (and in medical anthropology more broadly; see, eg Scheper-Hughes and Lock 1987), the dominant approach has been to critique the distinction between body and mind as an artificial or misleading imposition that misses the myriad ways that body and mind are mutually informing, or even a single domain. This line of social constructionist critique continues to the present with, for instance, insightful uses of the concept 'bodymind' to 'insis[t] on the inextricability of mind and body' (Schalk 2018: 5; see Price 2015).

In questioning the prosthetic metaphor, I am building on a line of analysis in disability studies that challenges the social constructionist idea that the body/mind dualism is an imposition. This line of analysis explores how *body and mind are in some ways distinct*, and how this is important to the understanding, experience, and politics of disability:

> Disability scholars have begun to insist that strong constructionism either fails to account for the difficult physical realities faced by people with disabilities or presents their body in ways that are conventional, conformist, and unrecognizable to them. These include the habits of privileging performativity over corporeality, favoring pleasure to pain, and describing social success in terms of intellectual achievement, bodily adaptability, and active political participation. The disabled body seems difficult for the theory of social construction to absorb: disability is at once its best example and a significant counterexample (Siebers 2001: 740).

In this regard it is striking that my disabled interlocutors often emphasised that they were not their bodies. As one Ethnographia Island resident put it:

> I used to be 'mind over matter,' push push push, but now unfortunately when the mind's the thing that's the matter, you have limits, and it's knowing your limits and accepting your limits in terms of accepting your new self. Because I will never be the self I used to

> be … It's hard to slow your mind down to the same, to be where your body is, actually I don't want to slow my mind down to be where my body is.[11]

Indeed, the ethnographic materials presented in this chapter show how digital embodiment in digital place permits forms of sociality and subjectivity that realise a sense of separation between mind and body. My interlocutors were clearly aware that just as the body can impinge on the mind (eg chronic pain, exhaustion), the physical world can impinge on digital place. This could include bodily limitations (for instance, hands that shook due to Parkinson's Disease, so that voice chat was preferable to typing). It could include limitations of one's computer or internet connection, reflecting how many disabled persons live on limited incomes due to unemployment and meagre-to-absent state support. It could include issues of interface. But all this was possible precisely because the online/offline binarism did not 'blur' (see Veerapen 2011). Online and offline are distinct, but as with any other binarism this does not imply the absence of a relation. The distinction makes relation possible.

Overall, this analysis suggests future pathways for research, three of which I briefly mention here. First, I have only touched on precisely how disabled persons build in Second Life. This includes interface tools that allow creating objects inworld, and also outside programs like Maya or Blender that more advanced builders use to create 'mesh' objects (which were added to Second Life in 2013).[12] Medicalised discussions of disability often focus on 'activities of daily living' like bathing and eating. How might the ability of 'disabled' persons to build in virtual worlds contribute to expanding notions of daily activities in the digital age?

The relation of gender to disability and digital place is another rich domain for continuing research, which can build on the scholarship on gender, design, and disability more generally.[13] Building and placemaking have typically been androcentric categories, and associations of women with the 'domestic' have long been of interest to feminist anthropologists (Rosaldo 1974). As noted earlier, women outnumber men in socially-oriented virtual worlds; they predominated on Ethnographia Island and I have focused on women's accounts. How does digital place relate to female agency when what is at issue is not avatar appearance but building as a social practice?

The relationship between 'virtual worlds' and 'virtual reality' is a third area where including disability in the discussion from the outset is of the utmost importance. Confusion between virtual worlds and virtual reality is rampant, leading designers, users, and critics to speak past each other. As should be abundantly clear, 'virtual worlds' are places online. 'Virtual reality' refers to three-dimensional

[11] This quotation is taken from Davis and Boellstorff 2016: 2015; see that article for additional ethnographic examples and discussion regarding disability and the mind/body dualism.

[12] Objects in Second Life are composed of 'primitives' (known as 'prims'). For instance, a table might be composed of five prims: a square prim for the tabletop, and four tall rectangular prims for the legs. However, if this table was composed in Maya or Blender and imported into Second Life as a 'mesh' object, it would use only one prim. This means that the table would load into the world more quickly. Additionally, land in Second Life has a 'prim count' limit regarding how many objects that parcel of land can contain. A mesh object counts less toward that prim limit, allowing for more objects in a place.

[13] See, inter alia, Guffey 2018; Hamraie 2017; Rembis 2017; Williamson 2019.

sensory immersion, usually with goggles for vision, headphones for sound, and tracking technology that allows for kinetic movement within a virtual space. But while virtual worlds and virtual reality share the word 'virtual,' they are distinct. Virtual worlds are typically experienced with a regular computer screen and can even be composed solely of text. On the other hand, virtual reality technology can be used with a flight simulator on a computer not connected to the internet.

Virtual worlds are about digital place, while virtual reality is about interface, which, as we have seen, can constitute a site of ableism. Virtual reality technology can represent a delightful way to experience virtual worlds. However, this benefit has thus far been limited by assumptions about 'sensory immersion' that discount persons who cannot see or walk around a room, or whose tremors make them unable to wear a headset. *The conflation of virtual reality and virtual worlds is ableist.* If future virtual worlds are predicated on the idea that you must be able to, for instance, see and hear, then persons with visual and auditory impairments will be excluded from those virtual worlds.

The study of disability and digital place, including the method of participant building, has much to offer the study of digital disability more broadly. Research thus far has focused on digital media (eg Goggin and Newell 2002; Hansen 2006). Some scholarship in this area has already begun addressing digital place (eg Ellis and Kent 2011). Adding that growing body of scholarship to the literature on digital media can, for instance, contribute to debates over the social construction of disability (eg Beckett and Campbell 2015; Shakespeare 2013): how does place versus media 'construct' ability diversity in everyday practice?

Finally, further work on disability's intersection with digital place holds great promise for anthropology. Embodiment has been important since the beginnings of the discipline (Csordas 1988; Mauss 1973), but this work has explored embodiment in the physical world. Linking this scholarship with interdisciplinary research on avatar embodiment (eg Mazalek et al 2011) can expand our ethnographic understanding of 'situated embodiment' (Lock 2017: 11) as distinct from, but intertwined with, questions of avatar appearance.

It is time to teleport away from Ethnographia Island, illuminated by a setting virtual sun and hosted by servers in the physical world. By the time you read this chapter the island may have disappeared; indeed, this whole virtual world will someday end. But virtual worlds as a phenomenon are here to stay as places of culture; their inhabitants will include those excluded by ableist discourse from the 'normal'. Lifeworlds of digital disability speak back to this exclusion, suggesting new possibilities for the virtual human.

References

Anderberg, P and Jönsson, B (2005) 'Being there' *Disability and Society* 20(7): 719–33. doi:10.1080/09687590500335733.

Ash, J, Kitchin, R and Leszczynski, A (2016) 'Digital turn, digital geographies?' *Progress in Human Geography* 42(1): 25–43. doi:10.1177/0309132516664800.

Balsamo, A (1996) *Technologies of the gendered body: reading cyborg women* (Durham NC, Duke University Press).
Bartle, RA (2004) *Designing virtual worlds* (Indianapolis IN, New Riders).
Bateson, G (1972) *Steps to an ecology of mind* (Chicago IL, University of Chicago Press).
Beckett, AE and Campbell, T (2015) 'The social model of disability as an oppositional device' *Disability and Society* 30(2): 270–83. doi:10.1080/09687599.2014.999912.
Boellstorff, T (2005) *The gay archipelago: sexuality and nation in Indonesia* (Princeton NJ, Princeton University Press).
—— (2011) 'Placing the virtual body: avatar, chora, cypherg' in FE Mascia-Lees (ed), *A companion to the anthropology of the body and embodiment* (New York, Wiley-Blackwell).
—— (2015) *Coming of age in second life: an anthropologist explores the virtually human*, 2nd edn (Princeton NJ, Princeton University Press).
—— (2019) 'The opportunity to contribute: disability and the digital entrepreneur' *Information, Communication, and Society* 22(4): 474–490, available online at: http://dx.doi.org/10.1080/13691 18X.2018.1472796.
Boellstorff, T, Nardi, B, Pearce, C and Taylor, TL (2012) *Ethnography and virtual worlds: a handbook of method* (Princeton NJ, Princeton University Press).
Broderick, AA and Ne'eman, A (2008) 'Autism as metaphor: narrative and counter-narrative' *International Journal of Inclusive Education* 12(5/6): 459–76. https://doi.org/10.1080/13603110802377490.
Casey, E (1997) *The fate of place: a philosophical history* (Berkeley CA, University of California Press).
Chib, A and Jiang, Q (2014) 'Investigating modern-day talaria: mobile phones and the mobility-impaired in Singapore' *Journal of Computer-Mediated Communication* 19(3): 695–711. doFi:10.1111/jcc4.12070.
Cosgrove, DE (1998) *Social formation and symbolic landscape* (Madison WI, University of Wisconsin Press).
Crary, J (1990) *Techniques of the observer: on vision and modernity in the nineteenth century* (Cambridge MA, MIT Press).
—— (1999) *Suspensions of perception: attention, spectacle, and modern culture* (Cambridge MA, MIT Press).
Csordas, TJ (1988) 'Embodiment as a paradigm for anthropology' *Ethos* 18(1): 5–47. doi:http://www.jstor.org/stable/640395.
Damer, B (1998) *Avatars! exploring and building virtual worlds on the internet* (Berkeley CA, Peachpit Press).
Davis, DZ and Boellstorff, T (2016) 'Compulsive creativity: virtual worlds, disability, and digital capital' *International Journal of Communication* 10: 2096–118.
Ellis, K and Kent, M (2011) 'Avatars with wheelchairs, but no virtual guide dogs: disability and Second Life' in *Disability and new media* (New York NY, Routledge).
Ferguson, J (1992) 'The cultural topography of wealth: commodity paths and the structure of property in rural Lesotho' *American Anthropologist* 94(1): 55–73. Available online at: www.jstor.org/stable/680037.
Friedberg, A (2006) *The virtual window: from Alberti to Microsoft* (Cambridge MA, MIT Press).
Garland-Thomson, R (2011) 'Misfits: a feminist materialist disability concept' *Hypatia: A Journal of Feminist Philosophy* 26(3): 591–609. doi:10.1111/j.1527-2001.2011.01206.x.
Ginsburg, F (2012) 'Disability in the digital age' in HA Horst and D Miller (eds), *Digital anthropology* (London, Berg).
Ginsburg, F and Rapp, R (2013) 'Disability worlds' *Annual Review of Anthropology* 42: 53–68. doi:10.1146/annurev-anthro-092412-155502.
Goggin, G and Newell, C (2002) *Digital disability: the social construction of disability in new media* (Lanham MA, Rowman & Littlefield).
Gubrium, A and Harper, K (2013) *Participatory visual and digital methods* (Walnut Creek CA, Left Coast Press).
Guffey, EE (2018) *Designing disability: symbols, space, and society* (London, Bloomsbury Academic).
Habermas, J (1987) *The theory of communicative action, volume 2. Lifeworld and system: a critique of functionalist reason*, translated by T McCarthy (Boston MA, Beacon Press).

Hamraie, A (2017) *Building access: universal design and the politics of disability* (Minneapolis MN, University of Minnesota Press).

Hansen, MBN (2006) *Bodies in code: interfaces with digital media* (London, Routledge).

Haraway, D (1991) 'A cyborg manifesto: science, technology, and socialist-feminism in the late twentieth century' in *Simians, cyborgs, and women: the reinvention of nature* (London, Routledge).

Healy, D (1997) 'Cyberspace and place: the internet as middle landscape on the electronic frontier' in D Porter (ed), *Internet culture* (New York NY, Routledge).

Heidegger, M (1962) *Being and time*, translated by J Macquarrie and E Robinson (New York NY, Harper and Row).

—— (2001) [1971] 'Building dwelling thinking' in *Poetry, Language, Thought*, translated by A Hofstadter (New York NY, Harper Perennial Modern Classics).

Hillis, K (1999) *Digital sensations: space, identity, and embodiment in virtual reality* (Minneapolis MN, University of Minnesota Press).

Husserl, E (1970) [1954] *The crisis of European sciences and transcendental phenomenology*, translated and with an introduction by D Carr (Evanston IL, Northwestern University Press).

Jain, SS (1999) 'The prosthetic imagination: enabling and disabling the prosthesis trope' *Science, Technology, and Human Values* 24(1): 31–54. doi:10.1177/016224399902400103.

Johnson, JL and Berrett, MT (2011) 'Cultural topography: a new research tool for intelligence analysis' *Studies in Intelligence* 55(2): 1–22, available online at: www.cia.gov/library/center-for-the-study-of-intelligence/csi-publications/csi-studies/studies/vol.-55-no.-2/pdfs-vol.-55-no.-2/Berrett-Cultural Topography-9June2011.pdf.

Kittler, F (2009) 'Towards an ontology of media' *Theory, Culture, and Society* 26(2–3): 23–31. doi:10.1177/0263276409103106.

Kohrman, M (1999) 'Motorcycles for the disabled: mobility, modernity, and the transformation of experiences in urban China' *Culture, Medicine and Psychiatry 23*(1): 133–55. https://doi.org/10.1023/A:1005455815637.

Kulick, D and Rydström, J (2015) *Loneliness and its opposite: Sex, disability, and the ethics of engagement* (Durham NC, Duke University Press).

Law, J (2004) *After method: mess in social science research* (London, Routledge).

Lefebvre, H (1991) *The production of space*, translated by D Nicholson-Smith (Oxford, Blackwell).

Lock, M (2017) 'Recovering the body' *Annual Review of Anthropology* 46(1): 1–14. doi:10.1146/annurev-anthro-102116-041253.

Low, SM (2017) *Spatializing culture: the ethnography of space and place* (London, Routledge).

Mauss, M (1973) 'Techniques of the body' *Economy and Society* 2(1): 70–88. doi:10.1080/03085147300000003.

Mazalek, A, Chandrasekharan, S, Nitsche, M, Welsh, T and Clifton, P (2011) 'Embodying self in virtual worlds' in A Peachey and M Childs (eds), *Reinventing ourselves: contemporary concepts of identity in virtual worlds* (London, Springer).

Merleau-Ponty, M (1962) *Phenomenology of perception* (London, Routledge & Kegan Paul).

Munn, ND (1986) *The fame of Gawa: a symbolic study of value transformation in a Massim (Papua New Guinea) society* (Cambridge MA, Cambridge University Press).

Ondrejka, C (2004) 'Escaping the gilded cage: user created content and building the metaverse' *New York Law School Law Review* 49(1): 81–101, available online at: www.nylslawreview.com/wp-content/uploads/sites/16/2013/11/49-1.Ondrejka.pdf.

Paterson, K and Hughes, B (1999) 'Disability studies and phenomenology: the carnal politics of everyday life' *Disability and Society* 14(5): 597–610. doi:10.1080/09687599925966.

Pearce, C, Symborski, C and Blackburn, BR (2015) 'Virtual worlds survey report: a trans-world study of non-game virtual worlds – demographics, attitudes, and preferences', corporate report, available online at: cpandfriends.com/wp-content/uploads/2015/03/vwsurveyreport_final_publicationedition1.pdf.

Petrick, ER (2015) *Making computers accessible: disability rights and digital technology* (Baltimore MD, Johns Hopkins University Press).

Phillips, S (2010) *Disability and mobile citizenship in postsocialist Ukraine* (Urbana IN, Indiana University Press).

Price, M (2015) 'The bodymind problem and the possibilities of pain' *Hypatia* 30(1): 268–84. doi:10.1111/hypa.12127.

Redfield, R (1955) *The little community: viewpoints for the study of a human whole* (Chicago IL, University of Chicago Press).

Rembis, M (ed) (2017) *Disabling domesticity* (New York NY, Palgrave Macmillan).

Rivers, WHR (1913) 'Report on anthropological research outside America' in WHR Rivers et al, *Reports upon the present condition and future needs of the science of anthropology* (Washington DC, Carnegie Institution of Washington).

Rosaldo, MZ (1974) 'Woman, culture, and society: a theoretical overview' in MZ Rosaldo and L Lamphere (eds), *Woman, culture, and society* (Stanford CA, Stanford University Press).

Rousso, H (2013) *Don't call me inspirational: a disabled feminist talks back* (Philadelphia PA, Temple University Press).

Saerberg, S (2015) 'Chewing accidents: a phenomenology of visible and invisible everyday accomplishments' *Journal of Contemporary Ethnography* 44(5): 580–97. doi:10.1177/0891241615587380.

Salamon, G (2007) 'The phenomenology of rheumatology: disability, Merleau-Ponty, and the fallacy of maximal grip' *Hypatia: A Journal of Feminist Philosophy* 27(2): 243–60. doi:10.1111/j.1527-2001.2012.01266.x.

Scheper-Hughes, N, and Lock, M (1987) 'The mindful body: a prolegomenon to future work in medical anthropology' *Medical Anthropology Quarterly* 1(1): 6–41.

Serres, M (2008) *The five senses: a philosophy of mingled bodies*, translated by M Sankey and P Cowley (London, Continuum).

Shakespeare, T (2013) 'The social model of disability' in L Davis (ed), *The disability studies reader* (London, Routledge).

Shalk, S (2018) *Bodyminds reimagined: (dis)ability, race, and gender in Black Women's speculative fiction* (Durham NC, Duke University Press).

Siebers, T (2013) 'Disability and the theory of complex embodiment' in L Davis (ed), *The disability studies reader* (London, Routledge).

—— (2001) 'Disability in theory: from social constructionism to the new realism of the body' *American Literary History* 13(4): 737–54. Available online at: www.jstor.org/stable/3054594.

Sinclair, J (2013) [1999] 'Why I dislike 'Person First' language' *Autonomy, the Critical Journal of Interdisciplinary Autism Studies* 1(2): 2–3, available online at www.larry-arnold.net/Autonomy/index.php/autonomy/article/view/OP1.

Stein, WW (2003) *Deconstructing development discourse in Peru: a meta-ethnography of the modernity project at Vicos* (Lanham MD, University Press of America).

Sterling, B (1992) *The hacker crackdown: law and disorder on the electronic frontier* (New York NY, Bantam Books).

Tanenbaum, J, El-Nasr, MS and Nixon, M (eds) (2014) *Nonverbal communication in virtual worlds: understanding and designing expressive characters* (Pittsburgh PA, Carnegie Mellon University ETC Press).

Titchkosky, T (2001) 'Disability: a rose by any other name? "Person-First" language in Canadian society' *Canadian Review of Sociology* 38(2): 125–40, available online at: doi.org/10.1111/j.1755-618X.2001.tb00967.x.

—— (2011) *The question of access: disability, space, meaning* (Toronto, University of Toronto Press).

Veerapen, M (2011) 'Encountering oneself and the other: a case study of identity formation in Second Life' in A Peachey and M Childs (eds), *Reinventing ourselves: contemporary concepts of identity in virtual worlds* (London, Springer).

Williamson, B (2019) *Accessible America: a history of disability and design* (New York NY, New York University Press).

INDEX

www.ingramcontent.com/pod-product-compliance
Ingram Content Group UK Ltd.
Pitfield, Milton Keynes, MK11 3LW, UK
UKHW021238300926
15471UKWH00013B/515

9 781509 974269